REAL WORLD
MICRO

TWENTY-FIRST EDITION

EDITED BY ROB LARSON, ALEJANDRO REUSS, BRYAN SNYDER, CHRIS STURR,

AND THE *DOLLARS & SENSE* COLLECTIVE

REAL WORLD MICRO, TWENTY-FIRST EDITION

Published by:
Economic Affairs Bureau, Inc. d/b/a *Dollars & Sense*
One Milk Street, 5th floor, Boston, MA 02109
617-447-2177; dollars@dollarsandsense.org.
For order information, contact Economic Affairs Bureau or visit: www.dollarsandsense.org.

Real World Micro is edited by the *Dollars & Sense* Collective, which also publishes *Dollars & Sense* magazine and the classroom books *Microeconomics: Individual Choice in Communities, Real World Macro, Current Economic Issues, The Economic Crisis Reader, Real World Globalization, America Beyond Capitalism, Labor and the Global Economy, Real World Latin America, Real World Labor, Real World Banking and Finance, The Wealth Inequality Reader, The Economics of the Environment, Introduction to Political Economy, Unlevel Playing Fields: Understanding Wage Inequality and Discrimination, Striking a Balance: Work, Family, Life,* and *Grassroots Journalism.*

The 2013 *Dollars & Sense* Collective:
Betsy Aron, Nancy Banks, John Miller, Kevin O'Connell, Linda Pinkow, Paul Piwko, Smriti Rao, Alejandro Reuss, Dan Schneider, Zoe Sherman, Bryan Snyder, Chris Sturr, and Jeanne Winner.

Co-editors of this volume: Rob Larson, Alejandro Reuss, Bryan Snyder, and Chris Sturr
Design and layout: Alejandro Reuss

Printed in U.S.A

CONTENTS

III

INTRODUCTION

It sometimes seems that the United States has not one, but two economies. The first economy exists in economics textbooks and in the minds of many elected officials. It is a free-market economy, a system of promise and plenty, a cornucopia of consumer goods. In this economy, people are free and roughly equal, and each individual carefully looks after him- or herself, making uncoerced choices to advance his or her economic interests. Government is but an afterthought in this world, since almost everything that people need can be provided by the free market, itself guided by the reassuring "invisible hand."

The second economy is described in the writings of progressives, environmentalists, union supporters, and consumer advocates as well as honest business writers who recognize that real-world markets do not always conform to textbook models. This second economy features vast disparities of income, wealth, and power manifested in a system of class. It is an economy where employers have power over employees, where large firms have the power to shape markets, and where large corporate lobbies have the power to shape public policies. In this second economy, government sometimes adopts policies that ameliorate the abuses of capitalism and other times does just the opposite, but it is always an active and essential participant in economic life.

If you are reading this introduction, you are probably a student in an introductory college course in microeconomics. Your textbook will introduce you to the first economy, the harmonious world of free markets. *Real World Micro* will introduce you to the second.

Why "Real World" Micro?

A standard economics textbook is full of powerful concepts. It is also, by its nature, a limited window on the economy. What is taught in most introductory economics courses today is in fact just one strand of economic thought—neoclassical economics. Fifty years ago, many more strands were part of the introductory economics curriculum, and the contraction of the field has imposed limits on the study of economics that can confuse and frustrate students. This is particularly true in the study of microeconomics, which looks at markets for individual goods or services.

Real World Micro is designed as a supplement to a standard neoclassical textbook. Its articles provide vivid, real-world illustrations of economic concepts. But beyond that, our mission is to address two major sources of confusion in the study of economics at the introductory level.

The first source of confusion is the striking simplification of the world found in orthodox microeconomics. Standard textbooks describe stylized economic

1

interactions between idealized buyers and sellers that bear scant resemblance to the messy realities of the actual economic activity that we see around us. There is nothing wrong with simplifying. In fact, every social science must develop simplified models; precisely because reality is so complex, we must look at it a little bit at a time in order to understand it. Still, these simplifications mystify and misrepresent actual capitalist social relations and excise questions of race, gender, and class from the analysis.

Mainstream economic analysis calls to mind the story of the tipsy party-goer whose friend finds him on his hands and knees under a streetlight. "What are you doing?" asks the friend. "I dropped my car keys across the street, and I'm looking for them," the man replies. "But if you lost them across the street, how come you're looking over here?" "Well, the light's better here." In the interest of greater clarity, economics often imposes similar limits on its areas of inquiry.

As the title *Real World Micro* implies, one of our goals is to confront mainstream microeconomic theory with a more complex reality to direct attention to the areas not illuminated by the streetlight, and particularly to examine how inequality, power, and environmental imbalance change the picture. The idea is not to prove the standard theory "wrong," but to challenge you to think about where the theory is more and less useful, and why markets may not operate as expected.

This focus on real-world counterpoints to mainstream economic theory connects to the second issue we aim to clarify. Most economics texts uncritically present key assumptions and propositions that form the core of standard economic theory. They offer much less exploration of a set of related questions: What are alternative propositions about the economy? Under what circumstances will these alternatives more accurately describe the economy? What differences do such propositions make? Our approach is not to spell out an alternative theory in detail, but to raise questions and present real-life examples that bring these questions to life. For example, textbooks carefully lay out "consumer sovereignty," the notion that consumers' wishes ultimately determine what the economy will produce. But can we reconcile consumer sovereignty with an economy where one of the main products in industries such as soft drinks, cars, and music is consumer desire itself? We think it is valuable to see ideas like consumer sovereignty as debatable propositions and that requires hearing other views in the debate.

In short, our goal in this book is to use real-world examples from today's economy to raise questions, stimulate debate, and dare you to think critically about the models in your textbook.

What's in This Book

Real World Micro is organized to follow the outline of a standard economics text. Each chapter leads off with a brief introduction, including study questions for the entire chapter, and then provides several short articles from *Dollars & Sense* magazine and other sources that illustrate the chapter's key concepts.

Here is a quick overview:

Chapter 1, Markets: Ideology and Reality, starts off the volume by taking a hard look at the strengths and weaknesses of actual markets, with special attention to weaknesses that standard textbooks tend to underemphasize.

Chapter 2, Supply and Demand, presents real-world examples of supply and demand in action. *Dollars & Sense* authors question the conventional wisdom on topics such as price volatility and bubbles, affordability of essential goods like food (and issues of hunger), and price regulations like the minimum wage and rent control.

Chapter 3, Consumers, raises provocative questions about utility theory and individual consumer choice. What happens when marketers shape buyers' tastes? What happens when important information is hidden from consumers? Does consumer society threaten the environment? How can consumer decisions include broader considerations like environmental sustainability or labor conditions? What roles should government play in consumer protection?

Chapter 4, Firms, Production, and Profit Maximization, illustrates how business strategies to maximize profits may come at the expense of the social good, and challenges students to think about alternative ways of organizing firms. The chapter considers issues like environmental pollution, executive compensation, and the relation between the profit motive and essential goods like health care.

Chapter 5, Market Structure and Monopoly, explores market power and monopoly, just one example of the unequal power relationships that pervade our economic system. The chapter critiques market power in such industries as pharmaceuticals, banking, and information technology, but also questions whether small business prevalence would be an improvement.

Chapter 6, Labor Markets, examines the ways in which labor-market outcomes can be affected by unionization, globalization, and a host of other factors largely left out of the standard supply-and-demand models. Among the issues discussed are the reasons for union decline, the causes of high unemployment today, the rise of "contingent" labor arrangements, and possible ways to improve labor conditions domestically and internationally.

Chapter 7, The Distribution of Income, discusses the causes and consequences of inequality, countering the mainstream view that inequality is good for growth. The chapter examines the contours of inequality, with particular attention to race and gender. It also questions conventional views attributing rising inequality to technological change and globalization, and considers the impact of a changing balance of power between workers and employers.

Chapter 8, Market Failure and Government Policy, addresses when and how public policy should address cases where markets do not fit the conventional model of perfect competition (known as "market failure"). It considers environmental pollution, and possible policy responses, as well as market failure in health insurance and medical care.

Chapter 9, Taxation, explores issues of incomes, wealth, and taxation, including who actually pays taxes and at what rates. It also explores whether changes in taxes lead to changes in economic behavior and outcomes. This proposition is explored in the areas of taxes on high-income individuals and their effects on savings and investment, as well as taxes on financial transactions and effects on speculative activity.

Chapter 10, Trade and Development, covers key issues in trade policy and the world economy. The chapter's articles question the value of free trade and foreign investment for development, consider the role of currency markets in global trade outcomes, and address the impacts of globalization on workers (in both high-income and low-income countries).

Chapter 11, A Coming Generational War?, this year's policy spotlight, explores major policy and social issues related to "intergenerational equity"—the distribution of economic benefits and costs between generations, including the older versus the younger today and current generations versus those yet to be born. It considers issues including investments in education, pensions and Social Security, government debt, and environmental protection.

Chapter 1

MARKETS:
IDEOLOGY AND REALITY

INTRODUCTION

Economics is all about tradeoffs. The concept of "opportunity cost" reminds us that in order to make a purchase, or even to make use of a resource that you control (such as your time), you must give up other possible purchases or other possible uses. Markets broaden the range of possible tradeoffs by facilitating exchange between people who do not know each other, and in many cases never meet at all. Think of buying a pair of athletic shoes in Atlanta from a company based in Los Angeles that manufactures shoes in Malaysia and has stockholders all over the world. As the idea of gains from trade suggests, markets allow many exchanges that make both parties better off.

But markets have severe limitations as well. The economic crisis that began in 2008 has made those limitations all too clear. Even lifelong free-marketeers such as former Federal Reserve chair Alan Greenspan have been forced to question their belief in the "invisible hand."

In the chapter's first article, economist Marty Wolfson critiques a mainstream "free market" ideology that views markets as delivering to each person their just rewards, based on their talent or effort. In fact, he argues, markets are often structured in ways that stack the deck in favor of the wealthy and powerful (Article 1.1).

Markets and price determination, in neoclassical economics, have been idealized into an elegant, utility-maximizing perfection. Chris Tilly, in "Shaking the Invisible Hand" (Article 1.2), uncovers the curious assumptions necessary to allow for the market mechanism to be the most efficient allocator of scarce resources. He provides us with eight "Tilly Assumptions" underlying perfectly functioning markets. If any of these assumptions is violated, then there is a possibility of "market failure," or less-than-optimal market results.

Alejandro Reuss provides us with a clear discussion of this idealized neoclassical view of exchange in "Freedom, Equity, and Efficiency" (Article 1.3). Ideal neoclassical markets offer the promise of freedom of choice, equity (fairness), and efficiency, but often fail to deliver on all three counts. Reuss walks us through these neoclassical standards and contrasts them to the not-so-rosy reality of unrestrained labor-market competition.

Mainstream theories justify increased consumption by arguing that this must reflect decisions made by consumers to maximize their happiness (utility). The late Alan Durning, in his seminal piece "Enough is Enough: Why More is Not Necessarily Better Than Less" (Article 1.4), shakes the very foundations of standard consumer theory. Durning argues that more is often worse, not better, and that the accumulation of material goods in affluent societies threatens the environment (is not sustainable), widens global inequalities, and hollows out our lives.

In "Sharing the Wealth of the Commons" (Article 1.5), Peter Barnes focuses our attention on the oft-ignored forms of wealth that we do not own privately, but are held in "commons." He challenges the way that conventional economists view the environment and other goods that are shared by many people.

For anyone who wants to explore questions of inequality and fairness, Gar Alperovitz and Lew Daly's article "The Undeserving Rich" (Article 1.6) provides some fascinating grist for the mill. They argue that growth is built on a base of collectively produced knowledge that each generation inherits—not merely on the efforts of individuals.

Finally, Doug Orr takes on the persistent myth of the stock market as an engine for turning savings (forgone consumption today) into investment (provision, through the purchase of durable goods, for consumption tomorrow). In "The Big Casino" (Article 1.7), Orr points out that, in fact, the stock market does little to provide companies with funding for investment. Instead, it is basically a den of speculation—that is, of gambling.

Discussion Questions

1. (General) What things should not be for sale? Beyond everyday goods and services, think about human bodies, votes, small countries, and other things that might be bought and sold. How do you draw the line between what should be bought and sold and what should not?

2. (General) If not markets, then what? What are other ways to organize economic activity? Which ways are most likely to resolve the problems brought up in this chapter?

3. (Article 1.1) Marty Wolfson argues that markets, far from being "free," are often rigged in favor of the wealthy and powerful. What are some examples?

4. (Article 1.2) Write out the eight "Tilly Assumptions" and corresponding realities using Tilly's exact terms for the assumptions. Are these assumptions reasonable?

5. (Article 1.2) For each of the eight "Tilly Assumptions," explain how the market mechanism would fail if the assumption were violated.

6. (Article 1.3) According to neoclassical theory, how do markets deliver "efficient" results if all "barriers" to exchange are removed? In what sense are these results "efficient?"

7. (Article 1.3) How is the word "freedom" defined by neoclassical economists? What freedoms do they argue workers lose under regulated labor markets?

8. (Article 1.3) Does the unfettered operation of the market mechanism deliver "equity" to society? In your view, what would fair labor-market outcomes look like?

9. (Article 1.4) Durning says that it's wrong for people in rich countries to consume so much when others in the world live in poverty. His viewpoint could be summarized as, "Live simply, so that others may simply live." Do you agree with this outlook?

10. (Article 1.4) Durning's argument implies that rather than seeking pleasure by consuming material goods, we should seek enjoyment through family, friends, and community. How could you use standard utility theory to describe this kind of choice? (Hint: Can family, friends, and community be "goods"?) What are some possible problems in using the theory in this way?

11. (Article 1.5) Peter Barnes says that we take for granted an enormous number of resources—including the natural environment, but also the laws and institutions that make business possible. Is his point the same as saying that there are market failures, such as pollution externalities, that prevent markets from taking into account the full value of the environment?

12. (Article 1.6) Consider the following quotation:

    > "I think we've been through a period where too many people have been given to understand that if they have a problem, it's the government's job to cope with it. ... They're casting their problem on society. And, you know, there is no such thing as society. There are individual men and women, and there are families."
    > —British Prime Minister Margaret Thatcher, talking to *Women's Own* magazine, October 31, 1987

    After reading Gar Alperovitz and Lew Daly's article "The Undeserving Rich," how do you think they would respond to Thatcher? How would you respond?

13. (Article 1.7) Doug Orr argues that, when the stock market is booming, it does little good for the majority of U.S. households. Stock-market crashes, however, do a great deal of harm. How is it possible, in Orr's view, for both of these claims to be true at the same time?

Article 1.1

"FREE MARKET" OUTCOMES ARE NOT FAIR—AND NOT FREE

BY MARTY WOLFSON

November/December 2012

"Since 1980, the U.S. government has reduced its intervention in the U.S. economy, which has become much more of a free market. Conservatives applaud this development because they think that free-market outcomes reward talent and hard work; progressives object to the income inequality of free-market outcomes and want to use government tax and transfer policy to reduce inequality."

Most people, whether conservative or progressive, would probably agree with this statement. This framing of the issue, however, plays into a right-wing story in which conservatives are the defenders of (free) market outcomes, including the success of the rich who have made it "on their own"; meanwhile, the "dependent poor" look to the government for handouts. This has been a basic element of the right-wing playbook for a long time. Then-presidential candidate Mitt Romney was drawing on this narrative when he complained about the 47% of the U.S. population "who are dependent upon government ... who believe that government has a responsibility to care for them."

This view has two main themes: 1) Because the U.S. free-market economy rewards talent and hard work, the middle class should emulate the wealthy for their success, not vilify them; and 2) those who have been failures in the market want the government to take care of them by redistributing income from those who have been successful. We can see these themes play out on all sorts of political issues. They form, for example, the basis for the attacks on the Affordable Health Care Act (or "Obamacare"). Middle-class Americans, in the conservative view, are being taxed—forced to pay—to provide health insurance for those "unsuccessful" elements of the population who have not earned it themselves.

The conservative argument assumes that the outcomes we observe are the result of a free-market economy. However, the right-wing objective has not been to create a free market; it has been to rig government policy and the market so as to redistribute income towards large corporations and the wealthy.

For example, conservatives themselves want to use government policy to bring about a different distribution of income from what we have now—a distribution that is more favorable to corporations and the very rich. A central policy objective for conservatives, ever since the Reagan Administration, has been to cut taxes on the wealthy. And by cutting government revenue, they have been able to make the argument that government programs for the poor and the middle class need to be cut in order to balance the budget.

Also, conservatives have eliminated restrictions on corporations and protections for workers, consumers, and the environment. They have attacked barriers to international capital mobility, deregulated industries, and reduced government regulations aimed at ensuring a safe workplace and a healthy environment.

Because conservative policies have often taken the form of reducing government programs and regulations, the ideology of a free market has been useful in rationalizing them. Other conservative interventions, however, have been less able to fit into the free-market mold, and therefore are especially revealing of conservatives' genuine aims.

When the financial crisis of 2008 threatened the survival of the large banks, they were quick to ask for the government to intervene with a large bailout. The "right-to-work" law recently passed in Indiana, designed to deprive unions of financial resources, is an explicit rejection of a market outcome—the private agreement between management and union to require all workers to pay their "fair share" of the costs of union representation. "Free-trade" agreements, ostensibly designed to eliminate restrictions on the movement of goods and capital, have nonetheless continued to restrict the free movement of people. Even the repeal of financial regulations in the 1980s and 1990s, ostensibly a free-market endeavor, created the anti-competitive giant financial firms that demanded to be bailed out in 2008.

The realization that the economy is rigged to benefit the rich and large corporations takes away the force of the right-wing argument that progressives want to use government to "vilify" the "successful" and reward the "slothful and incompetent." When the game has been rigged, it is wrong to say that the market simply rewards talent and hard work, and the outcomes that result can hardly be called fair. When the market outcomes that we observe are unfair, we need to both change the rules for how the economy works and use the government to restore fairness. ❏

Sources: Dean Baker, *The End of Loser Liberalism: Making Markets Progressive* (2011); Transcript of Mitt Romney video, *Mother Jones*, September 17, 2012 www.motherjones.com/politics/2012/09/full-transcript-mitt-romney-secret-video.

Article 1.2

SHAKING THE INVISIBLE HAND
The Uncertain Foundations of Free-Market Economics

BY CHRIS TILLY
November 1989; updated March 2011

> "It is not from the benevolence of the butcher, the brewer or the baker that we expect our dinner, but from their regard to their own interest... [No individual] intends to promote the public interest... [rather, he is] led by an invisible hand to promote an end which was no part of his intention."
>
> —*Adam Smith, The Wealth of Nations, 1776*

Seen the Invisible Hand lately? It's all around us these days, propping up conservative arguments in favor of free trade, deregulation, and tax-cutting.

Today's advocates for "free," competitive markets echo Adam Smith's claim that unfettered markets translate the selfish pursuit of individual gain into the greatest benefit for all. They trumpet the superiority of capitalist free enterprise over socialist efforts to supplant the market with a planned economy, and even decry liberal attempts to moderate the market. Anything short of competitive markets, they proclaim, yields economic inefficiency, making society worse off.

But the economic principle underlying this fanfare is shaky indeed. Since the late 19th century, mainstream economists have struggled to prove that Smith was right—that the chaos of free markets leads to a blissful economic order. In the 1950s, U.S. economists Kenneth Arrow and Gerard Debreu finally came up with a theoretical proof, which many orthodox economists view as the centerpiece of modern economic theory.

Although this proof is the product of the best minds of mainstream economics, it ends up saying surprisingly little in defense of free markets. The modern theory of the Invisible Hand shows that given certain assumptions, free markets reduce the wasteful use of economic resources—but perpetuate unequal income distribution.

To prove free markets cut waste, economists must make a number of far-fetched assumptions: there are no concentrations of economic power; buyers and sellers know every detail about the present and future economy; and all costs of production are borne by producers while all benefits from consumption are paid for by consumers (see box for a complete list). Take away any one of these assumptions and markets can lead to stagnation, recession, and other forms of waste—as in fact they do.

In short, the economic theory invoked by conservatives to justify free markets instead starkly reveals their limitations.

The Fruits of Free Markets

The basic idea behind the Invisible Hand can be illustrated with a story. Suppose that I grow apples and you grow oranges. We both grow tired of eating the same fruit all the time and decide to trade. Perhaps we start by trading one apple for one orange. This exchange satisfies both of us, because in fact I would gladly give up more than one apple to get an orange, and you would readily pay more than one orange for an apple. And as long as swapping one more apple for one more orange makes us both better off, we will continue to trade.

Eventually, the trading will come to a stop. I begin to notice that the novelty of oranges wears old as I accumulate a larger pile of them and the apples I once had a surplus of become more precious to me as they grow scarcer. At some point, I draw the line: in order to obtain one more apple from me, you must give me more than one orange. But your remaining oranges have also become more valuable to you. Up to now, each successive trade has made both of us better off. Now there is no further exchange that benefits us both, so we agree to stop trading until the next crop comes in.

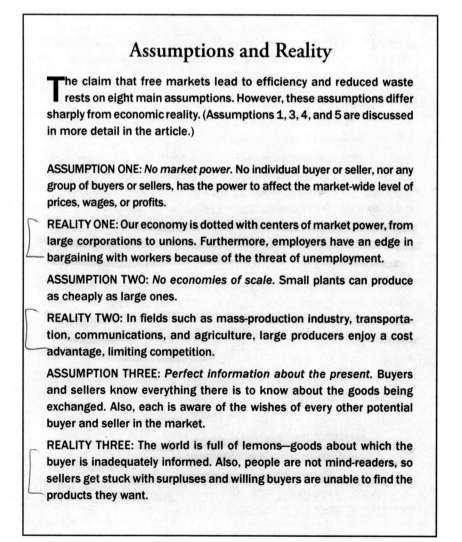

Assumptions and Reality

The claim that free markets lead to efficiency and reduced waste rests on eight main assumptions. However, these assumptions differ sharply from economic reality. (Assumptions 1, 3, 4, and 5 are discussed in more detail in the article.)

ASSUMPTION ONE: *No market power.* No individual buyer or seller, nor any group of buyers or sellers, has the power to affect the market-wide level of prices, wages, or profits.

REALITY ONE: Our economy is dotted with centers of market power, from large corporations to unions. Furthermore, employers have an edge in bargaining with workers because of the threat of unemployment.

ASSUMPTION TWO: *No economies of scale.* Small plants can produce as cheaply as large ones.

REALITY TWO: In fields such as mass-production industry, transportation, communications, and agriculture, large producers enjoy a cost advantage, limiting competition.

ASSUMPTION THREE: *Perfect information about the present.* Buyers and sellers know everything there is to know about the goods being exchanged. Also, each is aware of the wishes of every other potential buyer and seller in the market.

REALITY THREE: The world is full of lemons—goods about which the buyer is inadequately informed. Also, people are not mind-readers, so sellers get stuck with surpluses and willing buyers are unable to find the products they want.

Note several features of this parable. Both you and I end up happier by trading freely. If the government stepped in and limited fruit trading, neither of us would be as well off. In fact, the government cannot do anything in the apple/orange market that will make both of us better off than does the free market.

Adding more economic actors, products, money, and costly production processes complicates the picture, but we reach the same conclusions. Most of us sell our labor time in the market rather than fruit; we sell it for money that we then use to buy apples, oranges, and whatever else we need. The theory of the Invisible Hand tells us a trip to the fruit stand improves the lot of both consumer and seller; likewise, the sale of labor time benefits both employer and employee. What's more, according to the theory, competition between apple farmers insures that consumers will get apples produced at the lowest possible cost. Government intervention still can only make things worse.

ASSUMPTION FOUR: *Perfect information about the future.* Contracts between buyers and sellers cover every possible future eventuality.

REALITY FOUR: Uncertainty clouds the future of any economy. Futures markets are limited.

ASSUMPTION FIVE: *You only get what you pay for.* Nobody can impose a cost on somebody else, nor obtain a benefit from them, without paying.

REALITY FIVE: Externalities, both positive and negative, are pervasive. In a free market, polluters can impose costs on the rest of us without paying. And when a public good like a park is built or roads are maintained, everyone benefits whether or not they helped to pay for it.

ASSUMPTION SIX: *Price is a proxy for pleasure.* The price of a given commodity will represent the quality and desirability and or utility derived from the consumption of the commodity.

REALITY SIX: "Conspicuous Consumption" (Veblen) and or "snob effects" will often distort prices from underlying utility and marketers will try to position commodities accordingly.

ASSUMPTION SEVEN: *Self-interest only.* In economic matters, each person cares only about his or her own level of well-being.

REALITY SEVEN: Solidarity, jealousy, and even love for one's family violate this assumption.

ASSUMPTION EIGHT: *No joint production.* Each production process has only one product.

REALITY EIGHT: Even in an age of specialization, there are plenty of exceptions to this rule. For example, large service firms such as hospitals or universities produce a variety of different services using the same resources. —*Chris Tilly and Bryan Snyder*

This fable provides a ready-made policy guide. Substitute "Japanese autos" and "U.S. agricultural products" for apples and oranges, and the fable tells you that import quotas or tariffs only make the people of both countries worse off. Change the industries to airlines or telephone services, and the fable calls for deregulation. Or re-tell the tale in the labor market: minimum wages and unions (which prevent workers from individually bargaining over their wages) hurt employers and workers.

Fruit Salad

Unfortunately for free-market boosters, two major short-comings make a fruit salad out of this story. First, even if free markets perform as advertised, they deliver only one benefit—the prevention of certain economically wasteful practices—while preserving inequality. According to the theory, competitive markets wipe out two kinds of waste: unrealized trades and inefficient production. Given the right assumptions, markets ensure that when two parties both stand to gain from a trade, they make that trade, as in the apples-and-oranges story. Competition compels producers to search for the most efficient, lowest-cost production methods—again, given the right preconditions.

Though eliminating waste is a worthy goal, it leaves economic inequality untouched. Returning once more to the orchard, if I start out with all of the apples and oranges and you start out with none, that situation is free of waste: no swap can make us both better off since you have nothing to trade! Orthodox economists acknowledge that even in the ideal competitive market, those who start out rich stay rich, while the poor remain poor. Many of them argue that attempts at redistributing income will most certainly create economic inefficiencies, justifying the preservation of current inequities.

But in real-life economics, competition does lead to waste. Companies wastefully duplicate each other's research and build excess productive capacity. Cost-cutting often leads to shoddy products, worker speedup, and unsafe working conditions. People and factories stand idle while houses go unbuilt and people go unfed. That's because of the second major problem: real economies don't match the assumptions of the Invisible Hand theory.

Of course, all economic theories build their arguments on a set of simplifying assumptions about the world. These assumptions often sacrifice some less important aspects of reality in order to focus on the economic mechanisms of interest. But in the case of the Invisible Hand, the theoretical preconditions contradict several central features of the economy.

For one thing, markets are only guaranteed to prevent waste if the economy runs on "perfect competition": individual sellers compete by cutting prices, individual buyers compete by raising price offers, and nobody holds concentrated economic power. But today's giant corporations hardly match this description. Coke and Pepsi compete with advertising rather than price cuts. The oil companies keep prices high enough to register massive profits every year. Employers coordinate the pay and benefits they offer to avoid bidding up compensation. Workers, in turn, marshal their own forces via unionization—another departure from perfect competition.

Indeed, the jargon of "perfect competition" overlooks the fact that property ownership itself confers disproportionate economic power. "In the competitive model," orthodox economist Paul Samuelson commented, "it makes no difference whether capital hires labor or the other way around." He argued that given perfect competition among workers and among capitalists, wages and profits would remain the same regardless of who does the hiring. But unemployment—a persistent feature of market-driven economies—makes job loss very costly to workers. The sting my boss feels when I "fire" him by quitting my job hardly equals the setback I experience when he fires me.

Perfect Information?

In addition, the grip of the Invisible Hand is only sure if all buyers and sellers have "perfect information" about the present and future state of markets. In the present, this implies consumers know exactly what they are buying—an assumption hard to swallow in these days of leaky breast implants and chicken à la Salmonella. Employers must know exactly what skills workers have and how hard they will work—suppositions any real-life manager would laugh at.

Perfect information also means sellers can always sniff out unsatisfied demands, and buyers can detect any excess supplies of goods. Orthodox economists rely on the metaphor of an omnipresent "auctioneer" who is always calling out prices so all buyers and sellers can find mutually agreeable prices and consummate every possible sale. But in the actual economy, the auctioneer is nowhere to be found, and markets are plagued by surpluses and shortages.

Perfect information about the future is even harder to come by. For example, a company decides whether or not to build a new plant based on whether it expects sales to rise. But predicting future demand is a tricky matter. One reason is that people may save money today in order to buy (demand) goods and services in the future. The problem comes in predicting when. As economist John Maynard Keynes observed in 1934, "An act of individual saving means—so to speak—a decision not to have dinner today. But it does not necessitate a decision to have dinner or to buy a pair of boots a week hence...or to consume any specified thing at any specified date. Thus it depresses the business of preparing today's dinner without stimulating the business of making ready for some future act of consumption." Keynes concluded that far from curtailing waste, free markets gave rise to the colossal waste of human and economic resources that was the Great Depression—in part because of this type of uncertainty about the future.

Free Lunch

The dexterity of the Invisible Hand also depends on the principle that "You only get what you pay for." This "no free lunch" principle seems at first glance a reasonable description of the economy. But major exceptions arise. One is what economists call "externalities"—economic transactions that take place outside the market. Consider a hospital that dumps syringes at sea. In effect, the hospital gets a free lunch by passing the costs of waste disposal on to the rest of us. Because no market exists where the right to dump is bought and sold, free markets do nothing to compel the hospital to bear the costs of dumping—which is why the government must step in.

Public goods such as sewer systems also violate the "no free lunch" rule. Once the sewer system is in place, everyone shares in the benefits of the waste disposal, regardless of whether or not they helped pay for it. Suppose sewer systems were sold in a free market, in which each person had the opportunity to buy an individual share. Then any sensible, self-interested consumer would hold back from buying his or her fair share—and wait for others to provide the service. This irrational situation would persist unless consumers could somehow collectively agree on how extensive a sewer system to produce—once more bringing government into the picture.

Most orthodox economists claim that the list of externalities and public goods in the economy is short and easily addressed. Liberals and radicals, on the other hand, offer a long list: for example, public goods include education, health care, and decent public transportation—all in short supply in our society.

Because real markets deviate from the ideal markets envisioned in the theory of the Invisible Hand, they give us both inequality and waste. But if the theory is so far off the mark, why do mainstream economists and policymakers place so much stock in it? They fundamentally believe the profit motive is the best guide for the economy. If you believe that "What's good for General Motors is good for the country," the Invisible Hand theory can seem quite reasonable. Business interests, government, and the media constantly reinforce this belief, and reward those who can dress it up in theoretical terms. As long as capital remains the dominant force in society, the Invisible Hand will maintain its grip on the hearts and minds of us all. ❏

Article 1.3

FREEDOM, EQUITY, AND EFFICIENCY
Contrasting Views of Markets and Competition

BY ALEJANDRO REUSS
April 2012

The basic world-view of neoclassical economists is that, in markets, people engage voluntarily in exchanges with each other, and that this means market exchanges leave both parties better off. If someone cannot be forced to make a trade, they will only do so if it leaves them at least a little better off than they would have been otherwise. Left to their own devices, people will find and exhaust all the possibilities for trades that boost the overall social well-being. Policies that interfere with people's ability to make voluntary trades, then, can only subtract from the well-being of society as a whole.

The neoclassical narrative depends on many (often unspoken) *assumptions*. Individuals must be rational and self-interested. The assumption of "rationality" means they must act in ways that further their objectives, whatever these objectives may be. The assumption of "self-interest" means that, in making decisions, they must only take into account benefits and costs to themselves. They must have perfect information about all factors (past, present, and future) that could affect their decisions. Their actions must not affect any "third parties" (anyone other than those directly involved in the exchange and agreeing to its terms). There must be many buyers and sellers, so that no single buyer or seller (and no group of buyers or sellers colluding together) can impose the prices they want. Several other assumptions may also be important.

Implicitly, the neoclassical story appeals to ideas about freedom, equity (fairness), and efficiency. Very few people would say they are against any of these virtues, but different people embrace different definitions. Different people, for example, have different ideas about what people should have the freedom to do, and what "freedoms" would impinge on the freedoms, rights, or well-being of others. So really the issue is, when neoclassical economists say that unregulated market competition is desirable, for example, as a matter, of "freedom," what view of freedom are they basing this on?

Freedom

By "freedom," neoclassical economists mean freedom from force or threat of force. They would recognize that someone making an exchange when threatened with violence—when confronted with "an offer they can't refuse," in the *Godfather* sense of that phrase—is not really engaging in a voluntary transaction. That person could very well make an exchange leaving them worse off than they would have been otherwise (except that they may have saved their own neck). On the other hand, suppose a person is faced only with very undesirable alternatives to engaging in a trade. Suppose they have "no choice" but to accept a job, because the alternative is to starve. Neoclassical economists would point out that these circumstances are not of the potential employer's making. It is quite unlike, in their view, conditions that are directly imposed by the other party (like having a gun held to one's head). If the impoverished worker accepts a job offer, even at a very low wage or under very bad working conditions, the neoclassical economist would argue that this is evidence that he or she really is made better off by the exchange. Restricting his or her freedom to engage in this exchange, in the neoclassical view, only makes him or her worse off.

Equity

Neoclassical economists argue that restrictions on market competition can unfairly benefit some market participants (buyers or sellers) or potential market participants at the expense of others. This kind of equity concern enters into neoclassical theory in several ways:

First, restrictions on competition may affect the ability of different people (or firms) to participate in a market—to offer what they have for sale or to bid on what others offer for sale. Suppose that the government issues special licenses to some people or firms that permit them to engage in a certain trade, like driving a taxi, while denying such licenses to others. (Such policies create "barriers to entry," in the language of neoclassical economics.) Such restrictions are, in the neoclassical view, unfair to the unlucky (or less-influential) individuals or firms who do not receive licenses and so are locked out of the market.

Second, restrictions may affect the ability of different people to use whatever advantage they may have, to compete in a market. A price floor, for example, prevents lower-cost sellers from using their cost advantage (their willingness to accept a lower price) to compete in the market. In the neoclassical view, this favors higher-cost sellers at the expense of their lower-cost competitors.

Third, restrictions may affect the ability of sellers to fetch the highest price they can, constrained only by competition from other sellers, and of buyers to pay the lowest price they can, constrained only by bidding from other buyers. A price floor, by restricting producers from competing on price (preventing any from offering prices below the floor), may favor producers in general at the expense of consumers. By the same token, a price ceiling (a maximum legal price) may favor consumers at the expense of producers.

Efficiency

In the neoclassical view, a resource is used "efficiently" as long as the benefit from using that resource is greater than the cost. Let's think about a company—say, an auto company—that has to decide how many machines to rent or how many workers to hire for its operations. It will consider how many extra cars it can produce if it rents one additional machine, or hires one additional worker. The company will figure out how much income it will get from the sale of those additional cars. That is, it will multiply the number of additional cars by the price it will get per car. Ultimately, it will compare this extra income against the rental cost paid for the machine, or the wage paid to the worker. The company will rent a machine, or hire a worker, as long as the extra income it gets is more than the additional cost it has to pay.

In the neoclassical view, this is "efficient" not only from the standpoint of the company, but from the standpoint of society as a whole. If the cost of using an extra machine or hiring an extra worker is less than value of the extra cars produced, the use of the machine or worker is also "efficient" from the standpoint of society as a whole.

There's just one more problem. In the neoclassical view, for private actors to make decisions that are also "efficient" form the standpoint of society as a whole, the prices they base their decisions on have to be the *right* prices. That is, each price has to reflect the true cost of a good to society as a whole. So how do we know, in this view, what is the "right price"?

The "Right" Wage

Let's look at an example using, in the language of neoclassical economics, the "price of labor" (or wage). Suppose that the going wage in a certain place (for a certain kind of labor) is $20 per hour. According to neoclassical economists, a company will hire a worker as long as the extra benefit it gets from each extra hour of labor (the extra units produced times the price the company gets per unit) is at least as much as the additional cost it pays for that extra hour of labor ($20 per hour). Suppose, however, that the wage was only this high because there were barriers to competition in the labor market. If the wage without barriers would have only been, say, $10, then a company would hire an extra worker as long as the extra benefit it got from each extra hour of labor was at least $10 per hour.

How do we know whether the "right" wage is $20 or $10? In the view of neoclassical economists, the right wage—like any other right price—reflects the true cost to society of the good involved (here, an hour of labor). The cost of labor is whatever pains the worker endures as a result of that hour of work. This includes having to show up for work, when one might prefer to be someone else, having to follow the employer's orders, when one would rather be "doing one's own thing," putting up with the conditions at work, which could be dangerous, unhealthy, or unpleasant, and so on. It is competition in the labor market that makes workers reveal what they really require to compensate them for the burdens of labor.

If the price of labor, due to barriers to labor-market competition, is "too high," then employers will use "too little" labor. If the wage is $20, due to barriers, then employers will not hire an extra hour of labor unless it results in the production of at least $20 of additional goods. As a result of the inflated price of labor, society will have turned its back on who-knows-how-many opportunities to get between $10 and $20 of goods at a true cost of $10 worth of labor. In other words, wages that are inflated by barriers to competition result in an "inefficient" use of resources.

Critiques of the Neoclassical View

Economists associated with different schools of thought may use normative concepts like "freedom," "equity," or "efficiency," but mean something very different by these ideas than what neoclassical economists mean. (Some may choose not to use these terms, and instead invoke other normative concepts, like "justice," "equality," "the good life," and so on.) Here, however, we will focus on contrasts with the neoclassical views of freedom, equity, and efficiency described above.

Equity

Barriers to labor-market competition, neoclassical economists argue, favor some workers at the expense of others and workers at the expense of consumers. An alternative view is that restraints on labor-market competition allow workers to get a better deal (higher pay, better conditions, etc.) from employers. The absence of these restraints, on the other hand, may result in higher profits for employers while relegating workers to lower pay and worse conditions. Which outcome one prefers depends on how one values benefits to one group of people (workers) compared to benefits to another (employers).

There are several reasons that someone might favor the interests of workers over those of employers, and therefore approve of changes that benefit workers even if these benefits come at the expense of employers:

1. Ideas of "fairness" based on social "custom" or "convention." In most societies where people work for wages, there are evolving ideas about what is a "fair" wage or "decent" living. Partly, such ideas may be based on what people have become accustomed to in the past. Partly, they may reflect expectations that conditions of life will improve over time, and especially from one generation to the next.

2. Commitment to greater economic and social equality. People who get most of their income from property (ownership of businesses, land or buildings, or financial wealth) are likely to be at the top of the income ladder. Most of the people at the bottom or in the middle, on the other hand, get most of their income from work. Therefore, changes that benefit workers as a group (at the expense of employers) tend to bring about a more equal distribution of income in society.

3. Ideas about who creates and deserves to keep society's wealth. Some "radical" economists argue that labor is the source of all new wealth produced in society. Owners of property take a piece of this wealth by controlling things (like farms, mines, factories, etc.) that everyone else needs in order to work and live. In this view, there is no such thing as a "fair" distribution of income between workers and employers, since the employing class exists only by virtue of taking part of what workers produce.

Much of the history of labor movements around the world centers on attempts to *restrain* competition between workers, to keep workers from undercutting each other on the wages or conditions they will accept, and therefore to benefit workers as a group. Unions, for example, are compacts by which each member agrees *not* to accept a lower wage or worse conditions than the other members. Unions also set conditions on hours, benefits, and conditions of work. No individual can bargain a lower wage or worse conditions, in order to get a job, and thereby force other workers to do the same. Labor legislation like the minimum-wage laws, maximum hours (or overtime) laws, and laws regulating labor conditions, likewise, all restrain competition between workers.

Freedom

Neoclassical economists emphasize workers' freedom of choice to accept low wages, long hours, bad working conditions, and so on. Workers would not accept those conditions, they argue, unless doing so would leave them better off than they would be otherwise. In this view, institutions like unions or policies like minimum-wage laws interfere with workers' freedom to make a deal that would leave them better off.

Many liberal and almost all radical economists, on the other hand, emphasize how the conditions that an individual will "freely" accept depend on the alternatives available to them. If the only alternative is to starve in the street, most people would work even very long hours, under very bad conditions, for very low pay. Instead of seeing these workers as having "freely" accepted such agreements, however, one could view them as lacking any real freedom to *refuse* these conditions.

Union contracts, minimum-wage laws, and other restraints on competition between workers do, indeed, restrict each individual worker's "freedom" to accept lower wages, worse conditions, and so on, just as neoclassical economists argue. However, this view ignores the benefit to each worker—that these institutions also *protect* each worker from other workers undercutting him or her. Instead of seeing restraints on labor competition as robbing workers of the freedom to accept lower wages or worse conditions, one can instead see them as giving workers the freedom to demand higher wages or better conditions.

Efficiency

We have already described one concept of efficiency used by neoclassical economists: The key idea is that resources are used if (and only if) the benefit to society is greater than the cost. Neoclassical economists also use another concept of efficiency: An efficient condition is one in which nobody can be made better off without making someone worse off. This definition, pioneered by the Italian neoclassical economist Vilfredo Pareto, is known as "Pareto efficiency." The two definitions are connected: If resources were being wasted (used inefficiently), they could be used to make someone better off without making anyone worse off.

Neoclassical economists call a *change* that makes some people better off without making anyone worse off a "Pareto improvement." There are very few changes in public policies, however, that make some people better off while literally making nobody worse off. Most policy changes, potentially affecting millions of people, make some people better off and others worse off. In these cases, neoclassical economists apply what they call the "compensation test." They compare the benefits to the "winners" from some change in public policy to the losses to the "losers." If the total gains are greater than the total losses, neoclassical economists argue, the winners could compensate the losers—and leave everyone at least a little better off.

In most cases where there are both winners and losers due to a change in public policy, however, the winners do not actually compensate the losers. These are not, then, actual efficiency improvements in the sense that some people are made better off while nobody is made worse off. Restraints on labor-market competition, for example, may benefit workers at the expense of their employers. (Eliminating such policies, meanwhile, may have the opposite effect.)

Judging whether these changes are for the better, then, involves weighing the benefits to some people against the losses to others. How one resolves such an issue depends on one's normative ideas, or values, about whose interests should take precedence. In other words—whose side are you on? ❏

Article 1.4

ENOUGH IS ENOUGH

Why more is not necessarily better than less.

BY ALAN DURNING
June 1991, updated May 2009

> "Our enormously productive economy ... demands that we make consumption our way of life, that we convert the buying and use of goods into rituals, that we seek our spiritual satisfaction, our ego satisfaction, in consumption... We need things consumed, burned up, worn out, replaced, and discarded at an ever increasing rate."
>
> —*Victor Lebow, U.S. retailing analyst, 1955*

Across the country, Americans have responded to Victor Lebow's call, and around the globe, those who could afford it have followed. And many can: Worldwide, on average, a person today is four-and-a-half times richer than were his or her great-grandparents at the turn of the last century.

Needless to say, that new global wealth is not evenly spread among the earth's people. One billion live in unprecedented luxury; one billion live in destitution. Overconsumption by the world's fortunate is an environmental problem unmatched in severity by anything except perhaps population growth. Surging exploitation of resources threatens to exhaust or unalterably disfigure forests, soils, water, air, and climate. High consumption may be a mixed blessing in human terms, too. Many in the industrial lands have a sense that, hoodwinked by a consumerist culture, they have been fruitlessly attempting to satisfy social, psychological, and spiritual needs with material things.

Of course, the opposite of overconsumption—poverty—is no solution to either environmental or human problems. It is infinitely worse for people and bad for the natural world. Dispossessed peasants slash and burn their way into Latin American rain forests, and hungry nomads turn their herds out onto fragile African range land, reducing it to desert. If environmental destruction results when people have either too little or too much, we are left to wonder how much is enough. What level of consumption can the earth support? When does having more cease to add appreciably to human satisfaction?

The Consuming Society

Consumption is the hallmark of our era. The headlong advance of technology, rising earnings, and cheaper material goods have lifted consumption to levels never dreamed of a century ago. In the United States, the world's premier consuming society, people today on average own twice as many cars, drive two-and-a-half times as far, and travel 25 times further by air than did their parents in 1950. Air conditioning spread from 15% of households in 1960 to 64% in 1987, and color televisions from 1% to 93%. Microwave ovens and video cassette recorders reached almost two-thirds of American homes during the 1980s alone.

Japan and Western Europe have displayed parallel trends. Per person, the Japanese today consume more than four times as much aluminum, almost five times as much energy, and 25 times as much steel as they did in 1950. They also own four times as many cars and eat nearly twice as much meat. Like the Japanese, Western Europeans' consumption levels are only one notch below Americans'.

The late 1980s saw some poor societies begin the transition to consuming ways. In China, the sudden surge in spending on consumer durables shows up clearly in data from the State Statistical Bureau: Between 1982 and 1987, color televisions spread from 1% to 35% of urban Chinese homes, washing machines quadrupled from 16% to 67%, and refrigerators expanded their reach from 1% to 20%. By 2002 there were 126 color televisions, 93 washing machines, and 87 refridgerators for every 100 urban Chinese households.

Few would begrudge anyone the simple advantages of cold food storage or mechanized clothes washing. The point, rather, is that even the oldest non-Western nations are emulating the high-consumption lifestyle. Long before all the world's people could achieve the American dream, however, we would lay waste the planet.

The industrial world's one billion meat eaters, car drivers, and throwaway consumers are responsible for the lion's share of the damage humans have caused common global resources. Over the past century, the economies of the wealthiest fifth of humanity have pumped out two-thirds of the greenhouse gases threatening the earth's climate, and each year their energy use releases three-fourths of the sulfur and nitrogen oxides causing acid rain. Their industries generate most of the world's hazardous chemical wastes, and their air conditioners, aerosol sprays, and factories release almost 90% of the chlorofluorocarbons destroying the earth's protective ozone layer. Clearly, even one billion profligate consumers is too much for the earth.

Beyond the environmental costs of acquisitiveness, some perplexing findings of social scientists throw doubt on the wisdom of high consumption as a personal and national goal: Rich societies have had little success in turning consumption into fulfillment. Regular surveys by the National Opinion Research Center of the University of Chicago reveal, for example, that no more Americans report they are "very happy" now than in 1957.

Likewise, a landmark study by sociologist Richard Easterlin in 1974 revealed that Nigerians, Filipinos, Panamanians, Yugoslavians, Japanese, Israelis, and West Germans all ranked themselves near the middle of a happiness scale. Confounding any attempt to correlate affluence and happiness, poor Cubans and rich Americans were both found to be considerably happier than the norm.

If the effectiveness of consumption in providing personal fulfillment is questionable, perhaps environmental concerns can help us redefine our goals.

In Search of Sufficiency

By examining current consumption patterns, we receive some guidance on what the earth can sustain. For three of the most ecologically important types of consumption—transportation, diet, and use of raw materials—the world's people are distributed unevenly over a vast range. Those at the bottom clearly fall below the "too little" line, while those at the top, in the cars-meat-and-disposables class, clearly consume too much.

Approximately one billion people do their traveling, aside from the occasional donkey or bus ride, on foot. Unable to get to jobs easily, attend school, or bring their complaints before government offices, they are severely hindered by the lack of transportation options.

Another three billion people travel by bus and bicycle. Kilometer for kilometer, bikes are cheaper than any other vehicle, costing less than $100 new in most of the Third World and requiring no fuel.

The world's automobile class is relatively small: Only 8% of humans, about 400 million people, own cars. The automobile makes itself indispensable: Cities sprawl, public transit atrophies, shopping centers multiply, workplaces scatter.

The global food consumption ladder has three rungs. According to the latest World Bank estimates, the world's 630 million poorest people are unable to provide themselves with a healthy diet. On the next rung, the 3.4 billion grain eaters of the world's middle class get enough calories and plenty of plant-based protein, giving them the world's healthiest basic diet.

The top of the ladder is populated by the meat eaters, those who obtain close to 40% of their calories from fat. These 1.25 billion people eat three times as much fat per person as the remaining four billion, mostly because they eat so much red meat. The meat class pays the price of its diet in high death rates from the so-called diseases of affluence—heart disease, stroke, and certain types of cancer.

The earth also pays for the high-fat diet. Indirectly, the meat-eating quarter of humanity consumes nearly 40% of the world's grain—grain that fattens the livestock they eat. Meat production is behind a substantial share of the environmental strains induced by agriculture, from soil erosion to overpumping of underground water.

In consumption of raw materials, such as steel, cotton, or wood, the same pattern emerges. A large group lacks many of the benefits provided by modest use of nonrenewable resources—particularly durables like radios, refrigerators, water pipes, tools, and carts with lightweight wheels and ball bearings. More than two billion people live in countries where per capita consumption of steel, the most basic modern material, falls below 50 kilograms a year.

Roughly 1.5 billion live in the middle class of materials use. Providing each of them with durable goods every year uses between 50 and 150 kilograms of steel. At the top of the heap is the industrial world or the throwaway class. A typical resident of the industrialized fourth of the world uses 15 times as much paper, 10 times as much steel, and 12 times as much fuel as a Third World resident.

In the throwaway economy, packaging becomes an end in itself, disposables proliferate, and durability suffers. Americans toss away 180 million razors annually, enough paper and plastic plates and cups to feed the world a picnic six times a year, and enough aluminum cans to make 6,000 DC-10 airplanes. Similarly, the Japanese use 30 million "disposable" single-roll cameras each year, and the British dump 2.5 billion diapers.

The Cultivation of Needs

What prompts us to consume so much? "The avarice of mankind is insatiable," wrote Aristotle 23 centuries ago. As each of our desires is satisfied, a new one appears in its place. All of economic theory is based on that observation.

What distinguishes modern consuming habits, some would say, is simply that we are much richer than our ancestors, and consequently have more ruinous effects on nature. While a great deal of truth lies in that view, five distinctly modern factors play a role in cultivating particularly voracious appetites: the influence of social pressures in mass societies, advertising, the shopping culture, various government policies, and the expansion of the mass market into households and local communities.

In advanced industrial nations, daily interactions with the economy lack the face-to-face character prevailing in surviving local communities. Traditional virtues such as integrity, honesty, and skill are too hard to measure to serve as yardsticks of social worth. By default, they are gradually supplanted by a simple, single indicator—money. As one Wall Street banker put it bluntly to the *New York Times,* "Net worth equals self-worth."

Beyond social pressures, the affluent live completely enveloped in pro-consumption advertising messages. The sales pitch is everywhere. One analyst estimates that the typical American is exposed to 50 to 100 advertisements each morning before nine o'clock. Along with their weekly 22-hour diet of television, American teenagers are typically exposed to three to four hours of TV advertisements a week, adding up to at least 100,000 ads between birth and high school graduation.

Advertising has been one of the fastest-growing industries during the past half-century. In the United States, ad expenditures rose from $198 per capita in 1950 to $498 in 1989 to $930 for every man, woman, and child in the country in 2007. Worldwide, over the same period, per person advertising expenditures grew from $15 in 1950 to $46 in 1989 and $71 in 2002. In developing countries, the increases have been astonishing. Advertising billings in India jumped fivefold in the 1980s; newly industrialized South Korea's advertising industry grew 3540% annually in the late 1980s.

Government policies also play a role in promoting consumption and in worsening its ecological impact. The British tax code, for example, encourages businesses to buy thousands of large company cars for employee use. Most governments in North and South America subsidize beef production on a massive scale.

Finally, the sweeping advance of the commercial mass market into realms once dominated by family members and local enterprise has made consumption far more wasteful than in the past. More and more, flush with cash but pressed for time, households opt for the questionable "conveniences" of prepared, packaged foods, miracle cleaning products, and disposable everything—from napkins to shower curtains. All these things cost the earth dearly.

Like the household, the community economy has atrophied—or been dismembered—under the blind force of the money economy. Shopping malls, superhighways, and strips have replaced corner stores, local restaurants, and neighborhood theaters—the very places that help create a sense of common identity and community. Traditional Japanese vegetable stands and fish shops are giving way to supermarkets and convenience stores, and styrofoam and plastic film have replaced yesterday's newspaper as fish wrap.

All these things nurture the acquisitive desires that everyone has. Can we, as individuals and as citizens, act to confront these forces?

The Culture of Permanence

The basic value of a sustainable society, the ecological equivalent of the Golden Rule, is simple: Each generation should meet its own needs without jeopardizing the prospects of future generations to meet theirs.

For individuals, the decision to live a life of sufficiency—to find their own answer to the question "how much is enough?"—is to begin a highly personal process. Social researcher Duane Elgin estimated in 1981—perhaps optimistically—that 10 million adult Americans were experimenting "wholeheartedly" with voluntary simplicity. India, the Netherlands, Norway, Western Germany, and the United Kingdom all have small segments of their populations who adhere to a non-consuming philosophy. Motivated by the desire to live justly in an unjust world, to walk gently on the earth, and to avoid distraction, clutter, and pretense, their goal is not ascetic self-denial but personal fulfillment. They do not think consuming more is likely to provide it.

Realistically, voluntary simplicity is unlikely to gain ground rapidly against the onslaught of consumerist values. And, ultimately, personal restraint will do little if not wedded to bold political and social steps against the forces promoting consumption. Commercial television, for example, will need fundamental reorientation in a culture of permanence. As religious historian Robert Bellah put it, "That happiness is to be attained through limitless material acquisition is denied by every religion and philosophy known to humankind, but is preached incessantly by every American television set."

Direct incentives for overconsumption are also essential targets for reform. If goods' prices reflected something closer to the environmental cost of their production, through revised subsidies and tax systems, the market itself would guide consumers toward less damaging forms of consumption. Disposables and packaging would rise in price relative to durable, less-packaged goods; local unprocessed food would fall in price relative to prepared products trucked from far away.

The net effect might be lower overall consumption as people's effective purchasing power declined. As currently constituted, unfortunately, economies penalize the poor when aggregate consumption contracts: Unemployment skyrockets and inequalities grow. Thus arises one of the greatest challenges for sustainable economics in rich societies—finding ways to ensure basic employment opportunities for all without constantly stoking the fires of economic growth. ❏

Article 1.5

SHARING THE WEALTH OF THE COMMONS

BY PETER BARNES
November/December 2004

We're all familiar with private wealth, even if we don't have much. Economists and the media celebrate it every day. But there's another trove of wealth we barely notice: our common wealth.

Each of us is the beneficiary of a vast inheritance. This common wealth includes our air and water, habitats and ecosystems, languages and cultures, science and technologies, political and monetary systems, and quite a bit more. To say we share this inheritance doesn't mean we can call a broker and sell our shares tomorrow. It does mean we're responsible for the commons and entitled to any income it generates. Both the responsibility and the entitlement are ours by birth. They're part of the obligation each generation owes to the next, and each living human owes to other beings.

At present, however, our economic system scarcely recognizes the commons. This omission causes two major tragedies: ceaseless destruction of nature and widening inequality among humans. Nature gets destroyed because no one's unequivocally responsible for protecting it. Inequality widens because private wealth concentrates while common wealth shrinks.

The great challenges for the 21st century are, first of all, to make the commons visible; second, to give it proper reverence; and third, to translate that reverence into property rights and legal institutions that are on a par with those supporting private property. If we do this, we can avert the twin tragedies currently built into our market-driven system.

Defining the Commons

What exactly is the commons? Here is a workable definition: The commons includes all the assets we inherit together and are morally obligated to pass on, undiminished, to future generations.

This definition is a practical one. It designates a set of assets that have three specific characteristics: they're (1) inherited, (2) shared, and (3) worthy of long-term preservation. Usually it's obvious whether an asset has these characteristics or not.

At the same time, the definition is broad. It encompasses assets that are natural as well as social, intangible as well as tangible, small as well as large. It also introduces a moral factor that is absent from other economic definitions: it requires us to consider whether an asset is worthy of long-term preservation. At present, capitalism has no interest in this question. If an asset is likely to yield a competitive return to capital, it's kept alive; if not, it's destroyed or allowed to run down. Assets in the commons, by contrast, are meant to be preserved regardless of their return.

This definition sorts all economic assets into two baskets, the market and the commons. In the market basket are those assets we want to own privately and manage for profit. In the commons basket are the assets we want to hold in common and manage for long-term preservation. These baskets then are, or ought to be, the yin and yang of economic activity; each should enhance and contain the other. The role of the state should be to maintain a healthy balance between them.

The Value of the Commons

For most of human existence, the commons supplied everyone's food, water, fuel, and medicines. People hunted, fished, gathered fruits and herbs, collected firewood and building materials, and grazed their animals in common lands and waters. In other words, the commons was the source of basic sustenance. This is still true today in many parts of the world, and even in San Francisco, where I live, cash-poor people fish in the bay not for sport, but for food.

Though sustenance in the industrialized world now flows mostly through markets, the commons remains hugely valuable. It's the source of all natural resources and nature's many replenishing services. Water, air, DNA, seeds, topsoil, minerals, the protective ozone layer, the atmosphere's climate regulation, and much more, are gifts of nature to us all.

Just as crucially, the commons is our ultimate waste sink. It recycles water, oxygen, carbon, and everything else we excrete, exhale, or throw away. It's the place we store, or try to store, the residues of our industrial system.

The commons also holds humanity's vast accumulation of knowledge, art, and thought. As Isaac Newton said, "If I have seen further it is by standing on the shoulders of giants." So, too, the legal, political, and economic institutions we inherit—even the market itself—were built by the efforts of millions. Without these gifts we'd be hugely poorer than we are today.

To be sure, thinking of these natural and social inheritances primarily as economic assets is a limited way of viewing them. I deeply believe they are much more than that. But if treating portions of the commons as economic assets can help us conserve them, it's surely worth doing so.

How much might the commons be worth in monetary terms? It's relatively easy to put a dollar value on private assets. Accountants and appraisers do it every day, aided by the fact that private assets are regularly traded for money.

This isn't the case with most shared assets. How much is clean air, an intact wetlands,

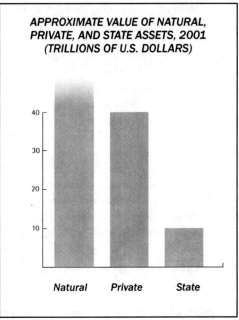

APPROXIMATE VALUE OF NATURAL, PRIVATE, AND STATE ASSETS, 2001 (TRILLIONS OF U.S. DOLLARS)

or Darwin's theory of evolution worth in dollar terms? Clearly, many shared inheritances are simply priceless. Others are potentially quantifiable, but there's no current market for them. Fortunately, economists have developed methods to quantify the value of things that aren't traded, so it's possible to estimate the value of the "priceable" part of the commons within an order of magnitude. The surprising conclusion that emerges from numerous studies is that the wealth we share is worth more than the wealth we own privately.

This fact bears repeating. Even though much of the commons can't be valued in monetary terms, the parts that can be valued are worth more than all private assets combined.

It's worth noting that these estimates understate the gap between common and private assets because a significant portion of the value attributed to private wealth is in fact an appropriation of common wealth. If this mislabeled portion was subtracted from private wealth and added to common wealth, the gap between the two would widen further.

Two examples will make this point clear. Suppose you buy a house for $200,000 and, without improving it, sell it a few years later for $300,000. You pay off the mortgage and walk away with a pile of cash. But what caused the house to rise in value? It wasn't anything you did. Rather, it was the fact that your neighborhood became more popular, likely a result of the efforts of community members, improvements in public services, and similar factors.

Or consider another fount of private wealth, the social invention and public expansion of the stock market. Suppose you start a business that goes "public" through an offering of stock. Within a few years, you're able to sell your stock for a spectacular capital gain.

Much of this gain is a social creation, the result of centuries of monetary-system evolution, laws and regulations, and whole industries devoted to accounting, sharing information, and trading stocks. What's more, there's a direct correlation between the scale and quality of the stock market as an institution and the size of the private gain. You'll fetch a higher price if you sell into a market of millions than into a market of two. Similarly, you'll gain more if transaction costs are low and trust in public information is high. Thus, stock that's traded on a regulated exchange sells for a higher multiple of earnings than unlisted stock. This socially created premium can account for 30% of the stock's value. If you're the lucky seller, you'll reap that extra cash—in no way thanks to anything you did as an individual.

Real estate gains and the stock market's social premium are just two instances of common assets contributing to private gain. Still, most rich people would like us to think it's their extraordinary talent, hard work, and risk-taking that create their well-deserved wealth. That's like saying a flower's beauty is due solely to its own efforts, owing nothing to nutrients in the soil, energy from the sun, water from the aquifer, or the activity of bees.

The Great Commons Giveaway

That we inherit a trove of common wealth is the good news. The bad news, alas, is that our inheritance is being grossly mismanaged. As a recent report by the advocacy group Friends of the Commons concludes, "Maintenance of the commons is terrible, theft is rampant, and rents often aren't collected. To put it bluntly, our common wealth—and our children's—is being squandered. We are all poorer as a result."

Examples of commons mismanagement include the handout of broadcast spectrum to media conglomerates, the giveaway of pollution rights to polluters, the extension of copyrights to entertainment companies, the patenting of seeds and genes, the privatization of water, and the relentless destruction of habitat, wildlife, and ecosystems.

This mismanagement, though currently extreme, is not new. For over 200 years, the market has been devouring the commons in two ways. With one hand, the market takes valuable stuff from the commons and privatizes it. This is called "enclosure." With the other hand, the market dumps bad stuff into the commons and says, "It's your problem." This is called "externalizing." Much that is called economic growth today is actually a form of cannibalization in which the market diminishes the commons that ultimately sustains it.

Enclosure—the taking of good stuff from the commons—at first meant privatization of land by the gentry. Today it means privatization of many common assets by corporations. Either way, it means that what once belonged to everyone now belongs to a few.

Enclosure is usually justified in the name of efficiency. And sometimes, though not always, it does result in efficiency gains. But what also results from enclosure is the impoverishment of those who lose access to the commons, and the enrichment of those who take title to it. In other words, enclosure widens the gap between those with income-producing property and those without.

Externalizing—the dumping of bad stuff into the commons—is an automatic behavior pattern of profit-maximizing corporations: if they can avoid any out-of-pocket costs, they will. If workers, taxpayers, anyone downwind, future generations, or nature have to absorb added costs, so be it.

For decades, economists have agreed we'd be better served if businesses "internalized" their externalities—that is, paid in real time the costs they now shift to the commons. The reason this doesn't happen is that there's no one to set prices and collect them. Unlike private wealth, the commons lacks property rights and institutions to represent it in the marketplace.

The seeds of such institutions, however, are starting to emerge. Consider one of the environmental protection tools the U.S. currently uses, pollution trading. So-called cap-and-trade programs put a cap on total pollution, then grant portions of the total, via permits, to each polluting firm. Companies may buy other firms' permits if they want to pollute more than their allotment allows, or sell unused permits if they manage to pollute less. Such programs are generally supported by business because they allow polluters to find the cheapest ways to reduce pollution.

Public discussion of cap-and-trade programs has focused exclusively on their trading features. What's been overlooked is how they give away common wealth to polluters.

To date, all cap-and-trade programs have begun by giving pollution rights to existing polluters for free. This treats polluters as if they own our sky and rivers. It means that future polluters will have to pay old polluters for the scarce—hence valuable—right to dump wastes into nature. Imagine that: because a corporation polluted in the past, it gets free income forever! And, because ultimately we'll all pay for limited pollution via higher prices, this amounts to an enormous transfer of wealth—trillions of dollars—to shareholders of historically polluting corporations.

In theory, though, there is no reason that the initial pollution rights should not reside with the public. Clean air and the atmosphere's capacity to absorb pollutants are "wealth" that belongs to everyone. Hence, when polluters use up these parts of the commons, they should pay the public—not the other way around.

Taking the Commons Back

How can we correct the system omission that permits, and indeed promotes, destruction of nature and ever-widening inequality among humans? The answer lies in building a new sector of the economy whose clear legal mission is to preserve shared inheritances for everyone. Just as the market is populated by profit-maximizing corporations, so this new sector would be populated by asset-preserving trusts.

Here a brief description of trusts may be helpful. The trust is a private institution that's even older than the corporation. The essence of a trust is a fiduciary relationship. A trust holds and manages property for another person or for many other people. A simple example is a trust set up by a grandparent to pay for a grandchild's education. Other trusts include pension funds, charitable foundations, and university endowments. There are also hundreds of trusts in America, like the Nature Conservancy and the Trust for Public Land, that own land or conservation easements in perpetuity.

If we were to design an institution to protect pieces of the commons, we couldn't do much better than a trust. The goal of commons management, after all, is to preserve assets and deliver benefits to broad classes of beneficiaries. That's what trusts do, and it's not rocket science.

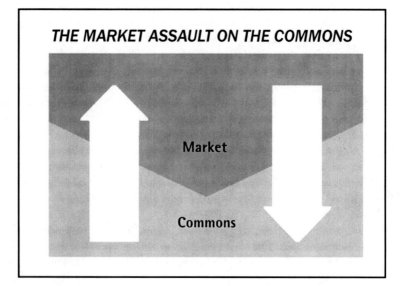

THE MARKET ASSAULT ON THE COMMONS

Market

Commons

Over centuries, several principles of trust management have evolved. These include:

- Trustees have a fiduciary responsibility to beneficiaries. If a trustee fails in this obligation, he or she can be removed and penalized.
- Trustees must preserve the original asset. It's okay to spend income, but don't invade the principal.
- Trustees must assure transparency. Information about money flows should be readily available to beneficiaries.

Trusts in the new commons sector would be endowed with rights comparable to those of corporations. Their trustees would take binding oaths of office and, like judges, serve long terms. Though protecting common assets would be their primary job, they would also distribute income from those assets to beneficiaries. These beneficiaries would include all citizens within a jurisdiction, large classes of citizens (children, the elderly), and/or agencies serving common purposes such as public transit or ecological restoration. When distributing income to individuals, the allocation formula would be one person, one share. The right to receive commons income would be a nontransferable birthright, not a property right that could be traded.

Fortuitously, a working model of such a trust already exists: the Alaska Permanent Fund. When oil drilling on the North Slope began in the 1970s, Gov. Jay Hammond, a Republican, proposed that 25% of the state's royalties be placed in a mutual fund to be invested on behalf of Alaska's citizens. Voters approved in a referendum. Since then, the Alaska Permanent Fund has grown to over $28 billion, and Alaskans have received roughly $22,000 apiece in dividends. In 2003 the per capita dividend was $1,107; a family of four received $4,428.

What Alaska did with its oil can be replicated for other gifts of nature. For example, we could create a nationwide Sky Trust to stabilize the climate for future generations. The trust would restrict emissions of heat-trapping gases and sell a declining number of emission permits to polluters. The income would be returned to U.S. residents in equal yearly dividends, thus reversing the wealth transfer built into current cap-and-trade programs. Instead of everyone paying historic polluters, polluters would pay all of us.

Just as a Sky Trust could represent our equity in the natural commons, a Public Stock Trust could embody our equity in the social commons. Such a trust would capture some of the socially created stock-market premium that currently flows only to shareholders and their investment bankers. As noted earlier, this premium is sizeable—roughly 30% of the value of publicly traded stock. A simple way to share it would be to create a giant mutual fund—call it the American Permanent Fund—that would hold, say, 10% of the shares of publicly traded companies. This mutual fund, in turn, would be owned by all Americans on a one share per person basis (perhaps linked to their Social Security accounts).

To build up the fund without precipitating a fall in share prices, companies would contribute shares at the rate of, say, 1% per year. The contributions would be the price companies pay for the benefits they derive from a commons asset, the large, trusted market for stock—a small price, indeed, for the hefty benefits. Over time, the mutual fund would assure that when the economy grows, everyone benefits. The top 5% would still own more than the bottom 90%, but at least every American would have some property income, and a slightly larger slice of our economic pie.

Sharing the Wealth

The perpetuation of inequality is built into the current design of capitalism. Because of the skewed distribution of private wealth, a small self-perpetuating minority receives a disproportionate share of America's nonlabor income.

Tom Paine had something to say about this. In his essay "Agrarian Justice," written in 1790, he argued that, because enclosure of the commons had separated so many people from their primary source of sustenance, it was necessary to create a functional equivalent of the commons in the form of a National Fund. Here is how he put it:

> There are two kinds of property. Firstly, natural property, or that which comes to us from the Creator of the universe—such as the earth, air, water. Secondly, artificial or acquired property—the invention of men. In the latter, equality is impossible; for to distribute it equally, it would be necessary that all should have contributed in the same proportion, which can never be the case .... Equality of natural property is different. Every individual in the world is born with legitimate claims on this property, or its equivalent.

Enclosure of the commons, he went on, was necessary to improve the efficiency of cultivation. But:

> The landed monopoly that began with [enclosure] has produced the greatest evil. It has dispossessed more than half the inhabitants of every nation of their natural inheritance, without providing for them, as ought to have been done, an indemnification for that loss, and has thereby created a species of poverty and wretchedness that did not exist before.

The appropriate compensation for loss of the commons, Paine said, was a national fund financed by rents paid by land owners. Out of this fund, every person reaching age 21 would get 15 pounds a year, and every person over 50 would receive an additional 10 pounds. (Think of Social Security, financed by commons rents instead of payroll taxes.)

A Progressive Offensive

Paine's vision, allowing for inflation and new forms of enclosure, could not be more timely today. Surely from our vast common inheritance—not just the land, but the atmosphere, the broadcast spectrum, our mineral resources, our threatened habitats and water supplies—enough rent can be collected to pay every American over age 21 a modest annual dividend, and every person reaching 21 a small start-up inheritance.

Such a proposal may seem utopian. In today's political climate, perhaps it is. But consider this. About 20 years ago, right-wing think tanks laid out a bold agenda. They called for lowering taxes on private wealth, privatizing much of government, and deregulating industry. Amazingly, this radical agenda has largely been achieved.

It's time for progressives to mount an equally bold offensive. The old shibboleths—let's gin up the economy, create jobs, and expand government programs—no longer excite. We need to talk about fixing the economy, not just growing it; about income for everyone, not just jobs; about nurturing ecosystems, cultures, and communities, not just our individual selves. More broadly, we need to celebrate the commons as an essential counterpoise to the market.

Unfortunately, many progressives have viewed the state as the only possible counterpoise to the market. The trouble is, the state has been captured by corporations. This capture isn't accidental or temporary; it's structural and long-term.

This doesn't mean progressives can't occasionally recapture the state. We've done so before and will do so again. It does mean that progressive control of the state is the exception, not the norm; in due course, corporate capture will resume. It follows that if we want lasting fixes to capitalism's tragic flaws, we must use our brief moments of political ascendancy to build institutions that endure.

Programs that rely on taxes, appropriations, or regulations are inherently transitory; they get weakened or repealed when political power shifts. By contrast, institutions that are self-perpetuating and have broad constituencies are likely to last. (It also helps if they mail out checks periodically.) This was the genius of Social Security, which has survived—indeed grown—through numerous Republican administrations.

If progressives are smart, we'll use our next New Deal to create common property trusts that include all Americans as beneficiaries. These trusts will then be to the 21st century what social insurance was to the 20th: sturdy pillars of shared responsibility and entitlement. Through them, the commons will be a source of sustenance for all, as it was before enclosure. Life-long income will be linked to generations-long ecological health. Isn't that a future most Americans would welcome? ❑

Article 1.6

THE UNDESERVING RICH

Collectively produced and inherited knowledge and the (re)distribution of income and wealth.

BY GAR ALPEROVITZ AND LEW DALY
March/April 2010

Warren Buffett, one of the wealthiest men in the nation, is worth nearly $50 billion. Does he "deserve" all this money? Why? Did he work so much harder than everyone else? Did he create something so extraordinary that no one else could have created it? Ask Buffett himself and he will tell you that he thinks "society is responsible for a very significant percentage of what I've earned." But if that's true, doesn't society deserve a very significant share of what he has earned?

When asked why he is so successful, Buffett commonly replies that this is the wrong question. The more important question, he stresses, is why he has *so much to work with* compared to other people in the world, or compared to previous generations of Americans. Buffett asks: how much money would he have if he had been born in Bangladesh, or in the United States in 1700?

Buffett may or may not deserve something more than another person working with what a given historical or collective context provides. As he observes, however, it is simply not possible to argue in any serious way that he deserves *all* of the benefits that are clearly attributable to living in a highly developed society.

Buffett has put his finger on one of the most explosive issues developing just beneath the surface of public awareness. Over the last several decades, economic research has done a great deal of solid work pinpointing much more precisely than in the past what share of what we call "wealth" society creates versus what share any individual can be said to have earned and thus deserved. This research raises profound moral—and ultimately political—questions.

Through No Effort of Our Own

Recent estimates suggest that U.S. economic output per capita has increased more than twenty-fold since 1800. Output per hour worked has increased an estimated fifteen-fold since 1870 alone. Yet the average modern person likely works with no greater commitment, risk, or intelligence than his or her counterpart from the past. What is the primary cause of such vast gains if individuals do not really "improve"? Clearly, it is largely that the scientific, technical, and cultural knowledge available to us, and the efficiency of our means of storing and retrieving this knowledge, have grown at a scale and pace that far outstrip any other factor in the nation's economic development.

A half century ago, in 1957, economist Robert Solow calculated that nearly 90% of productivity growth in the first half of the 20th century (from 1909 to 1949) could only be attributed to "technical change in the broadest sense." The supply of labor and capital—what workers and employers contribute—appeared almost incidental to this massive technological "residual." Subsequent research inspired by

Solow and others continued to point to "advances in knowledge" as the main source of growth. Economist William Baumol calculates that "nearly 90 percent . . . of current GDP was contributed by innovation carried out since 1870." Baumol judges that his estimate, in fact, understates the cumulative influence of past advances: Even "the steam engine, the railroad, and many other inventions of an earlier era, still add to today's GDP."

Related research on the sources of invention bolsters the new view, posing a powerful challenge to conventional, heroic views of technology that characterize progress as a sequence of extraordinary contributions by "Great Men" (occasionally "Great Women") and their "Great Inventions." In contrast to this popular view, historians of technology have carefully delineated the incremental and cumulative way most technologies actually develop. In general, a specific field of knowledge builds up slowly through diverse contributions over time until—at a particular moment when enough has been established—the next so-called "breakthrough" becomes all but inevitable.

Often many people reach the same point at virtually the same time, for the simple reason that they all are working from the same developing information and research base. The next step commonly becomes obvious (or if not obvious, very likely to be taken within a few months or years). We tend to give credit to the person who gets there first—or rather, who gets the first public attention, since often the real originator is not as good at public relations as the one who jumps to the front of the line and claims credit. Thus, we remember Alexander Graham Bell as the inventor of the telephone even though, among others, Elisha Gray and Antonio Meucci got there at the same time or even before him. Newton and Leibniz hit upon the calculus at roughly the same time in the 1670s; Darwin and Alfred Russel Wallace produced essentially the same theory of evolution at roughly the same time in the late 1850s.

Less important than who gets the credit is the simple fact that most breakthroughs occur not so much thanks to one "genius," but because of the longer historical unfolding of knowledge. All of this knowledge—the overwhelming source of all modern wealth—comes to us today *through no effort of our own*. It is the generous and unearned gift of the past. In the words of Northwestern economist Joel Mokyr, it is a "free lunch."

Collective knowledge is often created by formal public efforts as well, a point progressives often stress. Many of the advances which propelled our high-tech economy in the early 1990s grew directly out of research programs and technical systems financed and often collaboratively developed by the federal government. The Internet, to take the most obvious example, began as a government defense project, the ARPANET, in the early 1960s. Up through the 1980s there was little private investment or interest in developing computer networks. Today's vast software industry also rests on a foundation of computer language and operating hardware developed in large part with public support. The Bill Gateses of the world—the heroes of the "New Economy"—might still be working with vacuum tubes and punch cards were it not for critical research and technology programs created or financed by the federal government after World War II. Other illustrations range from jet airplanes and radar to the basic life science research undergirding many pharmaceutical industry advances. Yet the truth is that the role of collectively inherited knowledge is far, far greater than just the contributions made by direct public support, important as they are.

Earned Income?

A straightforward but rarely confronted question arises from these facts: If most of what we have today is attributable to advances we inherit in common, then why should this gift of our collective history not more generously benefit all members of society?

The top 1% of U.S. households now receives more income than the bottom 120 million Americans combined. The richest 1% of households owns nearly half of all investment assets (stocks and mutual funds, financial securities, business equity, trusts, non-home real estate). The bottom 90% of the population owns less than 15%; the bottom half—150 million Americans—owns less than 1%. If America's vast wealth is mainly a gift of our common past, what justifies such disparities?

Robert Dahl, one of America's leading political scientists—and one of the few to have confronted these facts—put it this way after reading economist Edward Denison's pioneering work on growth accounting: "It is immediately obvious that little growth in the American economy can be attributed to the actions of particular individuals." He concluded straightforwardly that, accordingly, "the control and ownership of the economy rightfully belongs to 'society.'"

Contrast Dahl's view with that of Joe the Plumber, who famously inserted himself into the 2008 presidential campaign with his repeated claim that he has "earned" everything he gets and so any attempt to tax his earnings is totally unjustified. Likewise, "we didn't rely on somebody else to build what we built," banking titan Sanford Weill tells us in a *New York Times* front-page story on the "New Gilded Age." "I think there are people," another executive tells the *Times*, "who because of their uniqueness warrant whatever the market will bear."

A direct confrontation with the role of knowledge—and especially inherited knowledge—goes to the root of a profound challenge to such arguments. One way to think about all this is by focusing on the concept of "earned" versus "unearned" income. Today this distinction can be found in conservative attacks on welfare "cheats" who refuse to work to earn their keep, as well as in calls even by some Republican senators to tax the windfall oil-company profits occasioned by the Iraq war and Hurricane Katrina.

The concept of unearned income first came into clear focus during the era of rapidly rising land values caused by grain shortages in early 19th-century England. Wealth derived *simply* from owning land whose price was escalating appeared illegitimate because no individual truly "earned" such wealth. Land values—and especially explosively high values—were largely the product of factors such as fertility, location, and population pressures. The huge profits (unearned "rents," in the technical language of economics) landowners reaped when there were food shortages were viewed as particularly egregious. David Ricardo's influential theory of "differential rent"—i.e., that land values are determined by differences in fertility and location between different plots of land—along with religious perspectives reaching back to the Book of Genesis played a central role in sharpening this critical moral distinction.

John Stuart Mill, among others, developed the distinction between "earned" and "unearned" in the middle decades of the 19th century and applied it to other forms of "external wealth," or what he called "wealth created by circumstances." Mill's approach fed into a growing sense of the importance of societal inputs which produce economic gains beyond what can be ascribed to one person working alone in nature without benefit of civilization's many contributions. Here a second element of what appears, historically, as a slowly evolving understanding also becomes clear: If contribution is important in determining rewards, then, Mill and others urged, since society at large makes major contributions to economic achievement, it too has "earned" and deserves a share of what has been created. Mill believed strongly in personal contribution and individual reward, but he held that in principle wealth "created by circumstances" should be reclaimed for social purposes. Karl Marx, of course, tapped the distinction between earned and unearned in his much broader attack on capitalism and its exploitation of workers' labor.

The American republican writer Thomas Paine was among the first to articulate a societal theory of wealth based directly on the earned/unearned distinction. Paine argued that everything "beyond what a man's own hands produce" was a gift which came to him simply by living in society, and hence "he owes on every principle of justice, of gratitude, and of civilization, a part of that accumulation back again to society from whence the whole came." A later American reformer, Henry George, focused on urban land rather than the agricultural land at the heart of Ricardo's concern. George challenged what he called "the unearned increment" which is created when population growth and other societal factors increase land values. In Britain, J. A. Hobson argued that the unearned value created by the industrial system in general was much larger than just the part which accrued to landowners, and that it should be treated in a similar (if not more radical and comprehensive) fashion. In a similar vein, Hobson's early 20th-century contemporary Leonard Trelawny Hobhouse declared that the "prosperous business man" should consider "what single step he could have taken" without the "sum of intelligence which civilization has placed at his disposal." More recently, the famed American social scientist Herbert Simon judged that if "we are very generous with ourselves, I suppose we might claim that we 'earned' as much as one fifth of [our income]."

The distinction between earned and unearned gains is central to most of these thinkers, as is the notion that societal contributions—including everything an industrial economy requires, from the creation of laws, police, and courts to the development of schools, trade restrictions, and patents—must be recognized and rewarded. The understanding that such societal contributions are both contemporary and have made a huge and cumulative contribution over all of history is also widely accepted. Much of the income they permit and confer now appears broadly analogous to the unearned rent a landlord claims. What is new and significant here is the further clarification that by far the most important element in all this is the accumulated *knowledge* which society contributes over time.

All of this, as sociologist Daniel Bell has suggested, requires a new "knowledge theory of value"—especially as we move deeper into the high-tech era through computerization, the Internet, cybernetics, and cutting-edge fields such as gene therapy and nanotechnology. One way to grasp what is at stake is the following: A person today working the same number of hours as a similar person in 1870—working just as hard but no harder—will produce perhaps 15 times as much economic output. It is clear that the contemporary person can hardly be said to have "earned" his much greater productivity.

Consider further that if we project forward the past century's rate of growth, a person working a century from now would be able to produce—and potentially receive as "income"—up to seven times today's average income. By far the greatest part of this gain will also come to this person as a free gift of the past—the gift of the new knowledge created, passed on, and inherited from our own time forward.

She and her descendents, in fact, will inevitably contribute less, relative to the huge and now expanded contribution of the past, than we do today. The obvious question, again, is simply this: to what degree is it meaningful to say that this person will have "earned" all that may come her way? These and other realities suggest that the quiet revolution in our understanding of how wealth is created has ramifications for a much more profound and far-reaching challenge to today's untenable distribution of income and wealth. ❑

Article 1.7

THE BIG CASINO

BY DOUG ORR
May/June 2014

> *Speculators may do no harm as bubbles on a steady stream of enterprise. But the position is serious when enterprise becomes the bubble on a whirlpool of specu-lation. When the capital development of a country becomes a by-product of the activities of a casino, the job is likely to be ill-done.*
> — John Maynard Keynes (1936)

On December 31, 2013, the Dow-Jones Industrial Average hit a new record high of 16,577. The media cheered this result and proclaimed that happy days are here again. Yet that same day, they reported that income inequality is continuing to increase, median family income is still 9% below what it was at the start of the recession, and the index of consumer sentiment is still 25% below pre-recession levels. Millions of people are still unemployed and Congress let long-term unemployment benefits expire. It appears that all of this suffering on Main Street is good for the stock market.

The media's constant reporting of stock market numbers so prominently and giving supposed links to the events of the day gives the impression that the stock market plays a central role in moving the economy forward and that everyone has a stake in these daily changes. In fact, the movement of these stock indices on a day-to-day basis has very little to do with the actual economy and, except in times of economic crisis, the stock market has almost no impact on the lives of most Americans. Fewer than half of American families own a single share of stock, and only about a third own shares totaling more than $5000. The stock market is the realm of the elite, and for the past several decades has had a negative impact on the real economy.

Who Are the "Investors"?

Economics textbooks tell us that financial markets play an important role in the economy, linking saving to investment. Some individuals have more income than they currently want to spend, so they engage in saving. Other individuals need money to engage in investment. "Investment" in this context means the creation of new, physically productive resources. If a firm builds a new factory, installs new machines, or buys new software to do its accounting, that is investment. When students spend time and money to acquire new skills that make them more productive, that is investment. So when a bank takes people's savings and lends it to the owner of a restaurant to buy a new stove, the bank plays an important economic role. Further, savers can get their money back if they need it in the future, because loans get repaid.

When you put money in the bank you receive interest. This is your reward for saving and giving the bank the use of your money. But you are not engaging in investment. The person who borrows the money and puts it to productive use is the investor. When you put money in the bank, you are a saver, not an investor.

Corporations, however, can bypass banks and gain access to financial capital by issuing stock. When a company issues new shares of stock, the money raised from the sale can be used to engage in productive investment. The issuing of new shares is called an "initial public offering," or IPO. IPOs are not done on stock exchanges. They are handled by investment banks. These IPOs transfer saving to firms and the firms can use the money for real investment. If these investments are successful, GDP will rise as consumers gain access to new products, the firm will grow and become more profitable, the price of their shares will rise, which provides savers a long-term capital gain as a return on their saving. This usually occurs over an extended period of time. But no one would buy a share of stock if they could not get their money back when they needed it. The useful role of the stock exchanges, what we call the "stock market," is to provide "liquidity." One individual who has money to save today can buy a share of stock from someone who needs to get their past savings back.

The words we use to describe things matter. Investors are usually seen as contributing to the economy because they hire workers to build new factories, new machines, and other productive assets, and these assets can make the real economy more productive. Workers create the assets, and the investors are given the credit. On the other hand, gamblers and speculators are usually seen as frivolous and destructive.

The biggest propaganda coup of the 20th century was convincing the media and the general public to call the speculators on the New York Stock Exchange (NYSE) "investors." They did it by blurring the positive role of the stock market with the speculative role. If you buy a share of Pacific Gas and Electric (PG&E) stock on the stock exchange, you will get a quarterly dividend payment, just like the interest you get from the money you put in a bank. But, PG&E does not get any new money to use for actual investment. The price you pay for the stock goes to the previous owner of the stock, not PG&E. Buying stock on the NYSE is not investing, but rather seeking a return on saving. But unlike saving at a bank, this saving involves a risk and is a form of speculation.

When the Dow-Jones index hit a record high of 16,577, that day NYSE market volume was 461 million shares, and another 1.34 billion shares were traded on the NASDAQ. That was a slow day because of the holidays. More than $50 billion changed hands, yet not a penny of all this money went to a corporation for use as productive investment.

The biggest casino in the world is located at the corner of Wall Street and Broad Street in New York City. Calling the players on the NYSE "investors" completely changes our understanding of the role they play. Consider rewording some recent stories: "Gamblers bet big on new Genentech drug," or "Speculators made 73% in one day buying Twitter's IPO in the morning and reselling later in the day to suckers caught up in the excitement." The Wall Street Journal does occasionally tell us the truth when they report on the "bets" made by "players" on the NYSE. Speculators betting that the price of a share will rise want to buy it and those betting that the price will fall want to sell it. If there are more buyers than sellers, the price will rise, regardless of anything that is happening in the real economy. Reporting a record high for the NYSE has about as much importance as reporting a record amount of gambling in Las Vegas. Except the gambling on the NYSE can have a much larger negative impact on the real economy.

Big Gambling Does Big Damage

The reason why the volume on the NYSE is so high is because speculators engage in high-frequency trading. An analyst predicts that, based on breaking news, the price of a particular stock may go up. If you can be the first to buy the stock before the price goes up, you can sell it a few minutes later (or even seconds, or fractions of a second, later) and make a profit. This is why brokerage houses now rely on "program trading." Computers can see price differentials and make trades much faster than humans can. Brokerage firms need to have the fastest possible computers and the fastest network connections because milliseconds matter. By 2010, this type of high-frequency, or "quant" trading made up 70% of the bloated stock trading volume.

If you buy a share of stock for $100 and sell it 30 minutes later for $100.50, you make a return of 50 cents, or 0.5%. If you buy a million shares, you make half a million dollars for a half an hour of "work." But the "work" was done by a computer program and you have done nothing to make the economy more productive, to create jobs, or to increase GDP. All you have done is to bring a large pile of money to the table at the casino. You have redistributed money from one person at the table to another, and for this, the Wall Street Journal calls you an "investor." You can use your winnings to hire the best and brightest minds to give you an edge at the table, and you will pay them well.

We are being told how important it is to get students into STEM fields (science, technology, engineering and math). Yet government funding for these fields is being cut and jobs prospects are uncertain. Stock market speculation diverts the best and brightest minds away from solving the real problems facing the world. Instead they are writing software to "read" news feeds looking for key phrases that might indicate a change in speculators' sentiment toward a particular stock, so that instantaneous trades can be made. They are writing algorithms to find the minutest correlations between economic indicators and changes in share prices. Landing a job at a big Wall Street firm can lead to annual bonuses in the millions of dollars. Jobs in basic scientific research and engineering cannot hope to compete.

Corporate managers are rewarded with bonuses for increases in stock prices, regardless of the long-term impacts on the firm. It forces managers to focus on quarterly profits and not on long-term economic growth. Cutting jobs and driving down wages can increase stock prices, but this has devastating impacts on the lives of ordinary people and reduces demand for products. If the price of a company's stock starts to fall, management may use the cash held by the company to buy back shares in order to prop up the price. This diverts resources that could have been used for productive investment into the hands of stock market speculators.

If enough of these speculators believe prices will continue to rise, they will pour more money into stocks, and share prices will rise. Speculation can be self-fulfilling and create price bubbles. The Dow-Jones was up by more than 35% for the year 2013. This run up in stock prices had several causes. Economists tell us that stock prices should reflect expected profitability, and despite the anemic recovery, corporate profits are soaring. The share of total national income going the owners of capital is now higher than at any point in modern U.S. history. But this is at the expense of the vast majority of the population. The share of national income going to wages and salaries continues to fall and is lower than in 1960. In the thirty three years since 1980, adjusted for inflation, labor productivity has gone up by 141% and wages have stagnated, going up by only 8%. The idea that each generation is better off than their parents' is no longer true. In the current recovery, 95% of the income gains have been taken by the top 1% of the population. The rise in stock prices is a reflection of the declining standard of living of the majority of Americans and the increasing incomes of the already wealthy. A recent Pew Center poll revealed that 64% of the population responded "no" when asked "does the U.S. offer everyone the same chance to get ahead." The share of income going to the richest 10% is higher than at any time since 1917. It is this richest 10% that own 91% all stocks, including all 401(k) accounts and mutual funds and 94% of other financial securities.

Some of the run up in stock prices may reflect this rise in profit, but another larger part is the result of speculation. Since the start of the recession, the Federal Reserve has pumped almost $4 trillion into the financial markets. All of this money has to go somewhere and banks are not lending it to businesses to engage in real investment. Some of it is being used by speculators to buy up foreclosed houses and either turning them into rentals or doing minor maintenance and then "flipping" them for a tidy profit (See Darwin BondGraham, "Whose Housing Recovery?" D&S March/April 2013). This is resulting in a massive redistribution of wealth from the middle class to the top 10% of wealth holders. In some cities, this is reigniting the housing bubble. But much of the money is finding its way into the stock market and this flood of money is driving up stock prices.

When speculators are optimistic they create bubbles. But if speculators turn pessimistic, they can also create stock market crashes. If this only affected the gamblers it would not be a problem. But as a company's stock price falls, it may be harder for the firm to borrow from banks or the bond market to pay for day-to-day operations. If this happens to enough companies, this can crash the real economy and drive up unemployment. As stock prices fall, the retirement savings of millions of workers (who have seen their defined-benefit pensions stolen and converted into 401(k) savings accounts) will also decline. Ordinary people reap little benefit from the daily speculation on the stock market, but millions experience real losses when the bets go bad. The Big Casino does very real damage to the real economy.

A Small Step Toward Taming the Casino

One way to reduce the damage would be to put a tax on the socially destructive behavior. We tax cigarettes and alcohol because of the damage they do. We tax gambling in Atlantic City at 8% and in Las Vegas at 6.25%. The sales taxes on socially useful items like shoes and computers are often more than 7%. There should also be a sales tax on the speculative buying and selling of stock.

To be sure, Wall Street lobbyists will try to scare the pubic in thinking that taxing speculation will somehow kill "investment" and jobs. Because unemployment is still high, anything that reduces employment growth will be seen as negative. But

SPECULATIVE TRADING VERSUS PRODUCTIVE FINANCING (FIGURES FOR 2007)		
EXISTING STOCKS TRADED	**NEW STOCKS ISSUED**	**RATIO OF TRADING TO NEW ISSUES**
$43.8 TRILLION	**$65.1 BILLION**	673:1
PERCENT OF TRADES GOING TO PRODUCTIVE FINANCING = 0.15%		

this tax will not reduce job creation. In fact, it is stock market speculation that does that. Between 2008 and 2013, the dollar value of shares repurchased by corporations was higher than the amount raised by IPOs. So the stock market has actually drained resources away from real investment and job creation.

In 2007, the year before the most recent collapse of a speculative bubble, $43.8 trillion in stocks changed hands on just the NYSE and the NASDAQ. That same year, only $65.1 billion was raised in IPOs. That is $673 dollars of speculation for every $1 allocated from savers to real investors. Putting a tax on stock speculation will have almost no impact on productive investment by businesses, but it will raise much needed revenue for public investments in education and infrastructure.

What we need is a "speculation-reduction tax." Some proponents of this type of tax call it a "financial transactions tax," or FTT. But the tax would not be on all financial transactions, just on speculation in the stock and bond markets. Gamblers and speculators are seen as frivolous and destructive, and a tax that would restrict their behavior would be positively received. To be fully effective, the tax should be "progressive" with respect to time. If a stock is held for less than a day, the tax on the trade should be 5% of the value of the trade. The tax on a stock held for a week would be 2%; for a month, 1%; and, for a year, 0.5%. But opponents will make the case that this is too complex and too costly, so a flat-rate tax is more feasible.

The European Union is likely to implement a FTT rate of 0.1% in 2014. This rate is too small to have much of an impact on speculation. The UK has had a tax rate of 0.5% since 1986. It has not restricted the basic functioning of their stock market, but a tax of this amount makes the short-term trade described above unprofitable. Since 2009, ten different FTT bills have been introduced in the U.S. House and four in the Senate, most at a rate less than 0.5%. If a 0.5% tax were implemented in the United States, the Congressional Research Service estimates revenue generation of $164 to $264 billion per year, depending on the decline in speculative trading. The left-leaning Center for Economic and Policy Research (CEPR) estimates revenues would be between $110 to $220 billion.

If the U.S. government implements this type of speculation-reduction tax, it will reallocate much needed resources to productive public investment and away from job-killing stock speculation. This idea, first proposed by John Maynard Keynes in 1936, is long over-due. As CEPR co-director Dean Baker put it in 1994, "Government is perfectly willingly to tax Las Vegas, Atlantic City and the lotteries, where working people place their bets with virtually no consequence to the country's economic future. Why then should it not also tax the preferred gambling venue of the wealthy, especially given the serious costs their activities impose on the economic prospects of the majority?" ❏

Sources: John Maynard Keynes, *The General Theory of Employment, Interest and Money* (1936); Dean Baker, et.al., "The Potential Revenue from Financial Transactions Taxes," Center for Economic and Policy Research, Dec. 2009; "A securities Transactions Tax: Brief Analytic Overview with Revenue Estimates," Congressional Research Service, June 2012; Robert Pollin and James Heintz, "Transaction Costs, Trading Elasticities and the Revenue Potential of Financial Transaction Taxes for the United States," Political Economy Research Institute, Dec. 2011; Dean Baker, Robert Pollin, and Marc Schaberg, "Taxing the Big Casino," *The Nation*, May 1994; Edward N. Wolff, The Asset Price Meltdown and the Wealth of the Middle Class, August 2012;NYSE Technologies Market Data (nyxdata.com); NASDAQ Trader (NASDAQtrader.com); PriceWaterhouse IPO Watch (pwc.com).

Chapter 2

SUPPLY AND DEMAND

INTRODUCTION

Textbooks tell us that supply and demand work like a well-oiled machine. The Law of Supply tells us that as the price of an item goes up, businesses will supply more of that good or service. The Law of Demand adds that as the price rises, consumers will choose to buy less of the item. Only one equilibrium price can bring businesses' and consumers' intentions into balance. Away from this equilibrium point, surpluses or shortages tend to drive the price back toward the equilibrium. Of course, government actions such as taxation or setting a price ceiling or floor can move the economy away from its market equilibrium, and create what economists call a "deadweight loss."

Our authors raise vexing issues about the mechanism of supply and demand. Chris Tilly and Marie Kennedy tell the complex story of a rise in the price of tortillas in Mexico, which turns out to be driven not by a shortage of corn, but by the multiple impacts of a nationwide shift towards free trade. The authors also go beyond an analysis of the causes of the price rise to explore its contribution to rising inequality in Mexico (Article 2.1).

Marc Breslow argues that supply and demand do not always produce the best outcomes for society. He notes that the "price gouging" that we suffer during shortages or feared shortages—especially for hard-to-substitute goods like gasoline—is simply supply and demand at work (Article 2.2).

With the "invisible hand of the market" efficiently allocating scarce resources, such as housing, what could possibly go wrong? In "The Bursting of the Housing Bubble" (Article 2.3), Dean Baker provides a trenchant analysis of the effects of the housing bubble in the United States, and a prescient view of the fallout from the bubble's inevitable demise.

The next two articles take on the mainstream textbook criticisms of price ceilings and price floors. Economist Ellen Frank questions the textbook models' conclusion that rent controls (and other price ceilings) lead to permanent shortages. She maintains that rent control helps to equalize power between landlords and tenants, and also to assure a supply of affordable housing (Article 2.4). Does raising the minimum wage cause layoffs, as mainstream models imply? Economist Jeannette Wicks-Lim says no, arguing that the minimum wage could go above $12 without causing substantial job loss (Article 2.5).

Finally, in "The Airfare Mystery" (Article 2.6), Arthur MacEwan argues that "supply and demand" is just a starting point for understanding what causes variation in air fares. We need to delve deeper, according to MacEwan, into issues of market power (does a particular airline monopolize a particular route?), price discrimination (are some buyers, like business travelers, charged more than others?), and government intervention (what roles do taxes and subsidies play?).

Taken together, these articles call into question the claims that markets always operate efficiently and lead to the best social allocation of resources. The articles also imply a constructive role for the "visible hand" of government.

Discussion Questions

1. (General) Several of these articles call for a larger government role in regulating supply and demand. What are some possible results of expanded government involvement, positive and negative? On balance, do you agree that government should play a larger role?

2. (Article 2.1) What reasons do Tilly and Kennedy provide for the rise in the price of tortillas in Mexico? Would you classify these reasons as being on the "supply side" or "demand side"? Do you think the authors' analysis deviates in any way from standard economic analyses of changing market prices?

3. (Article 2.1) In Tilly and Kennedy's article, how did the government of Mexico react to the tortilla price rise? What are the reactions of different members of the tortilla industry? What do you think it might take to lower tortilla prices in Mexico?

4. (Article 2.2) Breslow says that shortages have different effects on prices in the short run and the long run. Explain the difference. How is this difference related to the concepts of elasticity of demand and elasticity of supply?

5. (Article 2.3) What is a "bubble"? According to Baker, what was the evidence that a housing bubble was forming even back in 2005? What happened to the bubble and why? Does this "correction" support the views of economists how see markets as inherently self-correcting?

6. (Article 2.4) Frank states that because modern rent-control laws are "soft," they do not lead to housing shortages. Explain. Do you agree with her reasoning?

7. (Article 2.5) What is Wicks-Lim's argument against the claim that minimum-wage laws create unemployment?

8. (Article 2.6) MacEwan sees "supply and demand" as a shorthand for the various kinds of forces operating in real-world markets. What kinds of influences does he describe that may affect air fares? Which have an impact mainly on the supply side? Which on the demand side?

Article 2.1

SUPPLY, DEMAND, AND TORTILLAS

BY CHRIS TILLY AND MARIE KENNEDY

March/April 2007

The last year has been a fractious one in Mexico. Last May, in San Salvador Atenco in Mexico State, a group of street vendors and a wide range of allies protesting the vendors' expulsion from the central square were brutally repressed, with hundreds arrested, beaten, and sexually abused by police. To the south in Oaxaca, Governor Ulises Ruiz launched a similar police operation against striking teachers in June, sparking the formation of a broad front that occupied the center of the city for months despite constant attacks by police and armed goons, only to be swept out in November by a vicious federal-state police assault. Meanwhile, as the every-six-years presidential campaign heated up, a caravan of Zapatistas headed by *Subcomandante* Marcos toured the country arguing that only grass-roots mobilization, not a vote for one of the three major-party candidates, would change Mexican politics. July's presidential election put the right-wing National Action Party (PAN) candidate, Felipe Calderón, ahead of the center-left Party of the Democratic Revolution's (PRD) Andrés Manuel López Obrador by a razor-thin margin, amid evidence of large-scale irregularities. Supporters of López Obrador (popularly known as AMLO) took to the streets, creating a festive tent city stretching miles along Mexico City's main boulevard, La Reforma, and coming together in animated rallies of up to two million. Failing to change the election result, they declared a parallel government.

In early 2007, all of these struggles have been heating up once again. Key Atenco leaders are getting out of jail. Activists are marching in Oaxaca city once again, and a major Triqui indigenous community in that state just declared itself autonomous from the state, federal, and "official" local governments. AMLO and allies across the country are gearing up for what they call the Democratic National Convention, with the aim of building a new politics and writing a new constitution. The Zapatistas held a four day forum—"Encounter with the Peoples of the World"—hosting some 2,000 delegates in their base communities.

And across Mexico, the hot topic of the moment is…the price of tortillas. Prices for this Mexican staple, just a few months ago selling at 5 pesos (about 50 cents) per kilo (2.2 pounds, about 40 tortillas), had by mid-January spiked up to 8, 10, and in some places even 12 or 15 pesos per kilo. It's hard to convey to a U.S. audience how central tortillas are to the Mexican diet, but suffice it to say that *tortillerías* are sprinkled every couple of blocks across urban Mexico, and the great majority of families anchor their main meal with a kilo or two of tortillas. (When we first went to a *tortillería* and asked for ten tortillas, the vendor assumed she had heard us wrong and asked, "Ten kilos?") Perhaps the closest U.S. equivalent in terms of breadth of impact would be if the price of gas doubled and in some places even tripled. Other prices are also climbing—milk, eggs, sugar, meat, and natural gas—but it's the tortilla price surge that has grabbed Mexicans by the throat.

A Peculiar Crisis

A number of things are odd about the tortilla crisis. For one thing, there is no short-age of corn. Mexico had the largest corn harvest ever last year, more than twice as much as in 1980 (the country's population grew 60% over the same period). However, the structure of corn production has changed dramatically. Millions of family farmers in central and southern Mexico once dominated the crop, but free-trade policies have driven many of them off the land. Today, northern Mexican agri-business calls the tune. That plus NAFTA and other free trade agreements and the reduction of government subsidies mean that Mexico's corn price is now driven by the world price. The world price, in turn, increasingly responds to demand for etha-nol as well as for food products. So the price has trended up as oil prices made etha-nol more attractive—prompting *The Economist* to label corn "pure gold." Making matters worse, according to observers including the president of Mexico's central bank, speculation by large Mexican producers and traders is turbocharging the price hikes. Development expert Peter Rosset of the Center for the Study of Rural Change in Mexico points out that Mexican corn prices have spiked up far faster than those in the United States.

While one might expect the remaining small corn farmers in Mexico to ben-efit from rising prices, associations of small producers complain that they have not. Separated from consumers by layers of middlemen, they receive little or no trickle-down. The major beneficiaries are industry giants like Mexico's Maseca and U.S.-based Cargill, along with other large producers and traders. This pat-tern extends beyond Mexico. Guatemala's Institute for Agrarian and Rural Studies reports similar results of the Central American Free Trade Agreement in Guatemala: price increases for consumers, profits for the biggest corporations, and continued marginalization of small farmers.

Then there is the spectacle of a newly elected, pro-free trade president suddenly discovering the virtues of government intervention in the economy, at least to a lim-ited extent. President Calderón speedily negotiated an 8.5 peso cap with major corn meal and tortilla producers and retailers, promising to boost corn supplies so as to underwrite this price and stock the 24,000-odd government-run rural DICONSA stores that sell staples at subsidized prices. Ironically, he's increasing the supply by importing corn from the United States. (Mexico, the birthplace of corn, currently imports almost one-third of its corn consumption!)

Of course, once the price agreement was concluded, the tortilla industry began backing away from it. The corn meal giants clarified that this was a goodwill ges-ture on their part, not an ironclad commitment. Spokespeople for neighborhood *tortillerías* pointed out that they didn't work for the big companies, so the agree-ment wasn't binding on them. A few days after Calderón's tortilla handshake, we spot-checked tortillas in Tlaxcala (central Mexico, where we are living for six months)—the two *tortillerías* we priced were both selling at 9. That same day, the state government of Tlaxcala announced with much fanfare that it had concluded a separate 8.5 peso agreement with *tortillerías*. So the next day we returned to the same two shops: one was closed (we stopped by too late); the other was still charg-ing 9. Around the same time, federal government inspectors found prices over 8.5

at 53% of the *tortillerías* they visited nationwide. Still, two weeks after Calderón's pact, federal authorities had only managed to check prices at just over 3,000 shops out of an estimated 350,000. Even several weeks after the price *convenio*, tortilla sellers in the state of Aguascalientes announced that despite federal and state "agreements," they would not agree to a price ceiling under 10 pesos. On the other hand, the country's giant supermarket chains, including Wal-Mart, made a big show of discounting tortillas to 5 or 6 pesos (as a visit to our local Wal-Mart confirmed). Not a fair comparison, declared the *tortillería* industry: they mix all kinds of non-corn filler into their *nixtamal*, and besides, Mexicans prefer their tortillas fresh, hot, and local off a neighborhood *comal* (griddle).

"No to PAN, Yes to Tortillas!"

Naturally, Calderón's critics were not satisfied with his attempt to pull the tortillas out of the fire. AMLO and the PRD called for a six-peso ceiling on tortilla prices and a 35% increase in the minimum wage (currently set at a laughably low $US5 a day). Not to be outdone, the Con-federation of Revolutionary Workers and Peasants (CROC —despite its fiery name, a mainstream union federation long affiliated with the Institutional Revolutionary Party [PRI] that ruled Mexico for seventy years until 2000) demanded price ceilings on 30 items in the *canasta básica* (the basket of basic consumer necessities tracked by the government). On January 31, these groups and more organized a peaceful *megamarcha* to protest the growing gap between prices and wages and to demand a "new social contract." Left-leaning daily *La Jornada* described the turnout in Mexico City as "tens of thousands" or "one hundred thousand"—numerically disappointing compared to other recent demonstrations—but what was significant was the presence of activists from the PRI, two smaller parties, and a large number of worker and peasant organizations that had not previously joined PRD-initiated mobilizations. They jointly issued the broad-ranging "Declaración del Zócalo," named after the central Mexico City square where the demonstration took place, announcing, "We are starting a new stage of struggle for the demands of the majority sectors in Mexico."

Particularly noteworthy is the active participation of peasant groupings such as the Permanent Agrarian Congress, the National Council of Peasant Organizations, and the National Peasant and Fisheries Council in the nationwide mobilizations. Thanks to their involvement, the protest movement has embraced a "food sovereignty" program that goes well beyond wage and price demands. Such a program would include government support for small Mexican producers of staple grains such as corn and beans through government-sponsored research and technology transfer. They also demand a renegotiation of the agricultural section of NAFTA, which is currently scheduled to remove all trade protection from Mexican corn and beans in 2008. A wave of cheaper, subsidized corn and beans from the United States would most likely lead to a temporary drop in Mexican corn prices, but the devastating effect on small Mexican farmers would leave the country far more dependent on imports and more vulnerable to future price fluctuations.

Although we were unable to attend the Tlaxcala branch of the action, we joined a smaller pre-march in Tlaxcala the weekend before. A cheerful crowd of a couple of hundred, including a large contingent from the local chapter of the Social Security Administration union, rallied to slogans like, "No to PAN, yes to tortillas!" (PAN is both the name of the ruling party and the word for bread.) José Roberto Pérez Luna, head of the union, told us, "The system is not meeting the needs of the majority. That's what leads to revolutions. I'd hate to think that our government is fertilizing a revolution."

The "Employment President" Says No

For three weeks after the rally, the government of Calderón, who campaigned as "the employment president" but so far has presided over job losses of 178,000, kept mum about the key demands, apart from some vague promises to help support Mexican corn producers and some noises about prosecuting speculators. Finally on February 21, the government gave its answer: No. No to mandatory price controls. No to an increase in the minimum wage, using the old argument, widely discredited by recent research, that minimum-wage increases destroy jobs. (Around the same time, Calderón announced a 46% increase in wages for the army, a move many see as designed to bolster the harsh repression the government has meted out to protestors in Oaxaca and elsewhere. "In this country, we will no longer confuse illegality with human rights," he remarked recently in a not-very-veiled warning.) And no to reopening NAFTA. Mexico "will not change the rules of the game," the president declared.

In the absence of further government action, Mexican consumers "voted" with their pocketbooks, reducing tortilla consumption by 20% to 30% during January, according to the National Chamber of Tortilla and Corn Flour Producers. Unfortunately, as Marie Antoinette learned to her regret a few centuries ago, for the poorest the alternative to eating unaffordable staples is simply not eating. Nearly one-fifth of Mexicans live in extreme poverty. Poor Mexicans get 40% of their protein from tortillas, and while statistics on short-term changes in nutritional intake are not available, it is safe to assume that more of these people are going hungry. Calderón's secretary of social development, Beatriz Zavala, stirred much outrage when she claimed that tortilla price hikes would not affect food consumption by the rural poor, since so many of them are self-sufficient peasants. The reality is that in rural areas—as in the United States—family farmers are increasingly compelled to reduce planting in order to supplement their income with non-agricultural jobs, or are being forced off their land outright.

The groups that launched the January 31 protests promise further mobilizations. One of the coalition members, the National Peasant and Fisheries Council, also proposes to set up a network of 5,000 small producers who will sell directly to consumers in six states, plus the federal district that includes Mexico City, working with popular organizations wherever possible.

Tlaxcala union leader Pérez Luna is right to warn of "fertilizing a revolution." Whatever happens next with tortilla prices, the issues of the widening gap between most Mexicans' salaries and the cost of living, and the other widening gap between the rich and the rest, are not going away. These are some of the same issues that fueled the Zapatista rebellion, the street vendors' protest in Atenco, the teachers' strike in Oaxaca, and the wave of anger at the elite that has made AMLO's protests much more than the sour grapes of a losing candidate. Calderón's strategy—continued free-market reforms sprinkled with crowd-pleasing tactical concessions like the tortilla pact, and the mailed fist when protests get out of hand—seems more likely to accelerate these trends than halt them. In the coming years, expect Mexican politics to heat up as hot as a *tortillería's comal.* ❑

Resources: *La Jornada* (daily newspaper), www.jornada.unam.mx; "La declaración del Zócalo," www.jornada.unam.mx/2007/02/01/index.php?section=politica&article=006n1pol; Timothy Wise, "Policy space for Mexican maize," Global Development and Environment Institute, www. ase.tufts.edu/gdae/Pubs/wp/07-01MexicanMaize.pdf; Center for the Study of Rural Change in Mexico (CECCAM), "En defensa del maíz," www.ceccam.org.mx/ConclusionesDefensa.htm; Grassroots International, "Fixing the broken food system," grassrootsonline.org/food_is.html.

Article 2.2

PRICE GOUGING: IT'S JUST SUPPLY AND DEMAND

BY MARC BRESLOW
October 2000

- May 2000: Growing demand, along with supply cutbacks by OPEC, lead to soaring gasoline prices around the United States, especially in the upper Midwest, where they reach $2 a gallon, almost twice the levels of a year earlier.
- September 2000: Both presidential candidates, George W. Bush and Al Gore, offer plans to prevent dramatic increases in the price of heating oil during the coming winter, due to expected supply shortages.
- 1999 and 2000: red-hot high-tech economies in the San Francisco Bay and Boston areas draw in more professional workers, and raise the demand for housing. Vacancy rates dwindle to near zero, and prices for both rentals and house purchases rise out of sight. Moderate- and low-income renters are evicted for non-payment and forced to move into smaller quarters or out of these metropolitan areas.

Critics of the oil industry charge that the companies are conspiring to raise prices during shortages, ripping off consumers and gaining huge profits through illegal behavior. The industries respond that there is no conspiracy, prices are rising due to the simple functioning of supply and demand in the market. The media debate the question: can evidence be found of a conspiracy? Or are rising prices simply due to increased costs as supplies are short? Politicians ask whether companies are guilty of illegal activity, and demand that investigations be opened.

What's going on? In reality, critics of the industries are missing the point of how a capitalist "free market" operates during times of shortages. The industry spokespersons are more on target in their explanations—but that doesn't mean what the companies are doing is okay. In fact, they *are* profiting at the expense of everyone who is forced to pay outrageous prices.

Both the media and public officials want to know whether rising costs of operation are causing the high prices, and therefore the companies are justified. Why? Because simple textbook economics says that in a competitive market we should get charged according to costs, with companies only making a "normal" profit. But a careful reading of the texts shows that this is only in the "long run" when new supplies can come into the market. In the short run, when a shortage develops, "supply and demand" can force prices up to unbelievable levels, especially for any product or service that is really a necessity. It doesn't have any relationship to the cost of supplying the item, nor does it take a conspiracy. The industry spokespeople are right that market pressures are the cause.

What confuses consumers is why a relatively small shortage can cause such a huge price jump, as it did for gasoline and electricity. Why, if OPEC reduces world oil supplies by only 1% or 2%, can the price of gasoline rise by perhaps 50%? Why shouldn't prices rise by the 1% or 2%? The answer lies in a common-sense understanding of what happens during a shortage. Everyone who owns a car, and still needs to get to work, drop the kids off at child care, and buy groceries, still needs to drive. In the short run, you can't sell your car for a more energy-efficient one, nor move someplace where public transit is more available, nor find a new day care center closer to home. Even if there are subways or buses available where you live, tight work and family time schedules probably make it difficult for you to leave the car at home.

So, as prices rise, everyone continues trying to buy as much gasoline as they did before (in technical terms, the "short run price elasticity of demand" is very low). But there is 2% less gas available, so not everyone can get as much as they want. Prices will continue rising until some people drop out of the market, cutting back on their purchases because they simply can't afford to pay the higher prices. For something as essential to modern life as gasoline, this can take quite a price jump. If the price goes from $1.20 to $1.30 will you buy less? How about $1.50? Or $1.80? You can see the problem. Prices can easily rise by 50% before demand falls by the 2% needed for supply and demand to equalize.

Note that this situation has nothing to do with the costs of supplying gasoline, nor do oil companies in the United States have to conspire together to raise prices. All they have to do is let consumers bid for the available gasoline. Nothing illegal has taken place—OPEC is acting as a cartel, "conspiring," but the United States has no legal power over other countries. Profits can go up enormously, and they may be shared between OPEC, oil companies such as Exxon/Mobil and Royal Dutch Shell, and firms lower on the supply chain such as wholesalers and retail gas stations.

Housing is perhaps the worst of these situations, as no one should be forced to leave their home. But the "invisible hand" of the market will raise prices, and allocate housing, according to who has the greatest purchasing power, not who needs the housing. A highly-skilled computer programmer, moving into San Francisco from elsewhere, will get an apartment that some lesser-paid worker, maybe a public school teacher or a bus driver, has been living in, perhaps for many years.

In all these cases, the market has done what it does well—allocate sales to those who can afford to buy, without regard to need; and allocate profits to those who have a product in short supply, without regard to costs of production. The human costs to people of moderate- and low-incomes, who are priced out of the market, can be severe. But they can be prevented—by price controls that prevent price-gouging due to shortages. Such controls have been used many times in the United States—for rent in high-demand cities, for oil and gas during the "crises" of the 1970's, and for most products during World War II. Maybe it's time we made them a staple of sensible economic policy. ❑

Resources: "In Gas Prices, Misery and Mystery," Pam Belluck, *The New York Times*, 6/14/2000; "Federal action sought to cut power prices from May," Peter J. Howe, *The Boston Globe*, 8/24/2000; "Industry Blames Chemical Additives for High Gas Prices," Matthew L. Wald, *The New York Times*, 6/26/2000.

Article 2.3

THE BURSTING OF THE HOUSING BUBBLE

BY DEAN BAKER
August 2006; Truthout

Every day presents new evidence that the housing boom is turning into a housing bust. In the last week we have seen data showing that house sale prices are down from last year's levels in 26 major metropolitan areas, housing starts are down more than 15% from their bubble peaks, and applications for home purchase mortgages have dropped by more than 20%. A new poll of builders showed industry confidence at the lowest level since the middle of 1990-1991 recession.

At this point there is little doubt that the housing market is headed downward. The question is how low will it go and what will be the impact on the economy. If housing construction and sales prices revert to long-term trends, the decline will be severe, as will be the impact on the economy.

Over most of the post-World War II era, house prices have moved largely in step with other prices, keeping just about even with the overall rate of inflation. In the last decade, house prices suddenly exploded, increasing by more than 50%, after adjusting for inflation. This unprecedented run-up in house prices led to record levels of housing construction. The number of homes built in 2005 was almost 50% higher than it had been a decade earlier. This huge construction boom was a key factor in pulling the economy out of the recession.

The wealth created by the housing bubble also played a central role in propelling the economy. The run-up in housing prices has created more than $5 trillion in bubble wealth. Consumers have borrowed against this new wealth at a feverish pace, pulling more than $600 billion out of their homes in the last year. This borrowing fueled the consumption boom of the last five years, pushing savings into negative territory for the first time since the beginning of the Depression.

Of course, just like the stock bubble, the housing bubble could not be sustained. In the stock bubble, the supply of new issues of tech stocks eventually exceeded the demand from speculators. Similarly, the record levels of housing construction inevitably led to a glut of housing on the market. For a long time, speculators were willing to buy up anything that was built, but eventually the supply of speculators, or the supply of money to the speculators, reached a limit. Once they stopped buying, inventories began to grow, and the price boom came to an end.

There are desperate sellers in many of the areas where the housing market was booming just a year ago. In many cases, sellers are offering large concessions to unload their homes, such as paying buyers' closing costs, covering a year of condo fees, or offering lower than market mortgage rates. Since these concessions (which lower the real sale price) don't show up in the house price indexes used by economists, the decline in housing prices so far is actually considerably larger than most analysts recognize.

How far and fast prices will fall is difficult to know at this point, but a few things are predictable. Housing construction and sales will drop back toward trend level. Housing construction is already down by 15% from its peak. It is likely to fall at least this much more before stabilizing. Sales of existing homes, which are the life-blood of the real estate industry, are also likely to fall by 30-40% from peak levels.

In addition, the borrowing spree of the last five years is likely to come to an abrupt end as stagnant or declining home prices cut off this important source of credit. There is evidence that we are already seeing the effects of this credit squeeze, as credit card debt has begun to soar in the last few months. Families who can't get the money they need by borrowing against their homes will turn to credit cards as the best available alternative.

This does not paint a pretty picture for the economy. If housing construction and sales fall back to trend levels, it would mean a loss of more than 2 million jobs. The decline in consumption that will result because people can no longer borrow against their homes will have an even more dramatic impact on the economy. The financial system will also be shaken by an unprecedented wave of mortgage defaults.

Unfortunately, at this point there is no obvious way to avoid this scenario. The real problem was letting the housing bubble grow to such dangerous levels in the first place. The Federal Reserve Board, along with the economics profession, deserves to pay a serious price for such a momentous mistake. ❏

Article 2.4

DOES RENT CONTROL HURT TENANTS?

BY ELLEN FRANK
March/April 2003

> Dear Dr. Dollar:
> *What are the merits of the argument that rent control hurts tenants by limiting the incentives to create and maintain rental housing?*
> —Sarah Marxer, San Francisco, Calif.

The standard story of rent control, laid out in dozens of introductory economics textbooks, goes like this. In the housing market, landlords are willing to supply more rental units when prices are high, and tenants are willing to rent more units when prices are low. In an unregulated market, competition should result in a market-clearing price at which the number of apartments landlords are willing and able to provide just equals the number tenants are willing and able to rent. Thus, when prices are allowed to rise to their correct level, shortages disappear. Rent controls, in this story, disrupt the market mechanism by capping rents at too low a level. Artificially low rents discourage construction and maintenance, resulting in fewer available apartments than would exist without the controls. At the same time, low rents keep tenants in the area, searching for apartments that don't exist. The result: permanent housing shortages in rent-controlled markets.

What's wrong with this story? Just about everything.

First, the story ignores the unequal power that landlords and tenants exercise in an unregulated market. Boston College professor Richard Arnott notes that tenants are, for a number of reasons, averse to moving. This gives landlords inordinate pricing power even in a market where housing is not in short supply—and in areas where vacancy rates are low, land is scarce, and "snob zoning" commonplace, landlords can charge truly exorbitant prices. In Boston, rent controls were eliminated in 1997, and average apartment rents have since climbed nearly 100%. The city's spiraling rents show that without controls, landlords can—and do—gouge tenants.

Second, rent control opponents misrepresent the structure of controls. As practiced in the real world, rent control does not place fixed caps on rent. New York City enacted an actual rent freeze after World War II, and a small number of apartments still fall under this "old-law" rent control. But most rent-controlled apartments in New York and all controlled apartments in other U.S. cities fall under what Arnott calls "second generation" or "soft" controls, which simply restrict annual rent increases. Soft rent controls guarantee landlords a "fair return" on their properties and require that owners maintain their buildings. They allow landlords to pass along maintenance costs, and many allow improvement costs to be recouped on an accelerated schedule, making building upkeep quite lucrative.

Consequently, controlled apartments are not unprofitable. And as Occidental College professor and housing specialist Peter Dreier points out, landlords won't walk away as long as they are making a decent return. Residential landlords are not very mobile: they have a long-term interest in their properties, and only abandon them when *market* rents fall below even controlled levels as a result of poverty, crime, or economic depression. Rent controls themselves do not foster abandonment or poor maintenance.

Third, all second-generation rent control laws—enacted chiefly in the 1970s—exempted newly constructed buildings from controls. Thus, the argument that controls discourage new construction simply makes no sense. As for the oft-heard complaint that developers fear that rent controls, once enacted, will be extended to new buildings, the 1980s and 1990s construction booms in New York, Boston, San Francisco, and Los Angeles—all cities with controls—indicate that developers aren't all that worried. There is plenty of housing and construction in cities with and without rent controls.

Nevertheless, even in many cities with rent controls, there is a shortage of *affordable* apartments. Market housing costs have been rising faster than wages for at least two decades. That some apartments in New York and San Francisco are still affordable to low- and middle-income families is due primarily to rent control.

Indeed, limited as they might be, rent controls deliver real benefits. They prevent price-gouging and ration scarce apartments to existing tenants. The money tenants save in rent can be spent in the neighborhood economy, benefiting local businesses. Meanwhile, more secure tenants create neighborhoods that are stable, safe, and economically diverse. And rent controls are essential if tenants are to have credible legal protection against slumlords: the legal right to complain about lack of heat or faulty plumbing is meaningless if landlords can retaliate by raising rents.

There are many problems with the U.S. housing market. High prices, low incomes, and lack of public housing or subsidies for affordable housing all contribute to homelessness and housing insecurity in major American cities. Rent control is not the cause of these problems, nor is it the whole solution. But along with higher wages and expanded public housing, it is part of the solution. As Dreier puts it, "Until the federal government renews its responsibility to help poor and working-class people fill the gap between what they can afford and what housing costs to build and operate, rent control can at least help to keep a roof over their heads." ❏

Resources: Richard Arnott, "Time for Revisionism on Rent Control?" *Journal of Economic Perspectives*, Winter 1995. Dreier and Pitcoff, "I'm a Tenant and I Vote," *Shelterforce*, July/August 1997. Shelterforce website: <http://www.nhi.org/>.

Article 2.5

HOW HIGH COULD THE MINIMUM WAGE GO?

A 70% boost would help millions of workers, without killing jobs.

BY JEANNETTE WICKS-LIM
July/August 2012

The minimum wage needs a jolt—not just the usual fine-tuning—if it's ever going to serve as a living wage. Annual full-time earnings at today's $7.25 federal minimum wage are about $15,000 per year. This doesn't come anywhere near providing a decent living standard by any reasonable definition, for any household, least of all households with children. But among the seventeen states that either have active campaigns to raise their minimum wage or have raised them already this year, none have suggested raising the wage floor by more than 20%.

How high can the minimum wage go? As it turns out, a lot higher. Economists typically examine whether current minimum-wage laws hike pay rates up too high and cause employers to shed workers from their payrolls in response. But the current stockpile of economic research on minimum wages suggests that past increases have not caused any notable job losses. In other words, minimum wages in the United States have yet to be set too high. In fact, if we use past experience as a guide, businesses should be able to adjust to a jump in the minimum wage as great as 70%. That would push the federal minimum wage up to $12.30. In states with average living costs, full-time earnings at $12.30 per hour can cover the basic needs of the typical low-income working household (assuming both adults in two-adult households are employed).

Why is such a large increase possible? It's because minimum-wage hikes— particularly those in the 20-to-30% range adopted in the United States—impose very modest cost increases on businesses. This is true even for the low-wage, labor-intensive restaurant industry. And because these cost increases are so modest, affected businesses have a variety of options for adjusting to their higher labor costs that are less drastic than laying off workers.

Take, for example, the 31% rise in Arizona's state minimum wage in 2006, from $5.15 to $6.75. My colleague Robert Pollin and I have estimated that the average restaurant in Arizona could expect to see its costs rise between 1% and 2% of their sales revenue. What kind of adjustment would this restaurant need to make? A price hike of 1% or 2% would completely cover this cost increase. This would amount to raising the price of a $10.00 meal to $10.20.

To figure out what is the largest increase businesses can adjust to without laying off workers, we can take stock of what we know about how businesses have adjusted in the past and then figure out how much businesses can adjust along those lines.

Let's stick with the example of restaurants, since these businesses tend to experience the largest rise in costs. And let's start with a big increase in the minimum wage: 50%. If we add together all the raises mandated by such an increase in the minimum wage (assuming the same number of workers and hours worked), the raises employers would need to give workers earning wages above the minimum wage to maintain a stable wage hierarchy, and their higher payroll taxes, the total cost increase of a 50% minimum-wage hike would be 3.2% of restaurant sales.

The cost increase that these restaurants need to absorb, however, will actually be even smaller than 3.2% of their sales revenue. That's because when workers' wages rise, workers stay at their jobs for longer periods of time, saving businesses the money they would otherwise have spent on recruiting and training new workers. These savings range between 10% and 25% of the costs from raising the minimum wage. If the higher wage motivates workers to work harder, businesses would experience even more cost savings.

So what would happen if restaurants raised their prices to cover their minimum wage cost increases? One answer is that people may react to the higher prices by eating out less often and restaurant owners would lose business. With a large enough falloff in business, restaurants would have to cut back on their workforce. But it's unlikely that a price increase as small as 3% would stop people from eating out. Think about it: if a family is already willing to pay $40.00 to eat dinner out, it hardly seems likely that a price increase as small as $1.20 would to cause them to forgo all the benefits of eating out like getting together with family or friends and saving time in meal preparation, clean up, and grocery shopping.

Still, let's assume that a 3% price hike actually does influence people to eat out less. The key questions now are how much less and can restaurant owners make up their lost business activity? Economists have found that restaurant patrons do not react strongly to changes in menu prices (economists call this an "inelastic" demand). Estimates from industry research suggest that a price increase of 3% may reduce consumer demand by about 2%.

However, if these small price increases take place within a growing economy—even a slow-growing economy—restaurant owners will probably see basically no change in their sales. This is because as the economy expands and peoples' incomes rise, people eat out more. In an economy growing at a rate of 3% annually, which is slower than average for the U.S. economy, consumer demand for restaurant meals will typically rise by about 2.4%. This would boost sales more than enough to make up for any loss that restaurants may experience from a 3% price increase. In other words, consumers would still eat out more often even after a 50% minimum-wage hike.

After taking account of the ways that restaurants can adjust to the higher labor costs from a minimum wage hike, it turns out that the biggest minimum wage increase that restaurants can absorb while maintaining at least the same level of business activity is 70%. In 2004, Santa Fe, New Mexico, came close to this. Its citywide living-wage ordinance raised the wage floor by 65%—from $5.15 to $8.50. A city-commissioned report after it was put into effect found that "overall employment levels have been unaffected by the living wage ordinance."

However, even if the federal minimum rate were 70% higher, or $12.30, it would still fall short for two major groups of workers. First, one-worker families raising young children need generous income supports in addition to minimum wage earnings to help cover the high cost of raising children. Second, minimum-wage workers who live in expensive areas, such as New York City and Washington, D.C., require affordable housing programs.

A 70% minimum-wage hike is the biggest one-time increase that U.S. businesses can absorb without cutting jobs, but it's not the end of the story. In the future, the minimum wage can inch further upward. For example, it could rise in step with the expanding productive capacity of the U.S. economy, as it did in the 1950s and 1960s. A $12.30 minimum wage today rising each year with worker productivity would reach $17.00 in just over ten years (in 2011 dollars). This wage would be high enough so that a single parent with one child could support a minimally decent living standard. We would finally begin transforming the minimum wage into a living wage for all workers.

Policy discussions around the minimum wage need to move past the debate of whether or not it causes job loss. The evidence is clear: minimum wages, in the range of what's been adopted in the past, do not produce any significant job losses. Now it is time to focus on how we can use minimum wages to maximally support low-wage workers. Can we raise the minimum wage rate to a level we can call a living wage? By my reckoning, we can. ❑

Sources: Jeannette Wicks-Lim and Jeffrey Thompson, "Combining the Minimum Wage and Earned Income Tax Credit Policies to Guarantee a Decent Living Standard to All U.S. Workers" (Political Economy Research Institute, October 2010).

Article 2.6

THE AIRFARE MYSTERY

BY ARTHUR MacEWAN
January/February 2014

> Dear Dr. Dollar:
> *Boston is 3,280 air miles from London, only 27% further than the 2,580 air miles from Boston to San Diego. So why does a flight from Boston to London cost more than twice as much as a flight from Boston to San Diego, 100% more, for the same dates? Is it just supply and demand?* —Kathleen M. Gillespie, Lexington, Mass.

Airfares do seem to pose a mystery. Supply and demand may help explain things, but these are really little more than categories into which explanations can be placed. If someone says that the flights to London are so expensive because supply is limited relative to demand, we have no real explanation until we explain why supply is limited.

On the surface, the high price of flights on the Boston-London route suggests that this is a very profitable route. So why don't more airlines fly this route more often, expanding supply, to get a share of the profits?

Beneath the surface (on travel web sites), it turns out that a large part of the price difference between these two routes is not the actual payment to the airline, but taxes and fees. I found one Boston-London-Boston trip for $1,082, where taxes and fees accounted for $656 of that total. On the Boston-San Diego-Boston flight, however, taxes and fees accounted for only $33 out of the $436 cost.

In general, European governments charge much higher taxes and fees than is the case in the United States. From an environmental perspective, the Europeans are probably on the right track, as air travel is an especially polluting (greenhouse gas-creating) form of travel. The European governments, however, may simply be motivated by the opportunity to capture revenue.

There are seemingly strange airline fare differences within the United States that are not explained by tax and fee differences. For example, a non-stop round-trip Boston-Detroit flight (630 miles each way) costs about twice as much as a non-stop Boston-Chicago flight (860 miles each way)—$458 compared to $230 for the same times and dates.

This difference is explained by the fact that Delta has a lock on the Boston-Detroit route, while United, American, US Airways, and Jet Blue all fly the Boston-Chicago route. That is, Delta is a monopoly on the Boston-Detroit route and can charge high fares without facing competition. (Northwest used to control this route until it merged with Delta a couple of years ago.)

Why have no other airlines entered this apparently lucrative Boston-Detroit route? That's not clear. Perhaps Delta has long-term leases on Detroit airport gates. Or perhaps other airlines, recognizing the economic and population decline of Detroit, believe this market has limited potential. Whatever the reason, it is clear that monopoly control of this route is the issue.

Also, the Boston-Detroit fare portends an ominous future as airline mergers reduce competition further. Following the Delta-Northwest merger, Continental and United came together. American Airlines and US Airways have also been moving toward a merger. In August, however, the federal government acted to block the move. "According to the Justice Department," reported the *New York Times*, the proposed merger "would substantially reduce competition in over 1,000 city pairs served by the two airlines."

While monopolistic situations and taxes and fees explain some of the "mystery" of airline fares, there is more. Flights and times that are heavily used by business travelers tend to have high fares because business travelers are less concerned about the price. This is partly because they often have limited flexibility, but also because airfares are deductible as a cost of business—i.e., the taxpayers pick up part of the tab.

Also, on a flight with the same airline, prices can change dramatically within a day or even within hours. Trying to book a flight one evening, the cheapest ticket I could find was about $600, but by the next morning I got the ticket for about $300. I suspect that in this case the airline (using computer-based forecasting) recognized that the flight was not filling up and therefore reduced the price to attract more customers.

And things can work in the other direction. Making a reservation at the last minute, the potential passenger is often faced with a very high fare because the airline views the traveler as having little flexibility. For example, if I make a reservation to fly Boston-Chicago-Boston, leaving tomorrow and returning two days later, the fare would be over $900, as compared to the $230 I would pay if I made the reservation a few weeks in advance.

So, yes, supply and demand can help explain the variation in airfares. But to really understand what is going on we need to know a good deal more. ❏

Sources: "Airline Merger Mania," *New York Times*, June 22, 2013; James B. Stewart, "For Airlines, It May Be One Merger Too Many," *New York Times*, Aug. 16, 2013.

Chapter 3

CONSUMERS

INTRODUCTION

The "two economies" described in the introduction to this book—the textbook economy and the economy portrayed by critics of the status quo—come into sharp contrast when we consider the theory of consumer choice. In the textbook model of consumer choice, rational individuals seek to maximize their well-being by choosing the right mix of goods to consume and allocating their "scarce" resources accordingly. They decide for themselves how much they would enjoy various things, and make their choices based on full information about their options. More of any good is always better, but diminishing marginal utility says that each additional unit of a good consumed brings less additional enjoyment than the one before. The theory attempts to assess the utility of each individual uniquely. Yet, we soon discover that it is difficult if not impossible to "measure pleasure" for a single individual and impossible to compare utility between individuals.

The first contribution to this chapter, an interview with economist Juliet Schor (Article 3.1), explores the causes behind U.S. consumerism. Schor looks beyond some of the "usual suspects"—like advertising—by linking the rise of consumerism to labor-market forces that have prevented the reduction of work time. She argues that future changes in U.S. consuption behavior, and therefore long-term environmental sustainability, depend on reducing hours of work.

The second article in this chapter contends that the idea of consumer sovereignty—that consumer wishes determine what gets produced—does not fit the facts. Helen Scharber notes, in "The 800-Pound Ronald McDonald in the Room" (Article 3.2), how the advertising that saturates our daily lives constantly creates new wants. In recent years, advertisers have been increasingly targeting children in order to convince them to nag their parents into buying products they suddenly "need."

The next two articles focus on ways that consumers may bring more broadly social-minded concerns to their purchasing decisions, and the pitfalls they sometimes face. Today, consumers are increasingly conscious of environmental problems, and many are willing to pay premium prices for recycled, less-polluting, or otherwise "sustainably produced" goods. In "Way Beyond Greenwashing" (Article 3.3), however, Jonathan Latham documents the way that corporate "greenwashing" stands in the way of informed consumer decisions. "Big Conservation" organizations, he argues, sell "indulgences" to global agribusiness corporations over the issue of habitat destruction, allowing the companies to appear more environment-friendly than they really are.

In "Campus Struggles Against Sweatshops Continue" (Article 3.4), Sarah Blaskey and Phil Gasper turn our attention to activism around global labor conditions. They show how how people on the consumption side, in this case students and faculty at U.S. colleges and universties, have banded together with workers on the other side of the world to fight "sweatshop" conditions in apparel production.

In the chapter's final article, "How to Take on the Card Sharks—and Win!" (Article 3.5), Jim Campen describes a rare case of successful consumer-protection regulation in recent U.S. history. Credit card regulation has reined in what were widely seen as deceptive and abusive practices, designed to extract as much money in fees and fines as possible from unsuspecting card holders.

Discussion Questions

1. (Article 3.1) Schor argues that, far from being the consequence of human beings' inherently insatiable wants, consumerism is the result of various social and institutional factors. What does she see as the key factors pushing people to consume more and more? What are the main reasons, in her view, that consumer behavior in the United States has differed from that in other countries?

2. (Article 3.2) Standard consumer theory still applies if advertising is simply a way to inform consumers. But critics suggest that advertising shapes our tastes and desires. Think of some of your recent purchases. For which purchases was advertising primarily a source of information, and for which was it more of a taste-shaper?

3. (Article 3.2) According to Scharber, what are the negative impacts of advertising directed at children? Would you support a law banning advertising to young children? Why or why not?

4. (Articles 3.3 and 3.4) How can consumers overcome the problem of "asymmetric information" in making purchases? Consider cases when consumers are interested in something (like environmental impact or labor conditions) that they cannot directly observe from the product itself.

4. (Articles 3.5) Why does Campen think that government regulation was called for in the case of credit cards? Do you agree?

Article 3.1

TRUE WEALTH: WORK, LEISURE, AND CONSUMPTION

AN INTERVIEW WITH JULIET SCHOR
May/June 2014

Economist Juliet Schor is known worldwide for her research on the interrelated issues of work, leisure, and consumption. Her books on these themes include The Overworked American: The Unexpected Decline of Leisure, The Overspent American: Upscaling, Downshifting, and the New Consumer, *and* Plenitude: The New Economics of True Wealth *(retitled* True Wealth *for its paperback edition). She is also a professor of sociology at Boston College. — Eds.*

DOLLARS & SENSE: We wouldn't expect patterns of work, leisure, and consumption to change overnight, but we're now more than half a decade into a profound crisis. Obviously it's had a big impact on employment, incomes, and so forth, but do you see any lasting changes emerging?

JULIET SCHOR: Some of the trends that were pretty significant before the crash have abated. I'm thinking most particularly about what I've called the "fast fashion model" of consumption—cheap imports of manufactured goods that people were acquiring at accelerating rates, the acceleration of the fashion cycle, and the cycle of acquisition and discard. The trend was people buying things, holding them for shorter and shorter periods of time and then discarding them either into some kind of household storage, into a waste stream, or into secondary markets. You had an amazing period of acquisition of consumer goods. I first started looking at this in the realm of apparel, but it was also in consumer electronics, ordinary household appliances, and pretty much across the board in consumer goods.

Of course, a lot of it was financed by debt or longer working hours, but manufactured goods just became so cheap. The idea that you could buy a DVD player for $19—and yes, people were trampling each other in the stores on Black Friday to get them—but that's just an extraordinary period. So that has changed, because the economics of that have changed. Going forward, I don't think we're going to see that level of availability of cheap goods that we saw before. So I think that cycle has slowed down.

The other big thing has been the bifurcation of the consumer market. That's something that's been going on for a long time—the falling out of the middle as a result of the decline of the middle class, the growth of a really low-end in the consumer market with dollar stores and a retail sector where even Walmart is considered expensive. The other side was the expansion of the hyper-luxury market.

Trends in income and wealth are reflected in the consumer sphere. There's more reluctance to take on debt, so debt-fueled consumer buying is lessened. There's also less availability of consumer credit for households now. The other big thing that I've been looking at is the rise of "alternative cultures" of consumption; that is, people moving out of the branded, advertised goods and the mass-produced lifestyles that dominated in the last couple of decades into more ecologically aware lifestyles with more artisanal and self-production.

D&S: Stepping back and looking more broadly at the emergence of this mass consumer culture in the United States after the Second World War, what do you see that are the key factors that are at the root of consumer capitalism in the United States? It seems a little facile to focus too narrowly on just advertising. Some scholars point to mass media images and what kinds of lifestyles people aspire to. Galbraith pointed more generally to the relentless stream of new products fueling new desires—the so-called "dependence effect." How do you see those influences, as well as others, sorting out?

JS: I don't want to completely dismiss factors like the old monopoly capital idea or the advertising and marketing story, which is that shortfalls of demand led to a big effort to get people to buy things, but I don't buy that story, for the most part. If you think about the postwar period, you had a labor market in which firms were unwilling to use productivity growth to reduce hours of work, and I wrote a book about that, *The Overworked American*. Part of that was about firms and why they don't want to do that. So in the post-war period, you have, from the labor market side, a situation where all productivity growth is getting channeled into income—into expansion of output—so it goes to wages and profits.

Now, of course, workers aren't getting the benefits of productivity growth, but in the post-war era, they did. There were contracts that were explicitly tied—3% productivity, 3% real wage growth. So that creates consumer demand, because that income is getting into people's pockets. Now you can ask the question: Why don't they save it? I don't think it's advertising, primarily, that determines why people didn't save more. There, I think, you have to look at social competition, and the fact that you have an unequal society in which how you live, what you buy, and what you have are important determinants of social position. Rising income gives you a constantly rising norm, and people consume to keep up with that norm. I think it would have played out more or less similarly if there weren't any advertising. The products might have been different but this sort of "consumer escalator," the fact that you have growing levels of consumption, is really coming much more from the production side. So in that way, I'm much more Marxian than Keynesian, I would say.

D&S: Turning to the contrast between the United States and other high-income capitalist countries, especially in terms of the shape of the labor movement and the role of the state: How did working hours get reduced in other countries? In France or Germany, for example, the average employed person works about 300 hours less per year than in the United States. So that strikes me as quite central, in your analysis, in terms of understanding consumption patterns in different countries.

JS: In the United States in the post-war period, the state devoted a lot of energy to the promotion of consumption, whether it was the highway system or suburbanization. That was in part out of a fear of the "Keynesian problem" of inadequate demand after the Second World War. In Europe, I guess I would point to two things. First, after the war, they had a supply-side problem, which was that they had to rebuild productive capacity rather than what we had, which was the demand-side problem. So our state was much more oriented to promoting consumption than European states, which were more oriented towards rebuilding their societies. In Europe, working hours continued to fall and they didn't in the United States.

That's the way you need to think about it—everybody was on a common trajectory of work-hours decline from about 1870. Of course, the United States was the leader in all of that. We had the shortest working hours and we were the first ones to put in reforms of working hours: The United States was the leader on no Sunday work, no Saturday work, etc. I think the factors are the role of trade unions—both that trade unions were much stronger in Europe and also that in the United States, trade unions turned against the reduction of working hours after the Second World War. That has to do mostly with the Cold War, and with the conservative nature of U.S. trade unions. So in the 1950s, the AFL-CIO became—"hostile" may be too strong a word—became extremely disinterested in the idea of shorter hours of work. That's something that did not happen in Europe.

The other thing is that the incentives facing firms in the United States were really different, in terms of U.S. employers having much higher per worker fixed costs, because of health insurance. There are some European countries where health insurance is provided at the firm level, but mostly not. In the United States that turns out to be a powerful disincentive to reduce working hours, and it becomes a powerful incentive for raising working hours. The growth in inequality, which is more pronounced in the United States, also raised working hours. I think those are the key factors which lead the United States and Europe to diverge quite rapidly on the issue of work time. That divergence turns out to have all sorts of very important consequences.

One of the things you have seen in the patterns of leisure time activities in the United States is you've got time-stressed households doing really money-intensive things like going to the Caribbean for three days, or spending a lot of money to "de-stress," or spending money to reward themselves for working so hard. So we definitely have quite a bit of that in the United States because work is so demanding and stressful and that shapes the leisure patterns. You get what economists call goods- or income-intensive leisure.

D&S: If we think of consumption behavior as social—as aiming to enhance a person's social status—can we think of any important social constraints on the amounts or patterns of consumption? If many people disapprove of polluting or wasteful forms of consumption, like the Hummer, can we observe a social constraint on that? Or, in what are very difficult economic times for a lot of people, is there any effect on people reining in unseemly levels of luxury consumption?

JS: Well, I'll start with the latter. I was reading about and experiencing people's reluctance to engage in ostentatious displays at the time of the crash, and in its early aftermath. I think, by now, that didn't last very long. One of the things about the most ostentatious stuff is that we're increasingly a gated society, so the wealthy are consuming lavishly outside of the view of the ordinary and the poor. There is certainly less celebration of it, and you see it less in the culture now than before the crash, for sure. The Hummers are a very interesting case. I have a friend who did research on the war between Hummer drivers and the Prius drivers, the Prius drivers being referred to as "pious" drivers by the Hummer folks. Now the Hummer vehicle has collapsed as a consumer product. Hummer drivers were subjected to a lot of social disapproval. It also became economically less-desirable when the price of gas went up.

There is definitely a rising ecological consciousness that is attempting to moralize consumption in ways that yield social approval or disapproval of low-carbon versus high-carbon lifestyles. It isn't mainstream yet. It's much more prevalent in highly educated groups, it tends to be more bicoastal, it's a kind of "forward trend" in the consumer culture. You do see more and more, as you move into the mainstream, people attempting to do more ecologically. I think there's widespread sentiment about that. Then, of course, you also have so many people who are just trying to make ends meet that they feel it is not possible for them to think about ecological impact. Of course, the irony is that the people who are just trying to make ends meet are the ones with the low carbon footprints, but the discourse of environmental impact is permeating through consumer culture.

D&S: Going back to something about advertising: It seems to have become more pervasive, both in terms of physical spaces that are filled with advertising and products advertised to users. In the last couple of decades, we've seen the advent of direct marketing of prescription pharmaceuticals, for example, directly to the people who will end up using them. There's a pushback, such as criticism of advertising to children, but it seems largely that there's widespread tolerance of this pervasiveness of advertising in daily life.

JS: This is a little counterintuitive, but part of why advertising has become so pervasive is that the core of advertising, which is television spots, have become so unimportant. People don't have to watch them anymore, and that's huge for advertisers. I think the 30- or 60-second TV spots are much more powerful than the kinds of things that advertisers have moved towards in terms of the spatial expansion of advertising. I think that advertising on the web is much less powerful. So, that's one of the paradoxes of advertising in the contemporary moment: the moment when advertising is much more pervasive in terms of space and place, is a moment when it's much less powerful. Advertisers have been able to move in a few directions that have been productive for them, like word of mouth advertising, and so forth, but those forms are also being delegitimized. People know the person sitting next to them in a bar telling them to drink this vodka might be paid by the company.

Prescription drugs are a big exception, because that came about as a regulatory change. Drug companies weren't allowed to advertise directly to consumers before. If it weren't for pharmaceuticals and ads directed at kids, the advertising industry would be in big trouble. Now the kid story is, I think, a little bit different than the adult story, in the sense that you have a much more powerful approach to children now than you did in the past. The approach to children, I think, is a lot more effective than the approach to adults, which I think is declining in effectiveness. So, you can see a theme in what I'm saying about advertising. Today, I would say I feel less worried about advertising than I did before I started studying it. I think people tune it out. I don't want to go too far on this, but to me it's not where the main action is in terms of what's driving consumer patterns.

D&S: We see some examples of people, in their purchasing decisions, transcending a kind of narrow consumer mentality: They're thinking about environmental impacts, say, in buying a hybrid or electric car. In terms of other products they may be thinking about labor conditions, such as buying fair trade goods or no sweatshop apparel or footwear. On the other hand, one might look at this as reinforcing a core aspect of consumerist capitalism: That whatever it is that you may want, it's for sale and you can buy it.

JS: There's a debate in sociology and the social sciences more generally—because there are other disciplines that have weighed in on this question—about the critique of ethical consumption, political consumption, green consumption. Some argue that it's actually detrimental because it leads people to think that this purchasing behavior can solve problems, and it leads them to be less likely to join in collective solutions to environmental problems, labor problems, poverty, and development in the global South.

I did a study of that, and I used two different data sets: One was a random sample survey of all Americans. The other was an intentional survey of people who are political or ethical consumers, or what we called "conscious consumers," with about 2,000 participants. What we found is that there are actually very high levels of correlation between people engaging in this kind of purchasing and being socially and politically involved in trying to solve these problems in collective ways. And we also looked at the time sequencing and found a group of people who are politically involved already and then you add on this "walk the talk" aspect—if you're going to be fighting sweatshops, then don't buy sweatshop clothing, and if you're concerned about environmental impacts then you don't want to be buying things that are at odds with your values.

So you have people who were political first, then extended to their purchasing behavior, and you have people who got into both at around the same time, and you have people who moved in the other direction—who first did the conscious consuming and then became politically active. Certainly the idea that becoming a "green consumer" undermines your likelihood of engaging in collective action around this is not at all supported by the data in the United States, and there have also been some studies in Europe that show the same thing.

I think the fact of the matter is that changing marketplace behavior in the kind of society we have today is an important component in a broad-based campaign, whether it's on the environment or labor conditions or whatever. We see a lot of the NGOs involved in campaigns that have a market-based dimension—and those have been some of the most successful campaigns in recent years—because it's so hard to get the state to act to do these things, because it is captured by business. People have turned to the market in part because it's an arena where it looks like you can have some results, at least in the short term.

Ultimately, can you stop climate change through consumer behavior and through just market behavior? Definitely not. Can you ensure good working conditions merely by market-oriented activity? Definitely not. To think that it's sufficient is the real mistake, but I don't think that most people who work in this field, who try to work on transforming consumer behavior, have such a naïve view.

D&S: We've already talked about ways in which consumption is connected to people's lives at work, and the availability of leisure time, as well as some changes in patterns of consumption related to broader social objectives. What kinds of changes in consumption—and in the forces shaping consumption—do you envision?

JS: Well, I have a hard time thinking about the future without orienting all of my thinking about climate, because I just don't see much of a positive future unless we can address climate change very significantly. And that means, for wealthy countries, pretty radical emissions cuts in a pretty short period of time. It actually means that for most countries. So, as I think about the future, I think about what we could do both to address climate change through radical emissions reductions and also increase social justice, reduce inequality, and start solving the enormous problems that we have in this country. My most recent book, *True Wealth*, is about how to do that. Obviously, we need to get onto a renewable energy system, there's no question about that. We need a carbon tax or carbon regulation, and that's stuff that is very well known. What is not understood, I don't think, is that we can't successfully address climate change with a model in which we continue to try to expand the size of the economy.

We're going to have to deal with working hours, because that's the only way to stop expanding the size of the economy in any sensible way. So the core of what we need to do is to get back on the trajectory of using productivity growth to reduce hours of work. And that then opens up incredible possibilities in terms of rebalancing the labor market, integrating the unemployed, and having a fairer distribution of hours. We're talking about the distribution of income, but not about the distribution of hours, which is one of the things that drives the distribution of income. So, fair access to the work that exists, giving people more time off from work, and doing much more as a society—and probably a lot on the local and community level—to ensure basic needs for people.

With declining work hours, people's incomes are pretty much stabilized, so you need to bring the incomes of the bottom up, and you need to bring the incomes of the top down. Part of that has to be a redistribution of work opportunity and creating community provisioning of basic needs, like publicly owned utilities which provide power and heat for people at reasonable prices, enhanced public transportation, more public provisioning of food. There are really interesting things going on in global-South countries bringing farmers and consumers together in local food economies that are not just about high-priced organic food, which is what we have here, but low-priced food that ensures food security for people. So, shorter hours, basic needs being met—including housing, education, healthcare—that's the direction I would like to see us go, and I think that really it all flows out from a kind of commitment to climate protection. It could all flow out from a commitment to basic needs, too. They really integrate.

Time use is central, and I think you get a totally different culture of consumption if people's incomes are on a basically stabilized trajectory and what they're getting is more and more free time. So, you have a new culture of consumption that is not about the acquisition of the new, it's not the "work and spend" pattern as I've called it, it's not "throw away" or media driven, it's more "true materialist," where you really pay attention to the things you have, and it's a kind of earthier consumption. ❏

Article 3.2

THE 800-POUND RONALD McDONALD IN THE ROOM

BY HELEN SCHARBER

January 2007

W hen your child's doctor gives you advice, you're probably inclined to take it. And if 60,000 doctors gave you advice, ignoring it would be even more difficult to justify. Last month, the American Academy of Pediatrics (AAP) issued a policy statement advising us to limit advertising to children, citing its adverse effects on health. Yes, banning toy commercials might result in fewer headaches for parents ("Please, please, pleeeeeeease, can I have this new video game I just saw 10 commercials for????"), but the AAP is more concerned with other health issues, such as childhood obesity. Advertising in general—and to children specifically—has reached astonishingly high levels, and as a country, we'd be wise to take the doctors' orders.

Advertising to kids is not a new phenomenon, but the intensity of it is. According to Juliet Schor, author of *Born to Buy*, companies spent around $100 million in 1983 on television advertising to kids. A little more than 20 years later, the amount earmarked for child-targeted ads in a variety of media has jumped to at least $12 billion annually. That's over $150 per boy and girl in the U.S. And it's not as though kids only see ads for action figures and sugary cereal; the other $240 billion spent on advertising each year ensures that they see ads for all kinds of products, everywhere they go. According to the AAP report, "the average young person views more than 3,000 ads per day on television, on the Internet, on billboards, and in magazines." Ads are also creeping into schools, where marketers have cleverly placed them in "educational" posters, textbook covers, bathroom stalls, scoreboards, daily news programs, and bus radio programming.

If advertising to children is becoming increasingly ubiquitous, it's probably because it's becoming increasingly profitable. Once upon a time, kids didn't have as much market power as they do today. The AAP report estimates that kids under 12 now spend $25 billion of their own money annually, teenagers spend another $155 billion, and both groups probably influence around $200 billion in parental spending. Not too surprising, considering that 62 percent of parents say their children "actively participate" in car-buying decisions, according to a study by J.D. Power & Associates. Marketers are also becoming more aware of the long-term potential of advertising to children. While they may not be the primary market now, they will be someday. And since researchers have found that kids as young as two can express preferences for specific brands, it's practically never too early to begin instilling brand loyalty.

But while small children have an incredible memory for commercial messages, they may not have developed the cognitive skills necessary to be critical of them. In 2004, the American Psychological Association (APA) also called for setting limits on advertising to kids, citing research that "children under the age of eight are unable to critically comprehend televised advertising messages and are prone to accept advertiser messages as truthful, accurate and unbiased." Many people take offense at the idea that we might be manipulated by marketing. Aren't we, after all, intelligent enough to make up our own minds about what to buy? The research cited by the APA, however, shows that children are uniquely vulnerable to manipulation by advertising. Marketers therefore should not be allowed to prey on them in the name of free speech.

Such invasive advertising to children is not only an ethical problem. The American Academy of Pediatrics cited advertising's effects on health through the promotion of unhealthy eating, drinking and smoking as the main motivation for setting limits. Children's health issues certainly merit attention. The Center for Disease Control, for example, has found that the prevalence of overweight children (ages 6 to 11) increased from 7 percent in 1980 to about 19 percent in 2004, while the rate among adolescents (ages 12 to 19) jumped from 5 percent to 17 percent. In addition to physical health problems, Schor argues that extensive marketing has negative effects on children's emotional well being. In her research for Born to Buy, Schor found links between immersion in consumer culture and depression, anxiety, low self esteem and conflicts with parents. The big push to consume can also lead to financial health problems, as many Americans know all too well, with credit card debt among 18 to 24-year-olds doubling over the past decade.

Not even the staunchest critics of marketing to children would argue that advertisements are completely at fault for these trends. Yet, the commercialization of nearly everything is negatively affecting children's well being in rather profound ways. Why, then, is hardly anyone paying attention to the 800-pound Ronald McDonald in the room? Perhaps it's because advertising appears to be a necessary evil or a fair tradeoff—maybe little Emma's school couldn't afford a soccer team without Coke on the scoreboard, for example. Or perhaps some would argue that parents who don't approve of the commercial culture should limit their kids' exposure to it. Increasingly invasive marketing techniques make it practically impossible to simply opt out of commercial culture, though. Thus, decisions to limit marketing to children must be made by the country as a whole. Sweden, Norway, Greece, Denmark, and Belgium have already passed laws curbing kid-targeted advertising, and according to 60,000 pediatricians, if we care about the health of our kids, we should too. ❏

Sources: American Association of Pediatrics, Policy Statement on Children, Adolescents, and Advertising, December 2006 (pediatrics.aappublications.org/cgi/content/full/118/6/2563); American Psychological Association, "Television Advertising Leads to Unhealthy Habits in Childen" February 2004 (releasees/childrenads.html); Jennifer Saranow, "Car makers direct more ads at kids," *Wall Street Journal*, November 9th, 2006 (www.commercialexploitation.org/news/carmakers.html); David Burke, "Two-year olds branded by TV advertising" (www.whitedot.org/issue/isssory.aps?slug=Valkenburg); Center for a New American Dream, *Kids and Commercialism* (www.newdream.org/kids/);; Juliet Schor, Born to Buy: The Commercialized Child and the New Consumer Culture (New York: Scribner, 2004); Center for Disease Control, "Facts about Childhood Overweight" www.cdc.gov/Healthy Youth/overweight/index.html).

Article 3.3

WAY BEYOND GREENWASHING
Have corporations captured "Big Conservation"?

BY JONATHAN LATHAM
March/April 2012

Imagine an international mega-deal. The global organic food industry agrees to support international agribusiness in clearing as much tropical rainforest as they want for farming. In return, agribusiness agrees to farm the now-deforested land using organic methods, and the organic industry encourages its supporters to buy the resulting timber and food under the newly devised "Rainforest Plus" label. There would surely be an international outcry.

Virtually unnoticed, however, even by their own membership, the world's biggest wildlife conservation groups have agreed to exactly such a scenario, only in reverse. Led by the World Wide Fund for Nature (WWF, still known as the World Wildlife Fund in the United States), many of the biggest conservation nonprofits including Conservation International and the Nature Conservancy have already agreed to a series of global bargains with international agribusiness. In exchange for vague promises of habitat protection, sustainability, and social justice, these conservation groups are offering to greenwash industrial commodity agriculture.

The big conservation nonprofits don't see it that way, of course. According to WWF's "Vice President for Market Transformation" Jason Clay, the new conservation strategy arose from two fundamental realizations.

The first was that agriculture and food production are the key drivers of almost every environmental concern. From issues as diverse as habitat destruction to over-use of water, from climate change to ocean dead zones, agriculture and food production are globally the primary culprits. To take one example, 80-90% of all fresh water extracted by humans is for agriculture, according to the UN Food and Agriculture Organization's "State of the World's Land and Water" report.

This point was emphasized once again in an analysis published in the scientific journal *Nature* in October 2011. The lead author of this study was Professor Jonathan Foley. Not only is Foley the director of the University of Minnesota-based Institute on the Environment, but he is also a science board member of the Nature Conservancy.

The second crucial realization for WWF was that forest destroyers typically are not peasants with machetes but national and international agribusinesses with bulldozers. It is the latter who deforest tens of thousands of acres at a time. Land clearance on this scale is an ecological disaster, but Claire Robinson of Earth Open Source points out it is also "incredibly socially destructive," as peasants are driven off their land and communities are destroyed. According to the UN Permanent Forum on Indigenous Issues, 60 million people worldwide risk losing their land and means of subsistence from palm plantations.

By about 2004, WWF had come to recognize the true impacts of industrial agriculture. Instead of informing their membership and initiating protests and boycotts, however, they embarked on a partnership strategy they call "market transformation."

Market Transformation

With WWF leading the way, the conservation nonprofits have negotiated approval schemes for "Responsible" and "Sustainable" farmed commodity crops. According to WWF's Clay, the plan is to have agribusinesses sign up to reduce the 4-6 most serious negative impacts of each commodity crop by 70-80%. And if enough growers and suppliers sign up, then the Indonesian rainforests or the Brazilian Cerrado will be saved.

The ambition of market transformation is on a grand scale. There are schemes for palm oil (the Roundtable on Sustainable Palm Oil; RSPO), soybeans (the Round Table on Responsible Soy; RTRS), biofuels (the Roundtable on Sustainable Biofuels), Sugar (Bonsucro) and also for cotton, shrimp, cocoa and farmed salmon. These are markets each worth many billions of dollars annually and the intention is for these new "Responsible" and "Sustainable" certified products to dominate them.

The reward for producers and supermarkets will be that, reinforced on every shopping trip, "Responsible" and "Sustainable" logos and marketing can be expected to have major effects on public perception of the global food supply chain. And the ultimate goal is that, if these schemes are successful, human rights, critical habitats, and global sustainability will receive a huge and globally significant boost.

The role of WWF and other nonprofits in these schemes is to offer their knowledge to negotiate standards, to provide credibility, and to lubricate entry of certified products into international markets. On its UK website, for example, WWF offers its members the chance to "Save the Cerrado" by emailing supermarkets to buy "Responsible Soy." What WWF argues will be a major leap forward in environmental and social responsibility has already started. "Sustainable" and "Responsible" products are already entering global supply chains.

Reputational Risk

For conservation nonprofits these plans entail risk, one of which is simple guilt by association. The Round Table on Responsible Soy (RTRS) scheme is typical of these certification schemes. Its membership includes WWF, Conservation International, Fauna and Flora International, the Nature Conservancy, and other prominent nonprofits. Corporate members include repeatedly vilified members of the industrial food chain. As of January 2012, there are 102 members, including Monsanto, Cargill, ADM, Nestle, BP, and UK supermarket ASDA.

That is not the only risk. Membership in the scheme, which includes signatures on press-releases and sometimes on labels, indicates approval for activities that are widely opposed. The RTRS, for example, certifies soybeans grown in large-scale chemical-intensive monocultures. They are usually genetically modified organisms (GMOs). They are mostly fed to animals. And they originate in countries with hungry populations. When, according to an ABC News poll, 52% of Americans think GMOs are unsafe and 93% think GMOs ought to be labeled, for example, this is a risk most organizations dependent on their reputations probably would not consider.

The remedy for such reputational risk is high standards, rigorous certification, and watertight traceability procedures. Only credibility at every step can deflect the seemingly obvious suspicion that the conservation nonprofits have been hood-winked or have somehow "sold out."

So, which one is it? Are "Responsible" and "Sustainable" certifications indicative of a genuine strategic success by WWF and its fellows, or are the schemes nothing more than business as usual with industrial-scale greenwashing and a social-justice varnish?

Low and Ambiguous Standards

The first place to look is the standards themselves. The language from the RTRS standards (see sidebar), to stick with the case of soy, illustrates the tone of the RTRS principles and guidance.

There are two ways to read these standards. The generous interpretation is to recognize that the sentiments expressed are higher than what is actually practiced in many countries where soybeans are grown, in that the standards broadly follow common practice in Europe or North America. Nevertheless, they are far lower than organic or fair-trade standards; for example, they don't require crop rotation, or prohibit pesticides. Even a generous reading also needs to acknowledge the crucial point that adherence to similar requirements in Europe and North America has contaminated wells, depleted aquifers, degraded rivers, eroded the soil, polluted the oceans, driven species to extinction, and depopulated the countryside—to mention only a few well-documented downsides.

There is also a less generous interpretation of the standards. Much of the content is either in the form of statements, or it is merely advice. Thus section 4.2 reads: "Pollution is minimized and production waste is managed responsibly." Imperatives, such as: "must," "may never," "will," etc., are mostly lacking from the document. Worse, key terms such as "pollution," "minimized," "responsible," and "timely" (see sidebar) are left undefined. This chronic vagueness means that both certifiers and producers possess effectively infinite latitude to implement or judge the standards. They could never be enforced, in or out of court.

The Round Table on Responsible Soy Standards

RTRS standards (version 1, June 2010) cover five "principles." Principle 1: Legal Compliance and Good Business Practices. Principle 2: Responsible Labour Conditions. Principle 3: Responsible Community Relations. Principle 4: Environmental Responsibility. Principle 5: Good Agricultural Practice.

Language typical of the standards includes, under Principle 2 (Responsible Labour Conditions), section 2.1.1 states: "No forced, compulsory, bonded, trafficked, or otherwise involuntary labor is used at any stage of production," while section 2.4.4 states, "Workers are not hindered from interacting with external parties outside working hours."

Under Principle 3 (Responsible Community Relations), section 3.3.3 states: "Any complaints and grievances received are dealt with in a timely manner."

Under Principle 4 (Environmental Responsibility), section 4.2 states: "Pollution is minimized and production waste is managed responsibly," and section 4.4 states: "Expansion of soy cultivation is responsible."

Under Principle 5 (Good Agricultural Practice), Section 5.9 states: "Appropriate measures are implemented to prevent the drift of agrochemicals to neighboring areas."

Dubious Verification and Enforcement

Unfortunately, the flaws of RTRS certification do not end there. They include the use of an internal verification system. The RTRS uses professional certifiers, but only those who are members of RTRS. This means that the conservation nonprofits are relying on third parties for compliance information. It also means that only RTRS members can judge whether a principle was adhered to. Even if they consider it was not, there is nothing they can do, since the RTRS has no legal status or sanctions.

The "culture" of deforestation is also important to the standards. Rainforest clearance is often questionably legal, or actively illegal, and usually requires removing existing occupants from the land. It is a world of private armies and bribery. This operating environment makes very relevant the irony under which RTRS members, under Principle 1, volunteer to obey the law. The concept of volunteering to obey the law invites more than a few questions. If an organization is not already obeying the law, what makes WWF suppose that a voluntary code of conduct will persuade it? And does obeying the law meaningfully contribute to a marketing campaign based on responsibility?

Of equal concern is the absence of a clear certification trail. Under the "Mass Balance" system offered by RTRS, soybeans (or derived products) can be sold as "Responsible" that were never grown under the system. Mass Balance means vendors can transfer the certification quantity purchased, to non-RTRS soybeans. Such an opportunity raises the inherent difficulties of traceability and verification to new levels.

How Will Certification Save Wild Habitats?

A key stated goal of WWF is to halt deforestation through the use of maps identifying priority habitat areas that are off-limits to RTRS members. There are crucial questions over these maps, however. First, even though soybeans are already being traded, the maps have yet to be drawn up. Secondly, the maps are to be drawn up by RTRS members themselves. Thirdly, RTRS maps can be periodically redrawn. Fourthly, RTRS members need not certify all of their production acreage. This means they can certify part of their acreage as "Responsible," but still sell (as "Irresponsible"?) soybeans from formerly virgin habitat. This means WWF's target for year 2020 of 25% coverage globally and 75% in WWF's "priority areas" would still allow 25% of the Brazilian soybean harvest to come from newly deforested land. And of course, the scheme cannot prevent non-members, or even non-certified subsidiaries, from specializing in deforestation.

These are certification schemes, therefore, with low standards, no methods of enforcement, and enormous loopholes. Pete Riley of UK GM Freeze dubs their instigator the "World Wide Fund for naïveté" and believes "the chances of Responsible soy saving the Cerrado are zero." Claire Robinson of Earth Open Source agrees: "The RTRS standard will not protect the forests and other sensitive ecosystems. Additionally, it greenwashes soy that's genetically modified to survive being sprayed with quantities of herbicide that endanger human health and the environment." There is even a website (www.toxicsoy.org) dedicated to exposing the greenwashing of GMO soy.

Many other groups apparently share that view. More than 250 large and small sustainable farming, social justice, and rainforest preservation groups from all over the world signed a "Letter of Critical Opposition to the RTRS" in 2009. Signatories included the Global Forest Coalition, Friends of the Earth, Food First, the British Soil Association and the World Development Movement.

Other commodity certifications involving WWF have also received strong criticism. The Mangrove Action Project in 2008 published a "Public Declaration Against the Process of Certification of Industrial Shrimp Aquaculture" while the World Rainforest Movement issued "Declaration against the Roundtable on Sustainable Palm Oil (RSPO)," signed by 256 organizations in October 2008.

What Really Drives Commodity Certification?

Commodity certification is in many ways a strange departure for conservation nonprofits. In the first place the big conservation nonprofits are more normally active in acquiring and researching wild habitats. Secondly, these are membership organizations, yet it is hard to envisage these schemes energizing the membership. How many members of the Nature Conservancy will be pleased to find that their organization has been working with Monsanto to promote GM crops as "Responsible"? Indeed, one can argue that these programs are being actively concealed from their members, donors, and the public. From their advertising, their websites, and their educational materials, one would presume that poachers, population growth and ignorance are the chief threats to wildlife in developing countries. It is not true, however, and as WWF's Jason Clay and the very existence of these certification schemes make clear, senior management knows it well.

In public, the conservation nonprofits justify market transformation as cooperative; they wish to work with others, not against them. However, they have chosen to work preferentially with powerful and wealthy corporations. Why not cooperate instead with small farmers' movements, indigenous groups, and already successful standards, such as fair-trade, organic and non-GMO? These are causes that could use the help of big international organizations. Why not, with WWF help, embed into organic standards a rainforest conservation element? Why not cooperate with your membership to create engaged consumer power against habitat destruction, monoculture, and industrial farming? Instead, the new "Responsible" and "Sustainable" standards threaten organic, fair-trade, and local food systems—which are some of the environmental movement's biggest successes.

One clue to the enthusiasm for "market transformation" may be that financial rewards are available. According to Nina Holland of Corporate Europe Observatory, certification is "now a core business" for WWF. Indeed, WWF and the Dutch nonprofit Solidaridad are currently receiving millions of euros from the Dutch government (under its Sustainable Trade Action Plan) to support these schemes. According to the plan, 67 million euros have already been committed, and similar amounts are promised.

The Threat From the Food Movement

Commodity-certification schemes like RTRS can be seen as an inability of global conservation leadership to work constructively with the ordinary people who live in and around wild areas of the globe; or they can be seen as a disregard for fair-trade and organic labels; or as a lost opportunity to inform and energize members and potential members as to the true causes of habitat destruction; or even as a cynical moneymaking scheme. These are all plausible explanations of the enthusiasm for certification schemes and probably each plays a part. None, however, explains why conservation nonprofits would sign up to schemes whose standards and credibility are so low. Especially when, as never before, agribusiness is under pressure to change its destructive social and environmental practices.

The context of these schemes is that we live at an historic moment. Positive alternatives to industrial agriculture, such as fair trade, organic agriculture, agro-ecology, and the System of Rice Intensification, have shown they can feed the planet, without destroying it, even with a greater population. Consequently, there is now a substantial international consensus of informed opinion that industrial agriculture is a principal cause of the current environmental crisis and the chief obstacle to hunger eradication.

This consensus is one of several roots of the international food movement. As a powerful synergism of sustainability, social-justice, sustainability, food-quality, and environmental concerns, the food movement is a clear threat to the long-term existence of the industrial food system. Incidentally, this is why big multinationals have been buying up ethical brands.

Under these circumstances, evading the blame for the environmental devastation of the Amazon, Asia, and elsewhere, undermining organic and other genuine certification schemes, and splitting the environmental movement must be a dream come true for members of the industrial food system. A true cynic might surmise that the food industry could hardly have engineered it better had they planned it themselves.

Who Runs Big Conservation?

To guard against such possibilities, nonprofits are required to have boards of directors whose primary legal function is to guard the mission of the organization and to protect its good name. In practice, for conservation nonprofits this means overseeing potential financial conflicts and preventing the organization from lending its name to greenwashing.

So, who are the individuals guarding the mission of global conservation nonprofits? U.S.-WWF boasts (literally) that its new vice-chair was the last CEO of Coca-Cola, Inc. (a member of Bonsucro) and that another board member is Charles O. Holliday Jr., the current chairman of the board of Bank of America, who was formerly CEO of DuPont (owner of Pioneer Hi-Bred International, a major player in the GMO industry). The current chair of the executive board at Conservation International is Robert Walton, better known as chair of the board of Wal-Mart (which now sells "sustainably sourced" food and owns the supermarket chain ASDA). The boards of WWF and Conservation International do have more than a sprinkling of members with conservation-related careers. But they are heavily outnumbered by business represen-tatives. On the board of Conservation International, for example, are GAP, Intel, Northrop Grumman, JP Morgan, Starbucks, and UPS, among others.

The Nature Conservancy's board of directors has only two members (out of 22) who list an active affiliation to a conservation organization in their board CV (Prof. Gretchen Daly and Cristian Samper, head of the U.S. Museum of Natural History). Only one other member even mentions among his qualifications an interest in the subject of con-servation. The remaining members are like Shona Brown, who is an employee of Google and a board member of Pepsico, or Meg Whitman, the current president and CEO of Hewlett-Packard, or Muneer A. Satter, a managing director of Goldman Sachs.

So, was market transformation developed with the support of these boards or against their wishes? The latter is hardly likely. The key question then becomes: Did these boards in fact instigate market transformation? Did it come from the very top?

Never Ending

Leaving aside whether conservation was ever their true intention, it seems highly unlikely that WWF and its fellow conservation groups will leverage a positive trans-formation of the food system by bestowing "Sustainable" and "Responsible" stan-dards on agribusiness. Instead, it appears much more likely that, by undermining existing standards and offering worthless standards of their own, habitat destruc-tion and human misery will only increase.

Market transformation, as envisaged by WWF, nevertheless might have worked. However, WWF neglected to consider that successful certification schemes start from the ground up. Organic and fair-trade began with a large base of committed farmers determined to fashion a better food system. Producers willingly signed up to high standards and clear requirements because they believed in them. Indeed, many already were practicing high standards without certification. But when big players in the food industry have tried to climb on board, game the system and manipulate standards, problems have resulted, even with credible standards like fair-trade and organic. At some point big players will probably undermine these standards. They seem already to be well on the way, but if they succeed their efforts will only have proved that certification standards can never be a substitute for trust, commitment and individual integrity.

The only good news in this story is that it contradicts fundamentally the defeatist arguments of the WWF. Old-fashioned activist strategies, of shaming bad practice, boycotting products, and encouraging alternatives, do work. The market opportunity presently being exploited by WWF and company resulted from the success of these strategies, not their failure. Multinational corporations, we should conclude, really do fear activists, non-profits, informed consumers, and small pro-ducers all working together. ❏

Sources: Jonathan A. Foley et al. "Solutions for a Cultivated Planet" *Nature*, October 2011 (Nature.com); Jason Clay, "Economics, Behavior and Biodiversity Loss: Sustainability as a Pre-competitive Issue," March 25, 2011 (youtube.com); Food and Agriculture Organization of the United Nations, "Scarcity and degradation of land and water: growing threat to food security," November 28, 2011 (fao.org); State of the World's Land and Water Resources for Food and Agriculture (SOLAW), November 28, 2011 (fao.org); Mat McDermott, "More Dirty Deforestation: 55% of Indonesia's Logging Illegal + Cargill's Two Hidden Palm Oil Plantations," May 6, 2010 (treehugger.com); Earth Open Source (earthopensource.org); United Nations (UN; un.org); Roundtable on Sustainable Palm Oil (RSPO; rspo.org); Round Table on Responsible Soy (RTRS; responsiblesoy.org); Roundtable on Sustainable Biofuels (rsb.epfl.ch); Bonsucro (Bonsucro.com); WWF, "Save the Cerrado: What's happening in the Cerrado?" (wwf.org. uk); Gary Langer, "Behind the Label, Many Skeptical of Bio-engineered Food," June 19, 2001 (abcnews.com); Round Table on Responsible Soy, "Why certifying under the RTST Standard?" (responsiblesoy.org); Natural Resources Defense Council, "Atrazine: Poisoning the Well," May 2010 (nrdc.org); The *Capital-Journal* Editorial Board, "Time for action on rural depopulation," July 28, 2011 (cjonline.com); "State of the World's Indigenous Peoples Report, Chapter 7: Emerging Issues," January 2010 (un.org); "A Brief History of Rubber" (rainforests.mongabay.com); "Letter of critical opposition to the Round Table on Responsible Soy," April 2009 (bangmfood. org); Global Forest Coalition (globalforestcoalition.org); Public Declaration Against the Process of Certification of Industrial Shrimp Aquaculture, November 3, 2008 (mangroveactionproject. org); World Rainforest Movement, "Declarations against the Roundtable on Sustainable Palm Oil (RSPO) in Defence of Human Rights, Food Sovereignty," September 2008 (wrm.org); System of Rice Intensification (SRI-Rice; sri.ciifad.cornell.edu); Sarah Hills, "Coca-Cola snaps up first Bonsucro certified sugarcane," June 22, 2011 (foodnavigator.com); "Wal-Mart Unveils Global Sustainable Agriculture Goal," October 14, 2010 (walmartstores.com); "Largest Corporate Dairy, Biotech Firm and USDA Accused of Conspiring to Corrupt Rulemaking and Pollute Organics," January 23, 2012 (cornucopia.org); Dutch Ministry of Agriculture, "Nature and Food Quality Sustainable Food: Public Summary of Policy Document" (government.nl); Jonathan Latham and Allison Wilson, "How the Science Media Failed the IAASTD," April 7, 2008 (independentsciencenews.org).

Article 3.4

CAMPUS STRUGGLES AGAINST SWEATSHOPS CONTINUE

Indonesian workers and U.S. students fight back against Adidas.

BY SARAH BLASKEY AND PHIL GASPER
September/October 2012

Abandoning his financially ailing factory in the Tangerang region of Indonesia, owner Jin Woo Kim fled the country for his home, South Korea, in January 2011 without leaving money to pay his workers. The factory, PT Kizone, stayed open for several months and then closed in financial ruin in April, leaving 2,700 workers with no jobs and owed $3.4 million of legally mandated severance pay.

In countries like Indonesia, with no unemployment insurance, severance pay is what keeps workers and their families from literal starvation. "The important thing is to be able to have rice. Maybe we add some chili pepper, some salt, if we can," explained an ex-Kizone worker, Marlina, in a report released by the Worker Rights Consortium (WRC), a U.S.-based labor-rights monitoring group, in May 2012.

Marlina, widowed mother of two, worked at PT Kizone for eleven years before the factory closed. She needs the severance payment in order to pay her son's high school registration fee and monthly tuition, and to make important repairs to her house.

When the owner fled, the responsibility for severance payments to PT Kizone workers fell on the companies that sourced from the factory—Adidas, Nike, and the Dallas Cowboys. Within a year, both Nike and the Dallas Cowboys made severance payments that they claim are proportional to the size of their orders from the factory, around $1.5 million total. But Adidas has refused to pay any of the $1.8 million still owed to workers.

Workers in PT Kizone factory mainly produced athletic clothing sold to hundreds of universities throughout the United States. All collegiate licensees like Adidas and Nike sign contracts with the universities that buy their apparel. At least 180 universities around the nation are affiliated with the WRC and have licensing contracts mandating that brands pay "all applicable back wages found due to workers who manufactured the licensed articles." If wages or severance pay are not paid to workers that produce university goods, then the school has the right to terminate the contract.

Using the language in these contracts, activists on these campuses coordinate nationwide divestment campaigns to pressure brands like Adidas to uphold previously unenforceable labor codes of conduct.

Unpaid back wages and benefits are a major problem in the garment industry. Apparel brands rarely own factories. Rather, they contract with independent manufacturers all over the world to produce their wares. When a factory closes for any reason, a brand can simply take its business somewhere else and wash its hands of any responsibilities to the fired workers.

Brands like Nike and Russell have lost millions of dollars when, pressed by United Students Against Sweatshops (USAS), universities haver terminated their contracts. According to the USAS website, campus activism has forced Nike to pay severance and Russell to rehire over 1,000 workers it had laid off, in order to avoid losing more collegiate contracts. Now many college activists have their sights set on Adidas.

At the University of Wisconsin (UW) in Madison, the USAS-affiliated Student Labor Action Coalition (SLAC) and sympathetic faculty are in the middle of a more than year-long campaign to pressure the school to terminate its contract with Adidas in solidarity with the PT Kizone workers.

The chair of UW's Labor Licensing Policy Committee (LLPC) says that Adidas is in violation of the code of conduct for the school's licensees. Even the university's senior counsel, Brian Vaughn, stated publicly at a June LLPC meeting that Adidas is "in breach of the contract based on its failure to adhere to the standards of the labor code." But despite the fact that Vaughn claimed at the time that the University's "two overriding goals are to get money back in the hands of the workers and to maintain the integrity of the labor code," the administration has dragged its feet in responding to Adidas.

Instead of putting the company on notice for potential contract termination and giving it a deadline to meet its obligations as recommended by the LLPC, UW entered into months of fruitless negotiations with Adidas in spring of 2012. In July, when these negotiations had led nowhere, UW's interim chancellor David Ward asked a state court to decide whether or not Adidas had violated the contract (despite the senior counsel's earlier public admission that it had). This process will delay a decision for many more months--perhaps years if there are appeals.

Since the Adidas campaign's inception in the fall of 2011, SLAC members have actively opposed the school's cautious approach, calling both the mediation process and the current court action a "stalling tactic" by the UW administration and Adidas to avoid responsibility to the PT Kizone workers. In response, student organizers planned everything from frequent letter deliveries to campus administrators, to petition drives, teach-ins, and even a banner drop from the administration building that over 300 people attended, all in hopes of pressuring the chancellor (who ultimately has the final say in the matter) to cut the contract with Adidas.

While the administration claims that it is moving slowly to avoid being sued by Adidas, it is also getting considerable pressure from its powerful athletics director, Barry Alvarez, to continue its contract with Adidas. As part of the deal, UW's sports programs receive royalties and sports gear worth about $2.5 million every year.

"Just look at the money—what we lose and what it would cost us," Alvarez told the *Wisconsin State Journal*, even though other major brands would certainly jump at the opportunity to replace Adidas. "We have four building projects going on. It could hurt recruiting. There's a trickle-down effect that would be devastating to our whole athletic program."

But Tina Treviño-Murphy, a student activist with SLAC, rejects this logic. "A strong athletics department shouldn't have to be built on a foundation of stolen labor," she told Dollars & Sense. "Our department and our students deserve better.".

Adidas is now facing pressure from both campus activists in the United States and the workers in Indonesia--including sit-ins by the latter at the German and British embassies in Jakarta. (Adidas' world headquarters are in Germany, and the company sponsored the recent London Olympics.) This led to a meeting between their union and an Adidas representative, who refused to admit responsibility but instead offered food vouchers to some of the workers. The offer amounted to a tiny fraction of the owed severance and was rejected as insulting by former Kizone workers.

In the face of intransigence from university administrations and multinational companies prepared to shift production quickly from one location to another to stay one step ahead of labor-rights monitors, campus activism to fight sweatshops can seem like a labor of Sisyphus. After more than a decade of organizing, a recent fundraising appeal from USAS noted that "today sweatshop conditions are worse than ever."

Brands threaten to pull out of particular factories if labor costs rise, encouraging a work environment characterized by "forced overtime, physical and sexual harassment, and extreme anti-union intimidation, even death threats," says Natalie Yoon, a USAS member who recently participated in a delegation to factories in Honduras and El Salvador.

According to Snehal Shingavi, a professor at the University of Texas, Austin who was a USAS activist at Berkeley for many years, finding ways to build links with the struggles of the affected workers is key. "What I think would help the campaign the most is if there were actually more sustained and engaged connections between students here and workers who are in factories who are facing these conditions," Shingavi told *Dollars & Sense*. Ultimately, he said, only workers' self-activity can "make the kind of changes that I think we all want, which is an end to exploitative working conditions."

But in the meantime, even small victories are important. Anti-sweatshop activists around the country received a boost in September, when Cornell University President David Skorton announced that his school was ending its licensing contract with Adidas effective October 1, because of the company's failure to pay severance to PT Kizone workers. The announcement followed a sustained campaign by the Sweatfree Cornell Coalition, leading up to a "study in" at the president's office. While the contract itself was small, USAS described the decision as the "first domino," which may lead other campuses to follow suit. Shortly afterwards, Oberlin College in Ohio told Adidas that it would not renew its current four-year contract with the company if the workers in Indonesia are not paid severance.

Perhaps just as significant are the lessons that some activists are drawing from these campaigns. "The people who have a lot of power are going to want to keep that power and the only way to make people give some of that up is if we make them," Treviño-Murphy said. "So it's really pressure from below, grassroots organizing, that makes the difference. We see that every day in SLAC and I think it teaches us to be not just better students but better citizens who will stand up to fight injustice every time." ❑

Sources: Worker Rights Consortium, "Status Update Re: PT Kizone (Indonesia)," May 15, 2012 (workersrights.org); Andy Baggot, "Alvarez Anxiously Awaits Adidas Decision," *Wisconsin State Journal*, July 13, 2012 (host.madison.com); United Students Against Sweatshops (usas.org), PT Kizone update, June 15, 2012 (cleanclothes.org/urgent-actions/kizoneupdate).

Article 3.5

HOW TO TAKE ON THE CARD SHARKS—AND WIN!

New consumer-protection legislation has reined in predatory credit card lending.

BY JIM CAMPEN
November/December 2013

In the early 2000s, credit card companies, like other lenders, decided that there was lots of money to be made by exploiting vulnerable consumers. Up to that point, the credit card industry was a somewhat boring business that made its money by charging high—but not exorbitant—interest rates to borrowers who it judged likely to be able to make their monthly payments on time. Then, however, the giant banks that provide the bulk of the nation's credit cards switched to a business model based on what Elizabeth Warren, then a professor at Harvard Law School, memorably termed "tricks and traps." These were spelled out in the almost impossible-to-understand small print of the multi-page "agreements" that the banks provided to their customers. Anyone who did manage to read to the end found that the "agreement" allowed the credit card company to change any of its terms "at any time, for any reason."

The unfair and exploitative practices of the credit card companies, affecting millions of households, soon became widely known. Five years ago, it was almost impossible to avoid the avalanche of news articles, radio and TV reports, and Internet postings about them. Today, such stories are few and far between. This isn't because the media became bored with the story. It's because a powerful consumer movement publicized the abuses, built a strong campaign, and won two important legislative victories.

Tricks and Traps

Millions of consumers were enticed with offers of cards with "promotional" interest rates as low as 0% for the first few months and regular interest rates of between 12% and 14% after that, but ended up paying far more. They were slapped with late fees averaging over $33 each time their monthly payment arrived even one day late, even if the due date fell on a Sunday and their payment arrived on Monday. They faced stiff over-limit fees—sometimes multiple charges for a number of small purchases on the same day—if their charges exceeded their credit limit by even a single dollar, even though borrowers were generally not aware that they had exceeded their limit or that the credit card companies would authorize over-limit charges.

Most devastatingly, both of these minor mistakes were among those that could result in their interest rate being switched to a much higher "penalty rate." Some card companies adopted the policy of "universal default" whereby even a problem on an unrelated account (for example, being late on an electric bill) could result in a cardholder being subject to the penalty rate. By 2007, the average penalty rate was 16.9 percentage points higher than the regular interest rate, meaning that a 13% rate would jump to 29.9%.

Worst of all, the penalty rate applied not only to future purchases, but also to money already borrowed. For a household with the average 2008 credit card balance, about $10,700, this would result in additional interest charges of more than $1,800 per year. Once a household fell into this trap, it was almost impossible to get out—which is just the way the banks liked it.

Many of those trapped were low- and middle-income families who used their credit cards to pay for basic living expenses and unexpected medical bills. One recent survey, by the liberal policy organization Dēmos, found that two-fifths of such lower-income families used their credit cards in this way. Many other victims were college students, on their own for the first time, who fell prey to aggressive marketing on college campuses and ended up with debt that they couldn't repay as well as a damaged credit rating.

A Consumer Victory: The Credit CARD Act of 2009

As the credit card industry's abuses grew and spread, millions of outraged consumers demanded change. Led by a coalition of national consumer advocacy groups —including the Center for Responsible Lending, the Consumer Federation of America, Consumers Union, the National Consumer Law Center, and U.S. PIRG —a powerful grassroots movement pushed Congress to take action. The industry argued that the proposed legislation that eventually became the Credit Card Accountability, Responsibility, and Disclosure Act (known as the CARD Act) would end up hurting consumers by raising the cost and reducing the availability of credit card borrowing.

But credit card abuses were so widespread and so offensive that politicians were unwilling to defend them in the light of day. Although many Republicans worked behind the scenes to derail or weaken the bill, when the CARD Act came up for its final votes in May 2009, it passed overwhelmingly in both the Senate (90-5) and the House of Representatives (361-54).

The CARD Act effectively outlaws the worst of the credit card industry's tricks and traps. Most importantly, it prohibits retroactive interest rate increases on existing balances unless a borrower has missed two consecutive monthly payments on the account. And not only that: when a borrower is hit with a penalty rate, the company is required to restore the original interest rate if and when the borrower succeeds in making six consecutive on-time payments.

Late fees have been reduced by requiring that consumers have at least 21 days to make their payments, that payments due on a Sunday or holiday be regarded as on time if they arrive the next business day, that payments be due the same date each month, and that the fees be "reasonable and proportional." Over-limit fees are banned unless a cardholder opts-in to allow approval of charges over their credit limit, and are limited to one fee per month. The initial rate offered on a new account cannot be raised during the first year, and after that the borrower must be provided with 45-day advance notice and given the opportunity to cancel the card and pay off the existing balance over five years.

Credit card companies are prohibited from opening a new account or increasing a borrower's credit limit without assessing the consumer's ability to make timely loan payments. Those under 21 are given special protection from predatory credit card lenders by a prohibition on sending pre-approved offers of credit without advance permission, a ban on marketing on college campuses, and a new rule that no one under 21 years of age can get a card without either proving an independent ability to make the required monthly payments or obtaining a co-signer over 21.

Consumers Win Again: The CFPB

The enactment of the CARD Act was a major accomplishment. But simply passing laws doesn't make a difference unless those laws are enforced. And prohibiting existing abusive practices can't protect consumers against the credit card companies' endless ability to come up with imaginative new abuses that get around the law. The title of a December 2009 report from the Center for Responsible Lending spelled out the problem: "Dodging Reform: As Some Credit Card Abuses are Outlawed, New Ones Proliferate."

That's why a second consumer legislative victory—ensuring that the financial reform law passed in July 2010 (the Dodd-Frank Act) mandated the establishment of a Consumer Financial Protection Bureau (CFPB)—was perhaps even more important than the CARD Act itself.

The CFPB, which came into existence in July 2011, is charged not only with writing and enforcing the regulations that implement the CARD Act and other consumer-protection laws, but also with monitoring the operation of consumer-credit markets and taking action against unfair, deceptive, or abusive acts and practices. It seeks to improve consumers' ability to understand prices and risks upfront when shopping for credit, and to offer them a one-stop location for submitting complaints and seeking remedies for problems with credit card providers.

The Fruits of These Victories

That the CARD Act has produced major benefits for consumers, with none of the dire consequences predicted by the industry, has been documented in numerous reports and studies. For example, the group Consumer Action noted that while complaints about credit cards were regularly the number one reason for calls to its consumer hotline before 2009, they are no longer even among the top ten.

The most comprehensive assessment to date of the Act's impact on consumers and on the industry is provided by a major report released by the CFPB in October 2013. This report found that the average late fee had gone down from $33 to $27 and that over-limit fees had essentially disappeared. Together, these two changes were saving consumers an estimated $4 billion per year.

The CFPB also found that, while credit remains readily available to those with the ability to repay, the number of 18- to 20-year-olds with at least one credit card had fallen by half. (Meanwhile, of course, student loans have soared. These loans have their own problems, but at least their interest rates are much lower than those on credit cards and no repayment is required while students remain in school.)

The CFPB's publicly available consumer complaint database recorded over 36,000 complaints about credit cards in its first two years of operation, resulting in monetary payments to about 6,500 consumers, and increased public scrutiny of card-company performance. J. D. Power's 2013 *Credit Card Satisfaction Study* showed that customer satisfaction had risen every year since 2010, to the highest level since the study began in 2007.

The CFPB's report also highlighted areas where consumers continue to suffer from abusive practices of the credit card industry and promised to address these issues in a timely manner. In one of these areas—the selling of "add-on" products that purport to offer debt protection and identity protection—the CFPB has already required three big lenders (Chase, Capital One, and Discover) to refund over $700 million to consumers and to pay over $100 million in fines for deceptive marketing and charging for services that were never actually provided.

Crying Wolf

Data on what's happened during the three and one-half years since passage of the CARD Act demonstrate beyond any doubt what consumer advocates said at the time: that banks were "crying wolf," rather than warning of real dangers, when they predicted that the pending legislation would cause the cost of credit card borrowing to soar and their own profitability to plummet.

It is theoretically possible that all of the CARD Act's consumer benefits from the lower fees and rates noted earlier could have been offset by increases in other charges. This is what Jamie Dimon, CEO of JPMorgan Chase, was predicting when he said that "If you're a restaurant and you can't charge for the soda, you're going to charge more for the burger." But the CFPB investigated this possibility by measuring what it calls the "total cost of credit"—that is, it added up all fees and interest charges paid by credit card borrowers and calculated what percentage this represented of the total amount of credit card debt outstanding. The CFPB found that the total cost of credit declined from 16.4% in the last quarter of 2008 to 14.4% in the last quarter of 2012. It is impossible to know how much of this reduction is a result of the CARD Act, but it is crystal clear that predictions of an increase in borrowing costs were wrong.

Another October 2013 study on the impact of the CARD Act, this one by four academic economists, concluded that the resulting fee reductions have saved consumers $21 billion per year "with no evidence of an offsetting increase in interest charges or a reduction in access to credit." The savings were particularly great for the riskiest borrowers. While the fee reductions amounted to 2.8% of total credit card balances annually, they came to over ten percent of their credit card balances for the 17% of borrowers who were in the highest risk category as measured by their credit scores at the time they opened their accounts.

Did the consumer benefits from the CARD Act come at the expense of lender profitability? It's possible to get a remarkably clear answer to this question because the FDIC reports quarterly on the performance of different kinds of banks, categorized by specialization or size, and one of its categories consists of "credit card lenders." It turns out that all but one of the six largest credit card lenders (who together account for over two-thirds of total credit card balances) do their lending though separate banks that specialize in credit cards. This is true for Bank of

America, Chase, Capital One, Discover, and American Express; the only exception is Citibank.

Since 2010, "credit card banks" has been the most profitable single category, using the two measures of profitability reported by the FDIC—return on assets (ROA) and return on equity (ROE). In 2012, ROA was 3.14% for credit card banks, more than triple the 1.00% for all banks; ROE was 20.97% for credit card banks, more than double the 8.92% for all banks. The results for 2012 are very similar to those for 2011 and for the first half of 2013, and also to those for 2007, before the onset of the financial crisis and economic downturn.

Perhaps the credit card companies had been outsmarting themselves. A business model based on "tricks and traps" that aggressively pushed money into the hands of borrowers who lacked the ability to repay their debts may have worked in the short run, but ultimately was disastrous to the lenders themselves. Lending money only to those with the ability to repay it would seem like simple common sense. It's too bad that financial hardship for millions of borrowers, an act of Congress, and a new federal agency was necessary to make these lenders behave sensibly. ❏

Sources: The CARD ACT Report, October 1, 2013 (consumerfinance.gov); Sumit Agarwal, et al., "Regulating Consumer Financial Products: Evidence from Credit Cards"; Center for Responsible Lending (responsiblelending.org); Federal Deposit Insurance Corporation (FDIC), *Quarterly Banking Profile* (fdic.gov); Peter Dreier and Donald Cohen, "Credit Sharks Crying Wolf," The Cry Wolf Project, May 2009 (crywolfproject.org).

Chapter 4

FIRMS, PRODUCTION, AND PROFIT MAXIMIZATION

INTRODUCTION

How do producers make decisions? Textbooks describe a process that is rational, benign, and downright sensible. There is one best—least costly and most profitable—way to produce any given amount of goods or services. Given a particular scale of operations, there is one most profitable amount to produce. Businesses adjust their total output and the mix of inputs at the margin until they achieve these most profitable outcomes. They pay the going wage for labor, just as they pay the going price for any input. And when businesses have achieved the lowest possible costs, market competition ensures that they pass on savings to consumers.

This chapter describes a reality that is a bit more complicated, and in some ways uglier, than the textbook model. Very large companies are not the passive price-takers of neoclassical lore but do in fact affect the market-wide level of prices, profits, and wages, and manufacture their own demand. Thus, large corporations are the very embodiment of market power (volating Tilly Assumption #1, Article 1.2).

James Boyce opens the discussion, in "Pursuing Profits—Or Power?" (Article 4.1), by questioning the assumption that the firm seels to maximize profits alone. In Boyce's view, a great deal of business behavior (especially political behavior) suggests that corporate decision-makers often put the pursuit of power above profits.

Alejandro Reuss follows with a primer on corporations (Article 4.2). He describes the ways that corporations are "special"—that is, different from other capitalist enterprises—and why they have become the dominant form of business organization. He concludes by discussing how corporations' economic power—their control over investment and employment—can translate into political power.

Next, Dean Baker takes a look at the factors behind skyrocketing executive compensation at large corporations. In "Corporate Cronyism: The Secret to Overpaid CEOs" (Article 4.3), Baker argues that it is not CEOs' indiviual productivity, but rather their relationship to other corporate directors, that explains the executive-pay mystery.

In Article 4.4, "What's Good for Wal-Mart ...," John Miller provides a particularly salient example of firms' market power. He suggests that there may not be just "one best way" for retail businesses, but rather two: a "high road" based on high levels of service, skilled, decently paid employees, and higher prices, as exemplified by the business model at Costco; and a "low road" that offers low prices, no frills, and a low-paid, high-turnover workforce, which is Walmart's business model. Despite Walmart's growth and its position as the world's largest retailer, the author questions whether the business model has in fact proven beneficial for the U.S. economy as a whole.

In the next article, "Vultures in the E.R." (Article 4.5), Nicole Aschoff details how firms can profit at the expense of the social good. Aschoff focuses her attention on private-equity firms' increasingly common acquisition of hospitals. This may be profitable for the firms, she argues, while coming at the expense of patient care and sometimes jeopardizing the long term viability of the hospitals themselves.

The metals giant ASARCO provides another example of a corporation pursuing a particularly perverse "low road" profit-maximization strategy (Article 4.6). Fischel and her co-authors describe ASARCO's history of evading and actively violating worker and environmental safety laws. This history recently culminated in a successful bankruptcy declaration that released the corporation from its legal liabilities towards the affected communities. The authors also point out the regulatory failures of the American government along the way, including the striking failure of Congress to reinstate "polluter pays" fees to finance the "superfund" for environmental clean-up projects.

The final essay is economist Nancy Folbre's look at an alternative way of structuring the firm, "Co-op Economics" (Article 4.7). Folbre looks not only at the strength of workers' cooperatives, in which the workers are also the owners of the firm, but also the problems that they face in growing and becoming more widespread.

Discussion Questions

1. (General) The authors of the articles in this chapter present various firm strategies as a choice, rather than an imperative. How does this compare with the standard microeconomic analysis of business decision-making?

2. (General) Miller suggests that we should change the rules of the competitive game to steer businesses toward better treatment of workers. Present-day capitalism already has some such rules (such as those forbidding slavery). What rule changes do articles in this chapter propose? What do you think of these proposals?

3. (Article 4.1) Boyce argues that firms frequently put power before profits. If greater power goes hand in hand with higher profits, how can he tell what aim firms are actually pursuing?

4. (Article 4.2) How do corporations differ from other capitalist firms? How should the fact that corporations are chartered by the government, and shareholders given special protections (limited liability), affect our attitudes about government regulation of corporate operations?

5. (Article 4.3) Mainstrem neoclassical theory claims that, whatever CEOs' compensation, it must be justified by their contributions to production, or firms would not be willing to pay it. How does Baker dispute this view?

6. (Article 4.4) John Miller implies that there is more than one "best" way to organize production. Do you agree? If other ways of organizing production are equally good, why are certain ways dominant, at least in particular industries?

7. (Article 4.4) According to Cervantes (sidebar), how does Costco keep prices low while following very different labor practices?

8. (Article 4.5) Neoclassical economists argue that competitive markets align private incentives with the social good. Why does Aschoff think this is not the case with private-equity firms? Is this a special case, or does this point to a broader problem with the neoclassical view?

9. (Articles 4.5 and 4.6) Both Aschoff and Fischel and her co-authors discuss formally legal ways corporations can profit. When does the pursuit of profits cross the line? Would you draw the line at law-breaking, or are there some legal business practices—in addition to illegal ones—that you consider unacceptable?

10. (Article 4.7) Folbre proposes a dramatically different power structure at the level of the individual firm, with workers democratically contolling the enterprises where they work. Why does she think that this alternative strucutre could be desirable for workers and for society? If it is so desirable, why is it not more common?

Article 4.1

PURSUING PROFITS —OR POWER?

BY JAMES K. BOYCE
July/August 2013

Do corporations seek to maximize profits? Or do they seek to maximize power? The two may be complementary—wealth begets power, power begets wealth—but they're not the same. One important difference is that profits can come from an expanding economic "pie," whereas the size of the power pie is fixed. Power is a zero-sum game: more for me means less for you. And for corporations, the pursuit of power sometimes trumps the pursuit of profits.

Take public education, for example. Greater investment in education from preschool through college could increase the overall pie of well-being. But it would narrow the educational advantage of the corporate oligarchs and their privately schooled children—and diminish the power that comes with it. Although corporations could benefit from the bigger pie produced by a better-educated labor force, there's a tension between what's good for business and what's good for the business elite.

Similarly, the business elite today supports economic austerity instead of full-employment policies that would increase growth and profits. This may have something to do with the fact that austerity widens inequality, while full employment would narrow it (by empowering workers). If we peel away the layers of the onion, at the core again we find that those at the top of the corporate pyramid put power before profits.

As one more example, consider the politics of government regulation. Corporations routinely pass along to consumers whatever costs they incur as a result of regulation. In the auto industry, for instance, the regulations that mandated seat belts, catalytic converters, and better fuel efficiency added a few hundred dollars to car prices. They didn't cut automaker profit margins. If the costs of regulation are ultimately borne by the consumer, why do they face such stiff resistance from the corporations? The answer may have less to do with profits than with power. Corporate chieftains are touchy about their "management prerogatives." They simply don't like other folks telling them what to do.

In a famous 1971 memorandum to the U.S. Chamber of Commerce, future Supreme Court Justice Lewis Powell wrote, "The day is long past when the chief executive office of a major corporation discharges his responsibility by maintaining a satisfactory growth of profits." To counter what he described as an attack on the American free-enterprise system by labor unions, students, and consumer advocates, Powell urged CEOs to act on "the lesson that political power is necessary; that power must be assiduously cultivated; and that when necessary, it must be used aggressively and with determination." He was preaching to a receptive choir.

The idea that firms single-mindedly maximize profits is an axiom of faith of neoclassical Econ 101, but alternative theories have a long history in the broader profession. Thorstein Veblen, John Maynard Keynes, and Fred Hirsch all saw an individual's position relative to others as a key motivation in economic behavior.

Today a sound-bite version of this idea is encountered on bumper stickers: "He Who Dies with the Most Toys Wins."

In his 1972 presidential address to the American Economics Association, titled "Power and the Useful Economist," John Kenneth Galbraith juxtaposed the role of power in the real-world economy to its neglect in orthodox economics: "In eliding power—in making economics a nonpolitical subject—neoclassical theory ... destroys its relation with the real world."

On the free-marketeer side of the ideological spectrum, the pursuit of power is depicted as a pathology distinctive to the State. "Chicago school" economist William Niskanen theorized that public-sector bureaucrats seek to maximize the size of their budgets, taking this as a proxy for "salary, perquisites of the office, public reputation, power, patronage, ease of managing the bureau, and ease of making changes." He called this "the peculiar economics of bureaucracy."

But the pursuit of power isn't unique to government bureaucracies. It's commonplace in corporate bureaucracies, too. In his presidential address, Galbraith made the connection: "Between public and private bureaucracies—between GM and the Department of Transportation, between General Dynamics and the Pentagon—there is a deeply symbiotic relationship."

Recognizing the real-world pursuit of power not only helps us understand behavior that otherwise may seem peculiar. It also redirects our attention from the dichotomy between the market and the state toward a more fundamental one: the divide between oligarchy and democracy. ❏

Sources: Sarah O'Connor, "OECD warns of rising inequality as austerity intensifies," *Financial Times*, May 15, 2013 (ft.com); Lewis F. Powell, Jr., "Confidential Memorandum: Attack on American Free Enterprise System," Aug. 23, 1971 (law.wlu.edu); John Kenneth Galbraith, "Power and the Useful Economist," *American Economic Review*, March 1973; William A. Niskanen, "The Peculiar Economics of Bureaucracy," *American Economic Review*, May 1968.

Article 4.2

CORPORATIONS

BY ALEJANDRO REUSS
April 2012

When people use the word "corporation," they are usually referring to certain private, for-profit businesses, especially the largest businesses in the United States or other capitalist economies. When we think of corporations, we usually think of "big business." Besides size, people often picture other features of corporations when they hear the word. A corporation can have many shareholders—all part-owners of the company—instead of being owned by a single owner or a couple of partners. A corporation has a board of directors, elected by some or all of the shareholders, which may direct the overall way the corporation is managed. The board usually hires a few top executives, who then make decisions about how the corporation in managed on a day-to-day basis.

Corporations do not have to be large. There are corporations of all different sizes. Even a small company with a few employees could be a corporation. There are some large companies that are not corporations, but the very largest companies, which may have hundreds of thousands of employees and may sell billions of dollars of goods each year, are almost always corporations. Various different kinds of businesses can be corporations, including manufacturing companies (such as General Motors), retail companies (like Wal-Mart), or financial companies (like Bank of America or Liberty Mutual).

Even though some not for-profit entities are also—legally speaking—corporations, people usually use the word "corporation" as shorthand for for-profit companies like General Motors or Wal-Mart. A corporation, in this sense, is a particular type of capitalist enterprise—a "capitalist corporation."

What Is a Capitalist Enterprise?

By "capitalist enterprise," we just mean a private, for-profit business whose owners employ other people in exchange for wages. By this definition, a private business where a "self-employed" owner works, but which does not hire other people for wages, is not a capitalist enterprise.

In the United States and other similar economies, relatively few people are business owners. Farm workers do not usually own the farms where the work. Miners do not usually own the mines. Factory workers usually do not own the factories. People who work in shops or offices usually do not own those businesses. Most workers do not own the buildings where they go to work, the materials or tools they use, or the products they produce. Instead, they work for pay at capitalist enterprises that are owned by others.

Workers get paid a wage or salary by the owner of the business, who in turn owns whatever the worker produces using the materials and tools provided. The owners of a business, of course, do not usually want the goods that employees produce, but want to sell these goods. If a capitalist enterprise cannot sell these goods for more than what it cost to produce them, it cannot make a profit.

Even a business that makes a profit may not stay in business for very long if the profit is less than "normal" (whatever that may be). The owners may decide that it is not worth investing in that business, if it is possible for them to make a larger profit in another business. In addition, businesses that make higher profits can reinvest these profits to expand and modernize, and may put the less profitable business at a competitive disadvantage in the future. Therefore, owners of capitalist enterprises are under competitive pressure to make the most profit they can.

How Are Corporations Special?

In many ways, capitalist corporations are like other capitalist enterprises. However, corporations are also defined by their special legal status, which makes them different from other capitalist enterprises. Corporations are granted a "charter" by the government, which means that the corporation exists as a legal entity. (In the United States, state governments grant corporate charters.)

All the things that make corporations different from other capitalist enterprises are determined by government policy (in particular, the set of laws governing corporations). Corporate law creates certain special privileges for corporations that other businesses do not have. It also imposes special obligations on corporations (especially those whose shares are bought and sold on the stock market). The most important of these special characteristics are "limited liability," the "fiduciary responsibility" of management to the corporation's shareholders, "public disclosure" requirements, and the corporate "governance" structure.

Limited Liability

If a corporation cannot pay its debts, it can declare bankruptcy, and the people it owes can get paid off from the sale of its assets, like the buildings or machinery it owns. If the proceeds are not enough to pay off all the debts, however, the shareholders are not responsible (not "liable") to pay the rest. This is what we mean by the term "limited liability." Someone who buys stock in a corporation is risking whatever they paid for the stock, but cannot lose more than this amount. If the corporation goes bankrupt, the shareholders' stock becomes worthless, but the shareholders cannot be forced, legally, to pay whatever debts the corporation has left unpaid.

The justification usually given for the legal principle of limited liability is that it promotes economic growth and development. The idea is that, if companies were limited to what an individual or family, or perhaps a couple of partners, could scrape together to start a business, they would not be able to operate at the scale that modern corporations do. They would not have enough money to buy expensive machinery, let alone buy large factories or put together huge assembly lines.

Even if the reason given for limited liability is to fuel economic growth, however, we should remember that this is also a big favor from the government for the people who own shares in corporations. First, limited liability means that the government gives the shareholders of a corporation a certain kind a protection from other people's claims against it. Second, it means that corporations may take bigger risks in hopes of bigger profits, since the shareholders that they are not on the hook for all the corporation's liabilities if these risks do not pay off.

Fiduciary Responsibility

A single person who fully owns an entire company (known as a "privately held" company) can use the company's funds for whatever he or she likes, whether that is expanding the company's operations or buying luxury cars. In contrast, corporate executives receive a salary and other compensation (often lavish, in the case of large companies) decided by the board of directors or a committee of the board. They are legally free to spend this income as they wish.

Corporate executives also control how company funds are spent, but are not free to treat corporate funds as their own. This means that the chief executive of a company is not legally entitled to use company funds to remodel his or her house, buy fancy cars, take expensive vacations, and so on. Of course, executives still fly on private jets, take "business trips" to exotic locales, enjoy fancy "business dinners," and so on, but they have to justify these as necessary costs of doing business. If shareholders think that executives have failed in their fiduciary responsibility, they can actually sue the company.

Some legal scholars and economists have extended this idea to the logical extreme that corporate managers are legally obligated to the shareholders and only the shareholders. In this view, management decisions must be guided by the sole objective of enhancing "shareholder value" (in effect, the profitability of the corporation, and therefore the value of an ownership stake in it). This means that they cannot put other people's interests ahead of those of the shareholders. According to the "shareholder value" doctrine, if managers decide to pay workers more than they really have to, they are giving away the company's (that is, the shareholders') money. Likewise, they have no legal duty to the broader community, beyond abiding by the law. They do not have to "give back," say, by funding schools, libraries, or parks in the communities where they operate.

The shareholder value doctrine is not new, and it is not just something that pro-business comentators have made up. The doctrine was clearly articulated no later than 1919, in a Supreme Court opinion (*Dodge v. Ford Motor Company*) no less. However, in practice, the courts have been reluctant to intervene in disputes between shareholders and management (in effect, declining to open up the can of worms of deciding what the right business decisions would be).

Public Disclosure

Corporations that sell shares of stock on the stock market are called "publicly traded corporations." Each time a corporation sells a share of its stock to an individual or another company, it raises some money. This is one way the company can finance its operations. In actual fact, most stock sales do not involve a corporation selling stock to a member of the public, but one member of the public selling shares to another (that is, resale of shares that a corporation had previously issued). Therefore, most stock sales do not result in any money going to the corporation that originally issued it.

By law, publicly traded companies have to disclose certain business information. They have to file forms with the government (in particular, the Securities and Exchange Commission, or SEC) listing their officers (board members and top executives), the officers' compensation (salaries and other benefits), the company's profits or losses, and other information. The idea behind disclosure requirements is to protect shareholders or people who might consider purchasing shares in a company, often referred to as the "investing public."

In practice, corporate "insiders" (board members, top executives, etc.) have much more information about the financial condition of a corporation than members of the public. This has led to well-publicized scandals in recent years, such as the Enron case. Corporate executives sold the stock they owned when the price was high, knowing that in reality the company was not as profitable as the public thought, and that the stock price would soon plummet.

Corporate Governance

When an individual buys a share (or many shares) of a corporation, he or she gets certain property rights. Shareholders are not legally entitled to receive a share of the company's profits each year. The company management decides how much of this money to pay out to shareholders (as "dividends") and how much to keep. A corporation might keep cash reserves, use profits to buy existing businesses, use them to expand its existing operations (for example, by buying or renting additional factory or office buildings, buying new machinery, hiring additional workers, etc.). It is not necessarily preferable for shareholders to receive all or most of the company's profit for a year in the form of dividends. By using "retained earnings" to expand, a corporation may increase in overall value. This increases the value of an ownership share in the company (the value of the stock that shareholders own).

Shareholders have the right to sell their shares if and when they wish. This gives them a stake in the profitability of the corporation, since the price of a share (on the stock exchange) is likely to go higher the more profitable the company is. A shareholder who does not want to be a part owner of the company anymore is not entitled to sell back the shares to the company, nor to take "their" piece of the company with them. The corporation is not required to give the shareholder any tangible asset—the shareholder cannot claim any particular thing owned by the corporation—nor is the corporation forced to sell off tangible assets in order to pay a shareholder who does not want his or her shares anymore. This way, shareholders come and go, but the corporation itself stays intact.

Shareholders also have a say in the governance structure of the corporation. You can think of a corporation as a political entity, like a small (or, in some cases, not so small) country. Shareholders are like the citizens. They are entitled to attend annual shareholder meetings, where they can address questions or comments to the corporation's directors (board members) and executives. Shareholders are entitled to vote in elections to the board of directors (except for those holding certain classes of "nonvoting" or "preferred" stock). They can even run for election to the board of directors, if they so wish.

Corporate elections are different from government elections. First, in corporate elections, only shareholders are allowed to vote. The decisions made by a corporation's management may affect many other people—workers, people in communities where the corporation has operations, etc.—all around the world. However, if they are not shareholders in the corporation, they are not entitled to vote. In addition, in corporate elections, different shareholders do not get the same number of votes. Rather, each shareholder gets a number of votes equal to the number of shares he or she owns (excluding nonvoting stock). Someone who owns one share gets one vote; 10 shares, 10 votes; 100 shares, 100 votes.

In practice, a large shareholder does not need to own anywhere near a majority of the shares to effectively control a company. People who own very few shares in a company, if disgruntled with the management, are more likely to just sell their shares than to devote a lot of time and energy to getting the management replaced. Relatively small shareholders, in fact, usually just sign away their voting rights to other, larger shareholders. This way, a very wealthy individual may have effective control of a company even though he or she "only" owns, say, 5% of the total shares. Keep in mind that 5% of the stock in the largest corporate giants could be worth billions of dollars.

Corporations, Economic Power, and Political Power

Large corporations are certainly among the most powerful entities in the U.S. economy and politics. We can start by classifying the power of large corporations into economic power, on the one hand, and political power, on the other. Economic power has to do with the ability of large corporations to dictate to others (other businesses, workers, etc.) the conditions under which they will do business. Political power has to do with their ability to get what they want from the government, including both favors they can get from the government and influence over the overall direction of government policy.

Mainstream or "neoclassical" economists do not talk about economic power very much. Mostly, they talk about "market" economies as if nobody exercised any power over anyone else—buyers and sellers engaging in voluntary exchanges, each free from any kind of coercion from other buyers or sellers. The main form of economic power neoclassical economists do talk about is "market power"—basically, the ability of a seller (or buyer) to dictate higher (or lower) prices to others, because of a lack of competition.

In the view of radical political economists, employers as a group have economic power in a different sense. Most of the economic activity in capitalist economies depends on the economic decisions made by capitalist enterprises, such as how much output to produce, how many people to hire, whether to buy new machines or new buildings (this is what economists mean by "investment"), and so on. If capitalist employers decide not to hire people to produce goods and services, many people will be unemployed. Tax collections will be low, and governments are likely to experience budget deficits, unless they dramatically cut spending. Moreover, if capitalist enterprises are not hiring, unemployment is high, and many people are afraid of losing their jobs, the party in power probably will not survive the next election.

If the owners and managers of capitalist enterprises do not like the kinds of economic policies the government is putting in place, they may decide not to hire or invest. In some cases, where capitalists feel very threatened by government policies, they may actually do this with the conscious political aim of bringing down the government. More often, a decline in employment and investment can arise from a simple decline in "business confidence." The owners and managers of capitalist enterprises become pessimistic about being able to sell their goods at a profit, and make a business decision to cut back on production, employment, and investment. The effect, however, can still be to force the government to bend over backwards to maintain profitable conditions for business, in order to avoid an economic downturn. This way, the economic power of capitalist enterprises over the whole economy can result in their getting the kinds of government policies that favor them. ❑

Article 4.3

CORPORATE CRONYISM: THE SECRET TO OVERPAID CEOS

BY DEAN BAKER

February 2014; Truthout

It's hardly a secret that the heads of major corporations in the United States get mind-bending paychecks. While high pay may be understandable when a top executive turns around a failing company or vastly expands a company's revenue and profit, CEOs can get paychecks in the tens or hundreds of millions even when they did nothing especially notable.

For example, Lee Raymond retired from Exxon-Mobil in 2005 with $321 million. (That's 22,140 minimum wage work years.) His main accomplishment for the company was sitting at its head at a time when a quadrupling of oil prices sent profits soaring. Hank McKinnel walked away from Pfizer in 2006 with $166 million. It would be hard to identify his outstanding accomplishments.

But you don't have to be mediocre to get a big paycheck as a CEO. Bob Nardelli pocketed $240 million when he left Home Depot after six years. The company's stock price had fallen by 40% in his tenure, while the stock its competitor Lowe's had nearly doubled. And then we have the CEOs in the financial industry, heads of huge banks like Lehman's, Bear Stearns, and Merrill Lynch, or the insurer AIG. These CEOs took their companies to the edge of bankruptcy or beyond and still walked away with hundreds of millions of dollars in their pockets.

It's not hard to write contracts that would ensure that CEO pay bear a closer relationship to the company's performance. For example, if the value of Raymond's stock incentives at Exxon were tied to the performance of the stock of other oil companies (this can be done) then his going away package probably would not have been one-tenth as large. Also, there can be longer assessment periods so that it's not possible to get rich by bankrupting a company.

If anyone were putting a check on CEO pay, these sorts of practices would be standard, but they aren't for a simple reason. The corporate directors who are supposed to be holding down CEO pay for the benefit of the shareholders are generally buddies of the CEOs.

Corporate CEOs often have considerable input into who sits on their boards. (Some CEOs sit on the boards themselves.) They pick people who will be agreeable and not ask tough questions.

For example, corporate boards probably don't often ask whether they could get a comparably skilled CEO for lower pay, even though top executives of major companies in Europe, Japan, and South Korea earn around one-tenth as much as CEOs in the United States. Of course this is the directors' job. They are supposed to be trying to minimize what the company pays their top executives in the same way that companies try to cut costs by outsourcing production to Mexico, China, and elsewhere.

But friends don't try to save money by cutting their friends' pay. And when the directors themselves are pocketing hundreds of thousands of dollars a year for attending 4-10 meetings, there is little incentive to take their jobs seriously.

Instead we see accomplished people from politics, academia, and other sectors collecting their pay and looking the other way. For example, we have people like Erskine Bowles who had the distinction of sitting on the boards of both Morgan Stanley and General Motors in the years they were bailed out by the government. And we have Martin Feldstein, the country's most prominent conservative economist, who sat on the board of insurance giant AIG when it nearly tanked the world's financial system. Both Bowles and Feldstein were well-compensated for their "work."

Excessive CEO pay matters not only because it takes away money that rightfully belongs to shareholders, which include pension funds and individuals with 401(k) retirement accounts. Excessive CEO pay is important because it sets a pattern for pay packages throughout the economy. When mediocre CEOs of mid-size companies can earn millions or tens of millions a year, it puts upward pressure on the pay of top executives in other sectors.

It is common for top executives of universities and private charities to earn salaries in the millions of dollars because they can point to executives of comparably sized companies who earn several times as much. Those close in line to the boss also can expect comparably bloated salaries. In other words, this is an important part of the story of inequality in the economy.

To try to impose the checks that don't currently exist, the Center for Economic and Policy Research (CEPR) has created Director Watch. This site will highlight directors like Erskine Bowles and Martin Feldstein who stuff their pockets while not performing their jobs.

CEPR also worked with the Huffington Post to compile a data set that lists the directors for the Fortune 100 companies, along with their compensation, the CEOs' compensation, and the companies' stock performance. This data set is now available at the Huffington Post as Pay Pals.

Perhaps a little public attention will get these directors to actually work for their hefty paychecks. The end result could be to bring a lot of paychecks for those at the top back down to earth. ❏

Article 4.4

WHAT'S GOOD FOR WAL-MART . . .

BY JOHN MILLER
January/February 2006

"Is Wal-Mart Good for America?"

It is a testament to the public relations of the anti-Wal-Mart campaign that the question above is even being asked.

By any normal measure, Wal-Mart's business ought to be noncontroversial. It sells at low costs, albeit in mind-boggling quantities. ...

The company's success and size ... do not rest on monopoly profits or price-gouging behavior. It simply sells things people will buy at small markups and, as in the old saw, makes it up on volume. ... You may believe, as do service-workers unions and a clutch of coastal elites—many of whom, we'd wager, have never set foot in Wal-Mart—that Wal-Mart "exploits" workers who can't say no to low wages and poor benefits. You might accept the canard that it drives good local businesses into the ground, although both of these allegations are more myth than reality.

But even if you buy into the myths, there's no getting around the fact that somewhere out there, millions of people are spending billions of dollars on what Wal-Mart puts on its shelves. No one is making them do it. ... Wal-Mart can't make mom and pop shut down the shop anymore than it can make customers walk through the doors or pull out their wallets.

What about the workers? ... Wal-Mart's average starting wage is already nearly double the national minimum of $5.15 an hour. The company has also recently increased its health-care for employees on the bottom rungs of the corporate ladder.

—*Wall Street Journal* editorial, December 3, 2005

"Who's Number One? The Customer! Always!" The last line of Wal-Mart's company cheer just about sums up the *Wall Street Journal* editors' benign view of the behemoth corporation. But a more honest answer would be Wal-Mart itself: not the customer, and surely not the worker.

The first retail corporation to top the Fortune 500, Wal-Mart trailed only Exxon-Mobil in total revenues last year. With 1.6 million workers, 1.3 million in the United States and 300,000 offshore, Wal-Mart is the largest private employer in the nation and the world's largest retailer.

Being number one has paid off handsomely for the family of Wal-Mart founder Sam Walton. The family's combined fortune is now an estimated $90 billion, equal to the net worth of Bill Gates and Warren Buffett combined.

But is what's good for the Walton family good for America? Should we believe the editors that Wal-Mart's unprecedented size and market power have redounded not only to the Walton family's benefit but to ours as well?

Low Wages and Meager Benefits

Working for the world's largest employer sure hasn't paid off for Wal-Mart's employees. True, they have a job, and others without jobs line up to apply for theirs. But that says more about the sad state of today's labor market than the quality of Wal-Mart jobs. After all, less than half of Wal-Mart workers last a year, and turnover at the company is twice that at comparable retailers.

Why? Wal-Mart's oppressive working conditions surely have something to do with it. Wal-Mart has admitted to using minors to operate hazardous machinery, has been sued in six states for forcing employees to work off the books (i.e., unpaid) and without breaks, and is currently facing a suit brought by 1.6 million current and former female employees accusing Wal-Mart of gender discrimination. At the same time, Wal-Mart workers are paid less and receive fewer benefits than other retail workers.

Wal-Mart, according to its own reports, pays an average of $9.68 an hour. That is 12.4% below the average wage for retail workers even after adjusting for geography, according to a recent study by Arindrajit Dube and Steve Wertheim, economists at the University of California's Institute of Industrial Relations and long-time Wal-Mart researchers. Wal-Mart's wages are nearly 15% below the average wage of workers at large retailers and about 30% below the average wage of unionized grocery workers. The average U.S. wage is $17.80 an hour; Costco, a direct competitor of Wal-Mart's Sam's Club warehouse stores, pays an average wage of $16 an hour.

Wal-Mart may be improving its benefits, as the *Journal*'s editors report, but it needs to. Other retailers provide health care coverage to over 53% of their workers, while Wal-Mart covers just 48% of its workers. Costco, once again, does far better, covering 82% of its employees. Moreover, Wal-Mart's coverage is far less comprehensive than the plans offered by other large retailers. Dube reports that according to 2003 IRS data, Wal-Mart paid 59% of the health care costs of its workers and dependents, compared to the 77% of health care costs for individuals and 68% for families the average retailer picks up.

A recent internal Wal-Mart memo leaked to the *New York Times* confirmed the large gaps in Wal-Mart's health care coverage and exposed the high costs those gaps impose on government programs. According to the memo, "Five percent of our Associates are on Medicaid compared to an average for national employees of 4 percent. Twenty-seven percent of Associates' children are on such programs, compared to a national average of 22 percent. In total, 46 percent of Associates' children are either on Medicaid or are uninsured."

A considerably lower 29% of children of all large-retail workers are on Medicaid or are uninsured. Some 7% of the children of employees of large retailers go uninsured, compared to the 19% reported by Wal-Mart.

Wal-Mart's low wages drag down the wages of other retail workers and shutter downtown retail businesses. A 2005 study by David Neumark, Junfu Zhang, and Stephen Ciccarella, economists at the University of California at Irvine, found that Wal-Mart adversely affects employment and wages. Retail workers in a community with a Wal-Mart earned 3.5% less because Wal-Mart's low prices force other businesses to lower prices, and hence their wages, according to the Neumark study. The same study also found that Wal-Mart's presence reduces retail employment by 2% to 4%. While other studies have not found this negative employment effect, Dube's research also reports fewer retail jobs and lower wages for retail workers in metropolitan counties with a Wal-Mart. (Fully 85% of Wal-Mart stores are in metropolitan counties.) Dube figures that Wal-Mart's presence costs retail workers, at Wal-Mart and elsewhere, $4.7 billion a year in lost earnings.

In short, Wal-Mart's "everyday low prices" come at the expense of the compensation of Wal-Mart's own employees and lower wages and fewer jobs for retail workers in the surrounding area. That much remains true no matter what weight we assign to each of the measures that Wal-Mart uses to keep its costs down: a just-in-time inventory strategy, its ability to use its size to pressure suppliers for large discounts, a routinized work environment that requires minimal training, and meager wages and benefits.

How Low are Wal-Mart's Everyday Low Prices?

Even if one doesn't subscribe to the editors' position that it is consumers, not Wal-Mart, who cause job losses at downtown retailers, it is possible to argue that the benefit of Wal-Mart's low prices to consumers, especially low-income consumers, outweighs the cost endured by workers at Wal-Mart and other retailers. Jason Furman, New York University economist and director of economic policy for the 2004 Kerry-Edwards campaign, makes just such an argument. Wal-Mart's "staggering" low prices are 8% to 40% lower than people would pay elsewhere, according to Furman. He calculates that those low prices on average boost low-income families' buying power by 3% and more than offset the loss of earnings to retail workers. For Furman, that makes Wal-Mart "a progressive success story."

But exactly how much savings Wal-Mart affords consumers is far from clear. Estimates vary widely. At one extreme is a study Wal-Mart itself commissioned by Global Insight, an economic forecasting firm. Global Insight estimates Wal-Mart created a stunning savings of $263 billion, or $2,329 per household, in 2004 alone.

At the other extreme, statisticians at the U.S. Bureau of Labor Statistics found no price savings at Wal-Mart. Relying on Consumer Price Index data, the BLS found that Wal-Mart's prices largely matched those of its rivals, and that instances of lower prices at Wal-Mart could be attributed to lower quality products.

Both studies, which rely on the Consumer Price Index and aggregate data, have their critics. Furman himself allows that the Global Insight study is "overly simplistic" and says he "doesn't place as much weight on that one." Jerry Hausman, the M.I.T. economist who has looked closely at Wal-Mart's grocery stores, maintains that the CPI data that the Bureau of Labor Statistics relies on systematically miss the savings offered by "supercenters" such as Wal-Mart. To show the difference between prices at Wal-Mart and at other grocers, Hausman, along with Ephraim Leibtag, USDA Economic Research Service economist, used supermarket scanner data to examine the purchasing patterns of a national sample of 61,500 consumers from 1988 to 2001. Hausman and Leibtag found that Wal-Mart offers many identical food items at an average price about 15%-25% lower than traditional supermarkets.

While Hausman and Leibtag report substantial savings from shopping at Wal-Mart, they fall far short of the savings alleged in the Global Insight study. The Hausman and Leibtag study suggests a savings of around $550 per household per year, or about $56 billion in 2004, not $263 billion. Still, that is considerably more than the $4.7 billion a year in lost earnings to retail workers that Dube attributes to Wal-Mart.

But if "Wal-Mart hurts wages, not so much in retail, but across the whole country," as economist Neumark told *BusinessWeek*, then the savings to consumers from Wal-Mart's everyday low prices might not outweigh the lost wages to all workers. (Retail workers make up just 11.6% of U.S. employment.)

Nor do these findings say anything about the sweatshop conditions and wages in Wal-Mart's overseas subcontractors. One example: A recent Canadian Broadcasting Corporation investigative report found that workers in Bangladesh were being paid less than $50 a month (below even the United Nation's $2 a day measure of poverty) to make clothes for the Wal-Mart private label, Simply Basic. Those workers included ten- to thirteen-year-old children forced to work long hours in dimly lit and dirty conditions sewing "I Love My Wal-Mart" t-shirts.

Making Wal-Mart Do Better

Nonetheless, as Arindrajit Dube points out, the relevant question is not whether Wal-Mart creates more savings for consumers than losses for workers, but whether the corporation can afford to pay better wages and benefits.

Dube reasons that if the true price gap between Wal-Mart and its retail competitors is small, then Wal-Mart might not be in a position to do better—to make

---

The Costco Alternative? Wall Street Prefers Wal-Mart

In an April 2004 online commentary, *BusinessWeek* praised Costco's business model but pointed out that Costco's wages cause Wall Street to worry that the company's "operating expenses could get out of hand." How does Costco compare to low-wage Wal-Mart on overhead expenses? At Costco, overhead is 9.8% of revenue; at Wal-Mart, it is 17%. Part of Costco's secret is that its better paid workers are also more efficient: Costco's operating profit per hourly employee is $13,647; each Wal-Mart employee only nets the company $11,039. Wal-Mart also spends more than Costco on hiring and training new employees: each one, according to Rutgers economist Eileen Appelbaum, costs the company $2,500 to $3,500. Appelbaum estimates that Wal-Mart's relatively high turnover costs the company $1.5 to $2 million per year.

Despite Costco's higher efficiency, Wall Street analysts like Deutsche Bank's Bill Dreher complain that "Costco's corporate philosophy is to put its customers first, then its employees, then its vendors, and finally its shareholders. Shareholders get the short end of the stick." Wall Street prefers Wal-Mart's philosophy: executives first, then shareholders, then customers, then vendors, and finally employees.

In 2004, Wal-Mart paid CEO Lee Scott $5.3 million, while a full-time employee making the average wage would have received $20,134. Costco's CEO Jim Senegal received $350,000, while a full-time average employee got $33,280. And *BusinessWeek* intimates that the top job at Costco may be tougher than at Wal-Mart. "Management has to hustle to make the high-wage strategy work. It's up its wage and benefit gap and still maintain its price advantage. But if Wal-Mart offers consumers only minor price savings, then its lower wages and benefits hardly constitute a progressive success story that's good for the nation.

If Wal-Mart's true price gap is large (say, the 25% price advantage estimated by Hausman), then Wal-Mart surely is in a position to do better. For instance, Dube calculates that closing Wal-Mart's 16% overall compensation gap with other large retailers would cost the company less than 2% of sales. Raising prices by two cents on the dollar to cover those increased compensation costs would be "eminently absorbable," according to Dube, without eating away much of the company's mind-boggling $10 billion profit (2004).

Measures that set standards to force Wal-Mart and all big-box retailers to pay decent wages and provide benefits are beginning to catch on. Chicago, New York City, and the state of Maryland have considered or passed laws that would require big-box retailers to pay a "living wage" or to spend a minimum amount per worker-hour for health benefits. The Republican board of Nassau County on Long Island passed an ordinance requiring that all big-box retailers pay $3 per hour toward health care. Wal-Mart's stake in making sure that such proposals don't become law or spread nationwide goes a long way toward explaining why 80% of Wal-Mart's $2 million in political contributions in 2004 went to Republicans.

Henry Ford sought to pay his workers enough so they could buy the cars they produced. Sam Walton sought to pay his workers so little that they could afford to shop nowhere else. And while what was good for the big automakers was probably never good for the nation, what is good for Wal-Mart, today's largest employer, is undoubtedly bad for economic justice. ❑

---

constantly looking for ways to repackage goods into bulk items, which reduces labor, speeds up Costco's just-in-time inventory, and boosts sales per square foot. Costco is also savvier ... about catering to small shop owners and more affluent customers, who are more likely to buy in bulk and purchase higher-margin goods."

Costco's allegedly more affluent clientele may be another reason that its profit per employee is higher than Wal-Mart's and its overhead costs a lower percentage of revenue. However, Costco pays its employees enough that they could afford to shop there. As the *BusinessWeek* commentary noted, "the low-wage approach cuts into consumer spending and, potentially, economic growth."

—*Esther Cervantes*

Average Hourly Wage		Percentage of U.S. Workforce in Unions		Employees Covered by Company Health Insurance		Employees Who Leave After One Year	
Wal-Mart	Costco	Wal-Mart	Costco	Wal-Mart	Costco	Sam's Club*	Costco
$9.68	$16.00	0.0%	17.9%	48%	82%	21%	6%
* Sam's Club is the Wal-Mart unit that competes directly with Costco.							

Sources: "Is Wal-Mart Good for America?" *Wall Street Journal,* 12/3/05; "Gauging the Wal-Mart Effect," *WSJ,* 12/03/05; Arindrajit Dube & Steve Wertheim, "Wal-Mart and Job Quality—What Do We Know, and Should We Care?" 10/05; Jason Furman, "Wal-Mart: A Progressive Success Story," 10/05; Leo Hindery Jr., "Wal-Mart's Giant Sucking Sound," 10/05; A. Bernstein, "Some Uncomfortable Findings for Wal-Mart," *BusinessWeek* online, 10/26/05, and "Wal-Mart: A Case for the Defense, Sort of," *BusinessWeek* online, 11/7/05; Dube, Jacobs, and Wertheim, "The Impact of Wal-Mart Growth on Earnings Throughout the Retail Sector in Urban and Rural Counties," *Institute of Industrial Relations Working Paper,* UC Berkeley, 10/05; Dube, Jacobs, and Wertheim, "Internal Wal-Mart Memo Validates Findings of UC Berkeley Study," 11/26/05; Jerry Hausman and Ephraim Leibtag, "Consumer Benefits from Increased Competition in Shopping Outlets: Measuring the Effect of Wal-Mart," 10/05; Hausman and Leibtag, "CPI Bias from Supercenters: Does the BLS Know that Wal-Mart Exists?" *NBER Working Paper No. 10712,* 8/04; David Neumark, Junfu Zhang, and Stephen Ciccarella, "The Effects of Wal-Mart on Local Labor Markets," *NBER Working Paper No. 11782,* 11/05; Erin Johansson, "Wal-Mart: Rolling Back Workers' Wages, Rights, and the American Dream," American Rights at Work, 11/05; Wal-Mart Watch, "Spin Cycle"; CBC News, "Wal-Mart to cut ties with Bangladesh factories using child labour," 11/30/05; National Labor Committee, "10 to 13-year-olds Sewing 'I Love My Wal-Mart' Shirts," 12/05; Global Insight, "The Economic Impact of Wal-Mart," 2005.

Article 4.5

VULTURES IN THE E.R.

Private-equity firms target the U.S. health-care industry.

BY NICOLE ASCHOFF

January/February 2013

Public anger over increasing economic polarization and frustration with the seemingly unassailable power of big finance coalesced for a brief moment last summer in the public shaming of Bain Capital, the private-equity firm formerly run by Mitt Romney. Popular journalists like *Rolling Stone*'s Matt Taibbi turned their attention to the activities of powerful, secretive private equity firms, connecting the dots between private-equity investment and job loss, and people got mad. But, as with the leveraged-buyout kings of the 1980s, after the election furor subsided, Bain and its private-equity brethren dropped back under the radar, returning to business as usual.

However, the nature of "business as usual" for private equity warrants another look. Private-equity (PE) firms like Bain, Cerberus, Blackstone, Warburg Pincus, and Kohlberg, Kravis and Roberts (KKR) operate in nearly every sector of the economy, including manufacturing, business and financial services, food, entertainment, and health care. Cutthroat tactics, job loss, and bankruptcy are common themes in the PE world.

Health care is a particularly popular sector for PE firms. After a decline following the 2008 financial crisis, PE investment in health care has rebounded, both in the United States and globally. In particular, medical technology, pharmaceuticals, and medical services (like hospitals and nursing homes) are seeing sharp increases in PE investment. According to a recent report by Bain, the value of global private-equity deals in health care was over $30 billion in 2011, double the investment of 2010.

Growing PE interest in low-profit, or no-profit, sectors like hospitals may come as a surprise to many who assume that private investors prefer to channel their money toward industries with rapid growth or high profit potential, like medical technology and pharmaceuticals. But private-equity firms are not like most investors. Unlike venture capitalists, who bet their own money on the success of a company, in most cases private-equity firms put very little of their own capital into their investments, and instead arrange for outside investors (like pension funds) and the firm being taken over to fund the investment. The PE firms make their money from fees and dividends, which are often debt-financed by the acquired firm. This unique feature of private-equity firms means that any company with steady cash flow (or even just a substantial potential cash flow) is a possible target for acquisition.

The growing appetite for hospital takeovers by PE firms has its roots in the ongoing struggle for survival experienced by many hospitals. Hospitals—particularly small, community hospitals and those serving poor populations—are under intense pressure due to declining Medicare/Medicaid reimbursement rates, new government demands for technological upgrades, increasing numbers of under- and uninsured patients, and restricted access to credit markets. According to the American Hospital Association (AHA), roughly 30% of non-profit hospitals are operating at a loss. Many more hospitals find themselves breaking even each year, but unable to borrow and make investments to keep up with increasing costs and regulation.

The precarious financial situation of many community hospitals has led to a wave of mergers and acquisitions in recent years by for-profit hospital corporations and larger non-profit systems. Community hospitals believe that being absorbed by a larger hospital or hospital chain will result in improved access to capital to make necessary upgrades and maintain their patient base. Meanwhile, big, for-profit, and non-profit hospitals view the acquisition of smaller, community hospitals as an easy way to increase market share and improve economies of scale.

This consolidation trend is similar to the one that occurred in the hospital sector in the 1990s, but with one significant difference—the increasing role of PE investors. PE investors are betting that the growing needs of the baby-boomer generation, in combination with the Affordable Care Act, which will dramatically expand health-insurance coverage (an estimated 15-20 million new insured by 2014, and an additional 15 million by 2016), will create new profit opportunities. For example, in 2006, KKR, Bain, and Merrill Lynch acquired the mammoth Hospital Corporation of America (HCA), a for-profit hospital chain that owns hundreds of hospitals in the United States and England, for $31.6 billion. PE firms are also snapping up non-profit, community hospitals. In December 2010, Vanguard Health (owned at the time by Blackstone), bought the Detroit Medical Center for $1.3 billion. In the same year, Cerberus Capital Management paid $830 million to acquire the Caritas Christi chain of hospitals from the Archdiocese of Boston, folding the hospitals into a new, for-profit entity called Steward Health Care System. Although the AHA estimates that less than 20% of community hospitals are investor-owned, the number is growing rapidly. Josh Kosman, an expert on PE investment, estimates that half of the biggest for-profit hospital chains are now owned by private-equity firms.

One of the strategies followed by PE-backed, for-profit hospital chains like Vanguard and Steward is to gain control over urban market share by aggressively acquiring hospital groups. This strategy is a departure from earlier, more scattered, and somewhat opportunistic, acquisition patterns by for-profit hospital chains like HCA and Essent. Vanguard's purchase of Detroit Medical Center gave it control over 13.4% of Detroit's total market, while its 2010 purchase of Westlake Hospital and West Suburban Medical Center in Illinois gave it 47% of acute care inpatient beds in the immediate health planning area. Steward's recent acquisitions, including its purchase of the Caritas chain, give it control over a quarter of eastern Massachusetts acute care beds.

What's the Difference?

All hospitals are facing similar market conditions and are concerned with minimizing costs and increasing revenues. So what is the difference between not-for-profit systems like Partners, for-profit hospital chains such as Tenet and LifePoint, and PE-owned hospital chains like Steward? A recent report issued by the Congressional

Budget Office suggests that there is little difference in the behavior of non-profit and for-profit hospitals. The report found that not-for-profit hospitals on average provide slightly higher levels of uncompensated care than for-profit hospitals, while for-profit hospitals, on average, serve poorer populations with higher rates of people living with little or no health insurance.

However, Jill Horwitz, a professor at the University of Michigan, argues that nonprofit hospitals and for-profit hospitals exhibit important differences in the types of care they offer. For-profit firms emphasize surgical and acute care services, and cardiac and diagnostic services, while non-profit hospitals often provide less lucrative care such as mental health services, drug-and-alcohol treatment programs, and trauma-and-burn centers. When non-profit hospitals are converted into for-profits, they often discontinue or decrease these crucial, but less-profitable, services.

PE-backed hospital firms are particularly likely to jettison less-profitable services given their shorter investment timelines. Like most PE investments, PE firms' hospital acquisitions tend to last a short period (around five years). Then, the PE firm either takes the acquired firm public (offers stock for sale to the general public) or re-sells to other PE firms. For example, HCA was owned by two PE firms (KKR and Bain) for five years before a March 2011 initial public offering of stock (IPO), while Vanguard was owned by Morgan Stanley and Blackstone before going public in June 2011. The PE owners' goal during this period of time is to quickly increase profits and cash flow, enabling the PE firm to collect its fees and dividends, often by accessing credit and bond markets.

This investment timeline pushes PE firms to look for simple, and relatively fast, ways to increase revenues, such as eliminating less-profitable services. For example, in 2004, Vanguard's Weiss Hospital in Chicago failed a spot inspection for maternity-ward security. Staff failed to stop undercover inspectors from removing a baby (actually, for the purpose of the inspection, just an infant doll) from the ward without authorization. Rather than resolve the issue through increased staffing and a reexamination of hospital policy, Vanguard simply closed the maternity wing in 2007, eliminating a vital service for the surrounding community.

At the Vanguard-acquired Phoenix Memorial Hospital, located in a predominately urban, poor area of Phoenix, the company announced the closure of the emergency room despite earlier promises to the contrary. After a public outcry, Vanguard shelved the plan, but just a few years later closed the entire hospital and leased out the space. In the meantime, Vanguard invested heavily in surgical and ambulatory services at a nearby hospital in Phoenix's wealthier western suburbs.

In addition to reducing less-profitable services, PE-owned hospitals look for other ways to increase profits. These include centralizing and improving billing, records management, and financial services, and reducing staff, particularly registered nurses. In late 2011, nurses organized by the Massachusetts Nurses Association (MNA) gathered at Cerberus headquarters in New York to protest cuts of registered nurses on duty at Steward's Morton Hospital in southeastern Massachusetts. Since Steward's creation in 2010, the MNA and Steward have been at loggerheads. The MNA argues that Steward has cut the level of registered nurses to dangerously low levels at a number of its hospitals, including psychiatric units like the one at Carney Hospital in Boston, and has cut back on basics for patients. Nurses at Holy Family Hospital in northeastern Massachusetts complained that they were not allowed to give patients even a cup of coffee, while nurses at Norwood Hospital (in Norwood, Mass., south of Boston) brought loaves of bread to their floor to protest decreased food for patients. Nurses at Merrimack Valley Hospital, also in northeastern Massachusetts, claimed that administrators were turning down the temperature of electric blankets for chemotherapy patients to save pennies. The MNA and Steward are also fighting an ongoing battle over the MNA's pension plan. The MNA argues that Steward has refused to honor the pension agreement the union made with Caritas Christi, the former owner of the Steward chain, prior to the PE firm's 2010 acquisition.

PE-owned hospitals also engage in less-visible strategies to boost profits such as increasing lucrative surgical procedures. In 2005, the former chief compliance officer at the PE-owned Iasis hospital chain filed a complaint under the False Claims Act, alleging that doctors at St. Luke's Medical Center in Phoenix were installing a specific kind of heart implant—the intra-aortic pump—at ten times the normal rate. The alleged motive? Iasis could bill patients an additional $1000. In a 2012 exposé, the *New York Times* reported that an internal HCA memo showed that the company performed 1,200 cardiac procedures on patients without significant heart disease. The whistleblower, a registered nurse at a Florida HCA hospital, was fired for reporting the abuse.

The Biggest Difference: The Debt Trap

While service and staffing cuts, deteriorating patient care, and potentially unethical medical practices are easy to find at PE-owned hospitals and deserve urgent attention, they are not uniformly present at all PE-owned hospitals, and are also present at many non-PE-owned hospitals, both for-profit and non-profit. There is, however, another much bigger problem particular to PE hospital ownership.

PE firms are often portrayed as "turnaround" specialists and are viewed by many, including the hospitals themselves, as white knights bringing desperately needed investment and credit access. The problem with this view is that PE firms do not actually earn their money by turning around companies and making them successful. A PE firm's return on investment has little relation to whether the acquired hospital succeeds through improved patient care or increased cash flow. Instead, PE firms recoup their investment through fees (management fees, transaction fees, selling fees, etc.) from both the acquired firm and outside institutional investors. In fact, unlike other kinds of investment firms, PE firms generally put only a small percentage of the total equity down themselves, instead getting outside investors to cover the bulk of the initial equity investment. So even if the PE firm's investment fails to yield the imagined profits, the PE firm still earns a profit, or loses little or no money, because the risk is shouldered by outside investors, and in many cases, the acquired firm itself.

The primary source of risk for hospitals being acquired by PE firms is the debt load that comes with PE ownership. PE firms use the acquired hospital as a vehicle to earn profits by forcing it to sell bonds or shares, or take on bank debt, to pay the PE firm fees and dividends. For example, in January 2010, Vanguard took on $1.76

billion in debt, of which $300 million went to pay dividends to Blackstone. In June 2010, the hospital chain issued an additional $250 million in bonds and, in January 2011, the company recapitalized again. It paid a grand total of $775 million in debt-funded dividends to its PE sponsors between January 2010 and summer 2011.

When PE-backed hospital chains like Vanguard and HCA go public, they (and their PE sponsor) are able to make huge profits from their initial public offerings (IPOs). HCA raked in a record $3.8 billion at its 2011 IPO, but the money from the IPO went directly to chip away at the huge debt HCA incurred under KKR and Bain ownership. In the spring of the previous year, HCA's PE owners borrowed $2.5 billion to pay themselves a dividend, and then followed up in December with a junk-bond sale to pay themselves another nearly $2 billion dividend. As a result, under PE ownership, hospital companies like Vanguard and HCA, and all the community hospitals they have acquired along the way, become buried under a mountain of debt that stays with them long after their PE sponsor has moved on to other investments.

High levels of debt make hospitals vulnerable to changes in the industry as well as broader economic shifts. When credit markets are loose and the economy is growing, hospitals can manage their debt by issuing bonds to cover interest payments or by tapping revolving lines of credit from banks, enabling a steady inflow of funds. But these safety valves quickly disappear during broader economic downturns. A contraction in credit markets can make it difficult or impossible for hospitals to service debt by accessing new sources of liquidity. At the same time, because hospitals are saddled with so much debt, profits are channeled toward servicing the debt rather than building up cash reserves or making long-term investments in patient care or technology. This weakens the hospitals' ability to adjust to industry or economic shifts and makes them more likely to end up in bankruptcy.

The pitfalls associated with PE ownership have, in some cases, led to pushback against PE hospital acquisitions. For example, when Steward attempted to acquire Florida's non-profit Jackson Health System in 2011, it was met with public outcry from Miami residents and local politicians and was forced to back out of the deal. Unions have also been vocal opponents. In 2010, Council 31 of AFSCME in Chicago fought hard against the sale of Westlake Hospital and West Suburban Medical Center to Vanguard Health Systems, but ultimately failed to prevent the sale. Some states have attached conditions to deals involving the transformation of non-profit hospitals to for-profit, PE-owned entities. Michigan's attorney general forced Vanguard to agree to continue existing operations and services at the Detroit Medical Center for ten years after the 2010 purchase date, including commitments to charity care and research. However, the Michigan deal is exceptional, and most PE-hospital acquisitions come with few restrictions on the sale or closure of facilities.

The future of PE investment in hospitals depends on a number of factors, including the cost and availability of credit, health care legislation, and the public response to PE ownership. PE interest in the hospital sector hinges on cheap credit. If credit markets contract, and PE firms find it harder to arrange financing for their investment deals, they may lose interest in health care and instead restrict their investments to more profitable ventures. However, growing demand for health care, in the context of increased hospital obligations and restrictions as a result of the Affordable Care Act, may make community hospitals more vulnerable, and actually increase their attractiveness as takeover targets. Ultimately, the most promising avenue for restricting, or ideally, preventing PE takeovers of hospitals is to publicly scrutinize their behavior and demand alternative forms of financial support for the hospitals, doctors, and nurses struggling to provide affordable, high-quality care. ❑

Sources: Tim van Biesen and Karen Murphy, "Global Healthcare Private Equity Report 2012," Bain & Company, 2012; Advisen, "Private equity and hospitals: providence or problem," OneBeacon Professional Insurance, 2011; Lisa Goldstein, "New forces driving rise in not-for-profit hospital consolidation," Moody's Investor Service, 2012; Josh Kosman, *The Buyout of America: How Private Equity Will Cause the Next Great Credit Crisis* (New York: Portfolio, 2009); Congressional Budget Office, "Nonprofit hospitals and the provision of community benefits," Dec., 2006; Jill Horwitz, "Making Profits And Providing Care: Comparing Nonprofit, For-Profit, And Government Hospitals," *Health Affairs*, 24 (3), May 2005; Reed Abelson and Julie Creswell, "Hospital Chain Inquiry Cited Unnecessary Cardiac Work," *New York Times*, Aug. 6, 2012.

Article 4.6

BANKRUPTCY AS CORPORATE MAKEOVER

ASARCO demonstrates how to evade environmental responsibility.

BY ANNE FISCHEL, MARA KARDAS-NELSON, AND LIN NELSON
May/June 2010

> *"At around noon [every] July and August ... our folks would bring us into the house, because the smoke, the pollution, the sulfur, would settle into our community for about two or three hours ... when there was no breeze to take that away. When we would breathe that, we could not be outside because we were constantly coughing. So nobody can tell me that there was no ill effect on the majority of the folks that lived in Smeltertown."*
>
> —Daniel Solis, resident of Smeltertown, a Mexican-American neighborhood in El Paso, Texas, located next to an ASARCO smelter

After five long years in court, the bankruptcy of the American Smelting and Refining Company, or ASARCO, has finally been determined.

Hailed as one of the earliest and largest multinational corporations and responsible for the employment of hundreds of thousands, ASARCO has a long history of polluting both the environment and the workplace. After racking up billions in environmental damages, the company filed for bankruptcy in 2005.

It is billed as the largest environmental bankruptcy in United States history; 90 communities from 21 states will share a $1.79 billion settlement to cover the costs of environmental monitoring and cleanup and limited compensation to some of its workers. This figure, however, represents less than one percent of the funds originally identified as needed by claimants.

The ASARCO case emerged in the context of a diminished and disabled "Superfund," as the federal environmental program established to deal with hazardous waste sites is known. The fund was originally created by Congress to hold companies accountable for environmental damage and to ensure that communities are not left with large bills and no means to pay them. But years of corporate pressure on Capitol Hill has depleted Superfund, placing the financial burden of environmental cleanups on taxpayers, rather than on corporations.

This use of bankruptcies to avoid responsibility, coupled with a cash-strapped Superfund, offers a chilling glimpse into the world of corporate irresponsibility allowable under U.S. bankruptcy provisions and environmental policy. As the case closes, ASARCO is transforming from an aging corporation weighed down by shuttered factories and contaminated communities into a lean and profitable company. This is setting a precedent for how others can use legal loopholes to evade liability and undermine government protections.

Damaging Health and Environment, Yet Shaping Environmental Policy

ASARCO began operations in the late 1890s, mining, smelting, and refining essential ores (first lead, then copper) in order to provide base materials for industrial production. By the mid-20th century, the company had expanded to include holdings and operations in Latin America, Australia, Canada, Africa, and the Philippines. In 1914 company workers unionized through the Western Federation of Miners, which later became the Mine, Mill & Smelterworkers, eventually merging with the United Steelworkers in the 1960s. In its heyday, ASARCO operated in close to 90 U.S. communities in 22 states, employing thousands.

By the mid-1970s, employees and communities were growing concerned about environmental and public health risks resulting from company operations. Researchers, health departments, unions, and workers began tracking the impact of exposure to arsenic, lead, cadmium, and sulfur dioxide, all byproducts of the smelting process. In Tacoma, WA, site of one of ASARCO's largest smelting operations, dissident workers launched "The Smelterworker" newsletter, one of the first union-based occupational health efforts in the country. The Puget Sound Air Pollution Control Agency began to voice similar concerns when ASARCO's lobbying regarding federal laws and regulations successfully slowed development of a federal arsenic standard.

Health concerns also emerged in El Paso, Texas, site of a large ASARCO smelter that had polluted both sides of the U.S.-Mexico border. In 1970, following passage of the Clean Air Act, the City of El Paso sued ASARCO over its sulfur dioxide emissions. During the process of discovery, ASARCO submitted documentation of its emissions to the City for the first time. These reports showed that between 1969 and 1971, 1,012 metric tons of lead, 508 metric tons of zinc, eleven metric tons of cadmium, and one metric ton of arsenic had been released during operations.

By 1969 the city had a higher concentration of airborne lead than any other in the state. In the early 1970s a research team from the Centers for Disease Control (CDC), led by Dr. Philip Landrigan, confirmed a pattern of smelter-sourced lead threatening the children on the U.S. side.

The studies conducted by the CDC linked the high levels of lead in air, soil, and dust to the ASARCO smelter. They also linked the lead in soil and dust to elevated lead levels in children's blood. Landrigan's research team administered IQ tests and reaction time tests, and found significant differences in performance between lead-impacted children and those with lower blood levels. This pathbreaking research transformed scientific thinking about the impact of lead on children's development, and confirmed numerous dangers, even in children without obvious clinical symptoms.

At the time of research the threshold for lead in blood was 40 micrograms per deciliter. Today it is 10 micrograms per deciliter, and many health researchers and physicians want to see it set even lower. Yet some researchers had asserted that lead from smelters was not harmful to humans, and an El Paso pediatrician, in a study funded by an organization connected to the industry, claimed that levels of 40 to 80 micrograms were acceptable, as long as the children were properly nourished. As a result of the CDC studies, however, "it is now widely accepted in the scientific community that lead is toxic at extremely low levels," according to Landrigan.

Some of the affected children were treated with painful chelation therapy. Daniel Solis, a Smeltertown resident, recalls his siblings' reaction to the treatment:

They would get hysterical because of how much the treatment would hurt, they would literally go underneath their cribs and they would hold on to the bottom of the bed. I would literally have to go underneath and drag them out… It was excruciating. My mom would cry to see… the pain that her kids would be going through. But we had no other choice, you know, my siblings were that infected with lead that they had to get that treatment.

In 1991, through its subsidiary Encycle, ASARCO received highly hazardous waste, sourced from a Department of Defense site at Rocky Mountain Arsenal in Colorado. Napalm, sarin nerve gas, cluster bombs, and white phosphorous had all been produced at this site, and private pesticide companies also rented space in the facility. At Encycle, hazardous waste labels were removed and materials were shipped to ASARCO facilities in El Paso and in East Helena, Mont. Neither facility was licensed to manage hazardous waste; it is possible that the waste was shipped to other sites as well. In El Paso, workers were not informed of the risks of such incineration and were not trained to deal with these hazardous materials. This lack of protection and withholding of information violates the federal right-to-know workplace law.

The Government Accountability Office (GAO) has verified that from 1991 to 1999, the El Paso and East Helena plants received and incinerated waste meant only for licensed hazardous waste facilities. This illegal disposal potentially exposed hundreds of workers and both communities. In 1998, the federal government fined ASARCO $50 million for these violations and problems at other ASARCO sites. The settlement did not include provisions for testing workers, soil, air, water, or community members for exposure to potential contaminants. The El Paso community was not informed about these illegal activities; the extent of knowledge in East Helena is unclear. The wrist-slap against the company—and the actions that provoked it—became public only through the investigative work of citizen activists in El Paso, leading to a *New York Times* exposé in 2006.

Although many communities endure severe health effects and environmental problems, ASARCO's ties to powerful politicians gave it substantial influence on public health policy. During the George W. Bush years, James Connaughton, one of ASARCO's key attorneys, served as head of the White House Council for Environmental Quality. A key ASARCO scientist was positioned for the federal Lead Advisory Board, while other prominent, independent scientists were pushed to the margins. ASARCO has also promoted the corporate "audit privilege," allowing companies to self-monitor hazards.

Superfund: Hope and Disappointment for Polluted Communities

ASARCO was hardly the only company polluting communities throughout the industrial boom of the 20th century. As research linked contamination to birth defects, higher cancer rates, and other serious illnesses, community advocates and municipal and state leaders took collective action. In 1980, in response to the discovery of hazardous waste at Love Canal, N.Y., Congress passed the Comprehensive Environmental Response, Compensation & Liability Act (CERCLA), better known as "Superfund." The Act made companies legally and financially responsible for environmental degradation that occurred as a result of their operations. Additionally, cleanup costs for "orphan sites" where specific companies could not be identified or held responsible would draw money from the Superfund, made of a series of corporate taxes, or "polluter-pays fees," and supported by government revenue. The legislation authorized the Environmental Protection Agency (EPA) to place heavily contaminated sites on the National Priorities List. If identified as a "Superfund site," a community qualified for enforced cleanup and funds. Since the inception of Superfund, the EPA has identified over 1,200 sites, including 20 ASARCO operations. One in four Americans lives within four miles of a Superfund site.

In 1995, under the watch of President Clinton and a Republican Congress, Superfund's polluter-pays fees expired, thus shifting most of the financial burden onto taxpayers. As of 2010, these fees have yet to be reinstated. By 2003, all corporate funds were exhausted and the Superfund now relies solely on taxpayer-funded government revenues. According to the U.S. Public Interest Research Group, in 1995 taxpayers paid only 18% ($300 million) of the Superfund, but by 2005, they contributed 100%—approximately $1.2 billion.

As a result of under-financing and lack of political will, the number of Superfund sites undergoing cleanup has diminished. While the EPA averaged 87 completed cleanups a year from 1997 to 2000, in 2008 only 30 sites were processed, representing a drop of over 50% in the pace of cleanups. Without polluter-pays fees and in light of the bankruptcy, the affected communities at ASARCO sites are left with few options to ensure comprehensive cleanup and reparations.

Penny Newman of the Center for Community Action & Environmental Justice calls the fund "impotent" without corporate contributions: "It's disingenuous to pretend a program exists without the funding." In spring 2009, the Obama administration directed $600 million in stimulus money to 50 Superfund sites—including the ASARCO site in Tacoma—that have shown significant progress in their cleanups. Obama and the EPA call this a "stopgap measure," setting the restoration of the polluter-pays tax as an important environmental health goal.

The Bankruptcy "Solution"

As environmental and community health concerns mounted, public pressure increased, and projected cleanup costs skyrocketed, ASARCO closed most of its operations. All of ASARCO's sites—operating, shuttered, or in remediation—were affected by the 2005 Chapter 11 bankruptcy filing. The company cited environmental liabilities as a primary explanation for the action.

The bankruptcy was not a last-minute act of desperation. On the contrary, the company had been rearranging itself for some time, shedding liabilities and cutting costs through sales and mergers. In 1999, ASARCO was "bought" by its major subsidiary, Grupo México, a Mexican-based company that is one of the largest metal producers in the world. This sale is significant because ASARCO's assets and records were shifted outside of the United States and therefore no longer under U.S. government jurisdiction; citizens requesting records and remediation from the company now had difficulty doing so. In 2002, ASARCO sold one of its most valuable mining complexes, Southern Peru Copper, to its new parent company, transferring even more valuable resources beyond national boundaries. Fearing a potential bankruptcy, the Department of Justice forced ASARCO to set up a $100 million trust to cover liabilities for impacted U.S. communities.

Chapter 11 of the U.S. Bankruptcy Code permits corporate reorganization and invokes "automatic stay," in which most litigation is put on hold until it can be resolved in court, with creditors ceasing collection attempts. This status allowed ASARCO to legally avoid paying for environmental damage at sites that required it for the duration of the bankruptcy. Additionally, pension payments and other monies owed to workers as negotiated by the United Steelworkers, which represents most employees, were threatened and delayed. As a result of the bankruptcy, the Steelworkers, a member of the bankruptcy creditors' committee, settled with a one-year extension of their collective bargaining agreement.

Complexities stemming from ASARCO's multinational status became more apparent during the 2005-2009 bankruptcy proceedings. During the case, Grupo México, by court ruling, was removed as the controlling agent of ASARCO. As such, Grupo México battled with another corporate suitor, India-based Sterilite/Vedanta Corporation, for control; Grupo México eventually prevailed. This competition prolonged proceedings, as the judge assessed competing purchase offers and changing promises to affected communities and workers.

Through bankruptcy negotiations, ASARCO significantly reduced its debts to damaged communities. The *Tacoma News Tribune* reported that more than a dozen states and the federal government originally collectively filed $6 billion in environmental claims involving 20 ASARCO sites. Other estimates placed cleanup and liability costs as high as $25.2 billion. This figure was subsequently reduced to $3.6 billion in early bankruptcy court proceedings, which was later sliced to the final settlement of $1.79 billion.

In the days following the announcement of the settlement, government spokespeople and community members expressed a mix of relief and disappointment. According to U.S. Associate Attorney General Tom Perrelli, "The effort to recover this money was a collaborative and coordinated response by the states and federal government. Our combined efforts have resulted in the largest recovery of funds to pay for past and future cleanup of hazardous materials in the nation's history. Today is a historic day for the environment and the people affected across the country."

But activists and affected communities insist the ruling did not go far enough. In addition to paying less than originally projected, ASARCO's parent company, Grupo México, faces fewer responsibilities than it did before the bankruptcy. While the company had previously been pegged with penalty payments for the transfer of Southern Peru Copper, the bankruptcy decision, which reinstated Grupo México control, nullified this.

The $1.79 billion settlement will also be unevenly split between affected communities. While Washington State celebrated the perseverance of their attorneys and coordinated work of departments, Texas, which had relatively little sustained support and attention by federal authorities, will not be as well served. The El Paso area has a modest $52 million to address complex and hazardous contamination.

ASARCO's Legacy and Communities' Call for Responsibility

Throughout the bankruptcy proceedings, U.S. Senator Maria Cantwell (D-WA) warned that ASARCO's use of bankruptcy will be imitated by other companies aiming to minimize their liability for environmental and health damages. The *Tacoma News Tribune* has reported that companies in eight of the ten regions under EPA jurisdiction have considered bankruptcy in order to elude responsibility. A 2007 study identified six companies connected to approximately 120 Superfund sites in 28 states filing for bankruptcy, with four of these companies successfully avoiding over half a billion dollars in cleanup costs. In 2009, eleven states involved in the ASARCO bankruptcy and the Justice Department reaffirmed the warning that more companies will follow suit.

Twice Cantwell has introduced bills to curtail companies' use of bankruptcies and other "legal" techniques to avoid responsibility; twice the bills have failed.

Texas State Senator Shapleigh has witnessed the city of El Paso's struggle with the high cost of environmental cleanup and jeopardized public health. Commenting on the bankruptcy and echoing Cantwell's concerns, he warns, "This is a strategy that will be used over and over again in the United States. The corporations will play out this environmental saga…this is the first one."

A Familiar Story

The story of ASARCO is a complicated one. It is a story of environmental degradation, of countless hidden occupational health hazards, of a corporation comfortably connected to federal and state administrations, and of a broken safety net that offers little compensation for communities impacted by a century of industrial operations.

Yet the story of ASARCO is not an unfamiliar one. The company's evasion of corporate responsibility in the face of weakened federal regulations demonstrates how companies can shift billions of dollars of environmental cleanup costs onto affected communities.

The special brew of corporate bankruptcies and an under-funded Superfund leaves us extremely vulnerable to industrial contamination. ASARCO's bankruptcy left thousands of exposed workers and family members, 21 states, two Indian tribal communities, and unions in limbo for years, and now with very limited reparation for life-altering health effects and degraded environments. Despite the company's responsibility for extensive environmental and health damage, the settlement holds them accountable for only a sliver of originally projected cleanup costs. A lack of political will from Congress to ensure corporate funding for Superfund and to pass legislation that tightens legal loopholes has left communities who believed they were protected by the 1980 CERCLA legislation strapped for cash and with few legal protections to enforce corporate responsibility.

Current and former ASARCO employees, affected communities, and allies are organizing to push for corporate accountability and government regulations. In El

Paso, as a result of the bankruptcy, the Superfund dysfunction, and the special burden of illegal hazardous waste incineration, community advocates are working to shape a strategy for activating workplace right-to-know for former employees at high risk for illness. They are further insisting on transparency in the cleanup and corporate accountability for public health.

In February 2010, a group of over two dozen organizations and individuals, including current and former ASARCO employees and several Mexican government officials, wrote to the EPA with concerns that the cleanup plan for the El Paso site is "inadequate to protect the health of the [El Paso] community and does not address offsite-pollution in [New Mexico], Mexico and Texas." The current plan only addresses hazards in El Paso, but according to Mariana Chew of the Sierra Club, "Cuidad Juárez in Mexico and Sunland Park in [New Mexico] are the communities most affected by ASARCO's legal and illegal operations and yet are not taken in account." Chew and others are especially concerned about the health of children at an elementary school in Cuidad Juárez that sits just 400 feet downwind from the smelter.

The group demands larger payments from ASARCO, specifically for its illegal incineration of hazardous waste. In the interim, the group claims that federal monies from the Superfund should be used.

The 2010 National Latino Congress has also condemned ASARCO's contamination of the border region and the company's bankruptcy. The Congress, supported by hundreds of organizations and over 40 elected U.S. officials, demanded full disclosure of the illegal incineration of hazardous waste, and comprehensive testing and treatment for workers and community members who may have been exposed.

Meanwhile, in Hayden, Ariz., site of the company's only operating U.S. smelter, ASARCO officials have reassured residents that blowing dust from mine tailings is not a hazard. According to ASARCO vice president Thomas Aldrich, "Across the board these are very low in metals, about what you'd expect here, comparable to the background levels in soil."

Such statements offer little comfort for communities still struggling for information, protection, and accountability. ❑

This article is based on the project "No Borders: Communities Living and Working with Asarco" based at Evergreen State College and guided by Fischel and Nelson. The project examines the occupational and environmental health and social justice implications of ASARCO's operations with a focus on three communities: Ruston/Tacoma, Wash., Hayden, Ariz., and El Paso, Texas. A documentary film, "Borders of Resistance," to be released in the summer of 2010, documents the El Paso story of community and labor advocates pressing for accountability and health protections. Other films and writing are forthcoming.

Sources: Office of Texas Senator Eliot Shapleigh, "Asarco in El Paso," September 2008; Les Blumenthal, "Asarco Mess Reveals Superfund Failings," *Tacoma News Tribune*, March 21, 2006; Les Blumenthal, "Lawyers Dissect Asarco's cleanup obligation in the US," *Tacoma News Tribune*, May 20, 2006; Les Blumenthal, "Grupo México wins Asarco back in court ruling," *Tacoma News Tribune*, September 3, 2009; Joel Millman, "Asarco Bankruptcy Leaves Many Towns with Cleanup Mess," *Wall Street Journal*, May 24, 2006; Office of U.S. Senator Maria Cantwell,

"Cantwell Introduces Legislation to Prevent Corporate Polluters from Evading Toxic Cleanup Responsibilities," June 15, 2006; Center for Health, Environment and Justice, "Superfund: In the Eye of the Storm," March 2009; Center for Health, Environment and Justice, "America's Safety Net in Crisis: 25th Anniversary of Superfund," 2005; The Smelterworker rank-and-file union newsletter, circa 1970-75, Tacoma Wash.; Marianne Sullivan, "Contested Science and Exposed Workers: ASARCO and the Occupational Standard for Inorganic Arsenic," Public Health Chronicles, July 2007; Ralph Blumenthal, "Copper Plant Illegally Burned Hazardous Waste, EPA Says," *New York Times*, October 11, 2006; Government Accountability Office, "Environmental Liabilities: EPA Should Do More to Ensure That Liable Parties Meet Their Cleanup Obligations," August 2005; Government Accountability Office, "Hazardous Waste: Information about How DOD and Federal and State Regulators Oversee the Off-site Disposal of Waste from DOD Installations," November 2007; Department of Justice, "Largest Environmental Bankruptcy in US History Will Result in Payment of $1.79 Billion Towards Environmental Cleanup and Restoration," December 10, 2009; Seattle and King County Department of Public Health, Arsenic Facts, 2010; The Center for Health, Environment & Justice, "Letter to the Environmental Protection Agency," February 16 2010; The Center for Health, Environment & Justice, "News Release," February 16 2010; The 2010 National Latino Congress, "Draft Amended ASARCO Resolution," 2010; Interview, Dr. Philip Landrigan, Mt Sinai Medical School, August 27 2009; Interview, Daniel Solis, El Paso, Tex, August 2007.

Article 4.7

CO-OP ECONOMICS
What can economics teach us about the challenges and potential of cooperation?

BY NANCY FOLBRE
September/October 2013

I teach economics, a discipline largely inhabited by people skeptical of human potential for cooperation. But I live in a small New England town and work in a university environment that are, for the most part, cooperative. If I eat lunch on campus, I buy it from a student-managed, democratically run business that offers the tastiest, healthiest, cheapest provisions available. If I need to buy bread or milk on the way home, I pull into the Leverett Village Co-op. If my car needs attention, it goes to a worker-owned business, Pelham Auto, where I know both service managers by name. My money sits at the Five College Federal Credit Union, where it earns more interest and gains me better service than I've ever gotten at any other bank.

About four years ago, I began to weave economic theory more closely into my everyday life. The threads began coming together when Adam Trott and Michael Johnson, two members of the local Valley Alliance of Worker Cooperatives, reached out to tell me about their efforts to promote locally owned and democratically managed firms.

Although we lived in the same community, they found me as a result of a short post I wrote for the *New York Times*' "Economix" blog, describing a collaborative agreement between the United Steel Workers and the largest worker-owned business in the world, Mondragón Corporation. It seemed ironic, but also encouraging, that we first connected online, and that it might be possible to go from the global to the local and then back again.

Even in our cooperative-rich area of Western Massachusetts, Adam and Michael explained, most potential worker/owners knew virtually nothing about the principles involved (beyond liking the general idea). Why couldn't a public university provide better education and training for students potentially interested in starting up or joining a worker-owned business? Of course it could, and should. We decided to try to make that happen.

In a collaborative process that involved interested faculty and graduate students, as well as representatives from the Valley Alliance, we developed a new upper-division economics course and designed a Certificate Program for Applied Economic Research on Cooperative Enterprises centered on a summer research internship with a local cooperative.

Here, I want to share some of the ideas and opinions I've formed in the process of developing this program, which we believe could be a good model for other colleges and universities.

History Matters

Most people, including most college students, seem to think that cooperatives are a counter-cultural leftover from the 1960s, a niche phenomenon confined to hip neighborhoods and college towns. The economic history of the United States is typically portrayed as the steady march of corporate capitalism, trampling all other institutional forms. Many on the right see it as a march of progress; many on the left, as a march of doom.

Ironically, the traditional left preoccupation with corporate capitalism may simply feed the beast—overstating its hegemonic role, as though it can't be contained until the revolution comes. J.K. Gibson-Graham makes this point persuasively in *The End of Capitalism (As We Knew It)*: What we call "capitalism" involves many different creatures. Families, communities, non-profit organizations, and the state actually account for a larger share of economic activity—broadly defined—than capitalist firms.

Though standard economics texts hardly mention them, consumer cooperatives and worker-owned businesses have shaped our history. Their influence, however, has been uneven, greater in some industries and regions than others.

Marxist scholars have often associated cooperatives with the so-called "utopian socialists"—whom they have traditionally considered well-meaning but misguided. Efforts to establish alternative businesses have often been labeled a form of co-optation less politically virtuous than trade-union organizing or socialist political parties. Yet cooperative efforts have typically been closely linked to and complementary with larger anti-corporate organizing efforts. In a fascinating article entitled "Toward an Organizationally Diverse American Capitalism? Cooperative, Mutual, and Local, State-Owned Enterprise," sociologist Mark Schnaiberg traces the history of cooperative marketing efforts in the grain and dairy industries, originally dominated by large monopsonies that used their market power to pay farmers as little as possible. (A monopsony is a single buyer that dominates a market, just as a monopoly is a single seller.) When farmers successfully started up cooperatives, other members of the community also became more likely to organize on their own behalf.

Even when cooperative enterprises represent only a small proportion of market transactions in a local community, they often exercise a disproportionate influence, disciplining capitalist enterprises or pioneering innovations that are later adopted by them. Local food cooperatives were the first to begin marketing organic and local produce, and large supermarket chains gradually followed suit. Local credit unions have made it harder for large banking institutions to charge excessive fees. Worker-owned businesses have pulled the small-business community in a more progressive direction, serving as a counterweight to large, footloose firms.

By demonstrating the viability of businesses aimed to serve larger social goals, cooperatives have altered our economic ecology.

Culture Matters

As an economist, I was trained to emphasize the difference between for-profit and non-profit firms. But that difference may be less significant than the moral and cultural values central to the definition of cooperative enterprises.

Consumer cooperatives seek to provide high-quality products at minimal cost. Worker-owned businesses need to generate profits both to pay themselves and to finance investment. Both, however, are committed to seven "cooperative principles" (see box, p. 211) that include democracy and concern for community.

In this respect, cooperative enterprises can be seen as a subset of efforts to develop a solidarity economy, which also includes non-profit businesses and community organizations. They are also closely aligned with "buy local" efforts that urge consumers to shop in locally owned stores and build a local supply chain (for instance, by patronizing restaurants utilizing locally grown products).

Not that it's always clear how "concern for community" should be defined. Almost by their very nature as small, decentralized businesses, co-ops prioritize those with whom they are most likely to come into contact. But local solidarity is not automatically consistent with broader forms of solidarity. In fact, it risks a kind of parochialism that could lead to happy little enclaves embedded in a larger economy built on hierarchy and exploitation.

On the other hand, co-op culture can promote values that may lead people toward other forms of positive engagement, with the goal of steadily expanding the cooperative reach and linking many kinds of progressive efforts together. Co-op ventures also offer people the opportunity to build something new, rather than merely trying to tear down something old.

The Seven Cooperative Principles

Cooperatives around the world generally operate according to the same core principles and values, adopted by the International Co-operative Alliance (www.ica.coop) in 1995. Cooperatives trace the roots of these principles to the first modern cooperative, founded in Rochdale, England, in 1844.

1. **Voluntary and Open Membership**: Cooperatives are voluntary organizations, open to all people able to use its services and willing to accept the responsibilities of membership, without gender, social, racial, political or religious discrimination.
2. **Democratic Member Control**: Cooperatives are democratic organizations controlled by their members—those who buy the goods or use the services of the cooperative—who actively participate in setting policies and making decisions.
3. **Members' Economic Participation**: Members contribute equally to, and democratically control, the capital of the cooperative. This benefits members in proportion to the business they conduct with the cooperative rather than on the capital invested.
4. **Autonomy and Independence**: Cooperatives are autonomous, self-help organizations controlled by their members. If the co-op enters into agreements with other organizations or raises capital from external sources, it is done so based on terms that ensure democratic control by the members and maintains the cooperative's autonomy.
5. **Education, Training and Information**: Cooperatives provide education and training for members, elected representatives, managers and employees so they can contribute effectively to the development of their cooperative. Members also inform the general public about the nature and benefits of cooperatives.
6. **Cooperation among Cooperatives**: Cooperatives serve their members most effectively and strengthen the cooperative movement by working together through local, national, regional and international structures.
7. **Concern for Community**: While focusing on member needs, cooperatives work for the sustainable development of communities through policies and programs accepted by the members.

From the National Cooperative Business Association, International Year of Cooperatives (usa2012.coop).

The commitment to democratic decision-making distinguishes worker-owned businesses from other institutional forms that aim to enlarge economic goals (such as the new "social benefit" corporate charters) or to help incentivize workers (such as profit-sharing or employee-stock-ownership plans). This commitment reflects a cultural value—as well as a political principle. Other shared values encouraging respect and concern for others may help lubricate the democratic process by making collective decision-making less contentious.

Democratic values and skills may grow stronger in communities where they are consistently exercised, explaining why some regions of the world seem to foster more cooperative enterprises than others. The famous Mondragón cooperatives grew up in the Basque area of northern Spain, among people who felt embattled and impoverished by their minority status and strengthened by their progressive Catholic traditions. Many small cooperatives have prospered in northern Italy, an area with a long history of labor radicalism and a strong Communist Party. In Canada, the province of Quebec has successfully encouraged the cooperative provision of social services under the banner of the "social economy."

In the United States, cooperatives have often helped improve living standards in African-American communities, from a cooperative shipyard in 1860s Baltimore, to a co-op buying club in Depression-era Gary, Ind., to the Common Ground Collective in post-Katrina New Orleans. As Jessica Gordon-Nembhard and Ajowa Nzinga point out (see *Dollars & Sense*, July/August 2006), a common history of economic exclusion and hardship can foster cooperation.

Public policies have also played a role in developing these epicenters of cooperative development. But culture is surely one of the factors shaping the political alignments that generate such policies.

Efficiency Matters

Economists often overstate the value of efficiency, or define it in excessively narrow terms. But that doesn't mean it's not important. Efficiency is an important arbiter of success in competition and, in the world we live in, co-operators need to compete. Since competition between firms is, to some extent a "team sport," successful cooperation among team members can prove advantageous.

Democratically managed firms may be more efficient than others, even from the relatively narrow perspective of costs and benefits. The British economist John Stuart Mill made this argument in the mid-19th century, pointing out that workers who were also owners would be likely to work harder and smarter than those merely paid an hourly wage.

This issue never received much attention from early-twentieth-century Marxists convinced of the virtues of central planning. However, it came to the fore with Yugoslavian experiments in worker self-management in the mid-20th century and has since had a big impact on progressive economic thinking—in part because it helps frame a critique of both the traditional family firm and the modern corporation.

A long-standing favorite of neoclassical economists is an argument, developed by economists Armen Alchian and Harold Demsetz, that workers will have a tendency to shirk on the job unless they are overseen by an owner who can capture any profits (or "residual") left over after the workers are paid. This gives the "residual claimant" an incentive to crack the whip and make them work as hard as possible. Ownership in most modern corporations is highly fragmented, but owners presumably hire managers—from the chief executive officer or CEO down to supervisors and foremen—to fulfill this disciplinary role.

Radical economist Samuel Bowles effectively rebuts this argument, pointing out that it is difficult and costly to monitor effort. Workers seeking to resist capitalist exploitation may be especially likely to shirk unless managers can find a way to either secure their loyalty or threaten them with costly job loss.

Unfortunately, worker ownership alone doesn't necessarily solve this incentive problem. Workers either have to be really good at monitoring one another's efforts (so that no one can free ride without being sanctioned), or they have to feel such strong solidarity toward one another that no one even tries to free ride. (The latter is preferable, since it's often hard for a collective to fire someone who is slacking off.)

Other tensions among owner-workers can arise. For instance, young owner-workers have a stronger incentive to reinvest firm profits to increase their future earnings than older owner-workers, who would prefer to retain more earnings and/or fund their pensions. The success of a worker-owned enterprise depends on the ability of worker-owners to anticipate and creatively respond to such conflicts of interest. But the process of doing so—negotiating and resolving differences of opinion—can itself be quite costly, in two ways.

First, democratic decision-making can be quite time-consuming, especially if based on rules of consensus. Worker-owned firms generally treat time in meetings as part of their paid work, and the time they devote to it can cut down on directly productive activities.

Second, democratic decision-making can prove emotionally costly, as when good friends disagree about important matters and find it difficult to accommodate one another. On the other hand, conflict avoidance—such as a desire not to discipline a fellow worker who is also a friend—can also lower efficiency. This problem can be described as a "second order" free-rider problem—that is, a reluctance to openly point to or discourage free riding.

Representative democracy and delegation to a manager can help minimize these problems, but also at some cost. Majority rule can alienate the minority, and unstable factions can lead to lack of continuity in decision-making.

Worker-owned firms will be more likely to prosper if they cultivate an awareness of decision-making problems and develop the institutional structures and skills necessary to over-come them.

Here comes the Catch-22. Neither our educational system nor most employers do much to help people develop democratic management skills, so there's a big start-up problem. If we could just create more opportunities for people to develop and practice such skills, worker-owned businesses could enjoy more success.

Efficiency gains can also come at the macro level. Worker-owned businesses that get off the ground tend to be more stable than other small businesses, in part because workers have an incentive to hang in over the long haul, even if revenue slumps. This can buffer the effects of recession on the economy as a whole.

Most importantly, worker-owned businesses depend more on positive incentives than on the threat of job loss. Unlike employer-owned businesses, they don't rely on the labor discipline imposed by a high unemployment rate. And consistently high unemployment rates are among the most inefficient features of our current economic system.

Collaboration Matters

For all the reasons given above, the cooperative movement may need to reach a certain critical mass before it can really take off. More collaboration among cooperatives—and between cooperatives and other institutions such as public universities—could make a big difference.

Relatively few worker-owned businesses are started up in a given year, leading some to speculate that they are inherently less expansionary than capitalist firms (for the simple reason that worker-owners care about more than the rate of return on their capital investment). They also care about the quality of their work life and their place in the community. Some of the decision-making problems described above, moreover, may be more easily solved in small firms where everyone knows everyone else. Expansion can lead to complications.

However, collaboration and expansion could help worker-owned businesses in several ways. First, it could help them gain access to more and better financing. By definition, worker-owned firms can't sell equity shares in their business (because all owners must be workers). They can develop other forms of self-financing, including bonds that can be especially attractive to socially responsible investors. But they can also develop ways of pooling resources and helping to finance one another. Each firm belonging to the Valley Alliance of Worker Coops sets aside a percentage of its profits to promote local cooperative development. One can even imagine a kind of franchise model in which one firm could spin off smaller firms, which could become financially independent, but remain closely allied.

Second, vertical networking along the supply chain could increase efficiency and the ability to compete with large conglomerate capitalist enterprises. International networking among cooperatives holds particular promise, because it advances a larger fair-trade agenda, and also helps escape parochialism. Many examples of this kind of networking exist, such as the People's Market at UMass-Amherst buying only cooperatively produced coffee and actively seeking other cooperatively produced goods and services.

Third, more networking could help develop the distinctive managerial and decision-making skills described above. Indeed, the more worker-owners gain experience in different types of firms, the richer the skills they bring to the task of democratic management. And the more visible worker-owners become, the more young people are likely to become attracted to new prospects for more socially meaningful and economically rewarding work.

Finally, the more worker-owned businesses and other cooperative enterprises expand, the easier it becomes to build political coalitions and implement policies that promote their efforts. These synergies help explain how regional economies in the Basque area of Spain, northern Italy, and the Canadian province of Quebec have evolved.

A worker-owned business is what economists call a "microeconomic structure." But its ultimate success may depend on its ability to change the macroeconomic structure, which can, in turn, improve its microeconomic efficiency. Even a small cooperative firm can help a community enhance its standard of living and quality of life. More importantly, however, it can provide a catalyst for social and political changes that not only bring more and more worker-owned businesses into being, but also enable them to compete more effectively with capital-owned firms.

That's why worker-owned businesses fit the description of what the 20th-century Italian theorist and revolutionary Antonio Gramsci called a "non-reformist reform" and what sociologist Erik Olin Wright terms a "real utopia." Take another look at those seven cooperative principles. They offer a pretty good guide to running not just a business, but a whole society. ❏

Sources: J.K. Gibson-Graham, *The End of Capitalism (As We Knew It)* (University of Minnesota Press, 2006); Mark Schnaiberg, "Toward an Organizationally Diverse American Capitalism? Cooperative, Mutual, and Local, State-Owned Enterprise," *Seattle University Law Review*, Vol. 34, No. 4 (2011); Jessica Gordon-Nembhard and Ajowa Nzinga, "African-American Economic Solidarity," *Dollars & Sense*, July/August 2006; Erik Olin Wright, *Envisioning Real Utopias* (Verso, 2010).

Chapter 5

MARKET STRUCTURE AND MONOPOLY

INTRODUCTION

With monopoly, we finally encounter a situation in which most economists, orthodox and otherwise, agree that unfettered markets lead to an undesirable outcome. If a firm is able to create a monopoly, it faces a downward-sloping demand curve—that is to say, if it reduces output, it can charge a higher price. Economists argue that competitive forces tend to undermine any monopoly, but failing this, they support antitrust policy as a backstop. The concept of monopoly not only points to an important failing of markets, but it opens the door to thinking about many possible market structures other than perfect competition, including oligopoly, in which a small group of producers dominates the market. Monopoly and oligopoly are examples of market structures in which firms wield "market power" (violating Tilly Assumption #1—see Article 1.2). That is, individual firms can affect the market-wide level of prices, profits, and wages. Market power alters how markets function from the ideal of perfect competition and delivers significantly less optimal results.

We begin this chapter with another seminal article by Chris Tilly, "Is Small Beautiful? Is Bigger Better? Small and Big Businesses Both Have Their Drawbacks" (Article 5.1). This article walks through the pluses and minuses of large and small businesses, and finds both wanting.

The current financial crisis has provided particularly egregious examples of what happens when we institute *laissez-faire* (hands-off) regulatory regimens, especially in the area of finance. In "A Brief History of Mergers and Antitrust Policy" (Article 5.2), Edward Herman provides a long-term context for the discussion, reviewing the history of U.S. antitrust law over the last century. He also criticizes economists for justifying a hands-off policy toward big business mergers over the last few decades.

Next, Arthur MacEwan discusses the relevance of the concept of "monopoly capital" in an age of globalized competition (Article 5.3). MacEwan finds that firm size and market concentration have continued to grow throughout the era of globalization and that large firms still exhibit extraordinary market power.

In "Want Free Trade? Open the Medical and Drug Industry to Competition" (Article 5.4), Dean Baker describes how companies in this sector are protected from market competition. Doctors are protected form international competition, even as "free trade" agreements have put blue-collar workers squarely in competition with workers all over the world. Meanwhile, pharmaceutical companies enjoy monopoly protections lasting decades, thanks to patents, without a significant counterweight from government price regulation.

The last three articles look at the exercise of market power today. Rob Larson's "Not Too Big Enough" (Article 5.5) explores the phenomenon of the "too big to fail" banks as an expression of market power. Dean Baker's "Big Bank Immunity" (Article 5.6) examines what is now being called "too big to jail," where policymakers decline to prosecute cases of criminal misconduct by big banks, claiming that doing so could imperil the economy as a whole. Finally, Baker's "The False Libertarianism of the Silicon Valley Billionaires" (Article 5.7) shows how large tech firms acted to exercise market power in the labor market—colluding to hold down tech workers' wages.

Discussion Questions

1. (Article 5.1) List the pros and cons of large and small businesses that Tilly discusses. How does this compare with the problems associated with market structure that your textbook mentions? Be sure to compare Tilly's list of small-business flaws with what your textbook has to say about small business.

2. (Articles 5.1 and 5.2) In what ways do these articles show that corporations control "the marketplace of ideas"? What are the possible consequences? What, if anything, should be done about it?

3. (Article 5.3) Mainstream economists view competition among many small firms as a prerequisite for "efficient" market outcomes. Some touted globalization as a way to increase competition and benefit consumers. What problems, if any, result from the large size and market dominance of a few global firms? Should this change our view of globalization in any way? If so, how?

4. (Article 5.4) Baker argues that trade agreements have protected U.S. doctors and pharmaceutical companies from international competition. Why do you think this has been the case, when other kinds of workers and industries have borne the full brunt of global competition during the era of "globalization"? Would policies to reduce the prices charged by the medical sector be desirable? What policies?

5. (Articles 5.5 and 5.6) What is "moral hazard?" How does this concept relate to "too big to fail?" If the public cannot allow some firms to fail, is there anything that can replace the "discipline of the market" in restraining those companies' behavior? Is effective regulation possible if government officials are hesitant even to enforce existing law?

6. (Article 5.7) Silicon Valley firms have agued that competition restriains any company's ability to manipulate market coutcomes. How does their behavior show that they do not really believe that? Does this revelation help create a case for government regulation?

Article 5.1

IS SMALL BEAUTIFUL? IS BIG BETTER?

Small and big businesses both have their drawbacks.

BY CHRIS TILLY

July/August 1989, revised April 2002

Beginning in the late 1980s, the United States has experienced a small, but significant boom in small business. While big businesses have downsized, small enterprises have proliferated. Should we be glad? Absolutely, declare the advocates of small business. Competition makes small businesses entrepreneurial, innovative, and responsive to customers.

Not so fast, reply big business's boosters. Big corporations grew big because they were efficient, and tend to stay efficient because they are big—and thus able to invest in research and upgrading of technology and workforce skills.

But each side in this debate omits crucial drawbacks. Small may be beautiful for consumers, but it's often oppressive for workers. And while big businesses wield the power to advance technology, they also often wield the market power to bash competitors and soak consumers. In the end, the choices are quite limited.

Big and Small

Is the United States a nation of big businesses, or of small ones? There are two conventional ways to measure business size. One is simply to count the number of employees per firm. By this measure, small businesses (say, business establishments with less than 20 employees) make up the vast majority of businesses (Table 1). But they provide only a small fraction of the total number of jobs.

The other approach gauges market share—each firm's share of total sales in a given industry. Industries range between two extremes: what economists call "perfect competition" (many firms selling a standardized product, each too tiny to affect the market price) and monopoly (one business controls all sales in an industry). Economy-wide, as with employment, small businesses are most numerous, but control only a small slice of total sales. Sole proprietorships account for 73% of established businesses, far outnumbering corporations, which are 20% of the total (the remainder are partnerships). But corporations ring up a hefty 90% of all sales, leaving sole proprietors with only 6%. It takes a lot of mom and pop stores to equal General Motors' 1999 total of $177 billion in sales.

Industry by industry, the degree of competition varies widely. Economists consider an industry concentrated when its top four companies account for more than 40% of total sales in the industry (Table 2). At the high end of the spectrum are the cigarette, beer, and aircraft industries, where four firms account for the bulk of U.S. production.

No market comes close to meeting the textbook specifications for perfect competition, but one can still find industries in which a large number of producers compete for sales. The clothing and restaurant industries, for example, remain relatively competitive. Overall, about one-third of U.S. goods are manufactured in concentrated industries, about one fifth are made in competitive industries, and the rest fall somewhere in between.

Beating the Competition

Those who tout the benefits of small, competitive business make a broad range of claims on its behalf. In addition to keeping prices low, they say the quality of the product is constantly improving, as companies seek a competitive edge. The same desire, they claim, drives firms toward technological innovations, leading to productivity increases.

The real story is not so simple. Competition does indeed keep prices low. Believe it or not, clothing costs us less—in real terms—than it cost our parents. Between 1960 and 1999, while the overall price level and hourly wages both increased nearly sixfold, apparel prices didn't even triple. And small businesses excel at offering variety, whether it is the ethnic restaurants that dot cities or the custom machine-tool work offered by small shops. Furthermore, however powerful small business lobbies may be in Washington, they do not influence the legislative process as blatantly as do corporate giants.

But those low prices often have an ugly underside. Our sportswear is cheap in part because the garment industry increasingly subcontracts work to sweatshops— whether they be export assembly plants in Haiti paying dollar-a-day wages, or the "underground" Los Angeles stitcheries that employ immigrant women in virtual slavery. Struggling to maintain razor-thin profit margins, small businesses cut costs any way they can— which usually translates into low wages and onerous working conditions.

"There is a rule of survival for small business," Bill Ryan, president of Ryan Transfer Corporation, commented some years ago. "There are certain things you want to have [in paying workers] and certain things you can afford. You had better go with what you can afford." Bottom line, workers in companies employing 500 or more people enjoy average wages 30% higher than their counterparts in small businesses.

Part of this wage gap results from differences other than size—unionization, the education of the workforce, the particular jobs and industries involved. But University of Michigan economist Charles Brown and his colleagues

TABLE 1:
SMALL BUSINESS NATION?

Most businesses are small, but most employees work for big businesses

Company size (number of employees)	Percent of all firms	Percent of all workers
1–4	54%	6%
5–9	20%	8%
10–19	13%	11%
20–49	8%	16%
50–99	3%	13%
100–249	2%	16%
250–499	0.4%	10%
500–999	0.2%	7%
1,000 or more	0.1%	13%

Note: "Businesses" refers to establishments, meaning business locations.

Source: County Business Patterns, 1998.

controlled for all these differences and more, and still found a 10% premium for big business's employees. A note of caution, however: Other recent research indicates that this wage bonus is linked to long-term employment and job ladders. To the extent that corporations dissolve these long-term ties—as they seem to be rapidly doing—the pay advantage may dissolve as well.

Small business gurus make extravagant claims about small businesses' job-generation capacity. An oft-quoted 1987 report by consultant David Birch claimed that businesses with fewer than 20 employees create 88% of new jobs. The reality is more mundane: over the long run, businesses with 19 or fewer workers account for about one quarter of net new jobs. One reason why Birch's statistics are misleading is that new small businesses are created in great numbers, but they also fail at a high rate. The result is that the *net* gain in jobs is much smaller than the number created in business start-ups.

For companies in very competitive markets, the same "whip of competition" that keeps prices down undermines many of competition's other supposed benefits. The flurry of competition in the airline industry following deregulation, for example, hardly resulted in a higher quality product. Flying became temporarily cheaper, but also less comfortable, reliable, and safe.

Technological innovation from competition is also more myth than reality. Small firms in competitive industries do very little research and development. They lack both the cash needed to make long-term investments and the market power to guarantee a return on that investment. In fact, many of them can't even count on surviving to reap the rewards: only one-third to one-half of small business startups survive for five years, and only about one in five makes it to ten years. A 1988 Census Bureau survey concluded that in manufacturing, "technology use is positively correlated with plant size." Agriculture may be the exception that proves the rule. That highly competitive industry has made marked productivity gains, but its research is supported by the taxpayer, and its risks are reduced by government price supports.

Of course, the biggest myth about competition is that it is in any way a "natural state" for capitalism. In fact, in most markets the very process of competing for high profits or a bigger market share tends to create a concentrated, rather than a competitive, market structure.

TABLE 2: WHO COMPETES, WHO DOESN'T	
Industry	*Percent of sales by top four firms*
Light truck and utility vehicle manufacturing	96%
Breweries	91%
Home center stores	91%
Breakfast cereal manufacturing	78%
General book stores	77%
Credit card issuing	77%
Lawn equipment manufacturing	62%
Cable providers	63%
Computer and software stores	51%
Sock manufacturing	30%
Hotels and motels (excl. casinos)	22%
Gas stations	9%
Real estate	4%
Bars	2%

Source: 2002 Economic Census.

This process occurs in several ways. Big firms sometimes drive their smaller competitors out of business by selectively cutting prices to the bone. The smaller firms may lack the financial resources to last out the low prices. In the 1960s, several of IBM's smaller competitors sued it for cutting prices in a pattern that was designed to drive the smaller firms out of the market. Large corporations can also gain a lock on scarce resources: for example, large airlines like United and American operate the comprehensive, computerized information and reservation systems that travel agents tap into—and you can bet that each airline's system lists their own flights first. Or businesses may exploit an advantage in one market to dominate another, as Microsoft used its control of the computer operating system market to seize market share for its Internet browser.

Other firms eliminate competitors by buying them out—either in a hostile takeover or a friendly merger. Either way, a former competitor is neutralized. This strategy used to be severely limited by strict antitrust guidelines that prohibited most horizontal mergers—those between two firms that formerly competed in the same market. The Reagan administration's team at the Justice Department, however, loosened the merger guidelines significantly in the early 1980s. Since that time, many large mergers between former competitors have been allowed to go through, most notably in the airline industry.

The Power of Concentration

Concentration, then, is as natural to market economies as competition. And bigness, like smallness, is a mixed bag for us as consumers and workers. For workers, bigness is on the whole a plus. Whereas competition forces small businesses to be stingy, big firms are on average more generous, offering employees higher wages, greater job security, and more extensive fringe benefits. In 1993, 97% of businesses with 500 or more workers provided health insurance; only 43% of businesses with 25 or fewer employees did so. Large firms also provide much more employee training. The strongest unions, as well, have historically been in industries where a few firms control large shares of their markets, and can pass along increased costs to consumers—auto, steel, and tires, for example. When profits are threatened, though, firms in concentrated markets also have more resources with which to fight labor. They are better able to weather a strike, oppose unionization, and make agreements with rivals not to take advantage of each other's labor troubles. In addition, large companies, not surprisingly, score low on workplace autonomy.

What about consumers? Corporations in industries where there are few competitors may compete, but the competitive clash is seldom channeled into prolonged price wars. The soft drink industry is a classic example. David McFarland, a University of North Carolina economist, likens soft drink competition to professional wrestling. "They make a lot of sounds and groans and bounce on the mat, but they know who is going to win," he remarked.

Coke and Pepsi introduce new drinks and mount massive ad campaigns to win market share, but the net result is not lower prices. In fact, because competition between industry giants relies more on product differentiation than price, companies pass on their inflated advertising expenses to consumers. In the highly concentrated breakfast cereal market, the package frequently costs more than the contents. And of every dollar you pay for a box, nearly 20 cents goes for advertising.

It takes resources to develop and market a new idea, which gives large corporations distinct advantages in innovation. The original idea for the photocopier may have come from a patent lawyer who worked nights in his basement, but Xerox spent $16 million before it had a product it could sell. RCA invested $65 million developing the color television. RCA could take this gamble because its dominance in the television market ensured that it would not be immediately undercut by some other firm.

But market dominance can also translate into complacency. The steel industry illustrates the point. A few major producers earned steady profits through the 1950s and 1960s but were caught off-guard when new technologies vaulted foreign steel-makers to the top of the industry in the 1970s. Similarly, when IBM dominated the computer industry in the 1960s and early 1970s, innovation proceeded quite slowly, particularly compared to the frantic scramble in that industry today. With no competitors to worry about, it was more profitable for IBM to sit tight, since innovation would only have made its own machines obsolete.

And large corporations can also put their deep pockets and technical expertise to work to short-circuit public policy. In the 1980s, when Congress changed corporate liability laws to make corporate executives criminally liable for some kinds of offenses, General Electric's lobbyists and legal staff volunteered to help draft the final regulations, in order to minimize the damage.

Big businesses sometimes hide their lobbying behind a "citizen" smokescreen. The largest-spending lobby in Washington in 1986 was Citizens for the Control of Acid Rain. These good citizens had been organized by coal and electric utility companies to oppose tighter pollution controls. Along the same lines, the Coalition for Vehicle Choice (now, who could be against that?) was set up by Ford and General Motors in 1990 to fight higher fuel efficiency standards.

Concentration or Conglomeration

Over the last couple of decades, the mix of big and small businesses has changed, but the changes are small and—at first glance—contradictory. Over time, employment has shifted toward smaller firms, though the shift has been subtle, not revolutionary. Meanwhile, the overall level of industry-by-industry sales concentration in the economy has increased, but only slightly. As older industries become more concentrated, newer, more competitive ones crop up, leaving overall concentration relatively steady. In his book *Lean and Mean*, economist Bennett Harrison points out that there is actually no contradiction between the small business employment boomlet and big firms' continued grip on markets. Big businesses, it turns out, are orchestrating much of the flowering of small business, through a variety of outsourcing and subcontracting arrangements.

But if industry-by-industry concentration has changed little over the decades, conglomeration is a different matter. Corporate ownership of assets has become much more concentrated over time, reflecting the rise in conglomerates—corporations doing business in a variety of industries. Five decades ago, the top 200 manufacturing firms accounted for 48% of all sales in the U.S. economy. By 1993, the 200 biggest industrial businesses controlled 65% of sales.

Most mainstream economists see these groupings as irrelevant for the competitive structure of the economy. Antitrust laws place no restrictions on firms from different industries banding together under one corporate roof. But sheer size can easily affect competition in the markets of the individual firms involved. A parent company can use one especially profitable subsidiary to subsidize start-up costs for a new venture, giving it a competitive edge. And if one board of directors controls major interests in related industries, it can obviously influence any of those markets more forcefully.

A case in point is the mega-merger of Time Inc. and Warner, which will soon be joining with America Online. The resulting conglomerate will control massive sections of the home entertainment business, bringing together Time's journalists, film and television producers, and authors, Warner's entertainment machine, which includes Home Box Office, the nation's largest pay television channel, and AOL's huge share of the Internet access market. The conglomerate can influence the entertainment business from the initial point—the actors, writers, and directors—up to the point where the finished products appear on people's televisions or computers. Conglomeration also multiplies the political clout of large corportions. No wonder Disney and other entertainment giants have also hopped on the conglomeration bandwagon.

Choose your Poison

Competition, concentration, or conglomeration: The choice is an unsavory one indeed. Opting for lots of tiny, competing firms leaves labor squeezed and sacrifices the potential technological advantages that come with concentrated resources. Yet the big monopolies tend to dominate their markets, charge high prices, and waste countless resources on glitzy ad campaigns and trivial product differentiation. And the big conglomerate firms, while not necessarily dominant in any single market, wield a frightening amount of political and economic power, with budgets larger than those of most countries.

Of course, we don't have much to say about the choice, no matter how much "shopping for a better world" we engage in. Market competition rolls on—sometimes cutthroat, other times genteel. Industries often start out as monopolies (based on new inventions), go through a competitive phase, but end up concentrating as they mature. As long as bigness remains profitable and the government maintains a hands-off attitude, companies in both competitive and concentrated industries will tend to merge with firms in other industries. This will feed a continuing trend toward conglomeration. Since bigness and smallness both have their drawbacks, the best we can do is to use public policies to minimize the disadvantages of each. ❏

Resources: *Lean and Mean: The Changing Landscape of Corporate Power in the Age of Flexibility,* Bennett Harrison, 1994; *Employers Large and Small,* Charles Brown, James Hamilton, and James Medoff, 1990.

Article 5.2

A BRIEF HISTORY OF MERGERS AND ANTITRUST POLICY

BY EDWARD HERMAN
May/June 1998

Government efforts to prevent or break up monopolies are called antitrust policy. They assume that when a few companies dominate an industry, this weakens competition and hurts the public by reducing production, raising prices, and slowing technical advance. Antitrust has gone through cycles during this century. In some years, strongly pro-business presidencies (usually Republican) have allowed businesses to merge at will. These have often been followed by "reform" administrations, which tend to restrain, but not to reverse, concentrations of corporate power.

The federal government first took on a strong antitrust role with the Sherman Act of 1890, which outlawed monopoly and efforts to obtain it. In 1914 the Clayton Act also put restrictions on stock purchases and interlocking directorates that would reduce competition. This legislation responded to public anger and fears about "trusts," which brought separate firms under common control. Most notorious were Rockefeller's Standard Oil Trust and James Duke's American Tobacco Company, which employed ruthless tactics to drive their competitors out of business.

Early on the antitrust laws also treated organized labor as a "monopoly," and were used in breaking the Pullman strike in 1892. In 1908, the Supreme Court awarded damages to an employer against whom unions had organized a secondary boycott. This led to the Clayton Act exempting unions from its restrictions.

Otherwise, the federal government only minimally enforced the Sherman Act until Theodore Roosevelt was elected in 1900. Then in 1911 the Supreme Court decided that both the Standard Oil and American Tobacco trusts were "bad trusts," and ordered their dismantling. But in 1920 the Court refused to condemn the U.S. Steel consolidation, because it was a "good trust" that didn't attack its smaller rivals. This began a long period when the Antitrust Division and the courts approved mergers that produced industries with a few dominant firms, but which were "well-behaved." And in the 1920s, Republicans virtually ended antitrust enforcement.

The Golden Age

Franklin Roosevelt revived antitrust during 1938 to 1941, and antitrust law had its golden age from 1945 to 1974, fueled by a liberal Supreme Court, anti-merger legislation passed in 1950, and mildly progressive enforcement (though less so in the Republican years). During this period Alcoa's monopoly over aluminum production was broken (1945), and the Court found the tobacco industry guilty of "group monopoly" (1946), although the companies were only assessed a modest fine.

During the 1960s, when antitrust law blocked mergers among companies in the same industry, businesses adapted by acquiring firms in unrelated industries. Many such "conglomerate" mergers took place during 1964-68, when Lyndon Johnson was president. Companies like International Telephone and Telegraph, Ling-Temco-Vought, Gulf & Western, Tenneco, and Litton Industries grew rapidly.

The Reagan-Bush Collapse

Antitrust policy went into recession around 1974, then plunged during the presidencies of Ronald Reagan and George H. W. Bush. They aggressively dismantled antitrust, imposing drastic cuts in budgets and manpower, installing officials hostile to the antitrust mission, and failing to enforce the laws. During 1981-89, the Antitrust Division of the Justice Dept. challenged only 16 of over 16,000 pre-merger notices filed with them.

Despite his high-profile contest with Microsoft, Bill Clinton largely accepted the conservative view that most mergers are harmless. During his two terms, federal authorities approved or ignored many giant mergers. These included Westinghouse's buyout of CBS, the joining of "Baby Bells" Bell Atlantic and Nynex, and the combination of Chemical Bank and Manufacturers Hanover. During 1997 alone, 156 mergers of $1 billion or more, and merger transactions totalling more than *$1 trillion*, passed antitrust muster.

Clinton's failure to attack giant mergers rests nominally on the alleged efficiency of large firms and the belief that globalized markets make for competition. FTC head Robert Pitofsky said, "this is an astonishing merger wave," but not to worry because these deals "should be judged on a global market scale, not just on national and local markets."

But the efficiency of large size—as opposed to the profit-making advantages that corporations gain from market power and cross-selling (pushing products through other divisions of the same company)—is eminently debatable. And many markets are not global—hospitals, for example, operate in local markets, yet only some 20 of 3,000 hospital mergers have been subjected to antitrust challenge. Even in global markets a few firms are often dominant, and a vast array of linkages such as joint ventures and licensing agreements increasingly mute global competition.

The Clinton administration's failure to contest many giant mergers did not rest only on intellectual arguments. It also reflected political weakness and an unwillingness to oppose powerful people who fund elections and own or dominate the media. This was conspicuously true of the great media combinations—Disney and Cap-Cities/ABC, and TimeWarner and Turner—and the merger of Boeing and McDonnell-Douglas, which involved institutions of enormous power, whose mergers the stock market greeted enthusiastically.

The Economists Sell Out

Since the early 1970s, powerful people and corporations have funded not only elections but conservative economists, who are frequently housed in think-tanks such as the American Enterprise, Hoover, and Cato Institutes, and serve as corporate consultants in regulatory and anti-trust cases. Most notable in hiring economic consultants have been AT&T and IBM, which together spent hundreds of millions of dollars on their antitrust defenses. AT&T hired some 30 economists from five leading economics departments during the 1970s and early 1980s.

Out of these investments came models and theories downgrading the "populist" idea that numerous sellers and decentralization were important for effective competition (and essential to a democratic society). They claimed instead that the market can do it all, and that regulation and antitrust actions are misconceived. First, theorists showed that efficiency gains from mergers might reduce prices even more than monopoly power would cause them to rise. Economists also stressed "entry," claiming that if mergers did not improve efficiency any price increases would be wiped out eventually by new companies entering the industry. Entry is also the heart of the theory of "contestable markets," developed by economic consultants to AT&T, who argued that the ease of entry in cases where resources (trucks, aircraft) can be shifted quickly at low cost, makes for effective competition.

Then there is the theory of a "market for corporate control," in which mergers allow better managers to displace the less efficient. In this view, poorly-managed firms have low stock prices, making them easy to buy. Finally, many economists justified conglomerate mergers on three grounds: that they function as "mini capital markets," with top managers allocating capital between divisions of a single firm so as to maximize efficiency; that they reduce transaction costs; and that they are a means of diversifying risk.

These theories, many coming out of the "Chicago School" (the economics department at the University of Chicago), suffer from over-simplification, a strong infusion of ideology, and lack of empirical support. Mergers often are motivated by factors other than enhancing efficiency—such as the desire for monopoly power, empire building, cutting taxes, improving stock values, and even as a cover for poor management (such as when the badly-run U.S. Steel bought control of Marathon Oil).

Several researchers have questioned the supposed benefits of mergers. In theory, a merger that improves efficiency should increase profits. But one study by Dennis Mueller, and another by F. W. Scherer and David Ravenscraft, showed that mergers more often than not have reduced returns to stockholders. A study by Michael Porter of Harvard University demonstrated that a staggering 74% of the conglomerate acquisitions of the 1960s were eventually sold off (divested)—a good indication that they were never based on improving efficiency. William Shepherd of the University of Massachusetts investigated the "contestable markets" model, finding that it is a hypothetical case with minimal applicability to the real world.

Despite their inadequacies, the new apologetic theories have profoundly affected policy, because they provide an intellectual rationale for the agenda of the powerful. ❑

Sources: "Competition Policy in America: The Anti-Antitrust Paradox," James Brock, *Antitrust Bulletin*, Summer 1997; "The Promotional-Financial Dynamic of Merger Movements: A Historical Perspective," Richard DuBoff and Edward Herman, *Journal of Economic Issues*, March 1989; "Antimerger Policy in the United States: History and Lessons," Dennis C. Mueller, *Empirica*, 1996; "Dim Prospects: effective competition in telecommunications, railroads and electricity," William Shepherd, *Antitrust Bulletin*, 1997.

Article 5.3

MONOPOLY CAPITAL AND GLOBAL COMPETITION

BY ARTHUR MacEWAN
September/October 2011

Dear Dr. Dollar:
Is the concept of monopoly capital relevant today, considering such things as global competition?
—Paul Tracy, Oceanside, Calif.

In 1960, the largest 100 firms on *Fortune* magazine's "annual ranking of America's largest corporations" accounted for 15% of corporate profits and had revenues that were 24% as large as GDP. By the early 2000s, each of these figures had roughly doubled: the top 100 firms accounted for about 30% of corporate profits and their revenues were over 40% as large as GDP.*

The banking industry is a prime example of what has been going on: In 2007 the top ten banks were holding over 50% of industry assets, compared with about 25% in 1985.

If by "monopoly capital" we mean that a relatively small number of huge firms play a disproportionately large role in our economic lives, then monopoly capital is a relevant concept today, even more so than a few decades ago.

Global competition has certainly played a role in reshaping aspects of the economy, but it has not altered the importance of very large firms. Even while, for example, Toyota and Honda have gained a substantial share of the U.S. and world auto markets, this does not change the fact that a small number of firms dominate the U.S. and world markets. Moreover, much of the rise in imports, which looks like competition, is not competition for the large U.S. firms themselves. General Motors, for example, has established parts suppliers in Mexico, allowing the company to pay lower wages and hire fewer workers in the states. And Wal-Mart, Target, and other large retailers obtain low-cost goods from subcontractors in China and elsewhere.

Economics textbooks tell us that in markets dominated by a few large firms, prices will be higher than would otherwise be the case. This has generally been true of the auto industry. Also, this appears to be the case in pharmaceuticals, telecommunications, and several other industries.

Wal-Mart and other "big box" stores, however, often do compete by offering very low prices. They are monopsonistic (few buyers) as well as monopolistic (few sellers). They use their power to force down both their payments to suppliers and the wages of their workers. In either case—high prices or low prices—large firms are exercising their market power to shift income to themselves from the rest of us.

Beyond their operation within markets, the very large firms shift income to themselves by shaping markets. Advertising is important in this regard, including, for example, the way pharmaceutical firms effectively create "needs" in pushing their products. Then there is the power of large firms in the political sphere. General

Electric, for example, maintains huge legal and lobbying departments that are able to affect and use tax laws to reduce the firm's tax liability to virtually nothing. Or consider the success of the large banks in shaping (or eliminating) financial regulation, or the accomplishments of the huge oil companies and the military contractors that establish government policies, sometimes as direct subsidies, and thus raise their profits. And the list goes on.

None of this is to say that everything was fine in earlier decades when large firms were less dominant. Yet, as monopoly capital has become more entrenched, it has generated increasingly negative outcomes for the rest of us. Most obvious are the stagnant wages and rising income inequality of recent years. The power of the large firms (e.g., Wal-Mart) to hold down wages is an important part of the story. Then there is the current crisis of the U.S. economy—directly a result of the way the very large financial firms were able to shape their industry (deregulation). Large firms in general have been prime movers over recent decades in generating deregulation and the free-market ideology that supports deregulation.

So, yes, monopoly capital is still quite relevant. Globalization does make differences in our lives, but globalization has in large part been constructed under the influence and in the interest of the very large firms. In many ways globalization makes the concept of monopoly capital even more relevant. ❑

* The profits of the top 100 firms (ranked by revenue) were quite low in 2010, back near the same 15% of total profits as in 1960, because of huge losses connected to the financial crisis incurred by some of the largest firms. Fannie Mae, Freddie Mac, and AIG accounted for combined losses of over $100 billion. Also, the revenues of all firms are not the same as GDP; much of the former is sales of intermediate products, but only sales of final products are included in GDP. Thus, the largest firms' revenues, while 40% as large as GDP, do not constitute 40% of GDP.

Article 5.4

WANT FREE TRADE?
Open the Medical and Drug Industry to Compeititon

BY DEAN BAKER
November 2013; The Guardian Unlimited

Free trade is like apple pie, everyone is supposed to like it. Economists have written thousands of books and articles showing how everyone can gain from reducing trade barriers. While there is much merit to this argument, little of it applies to the trade pacts that are sold as "free-trade" agreements.

These deals are about structuring trade to redistribute income upward. In addition, these agreements also provide a mechanism for over-riding the democratic process in the countries that are parties to the deals. They are a tool whereby corporate interests can block health, safety, and environmental regulations that might otherwise be implemented by democratically elected officials. This is the story with both the Trans-Pacific Partnership (TPP) now being negotiated by General Electric, Merck, and other major corporations who have been invited to the table, as well as the European Union-United States (EU-U.S.) trade agreement.

But trade agreements don't have to be designed to make the rich richer. It is possible to envision trade deals that actually would liberalize trade. NAFTA and it successors were designed to push down the wages of manufacturing workers by making it as easy as possible to set up operations overseas. This put U.S. steelworkers and autoworkers in direct competition with the low-wage workers in the developing world, pushing down wages of manufacturing workers in the United States, and by reducing the number of manufacturing jobs, the wages of less educated workers more generally.

This is all very simple and straightforward. But suppose that instead of designing trade deals to give us cheaper manufacturing workers we designed trade deals to give us cheaper doctors. In the United States, we pay our doctors almost twice as much as the average in other wealthy countries, and almost three times as much as in countries like Sweden or Norway. Suppose we structured a trade deal to get our doctors' pay in line with pay in other wealthy countries.

If we could save an average of $100,000 per doctor, this would translate to savings of roughly $85 billion a year, which would come to more than $1 trillion over the next decade. Throw in dentists and a few other highly paid professions and we would be talking real money. Just the savings on doctors' pay would come to more than $12,000 for an average family of four over ten years. This dwarfs the potential gains that are projected even by supporters of the trade agreements now being negotiated.

But we can be sure that freer trade in physicians' services will not be on the agenda in these trade deals. While the United States brings in Stem workers, nurses, and even teachers from other countries in order to keep their wages down in the United States, no one in a policy position will talk about doing the same with doctors.

The reason is very simple: doctors have lots of money and power. Roughly a third of them can be found in the top 1%, and nearly all would be in the top 3% of the income distribution.

Of course, trade can be used to bring down prices in other areas as well. The United States pays close to twice as much for its prescription drugs as people in other wealthy countries. This is the deliberate result of a patent policy that gives unchecked monopolies to drug companies for decades. In contrast, every other wealthy country couples patent monopolies with price controls, negotiated prices or some other policy that limits the extent to which drug companies can exploit their monopoly.

The United States could simply change its patent policy, but with that route being politically blocked, it could in principle use free trade to bring about the same result. With the country spending over $300 billion a year on drugs at present, the potential gains here also could be well over $1 trillion over the course of a decade.

The industry will claim that lower drug prices will hurt the incentive to develop new drugs, but we can switch to more modern and efficient methods for financing research. By raising prices by tens or even hundreds of times above their free market price, drug patents create the same sort of distortions and waste that we would expect from tariffs of several thousand percent. It's not hard to envision a system that leads to less waste and corruption.

There are many other areas where trade could, in principle, be used to bring about gains for large segments of the U.S. population as well as its trading partners. Unfortunately, we are not likely to see trade agreements that will produce such broad gains. This has nothing to do with trade per se, it has due to with the fact that these trade deals are developed and negotiated by corporate interests for corporate interests.

With the drug companies sitting at the negotiating table at the TPP, does anyone think the deal will actually lower drug prices? Do we expect good rules regulating fracking when the oil and gas industries are writing them? And will the big banks working on the financial section produce good rules for regulating finance?

Yes, free trade can benefit the country as a whole. But the trade deals we will see in the next year have nothing to do with free trade, they are just one more item on the agenda for redistributing wealth upward. ❑

Article 5.5

NOT TOO BIG ENOUGH
Where the big banks come from.

BY ROB LARSON
April 2010

The government bailout of America's biggest banks set off a tornado of public anger and confusion. When the House of Representatives initially rejected the bailout bill, the *Wall Street Journal* attributed it to "populist fury," and since then the public has remained stubbornly resentful over the bailout of those banks considered "too big to fail." Now, the heads of economic policy are trying to gracefully distance themselves from bailouts, claiming that future large-scale bank failures will be avoided by stronger regulation and higher insurance premiums.

Dealing with the collapse of these "systemically important banks" is a difficult policy issue, but the less-discussed issue is how the banking industry came to this point. If the collapse of just one of our $100 billion megabanks, Lehman Brothers, was enough to touch off an intense contraction in the supply of essential credit, we must know how some banks became "too big to fail" in the first place. The answer lies in certain incentives for bank growth, which after the loosening of crucial industry regulations drove the enormous waves of bank mergers in the last thirty years.

Geographical Growth

Prior to the 1980s, American commercial banking was a small-scale affair. State-chartered banks were prohibited by state laws from running branches outside their home state, or sometimes even outside their home county. Nationally chartered banks were likewise limited, and federal law allowed interstate acquisitions only if a state legislature specifically decided to permit out-of-state banks to purchase local branches. No states allowed such acquisition until 1975, when Maine and other states began passing legislation allowing at least some interstate banking. The trend was capped in 1994 by the Riegle-Neal Act, which removed the remaining restrictions on interstate branching and allowed direct cross-state banking mergers.

This geographic deregulation allowed commercial banks to make extensive acquisitions, in state and out. When Wells Fargo acquired another large California bank, Crocker National, in 1986 it was the largest bank merger in U.S. history. Since "the regulatory light was green," a single banking company could now operate across the uniquely large U.S. market, opening up enormous new opportunities for economies of scale in the banking industry.

Economies of scale are savings that companies enjoy when they grow larger and produce more output. The situation is similar to a cook preparing a batch of cookies for a Christmas party, and then preparing a batch for New Year's while all the ingredients and materials are already out. Producing more output (cookies) in one afternoon is more efficient than taking everything out again later to make the New Year's batch separately. In enterprise, this corresponds to spreading the large costs of startup investment over more and more output, and is often thought of as lower per-unit costs as the level of production increases. In other words, there's less effort per cookie if you make them all at once. Economies of scale, when present in an industry, create a strong incentive for firms to grow larger, since profitability will improve. But they also give larger, established firms a valuable cost advantage over new competitors, which can put the brakes on competition.

Once unleashed by the policy changes, these economies of scale played a major role in the industry's seemingly endless merger activity. "In order to compete, you need scale," said a VP for Chemical Bank when buying a smaller bank in 1994. Of course, in 1996 Chemical would itself merge with Chase Manhattan Bank.

Economies of Scale in Banking and Finance

Economies of scale are savings that companies benefit from as they grow larger and produce more output. While common in many industries, in banking and finance, these economies drove bank growth after industry deregulation in the 1980s and 90s. Some of the major scale economies in banking are:

- **Spreading investment over more output.** With the growth in importance of large-scale computing power and sophisticated systems management, the costs of setting up a modern banking system are very large. However, as a firm grows it can "spread out" the cost of that initial investment over more product, so that its cost per unit decreases as more output is produced.

- **Consolidation of functions.** The modern workforce is no stranger to the mass firings of "redundant" staff after mergers and acquisitions. If one firm's payroll staff and computer systems can handle twice the employees with little additional expense, an acquired bank may see its payroll department harvest pink slips while the firm's profitability improves. When Citicorp merged with the insurance giant Travelers Group in 1998, the resulting corporation laid off over 10,000 workers—representing 6% of the combined company's total workforce and over $500 million in reduced costs for Citigroup. This practice can be especially lucrative in a country like the United States, with a fairly unregulated labor market where firms are quite free to fire. Despite the economic peril inflicted on workers and their families, this consolidation is key to increasing company efficiency post-merger. Beyond back-office functions, core profit operations may also benefit from consolidation. When Bank of America combined its managed mutual funds into a single fund, it experienced lower total costs, thanks to trimming overhead from audit and prospectus mailing expenses. Consolidating office departments in this fashion can yield savings of 40% of the cost base of the acquired bank.

- **Funding mix.** The "funding mix" used by banks refers to where banks get the capital they then package into loans. Smaller institutions, having only limited deposits from savers, must "purchase funds" by borrowing from other institutions. This increases the funding cost of loans for banks, but larger banks will naturally have access to larger pools of deposits from which to arrange loans. This funding cost advantage for larger banks relative to smaller ones represents another economy of scale.

- **Advertising.** The nature of advertising requires a certain scale of operation to be viable. Advertising can reach large numbers of potential customers, but if a firm is small or local, many of those customers will be too far afield to act on the marketing. Large firm size, and especially geographic reach, can make the returns on ad time worth the investment.

Spreading big investment costs over more output is the main source of generic economies of scale, and in banking, the large initial investments are in sophisticated computer systems. The cost of investing in new computer hardware and systems development is now recognized as a major investment obstacle for new banks, although once installed by banks large enough to afford them, they are highly profitable. The *Financial Times* describes how "the development of bulk computer processing and of electronic data transmission...has allowed banks to move their back office operations away from individual branches to large remote centers. This had helped to bring real economies of scale to banking, an industry which traditionally has seen diseconomies set in at a very modest scale."

Economies of scale are common in manufacturing, and in the wake of deregulation the banking industry was also able to exploit a number of them. Besides spreading out the cost of computer systems, economies of scale may be present in office consolidation, in the funding mix used by banks, and in advertising (see sidebar).

Industry-to-Industry Growth

BusinessWeek's analysis is that the banking industry "has produced large competitors that can take advantage of economies of scale...as regulatory barriers to interstate banking fell," although not until the banks could "digest their purchases." The 1990s saw hundreds of bank purchases annually and hundreds of billions in acquired assets.

But an additional major turn for the industry came with the Gramm-Leach-Bliley Act of 1999 (GLB), which further loosened restrictions on bank growth, this time not geographically but industry-to-industry. After earlier moves in this direction by the Federal Reserve, GLB allowed for the free combination of commercial banking, insurance, and the riskier field of investment banking. These had been separated by law for decades, on the grounds that the availability of commercial credit was too important to the overall economy to be tied to the volatile world of investment banking.

GLB allowed firms to grow further, through banks merging with insurers or investment banks. The world of commercial credit was widened, and financial mergers this time exploited economies of scope—where production of multiple products jointly is cheaper than producing them individually. As commercial banks, investment banks, and insurers have expanded into each others' fields in the wake of GLB, their different lines of business can benefit from single expenses—for example, banks perform research on loan recipients that can also be used to underwrite bond issues. Scope economies such as these allow the larger banks to both run a greater profit on a per-service basis and attract more business. Thanks to the convenience of "one stop shopping," Citigroup now does more business with big corporations, like IT giant Unisys, than its component firms did pre-merger.

Exploiting economies of scope to diversify product lines in this fashion can also help a firm by reducing its dependence on any one line of business. Bank of America weathered the stock market downturn of 2001 in part because its corporate debt underwriting business was booming. Smaller, more specialized banks can become "one-trick ponies" as the *Wall Street Journal* put it—outdone by larger competitors with low-cost diversification thanks to scope economies.

These economies of scope are parallel to the scale economies, since both required deregulatory policy changes to be unleashed. Traditionally, banking wasn't seen as an industry with the strong economies of scale seen in, say, manufacturing. But the deregulation and computerization of the industry have allowed these firms to realize returns to greater scale and wider scope, and this has been a main driver of the endless acquisitions in the industry in recent decades.

Market Power

The enormous proportions that the banking institutions have taken on following deregulation have meant serious consequences for market performance. A number of banks have reached sufficient size to exercise market power—the ability of firms to influence prices and to engage in anticompetitive behavior. The market power of our enormous banks allows them to take positions as price leaders in local markets, where large firms use their dominance to elevate prices (i.e., increase fees and rates on loans, and decrease interest rates on deposits). Large firms can do this because smaller firms may perceive that lowering their prices to take market share could be met by very drastic reductions in prices from the larger firm in retaliation. Large firms, having deeper pockets, may be able to withstand longer periods of operating at a loss than the smaller firms.

Small banks are likely to perceive that the colossal size and resources of the megabanks make them unprofitable to cross—better to follow along and charge roughly what the dominant, price-leading firm does. Empirical research by Federal Reserve Board senior economist Steven Pilloff supported this analysis, finding that the arrival of very large banks in local markets tended to increase bank profitability for reasons of price leadership, due to the larger banks' economies of scale and scope, financial muscle, and diversification.

Examples of the use of banking industry market power are easy to find. Several bills now circulating in Congress deal with the fees retail businesses pay to the banks and the credit card companies. When consumers make purchases with their Visas or MasterCards, an average of two cents of each dollar goes not to the retailer but to the credit card companies that run the payment network and the banks that supply the credit. These "interchange fees" bring in over $35 billion in profit in the United States alone, and they reflect the strong market power of the banks and credit card companies over the various big and small retailers. The 2% charge comes to about $31,000 for a typical convenience store, just below the average per-store yearly profit of $36,000, and this has driven a coalition of retailers to press for congressional action.

Visa has about 50% of the credit card market (including debit cards), and MasterCard has 25%, which grants them profound market power and strong bargaining positions. Federal Reserve Bank of Kansas City economists found the United States "maintains the highest interchange fees in the world, yet its costs should be among the lowest, given economies of scale and declining cost trends." The *Wall Street Journal*'s description was that "these fees…have also been paradoxically tending upward in recent years when the industry's costs due to technology and economies of scale have been falling." Of course, there's only a paradox if market power is omitted from the picture. The dominant size and scale economies of the banks and the credit card oligopoly allow for high prices to be sustained—bank muscle in action against a less powerful sector of the economy. The political action favored by the retailers includes proposals for committees to enact price ceilings or (interestingly) collective bargaining by the retailers. As is often the case, the political process is the reflection of the different levels and positions of power of various corporate institutions, and the maneuvering of their organizations.

Market power brings with it a number of other advantages. A powerful company is likely to have a widespread presence, make frequent use of advertising, and be able to raise its profile by contributing to community organizations like sports leagues. This allows the larger banks to benefit from stronger brand identity—their scale and resources make customers more likely to trust their services. This grants a further advantage in the form of customer tolerance of higher prices due to brand loyalty.

Political Clout

Crucially, large firms with market power are free to participate meaningfully in politics—using their deep pockets to invest in electoral campaigns and congressional lobbying. The financial sector is among the highest-contributing industries in the United States, with total 2008 campaign contributions approaching half a billion dollars, according to the Center For Public Integrity. So it's unsurprising that they receive so many favors from the government, since they fund the careers of the decision-making government personnel. This underlying reality is why influential Senator Dick Durbin said of Congress, "The banks own the place."

Finally, banks may grow so large by exploiting scale economies and market power that they become "systemically important" to the nation's financial system. In other words, the scale and interconnectedness of the largest banks is considered to have reached a point where an abrupt failure of one or more of them may have "systemic" effects—meaning the broader economic system will be seriously impaired. These "too big to fail" banks are the ones that were bailed out by act of Congress in the fall 2008. Once a firm becomes so enormous that the government must prevent its collapse for the good of the economy, it has the ultimate advantage of being free to take far greater risks. Riskier investments come with higher returns and profits, but the greater risk of collapse that accompanies them will be less intimidating to huge banks that have an implied government insurance policy.

Some analysts have expressed doubt that such firms truly are too large to let fail, and that the banks have pulled a fast one. It might be pointed out in this connection that in the past the banks themselves have put their money where their mouths are—they have paid out of pocket to rescue financial institutions they saw as too large and connected to fail. An especially impressive episode took place in 1998, when several of Wall Street's biggest banks and financiers agreed to billions in emergency loans to rescue Long Term Capital Management. LTCM was a high-profile hedge fund that borrowed enormous sums of capital to make billion-dollar gambles on financial markets.

America's biggest banks aren't in the habit of forking over $3.5 billion of good earnings, but they had loaned heavily to LTCM and feared losing their money if the fund went under. The Federal Reserve brought the bankers together, and in the end, they paid up to bail out their colleagues, and the *Wall Street Journal* reported that it was the Fed's "clout, together with the self-interest of several big firms that already had lent billions of dollars to Long-Term Capital, that helped fashion the rescue." Interestingly, the banks insisted on real equity in the firm they were pulling out of the fire, and they gained a 90% stake in the hedge fund. Comparing this to the less-valuable "preferred stock" the government settled for in its 2008 bailout package of the large banks is instructive. The banks also got a share of control in the firm they rescued, again in stark contrast to the public bailout of some of the same banks.

Even Bigger?

In fact, the financial crisis and bailout led only to further concentration of the industry. The crisis gave stronger firms an opportunity to pick up sicker ones in another "wave of consolidation," as *BusinessWeek* put it. And a large part of the government intervention itself involved arranging hasty purchases of failing giants by other giants, orchestrated by the Federal Reserve. For example, the Fed helped organize the purchase of Bear Stearns by Chase in March 2008 and the purchase of Wachovia by Wells Fargo in December 2008. Even the bailout's "capital infusions" were used for further mergers and acquisitions by several recipients. The Treasury Department was "using the bailout bill to turn the banking system into the oligopoly of giant national institutions," as the *New York Times* reported.

The monumental growth of the largest banks owes a lot to the industry's economies of scale and scope, once regulations were relaxed so firms could exploit them. While certainly not unique to finance, these dynamics have brought the banks to such enormous size that their bad bets can put the entire economy in peril. Banking therefore offers an especially powerful case for the importance of these economies and the role of market power, since it's left the megabanks holding all the cards.

In fact, many arguments between defenders of the market economy and its critics center on the issue of competition vs. power—market boosters reliably insist that markets mean efficient competition, where giants have no inherent advantage over small, scrappy firms. However, the record in banking clearly shows that banks have enjoyed a variety of real benefits from growth. The existence of companies of great size and power is a quite natural development in many industries, due to the appeal of returns to scale and power. This is why firms end up with enough power to influence government policy, or such absurd size that they can blackmail us for life support.

And leave us crying all the way to the bank. ❑

Sources: Judith Samuelson and Lynn Stout, "Are Executives Paid Too Much?" *Wall Street Journal*, February 26, 2009; Tom Braithwaite, "Geithner Presses Congress for Action on Reform," *Financial Times*, September 23, 2009; Phillip Zweig, "Intrastate Mergers Between Banking Giants Might Not Be Out of the Question Anymore," *Wall Street Journal*, March 25, 1986; Bruce Knecht, "Chemical Banking plans acquisition of Margaretten," *Wall Street Journal*, May 13, 1994;

Eric Weiner, "Banks Will Post Good Quarterly Results," *Wall Street Journal*, January 10, 1997; Gabriella Stern, "Four Big Regionals To Consolidate Bank Operations," *Wall Street Journal*, July 22, 1992; "Pressure for change grows," *Financial Times*, September 27, 1996; Tracy Corrigan and John Authers, "Citigroup To Take $900 million charge: Cost-cutting Program to Result in Loss of 10,400 Jobs," *Financial Times*, December 16, 1998; Eleanor Laise, "Mutual-Fund Mergers Jump Sharply," *Wall Street Journal*, March 9, 2006; Steven Pilloff, "Banking, commerce and competition under the Gramm-Leach-Bliley Act," *The Antitrust Bulletin*, Spring 2002; David Humphrey, "Why Do Estimates of Bank Scale Economies Differ?" *Economic Review* of Federal Reserve Bank of Richmond, September/October 1990, note four; Michael Mandel and Rich Miller, "Productivity: The Real Story," *BusinessWeek*, November 5, 2001; John Yang, "Fed Votes to Give 7 Bank Holding Firms Additional Power in Securities Sector," *Wall Street Journal*, July 16, 1987; "Banking Behemoths—What Happens Next: Many companies Like to Shop Around For Their Providers of Financial Services," *Wall Street Journal*, September 14, 2000; Carrick Mollenkamp and Paul Beckett, "Diverse Business Portfolios Boost Banks' Bottom Lines," *Wall Street Journal*, July 17, 2001; *Journal of Financial Services Research*, "Does the Presence of Big Banks Influence Competition in Local Markets?" May 1999; "Credit-Card Wars," *Wall Street Journal*, March 29, 2008; *Economic Review* of the Federal Reserve Bank of Kansas City, "Interchange Fees in Credit and Debit Card Markets: What Role for Public Authorities," January-March 2006; "Credit Where It's Due," *Wall Street Journal*, January 12, 2006; Keith Bradsher, "In One Pocket, Out the Other," *New York Times*, November 25, 2009; Center For Public Integrity, Finance/Insurance/Real Estate: Long-Term Contribution Trends, opensecrests.org; Dean Baker, "Banks own the U.S. government," *Guardian*, June 30, 2009; Anita Raghavan and Mitchell Pacelle, "To the Rescue? A Hedge Fun Falters, So the Fed Persuades Big Banks to Ante Up," *Wall Street Journal*, September 24, 1998; Theo Francis, "Will Bank Rescues Mean Fewer Banks?" *BusinessWeek*, November 25, 2008; Joe Nocera, "So When Will Banks Give Loans?" *New York Times*, October 25, 2008.

Article 5.6

BIG BANK IMMUNITY
When do we crack down on Wall Street?

BY DEAN BAKER
March 2013; Truthout

The Wall Street gang must really be partying these days. Profits and bonuses are as high as ever as these super-rich takers were able to use trillions of dollars of below-market government loans to get themselves through the crisis they created. The rest of the country is still struggling with high unemployment, stagnant wages, underwater mortgages and hollowed out retirement accounts, but life is good again on Wall Street.

Their world must have gotten even brighter last week when Attorney General Eric Holder told the Senate Judiciary Committee that the Justice Department may have to restrain its prosecutors in dealing with the big banks because it has to consider the possibility that a prosecution could lead to financial instability. Not only can the big banks count on taxpayer bailouts when they need them; it turns out that they can share profits with drug dealers with impunity. (The case immediately at hand involved money laundered for the Mexican drug cartel.) And who says that times are bad?

It's hard to know where to begin with this one. First off, we should not assume that just because the Justice Department says it is concerned about financial instability that this is the real reason that they are not prosecuting a big bank. There is precedent for being less than honest about such issues.

When Enron was about to collapse in 2002 as its illegal dealings became public, former Treasury Secretary Robert Rubin, who was at the time a top Citigroup executive, called a former aide at Treasury. He asked him to intervene with the bond rating agencies to get them to delay downgrading Enron's debt. Citigroup owned several hundred million dollars in Enron debt at the time. If Rubin had gotten this delay Citigroup would have been able to dump much of this debt on suckers before the price collapsed.

The Treasury official refused. When the matter became public, Robert Rubin claimed that he was concerned about instability in financial markets.

It is entirely possible that the reluctance to prosecute big banks represents the same sort of fear of financial instability as motivated Robert Rubin. In other words, it is a pretext that the Justice Department is using to justify its failure to prosecute powerful friends on Wall Street. In Washington this possibility can never be ruled out.

However, there is the possibility that the Justice Department really believes that prosecuting the criminal activities of Bank of America or JP Morgan could sink the economy. If this is true then it make the case for breaking up the big banks even more of a slam dunk since it takes the logic of too big to fail one step further.

Just to remind everyone, the simple argument against too-big-to-fail is that it subsidizes risk-taking by large banks. In principle, when a bank or other company is engaged in a risky line of business those who are investing in the company or lending it money demand a higher rate of return in recognition of the risk.

However, if they know that government will back up the bank if it gets into trouble then investors have little reason to properly evaluate the risk. This means that more money will flow to the TBTF bank since it knows it can undertake risky activities without paying the same interest rate as other companies that take on the same amount of risk. The result is that we have given the banks an incentive to engage in risky activity and a big subsidy to their top executives and creditors.

If it turns out that we also give them a get-out-of-jail-free card when it comes to criminal activity then we are giving these banks an incentive to engage in criminal activity. There is a lot of money to be gained by assisting drug dealers and other nefarious types in laundering their money. In principle the laws are supposed to be structured to discourage banks from engaging in such behavior. But when the attorney general tells us that the laws cannot be fully enforced against the big banks he is saying that we are giving them incentive to break the law in the pursuit of profit.

Our anti-trust laws are supposed to protect the country against companies whose size allows them inordinate market power. In principle, we would use anti-trust law to break up a phone company because its market dominance allowed it to charge us $10 a month too much on our cable. How could we not use anti-trust policy to break up a bank whose size allows it to profit from dealing with drug dealers and murderers with impunity? ❑

Article 5.7

THE FALSE LIBERTARIANISM OF THE SILICON VALLEY BILLIONAIRES

BY DEAN BAKER
January 2014; The Guardian

L ast week Mark Ames published an article that should forever destroy any connection between the Silicon Valley tech billionaires and libertarian worldviews.
The article reports on a court case that alleges that Apple, Google, and other Silicon
Valley powerhouses actively conspired to keep their workers' wages down. According
to documents filed in the case, these companies agreed not to compete for each others' workers dating at least as far back as 2005. Workers in the industry have filed a
class action suit that could lead to the payment of billions of dollars in lost wages.

This case is striking at many levels, the most obvious being the effective theft
of large amounts of money by some of the richest people on the planet from their
employees. This is pernicious, but not altogether surprising. After all, the boss stealing from the workers is as dog bites man as it gets. Few would be surprised that rich
people were willing to break the law to get even richer.

The real news here is how the Silicon Valley barons allegedly broke the law. The
charge is that they actively colluded to stifle market forces. They collectively acted
to prevent their workers from receiving the market-clearing wage. This means not
only that they broke the law, and that they acted to undermine the market, but that
they really don't think about the market the way libertarians claim to think about
the market.

The classic libertarian view of the market is that we have a huge number of
people in the market actively competing to buy and sell goods and services. They
acknowledge the obvious—some actors are much bigger than others—but there is
so much competition that no individual or company can really hope to have much
impact on market outcomes.

This point is central to their argument that the government should not interfere with corporate practices. For example, if we think our local cable company is
charging too much for cable access, our libertarian friends will insist that the phone
company, satellite television, or other competitors will step in to keep prices in line.
They would tell the same story if the issue were regulating the airlines, banks, health
insurance, or any other sector where there is reason to believe that competition
might be limited.

They would tell the same story on the labor side. If we are concerned that
workers are getting low wages then the answer is to improve their skills through
education and training rather than raise the minimum wage. If workers were worth
more than the minimum wage, then the market would already be paying them more
than the minimum wage.

They have the same story when it comes to requiring family leave, sick days, or
other benefits. Libertarians would say that if workers value these benefits they would

negotiate for them and be willing to trade off wages. There is no reason for the government to get involved.

This story about the wonders of the free market is simple in its appeal and it has the great implication that nothing should be done to keep the rich from getting ever richer. However, the Silicon Valley non-compete agreements show that this is not how the tech billionaires believe the market really works. This is just a story they peddle to children and gullible reporters.

If they really believed the market had a deep sea of competitors in which no individual actor could count for much, then their non-compete agreements would serve no purpose. If Google, Apple, Intel, and the other biggies agreed not to hire each others' workers, it really wouldn't affect their pay since there would always be new upstarts ready to jump in and hire away underpaid engineers.

The fact the Silicon Valley honchos took the time to negotiate and presumably enforce these non-compete agreements was because they did not think that there were enough competitors to hire away their workers. They believed that they had enough weight on the buy-side of the market for software engineers that if they agreed to not to compete for workers, they could keep their wages down.

It shouldn't be surprising that the Silicon Valley billionaires really are not libertarians. After all, much of their fortunes rest on patents and copyrights, both of which are government granted monopolies: the opposite of a free market.

But for some reason, seeing the tech whiz-kids forming a cartel to keep down their workers' wages seems an even more direct violation of any belief in libertarian principles. This is the same sort of cartel behavior that we associate with the cigar-chomping robber barons of the late 19th century. It turns out that the biggest difference between the tech billionaires of the Internet Age and the high rollers of the railroad age is the cigars. ❑

Chapter 6

LABOR MARKETS

INTRODUCTION

Mainstream economics textbooks emphasize the ways that labor markets are similar to other markets. In the standard model, labor suppliers (workers) decide how much to work in the same way that producers decide how much to supply, by weighing the revenues against the costs—in this case, the opportunity costs of foregone leisure, and other potential costs of having a job, like physical injury. Workers are paid their marginal product, the extra output the firm gets from employing one extra unit (e.g., hour) of labor. Workers earn different wages because they contribute different marginal products to output. Of course, economists of every stripe acknowledge that, in reality, many non-market factors, such as government assistance programs, unionization, and discrimination, affect labor markets. But in most economics textbooks, these produce only limited deviations from the basic laws of supply and demand.

Starting off the chapter, Alejandro Reuss addresses the reasons behind union decline in the United States (Article 6.1), pointing especially to the aggressiveness of employers in fighting both existing unions and new unionization drives (the "employers' offensive") since the 1970s. Government policy, Reuss argues, has also played an important role, especailly in the failure to protect workers' rights to form unions or to strike.

John Miller and Jeannette Wicks-Lim take apart the argument, increasingly heard in policy circles, that a large share of unemployment today is a result not of the generalized lack of demand caused by the recession, but of workers not having the skills that employers desire (Article 6.2). In this article, Miller and Wicks-Lim show that this argument has little empirical support and that it shifts the blame for unemployment onto workers themselves.

Miller follows with an article on so-called "right to work" laws, which make it illegal to require union membership as a condition of employment. (These laws encourage workers to "free ride"—not contribute union dues even if they benefit from union representation—and so undermine union strength.) In "Wrong About Right-to-Work" (Article 6.3), Miller debunks the view, touted by conservative economists Arthur Laffer and Stephen Moore, that states with right-to-work laws enjoy superior rates of economic growth or job creation.

Next, Miller argues against the *Wall Street Journal* edtiors' view that the Affordable Care Act (ACA, or "Obamacare") wrongly "skews" labor-market decisions. A Congressional Budget Office report does, indeed, say that some workers will drop out of the labor force as a result of the health-care reform law. The reason, however, is that they will no longer have to stay in bad jobs just to keep their health insurance. This new freedom to quit will, in turn, boost workers' bargaining power. A more comprehensive and universal health reform, such as a single-payer system, Miller argues, could do more.

In "We're Not Lovin' It" (Article 6.5), Nicole Aschoff looks at the recent upsurge in protests and strikes against low wages and poor working conditions in the retail and fast-food sectors. Companies could raise wages and improve conditions, Aschoff argues, and still remain profitable.

Next, Gerald Friedman chronicles the rise of "contingent labor," or what he calls the "gig economy" in the United States. In "Dog Walking and College Teaching" (Article 6.6), Friedman shows how labor contracts with little job security have been on the rise in everything from construction and office work to higher education.

Wrapping up the chapter, two articles address labor conditions internationally. John Miller describes the struggle to improve sweatship conditions in global apparel production—and apparel retailers' reistance—in "After Horror, Apologetics" (Article 6.7). Arthur MacEwan, meanwhile, addresses the merits of international labor standards and whether labor and progressive groups should support the inclusion of such standards in trade agreements (Article 6.8).

Discussion Questions

1. (Article 6.1) Why has the number of workers represented by unions fallen in the United States over the last few decades? Which areas of the American economy remain highly unionized? Which areas of the American economy are experiencing growth in union membership?

2. (Article 6.2) What data support the case that today's high unemployment rates can be attributed to a mismatch between job openings and workers' skills? How do Miller and Wicks-Lim respond to these arguments?

3. (Article 6.3) What are "right to work" laws? How are these laws designed to undermine the ability of a union to function? Is there really a correlation between "right to work" laws and economic growth? If so, in what direction?

4. (Article 6.4) Why would the availability of public benefits, like health coverage, cause people to reduce their work hours? What positive effects does Miller believe would result?

5. (Article 6.5) What explains the recent upsurge in labor protests and strikes in the retail and fast-food sectors? Why have companies been so adamant on a low-wage strategy when there are examples showing how that a high-wage approach can be consistent with profitability?

6. (Article 6.6) Why have "contingent" labor arrangements increased so much in recent decades? How do employers benefit from these arrangements? If workers, on balance, are harmed, why do employers not have a hard time finding people willing to work under such contracts?

7. (Article 6.7) Is it true that poor countries simply cannot afford better and safer working conditions? How does Miller argue this is not the case? Does the existence of employment under unsafe conditions show that workers prefer the incomes from this employment over safety? Is there a strong case for regulation, if workers enter into such labor arrangements willingly?

8. (Article 6.8) What is MacEwan's argument for supporting international labor standards in trade agreements? What pitfalls does he describe, which could unintentionally harm some workers in developing countries? Why does he believe that supporting the right of workers to form unions avoids these pitfalls?

Article 6.1

WHAT'S BEHIND UNION DECLINE IN THE UNITED STATES?

The role of the "employers' offensive" has been key.

BY ALEJANDRO REUSS
May/June 2011

The total number of union members in the United States peaked in the late 1970s and early 1980s, at over 20 million. As of 2010, it remained near 15 million. The story of union decline in the United States, however, does not begin in the 1980s, nor is it as modest as these figures would suggest.

Union density (or the "unionization rate"), the number of workers who are members of unions as a percentage of all employed workers, has been declining in the United States for over half a century. The share of U.S. workers in unions peaked in 1954, at just over 25%. For nonagricultural workers, the high-water mark—at more than one third of employed workers—came even earlier, in 1945. It would reach nearly the same percentage again in the early 1950s, before beginning a long and virtually uninterrupted decline.

By 2010, the U.S. unionization rate was less than 12%. It would be even lower were it not for the growth of public-sector unions since the 1960s. For private-sector workers, the unionization rate is now less than 7%.

There are multiple reasons for union decline, including shrinking employment in highly unionized industries, falling unionization rates within these traditional bastions of unionism, and failures to unionize in new, growing sectors.

Employers' determination to rid themselves of unions has certainly played a major role in declining unionization rates. Where employers could not break unions by frontal assault, they were determined to find ways around them. Unionized companies established parallel non-union operations, a practice sometimes known as "double breasting," gradually shifting production and employment away from their unionized facilities. Some employers began contracting out work formerly done by union employees to non-union subcontractors (the original meaning of "outsourcing"). Some established new operations far from their traditional production centers, especially in less unionized and lower-wage areas. Many companies based in the Northeast and Upper Midwest, for example, set up new production sites in the South and West, and eventually in other countries. Finally, new employers entering highly unionized sectors usually remained non-union. The auto industry is a good example. So-called "transplants" (factories owned by non-U.S. headquartered companies) have accounted for an increasing share of the industry's shrinking labor force, and have remained largely non-union.

Historically, union growth has come primarily in short spurts when unions expand into new industries. Since the 1940s, however, U.S. unions have failed to organize in growing industries to compensate for the declines in employment and unionization rates in traditional union strongholds. The public sector represents the one major exception. Since the early 1970s, union density for public-sector workers has increased from about 20% to over 35%. This has not been nearly enough, however, to counteract the decline among private-sector workers. To maintain the

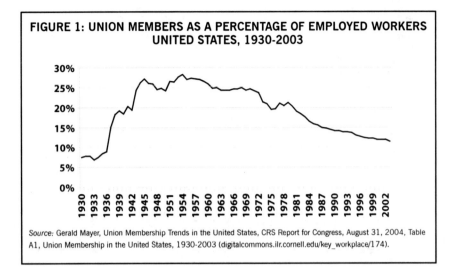

FIGURE 1: UNION MEMBERS AS A PERCENTAGE OF EMPLOYED WORKERS UNITED STATES, 1930-2003

Source: Gerald Mayer, Union Membership Trends in the United States, CRS Report for Congress, August 31, 2004, Table A1, Union Membership in the United States, 1930-2003 (digitalcommons.ilr.cornell.edu/key_workplace/174).

overall unionization rates of the 1950s or 1960s, unions would have had to enlist millions more workers in the private sector, especially in services.

Since the 1970s, employers have fought unions and unionization drives with increasing aggressiveness, as part of what labor historian Michael Goldfield calls the "employer offensive." Many employers facing unionization drives fire vocal union supporters, both eliminating pro-union campaigners and spreading fear among the other workers. Researchers at the Center for Economic and Policy Research (CEPR) have found that, between 2001 and 2005, pro-union workers were illegally fired in around one-fourth of all union election campaigns. Meanwhile, during many campaigns, employers threaten to shut down the facility (at least in part) if the union wins. Labor researcher Kate Bronfenbrenner reports, in a study from the mid 1990s, that employers threatened plant closings in more than half of all unionization campaigns, and that such threats cut the union victory rate (compared to those in which no such threat was made) by about 30%.

The employer offensive has unfolded, especially since the 1980s, against a bacdrop of government hostility towards unions. The federal government has often turned a blind eye to illegal tactics (or "unfair labor practices") routinely used by employers to fight unionization drives. Employer retaliation against workers (by firing or otherwise) for union membership, union activity, or support for unionization is illegal. So is an employer threatening to close a specific plant in response to a unionization drive. However, since the 1980s, union supporters argue, the government agencies tasked with enforcing labor law have increasingly ignored such practices, imposed only "slap on the wrist" punishments, or delayed judgment, somtimes for years, long after the unionization drive is over and done with.

Many labor historians point to the Reagan administration's mass firing of striking air-traffic controllers (members of the Professional Air Traffic Controllers Organization, or PATCO) in 1981 as a signal that the government approved of private employers' own union-busting activities. Before the PATCO strike, it was relatively rare for employers to fire striking workers and hire "permanent replacements." (Sometimes, employers would bring in replacements during a strike, but

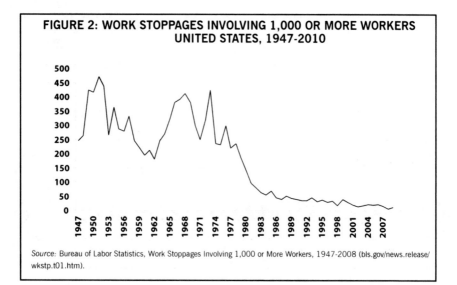

FIGURE 2: WORK STOPPAGES INVOLVING 1,000 OR MORE WORKERS UNITED STATES, 1947-2010

Source: Bureau of Labor Statistics, Work Stoppages Involving 1,000 or More Workers, 1947-2008 (bls.gov/news.release/wkstp.t01.htm).

striking workers would get their jobs back after a settlement was reached.) After PATCO, private employers increasingly responded to strikes by firing the strikers and bringing in permanent replacements—a practice that is illegal in many countries, but not in the United States. The number of large strikes, already in sharp decline during the preceding few years (possibly due to the employer offensive, rising unemployment, and other factors), has since declined to microscopic proportions.

At this point, unions in the United States—including less than a tenth of private-sector workers—are almost back down to the level they were on the eve of the Great Depression. The 1930s turned out to be the greatest period of union growth in U.S. history, with substantial additional growth in the 1940s and 1950s largely an aftershock of that earlier explosion. There is no guarantee, however, that history will repeat itself, and that the weakness of organized labor today will give way to a new burst of energy. In the midst of a deep recession, and now the beginnings of a halting recovery, there have been few signs of a labor revival. Ironically, only the recent attacks on public-sector workers and unions have provoked a mass-movement fightback. Labor supporters, however, should understand this, soberly, as coming from a very defensive position. ❑

Sources: Michael Goldfield, "Labor in American Politics—Its Current Weakness," *The Journal of Politics,* Vol. 48, No. 1. (Feb., 1986), pp. 2-29; Kate Bronfenbrenner, "Final Report: The Effects of Plant Closing or Threat of Plant Closing on the Right of Workers to Organize," *International Publications,* Paper 1, 1996 (digitalcommons.ilr.cornell.edu/intl/1); Gerald Friedman, *Reigniting the Labor Movement: Restoring Means to Ends in a Democratic Labor Movement* (New York: Routledge, 2008); Gerald Mayer, "Union Membership Trends in the United States," CRS Report for Congress, August 31, 2004, Table A1, Union Membership in the United States, 1930-2003 (digitalcommons.ilr.cornell.edu/key_workplace/174); Bureau of Labor Statistics, "Work Stoppages Involving 1,000 or More Workers," 1947-2008 (www.bls.gov/news.release/wkstp.t01.htm); John Schmitt and Ben Zipperer, "Dropping the Ax: Illegal Firings During Union Election Campaigns," Center for Economic and Policy Research, January 2007 (www.cepr.net/documents/publications/unions_2007_01.pdf).

Article 6.2

UNEMPLOYMENT: A JOBS DEFICIT OR A SKILLS DEFICIT?

BY JOHN MILLER AND JEANNETTE WICKS-LIM
January/February 2011

Millions of Americans remain unemployed nearly a year and a half after the official end-date of the Great Recession, and the nation's official unemployment rate continues at nearly 10%.

Why? We are being told that it is because—wait for it—workers are not qualified for the jobs that employers are offering.

Yes, it's true. In the aftermath of the deepest downturn since the Great Depression, some pundits and policymakers—and economists—have begun to pin persistently high unemployment on workers' inadequate skills.

The problem, in this view, is a mismatch between job openings and the skills of those looking for work. In economics jargon, this is termed a problem of "structural unemployment," in contrast to the "cyclical unemployment" caused by a downturn in the business cycle.

The skills-gap message is coming from many quarters. Policymaker-in-chief Obama told Congress in February 2009: "Right now, three-quarters of the fastest-growing occupations require more than a high school diploma. And yet, just over half of our citizens have that level of education." His message: workers need to go back to school if they want a place in tomorrow's job market.

The last Democrat in the White House has caught the bug too. Bill Clinton explained in a September 2010 interview, "The last unemployment report said that for the first time in my lifetime, and I'm not young ... we are coming out of a recession but job openings are going up twice as fast as new hires. And yet we can all cite cases that we know about where somebody opened a job and 400 people showed up. How could this be? Because people don't have the job skills for the jobs that are open."

Economists and other "experts" are most likely the source of the skills-gap story. Last August, for instance, Narayana Kocherlakota, president of the Federal Reserve Bank of Minneapolis, wrote in a Fed newsletter: "How much of the current unemployment rate is really due to mismatch, as opposed to conditions that the Fed can readily ameliorate? The answer seems to be a lot." Kocherlakota's point was that the Fed's monetary policy tools may be able to spur economic growth, but that won't help if workers have few or the wrong skills. "The Fed does not have a means to transform construction workers into manufacturing workers," he explained.

The skills-mismatch explanation has a lot to recommend it if you're a federal or Fed policymaker: it puts the blame for the economic suffering experienced by the 17% of the U.S. workforce that is unemployed or underemployed on the workers themselves. Even if the Fed or the government did its darndest to boost overall spending, unemployment would be unlikely to subside unless workers upgraded their own skills.

The only problem is that this explanation is basically wrong. The weight of the evidence shows that it is not a mismatch of skills but a lack of demand that lies at the heart of today's severe unemployment problem.

High-Skill Jobs?

President Obama's claim that new jobs are requiring higher and higher skill levels would tend to support the skills-gap thesis. His interpretation of job-market trends, however, misses the mark. The figure that Obama cited comes from the U.S. Department of Labor's employment projections for 2006 to 2016. Specifically, the DOL reports that among the 30 fastest growing occupations, 22 of them (75%) will typically require more than a high school degree. These occupations include network systems and data communications analysts, computer software engineers, and financial advisors. What he fails to say, however, is that these 22 occupations are projected to represent less than 3% of all U.S. jobs.

What would seem more relevant to the 27 million unemployed and underemployed workers are the occupations with the *largest* growth. These are the occupations that will offer workers the greatest number of new job opportunities. Among the 30 occupations with the largest growth, 70%—21 out of 30—typically do not require more than a high school degree. To become fully qualified for these jobs, workers will only need on-the-job training. The DOL projects that one-quarter of all jobs in 2016 will be in these 21 occupations, which include retail salespeople, food-preparation and food-service workers, and personal and home care aides.

In fact, the DOL employment projections estimate that more than two-thirds (68%) of the jobs in 2016 will be accessible to workers with a high school degree

---

LABOR MARKET MUSICAL CHAIRS

To understand the data discussed here, try picturing the U.S. labor market as a game of musical chairs, with a few twists. At any time, chairs (job openings) can be added to the circle and players can sit down (get hired). When the music stops at the end of the month, not all the chairs are filled. Still, many people—far more people than the number of empty chairs—are left standing.

Each month, the Bureau of Labor Statistics reports on what happened in that month's game of labor market musical chairs in its various measures of unemployment and in the Job Openings and Labor Turnover Survey (JOLTS). Here's how the BLS scorecard for labor market musical chairs works.

- **Job openings** is a snapshot of the number of jobs available on the last day of the month—the number of empty chairs when the music stops.
- **Hires** are all the new additions to payroll during the month—the number of people who found a chair to sit in while the music was playing. Because many chairs are added to the circle and filled within the same month, the number of hires over a month is typically greater than the number of openings available on the last day of that month.
- **Unemployed persons** are those who looked for a job that month but couldn't find one—the number of people who played the game but were left standing when the music stopped at the end of the month.

or less. Couple this with the fact that today, nearly two-thirds (62%) of the adult labor force has at least some college experience, and an alleged skills gap fails to be convincing as a driving force behind persistent high unemployment.

Low-Skill Workers?

If employers were having a hard time finding qualified workers to fill job openings, you'd think that any workers who are qualified would be snapped right up. But what the unemployment data show is that there remains a substantial backlog of experienced workers looking for jobs or for more hours in their existing part-time jobs in those major industries that have begun hiring—including education, healthcare, durable goods manufacturing, and mining.

Most telling are the *underemployed*—those with part-time jobs who want to work full-time. Today there are more underemployed workers in each of the major industries of the private economy than during the period from 2000 to 2007, as Arjun Jayadev and Mike Konczal document in a 2010 paper published by the Roosevelt Institute. Even in the major industries with the highest number of job openings— education and health services, professional and business services, transportation and utilities, leisure and hospitality, and manufacturing—underemployment in 2010 remains at levels twice as high or nearly twice as high as during the earlier period (measured as a percentage of employed workers).

Purveyors of the mismatch theory would have a hard time explaining how it is that underemployed workers who want full-time work do not possess the skills to do the jobs full time that they are already doing, say, 20 hours a week.

More broadly, workers with a diverse set of skills—not just construction work- ers—lost jobs during the Great Recession. Workers in manufacturing, professional and business services, leisure and hospitality, transportation and utilities, and a host of other industries were turned out of their jobs. And many of these experienced workers are still looking for work. In each of the 16 major industries of the economy unemployment rates in September 2010 were still far higher than they had been at the onset of the Great Recession in December 2007. In the industries with a large number of (cumulative) job openings during the recovery—education and health services, professional and business services, and manufacturing—experienced work- ers face unemployment rates twice what they were back in December 2007.

There are plenty of experienced workers still looking for work in the industries with job openings. To be faithful to the data, Kocherlakota and the other mismatch proponents would need to show that experienced workers no longer possess the skills to work in their industry, even though that industry employed them no more than three years ago. That seems implausible.

Statistical Errors

Still, the statistical oddity that Bill Clinton and many economists have pointed to does seem to complicate the picture. If the number of job openings is rising at a good clip yet the number of new hires is growing more slowly and the unemploy- ment rate is stagnant, then maybe employers *are* having trouble finding qualified folks to hire. Once you take a closer looks at the numbers, though, there is less here than meets the eye.

First, the *rate* at which job openings and new hires numbers change over time is not the right place to look. What we really need to know is how the number of unfilled job posts compares to the number of qualified workers employers hire over the same month. If employers in today's recovery are having a hard time finding workers, then the job openings left unfilled at the end of the month should be relatively high compared to the number of newly hired workers that month. In other words, if the number of positions left unfilled at the end of the month relative to the number of new hires rises *above* what we've seen during past recoveries, this would mean that employers are finding it harder to fill their positions with the right workers this time around.

But it turns out that the ratio of unfilled job openings to new hires is approximately the same during this recovery as in the recovery from the 2001 recession. In September 2010, fifteen months into the current economic recovery, the ratio of job posts left unoccupied at the end of the month to the number of monthly new hires stood at 69%—very close to its 67% level in February 2003, fifteen months into the

---

WHERE MISMATCHES MAY MATTER

The skills-mismatch theory does not go very far toward explaining stubbornly high U.S. unemployment. Still, there are unquestionably some unemployed and underemployed workers whose job prospects are limited by "structural" factors.

One kind of structural unemployment that does seem to fit the contours of the Great Recession to at least some degree is that caused by a mismatch of geography: the workers are in one part of the country while the jobs they could get are in another. The housing crisis surely has compromised the ability of unemployed workers to unload their single largest asset, a house, and move to another part of the country. Plus, job losses have been particularly heavy in regions where the housing crisis hit hardest.

But at the same time, lost jobs have been widespread across industries and there is little real evidence of geographic mismatch between job openings and unemployed workers. As labor economist Michael Reich reports, "economic decline and the growth of unemployment have been more widespread than ever before, making it unclear where the unemployed should migrate for greater job opportunities."

Even where there is a skills mismatch, that doesn't mean the government shouldn't get involved. On the contrary, government policies to boost economic demand can help significantly. When demand is high, labor markets become very tight and there are few available workers to hire. Workers previously viewed as "unemployable" get hired, get experience and on-the-job training, and see their overall career prospects brighten.

And, of course, government can fund expanded job-training programs. If the economy continues to slog along with low growth rates and persistent unemployment, the ranks of the long-term unemployed will rise. As they go longer and longer without work, their skills will atrophy or become obsolete and they will face a genuine skills-mismatch problem that will make job-training programs more and more necessary.

last recovery. In other words, today's employers are filling their job openings with the same rate of success as yesterday's employers.

Comparisons that focus on the unemployment rate rather than on the number of new hires are even less meaningful. As hiring picks up at the beginning of an economic recovery, workers who had given up the job search start looking again. This brings them back into the official count of the unemployed, keeping the unemployment rate from dropping even as both job openings and new hires rise.

Not Enough Jobs

The reality of the situation—the widespread job losses and the long, fruitless job searches of experienced workers—make it clear that today's employment problem is a jobs deficit across the economy, not a skills deficit among those looking for work.

While it's true that any given month ends with some number of unfilled job openings, the total number of jobs added to the economy during this recovery has simply been inadequate to put the unemployed back to work. In fact, if every job that stood open at the end of September 2010 had been filled, 11.7 million officially unemployed workers would still have been jobless.

This recovery has seen far fewer job openings than even the so-called "jobless" recovery following the 2001 recession. Economists Lawrence Mishel, Heidi Shierholz, and Kathryn Edwards of the Economic Policy Institute report that cumulative job openings during the first year of this recovery were roughly 25% lower than during the first year of the recovery following the 2001 recession—that's 10 million fewer jobs. Even in the industries generating the most job openings in the current recovery—education and health services, professional and business services, leisure and hospitality, and manufacturing—the cumulative number of job openings has lagged well behind the figure for those industries during the first year of the recovery from the 2001 recession. (Only the mining and logging category, which accounted for just 0.5% of employment in 2007, has had more job openings during the first year of this recovery than during the first year of the 2001 recovery.)

Why has the pick-up in jobs following the Great Recession been worse than usual? The simple answer is that the recession was worse than usual. The sharp and extreme decline of output and employment in the Great Recession has severely dampened demand—that is, people have not had money to buy things. With the resulting lack of sales, businesses were not willing to either invest or hire; and this in turn has meant a continuing lack of demand.

If businesses have barely resumed hiring, it has not been for lack of profits. By the middle of 2010, corporate profits (adjusted for inflation) were about 60% above their low point at the end of 2008, well on their way back to the peak level of mid-2006. Also, in early 2010 non-financial firms were sitting on almost $2 trillion in cash. There was no lack of ability to invest and hire, but there was a lack of incentive to invest and hire, that is, a lack of an expectation that demand (sales) would rise. As is well known, small businesses have generally accounted for a disproportionately large share of job growth. Yet, since the onset of the Great Recession, small business owners have consistently identified poor sales as their single most important problem—and thus, presumably, what has prevented them from expanding employment.

The Role of Demand

Regardless of the lack of evidence to support it, the skills-mismatch story has seeped into media coverage of the economy. Take, for example, National Public Radio's recent Morning Edition series titled "Skills gap: holding back the labor market." In one segment, reporter Wendy Kaufman presents anecdotes about employers turning down record numbers of applicants and leaving job openings unfilled. Economist Peter Capelli then comes on and remarks, "You know, a generation ago you'd never expect that somebody could come into a reasonably skilled, sophisticated position in your organization and immediately make a contribution. That's a brand new demand." Now, that comment does not point to today's workers possessing fewer skills or qualifications. Rather, it suggests that employers have raised the bar: they are pickier than in the past.

That makes sense. We've seen that employers are successfully filling positions at about the same rate as in the recent past. What's different this time around is that employers have had up to six unemployed workers competing for every job opening left vacant at the close of the month. This is by far the highest ratio on record with data back to 2000. During the 2001 recession, that ratio rose to just over two unemployed workers for each opening. (In the first years of the "jobless recovery" following the 2001 recession, the ratio continued to rise, but it remained below three to one.) Clearly, these numbers favor the alternative explanation. Unfortunately, Kaufman doesn't even consider it.

That's too bad. Recognizing that a lack of demand for goods and services is to blame for the severe crisis of unemployment puts the focus squarely back on the federal government and on the Fed, which could help to remedy the problem —*if* they had the political will to do so. Millions of unemployed workers, organized and armed with an accurate diagnosis of the problem, could create that political will— unless they are distracted by a wrong-headed diagnosis that tries to blame them for the problem. ❏

Sources: Bureau of Labor Statistics Table A-14, Unemployed persons by industry and class of workers, not seasonally adjusted, historical data (bls.gov); Lawrence Mishel, Heidi Shierholz, and Kathryn Anne Edwards, "Reasons for Skepticism About Structural Unemployment," Economic Policy Institute, Briefing Paper #279, September 22, 2010 (epi.org); Arjun Jayadev and Mike Konczal, "The Stagnating Labor Market," The Roosevelt Institute, September 19, 2010 (rooseveltinstitute. org); Bureau of Labor Statistics, Job Openings and Labor Turnover (JOLTS) Highlights, September 2010 (bls.gov); Michael Reich, "High Unemployment after the Great Recession: Why? What Can We Do?," Policy Brief from the Center on Wage and Employment Dynamics, Institute for Research on Labor and Employment, University of California, Berkeley, June 2010 (irle.berkeley.edu/cwed); Narayana Kocherlakota, President Federal Reserve Bank of Minneapolis, "Inside the FOMC," Marquette, Michigan, August 17, 2010 (minneapolisfed.org); Lawrence Mishel and Katherine Anne Edwards, "Bill Clinton Gets It Wrong," Economic Policy Institute, Economic Snapshot, September 27, 2010 (epi.org); "Remarks of President Barack Obama—Address to Joint Session of Congress," February 24, 2009 (whitehouse.gov); "The Skills Gap: Holding Back the Labor Market," Morning Edition, National Public Radio, November 15, 2010 (npr.org).

Article 6.3

WRONG ABOUT RIGHT-TO-WORK

Laffer throws another curve-ball.

BY JOHN MILLER
July/August 2011

BOEING AND THE UNION BERLIN WALL

Two policies have consistently stood out as the most important in pre-dicting where jobs will be created and incomes will rise. First, states with no income tax generally outperform high income tax states. Second, states that have right-to-work laws grow faster than states with forced unionism.

As of today there are 22 right-to-work states and 28 union-shop states. Over the past decade (2000-09) the right-to-work states grew faster in nearly every respect than their union-shop counterparts: 54.6% versus 41.1% in gross state product, 53.3% versus 40.6% in personal income, 11.9% versus 6.1% in population, and 4.1% versus -0.6% in payrolls.

The Boeing incident makes it clear that right-to-work states have a competitive advantage over forced-union states. So the question arises: Why doesn't every state adopt right-to-work laws?

—Arthur B. Laffer and Stephen Moore, *Wall Street Journal* op-ed, May 13, 2011

What do you get when you mix a *Wall Street Journal* editorial writer with a sup-ply-side economist?

That's right: more of the same.

This time, however, it's right-to-work laws, not taxes, that come in for the full Laffer treatment (although without the illustration on the back of a cocktail napkin).

In May 2011, the National Labor Relations Board (NLRB) issued an injunction to stop defense giant Boeing from moving a jet production line from its unionized factories in Washington state to right-to-work South Carolina. The International Association of Machinists & Aerospace Workers union had filed a complaint that the planned move was in retaliation against strikes the union conducted over the last decade, and thus illegal.

The NLRB decision amounts to "a regulatory wall with one express purpose: to prevent the direct competition of right-to-work states with union-shop states," insist Arthur Laffer, the supply-side economist, and Stephen Moore, former head of the far-right economics think tank Club for Growth and now on the *Wall Street Journal*'s editorial board. Right-to-work laws enforced in 22 states, mostly in the southern and western United States, prohibit businesses and unions from agree-ing to contracts that stipulate that an employer will hire only workers who join the union or pay union dues. In right-to-work states, unions confront a free-rider problem: they have to organize workers who can benefit from collective bargaining without joining (or staying in) the union or paying dues.

The disadvantages that right-to-work states impose on unions give those states a competitive advantage that will enrich them, according to Laffer and Moore. And their report, "Rich States, Poor States," has the numbers to prove it, or so they claim. Right-to-work states grow faster, add more income, create more jobs, and attract more people than states hamstrung by pro-union labor laws.

But it turns out that the claim that right-to-work laws lead states to prosper is no more credible than Laffer's earlier claim that cutting income taxes would spur such an explosion of economic growth that government revenues would actually rise despite the lower tax rates. Much like what Laffer had to say about tax cuts and economic growth, Laffer and Moore make the case for right-to-work laws as the key to economic prosperity through sleight of hand and half-truths.

Let's take a look at exactly where their story goes wrong.

Something Up Their Sleeve

To begin with, Laffer's and Moore's report needs to be read carefully. Their claim is that the economies of states with right-to-work laws grow faster, not that their citizens are better off.

And they are not. For instance, while it is true that both output and income have grown faster in right-to-work states than in other states over the last decade, the growth is from a much lower starting point. In fact, output and income in those states still lag well behind the levels in non-right-to-work states. Personal income per capita averaged $37,134 (in 2010) and real GDP per capita averaged $39,365 (in 2009) in right-to-work states, but $41,312 and $42,513 respectively in the other 28 states.

The positive job creation numbers that Laffer and Moore report for right-to-work states over the last decade haven't resulted in superior job prospects for those out of work. With their faster growing populations, right-to-work states had unemployment rates averaging 8.0% in April of this year, just below the 8.2% average in non-right-to-work states.

And in practice, right-to-work laws are very much "right-to-work-for-less" laws, as union critics call them. In a recent Economic Policy Institute briefing paper, economists Elise Gould and Heidi Shierholz looked closely at the differences in compensation between right-to-work and non-right-to-work states. Controlling for the demographic and job characteristics of workers as well as state-level economic conditions and cost-of-living differences across states, they found that in 2009:

- Wages were 3.2% lower in right-to-work states vs. non-right-to-work states–about $1,500 less annually for a full-time, year-round worker.

- The rate of employer-sponsored health insurance was 2.6 percentage points lower in right-to-work states compared with non-right-to-work states.

- The rate of employer-sponsored pensions was 4.8 percentage points lower in right-to-work states. On top of that, in 2008 the rate of workplace deaths was 57% higher in right-to-work states than non-right-to-work states, while the 2009,poverty rate in right-to-work states averaged 15.0%, considerably above the 12.8% average for non-right-to-work states.

But here is the real kicker: once their effect is isolated from the effects of other factors, right-to-work laws seem to have little or no impact even on economic growth itself. For instance, a 2009 study conducted by economist Lonnie Stevans concludes that:

> While … right-to-work states are likely to have more self-employment and less bankruptcies on average relative to non-right-to-work states, there is certainly no more business capital. … Moreover, from a state's economic standpoint, being right-to-work yields little or no gain in employment and real economic growth. Wages and personal income are both lower in right-to-work states, yet proprietors' income is higher.

Those lower wages and lower personal incomes are especially detrimental in today's fragile economic recovery, still plagued by a lack of consumer spending.

A Bad Move

The evidence above militates against the notion that right-to-work laws are the key to economic prosperity for state economies, and in favor of the notion that anti-union laws, much like deregulation and tax cuts targeted at the rich, are another mechanism for securing more and more for the well-to-do at the expense of most everyone else.

That is especially clear when it comes to Boeing's planned move from Washington state to South Carolina. Ironically, union-heavy Washington tops right-to-work South Carolina in Laffer's and Moore's Economic Outlook Rankings for 2010 and in their Economic Performance Rankings for 1998- 2008. Personal income, output, and employment all grew considerably faster in Washington state than in South Carolina from 1998 to 2008. And personal income per capita and GDP per capita in Washington state ($43,564 and $45,881 respectively) far exceed their levels in South Carolina ($33,163 and $30,845).

Beyond that, unemployment and poverty rates in Washington state are both well below those in South Carolina. By all those measures, Washington's economy is far and away the more vibrant of the two.

Working conditions are a lot better in Washington state too, something not lost on Boeing. Wage workers in Washington state on average make $11,020 a year more than their counterparts in South Carolina. Production workers in Washington state earn $5,560 a year more. South Carolina workers are 69% more likely to die on the job than workers in Washington. And not surprisingly, just 6.2% of wage and salary workers in right-to-work South Carolina were union members in 2010, versus more than 20% in Washington.

So then why does Boeing want to leave the Evergreen State for the Palmetto State? To benefit from a more vibrant economy? Or to take advantage of workers whose ability to organize is hindered by right-to-work laws, whose bargaining power has been eroded by high unemployment and poverty, who have few alternatives than to endure working in far more dangerous conditions while getting paid less than workers in Washington? The numbers speak for themselves.

No wonder the NLRB filed an injunction against Boeing's planned move. Labor board members saw it for what it is: not a mere relocation, but an exercise of raw power intended to bust a union. ❏

Sources: Arthur B. Laffer and Stephen Moore, "Rich States, Poor States: ALEC-Laffer State Economic Competitiveness Index, 3rd edition," Wall Street Journal, April 7, 2010; Lonnie K. Stevans, "The Effect of Endogenous Right-to-Work Laws on Business and Economic Conditions in the United States: A Multivariate Approach," Review of Law & Economics, Vol. 5, Issue 1, 2009; Elise Gould and Heidi Shierholz, "The Compensation Penalty of 'Right-to-Work' Laws," Economic Policy Institute Briefing Paper #299, February 17, 2011 (epi.org); Gordon Lafar, "'Right-to-Work': Wrong in New Hampshire," Economic Policy Briefing Paper #302, April 5, 2011 (epi.org); Carl Horowitz, "NLRB Sues Boeing; Seeks End to Commercial Jet Production in South Carolina," National Legal and Policy Center, May 4, 2011 (nlpc.org).

Article 6.4

SKEW YOU!

WSJ *editors are upset that Obamacare makes workers less desperate.*

BY JOHN MILLER
March/April 2014

No less than the Congressional Budget Office reported that the health law is causing Americans to work less or not at all. CBO says the economy will lose the equivalent of two million full-time workers by 2017 and 2.5 million over the next decade.

CBO's conclusion is that ObamaCare will encourage people to supply less labor by deciding not to take a job or by working fewer hours. CBO doesn't note, though we will, that simply extending "free" coverage skews job search decisions by offering an in-kind bonus for unemployment.

The White House seems to [think] that the report is positive because "individuals will be empowered to make choices about their own lives and livelihoods" and "have the opportunity to pursue their dreams." There you have it: the new American dream of not working.

—"The Jobless Care Act," Review and Outlook, *Wall Street Journal*, Feb. 4, 2014.

They just couldn't help themselves. It wasn't enough for the *Wall Street Journal* editors that the Congressional Budget Office (CBO) reported in February that the Affordable Care Act (ACA) was likely to reduce the size of the U.S. workforce by the equivalent of 2.5 million full-time workers in the next decade.

No, the *Journal* editors just had to add, "CBO doesn't note, though we will, that simply extending 'free' coverage skews job search decisions by offering an in-kind bonus for unemployment."

I guess we should be grateful. It's not that often that the *Journal* editors lay bare their dedication to maintaining the tremendous power enjoyed by owners and employers and the paucity of alternatives available to workers and job-seekers in today's labor market. The editors' conception of freedom for workers amounts to little more than nothing left to lose—the right to seek jobs under conditions dictated by employers and enforced by markets, without public-policy interventions, however modest, that might empower job-seekers.

The ACA is a largely pro-business type of reform. A conservative (Heritage Foundation) designed policy, the ACA built reform on the existing private employer-provided health insurance system, and protects the interests of all the big players in the industry (health-care providers, pharmaceutical companies, and especially insurance companies). So what is it, exactly, about the ACA—and the CBO report—that provoked the *Wall Street Journal* to lay bare the power relations of the labor market for all to see?

Inside the CBO Report

To begin with, what the CBO report, "Labor Market Effects of the Affordable Care Act," didn't say seemed to tick off the editors as much as the White House's insistence that the report was good news. None of the CBO's projection of a smaller labor force comes from a decrease in the demand for labor or the numbers of available jobs—a finding that surely would have been a problem for workers and job-seekers, and would have helped the *Journal* editors build their case against the ACA.

The CBO could not be clearer on this point. Its estimate of the decline in number of hours worked over the next decade, in the words of the report, "stems almost entirely from a net decline in the amount of labor that workers choose to supply, rather than from a net drop in businesses' demand for labor." The CBO calculates that the expansion of Medicaid benefits and health-care subsidies for low-income households in the ACA will boost spending in the economy (net of higher taxes) and, in turn, "boost demand for labor over the next few years."

A decrease in the supply of labor is quite a different story than a decrease in the demand for labor. A decrease in the supply of labor says that workers will choose to work fewer hours, not that they will be unable to find work because of Obamacare.

Why would workers choose to work fewer hours over the next decade? Most fundamentally, fewer workers will be stuck in their jobs because they are afraid of losing their health insurance, as the White House emphasized. A *New York Times* editorial referred to this as just what it is: "freeing workers from the insurance trap." The ACA's subsidy for low-income individuals to purchase private insurance is the most important reason for this effect, according to CBO, followed by the health-care law's expansion of Medicaid.

Skewing in the Right Direction

The CBO's empirical estimates are, as they admit, "subject to substantial uncertainty." But a reduction in the supply of labor, whatever its exact size, will surely alter labor-market outcomes. For the *WSJ* editors, that amounts to a "skewing" of job-seekers' decision making that needs to opposed. But those changes will empower workers, especially low-income workers.

The CBO's findings show that the ACA will reduce unemployment. The equivalent of 2.5 million full-time workers—counting both those who are unemployed and those who are employed but unable to find full-time work—are looking for jobs. Due to the ACA, the number of unemployed and involuntarily part-time workers will drop. And when full-time workers are harder for employers to come by, job-seekers should find their bargaining power enhanced.

This should also drive up wages of those who do have jobs. That's a result that most any introductory economics student would anticipate. A decrease in the supply of labor reduces the equilibrium quantity of labor (employment) and increases the equilibrium price (the wage rate). In addition, the ACA will reduce federal budget deficits. The report directs the reader to a letter the CBO sent to House Speaker Boehner estimating that the likely effect of repealing the ACA would be "a net increase in the in federal budget deficits of $109 billion over the 2013-22 period." The *WSJ* editors, who have spilled a lot of ink railing against budget deficits, never mention that the ACA will reduce the deficit.

All told, the access to health care afforded by Obamacare undoes the necessity for job-seekers to take undesirable jobs to get health coverage and for workers to stay in undesirable jobs to keep it. The ACA also lowers the unemployment rate, puts upward pressure on wages, and reduces the federal budget deficit.

That's hardly the jobless catastrophe the editors predict. The ACA, however, will "skew" the balance of decision making in favor of job-seekers at the expense of employers, just as the *Journal* editors complain it will. Coming in wake of over three decades of ever-worsening inequality, in which wages have stagnated and profits boomed, while the economy has faltered, a little skewing seems in order.

Universal Health Care and Power

It will take more than the ACA to turn around the profound inequalities of income and power that plague today's economy and that are enforced by the free-market ideology espoused by the *WSJ* editors and their ilk. Surely a single-payer health-insurance system, or "Medicare for all," would have done more to right the imbalance of power that has crippled our economy and concentrated income gains almost exclusively among the most well-to-do.

While even genuinely universal social programs cannot do it alone—not without other equally fundamental changes, like bigger and stronger labor unions or checks on finance and globalization—they can do some real good for most of us.

Truly universal health care would tend to redistribute income and power in society because it provides all workers—not just low-income workers—with the option of switching jobs without risking the loss of health care. Workers with more options can push for higher wages. Universal health-care coverage would create a share of people's income that comes to them as members of society, and is not proportional to their market incomes or dependent on having a job. That contributes to greater income equality and economic security. And to the extent that people have greater economic security, their political as well as their economic power tends to grow.

Finally, a universal health-care program that, unlike the ACA, operates largely outside of the market would help to show that problems can be solved through shared responsibility. In that way, healthcare as a right—a service provided by all of us to all of us—would also contribute to undoing the notion, so prevalent for the last few decades, that just about everything should be "left to the market."

If Obamacare turns out to be the first step toward universal health care, then perhaps it truly is a threat to the powers-that-be and the free-market ideologues. Imagine that not only healthcare, but also things like education, from daycare to college, were provided universally—to all of us as a right. That just might usher in an era of economic security and well-being, dramatically reducing the desperate choices many face in today's labor market. Now that surely would render the *Journal* editors apoplectic.

But I say—skew them. ❑

Sources: Congressional Budget Office, The Budget and Economic Outlook: 2014 to 2024, Appendix B and Appendix C, February 2014; CBO, Letter to Honorable John Boehner, July 24, 2012; *New York Times*, "Freeing Workers From the Insurance Trap," Feb. 4, 2014.

Article 6.5

WE'RE NOT LOVIN' IT

Low-wage workers fight to make bad jobs better.

BY NICOLE ASCHOFF
September/October 2013

There's a line in Johnny Paycheck's 1977 hit song that goes "I'd give the shirt right off my back, if I had the guts to say ... Take this job and shove it, I ain't working here no more." In the past year, fast-food, retail, and warehouse workers have shown they do have the guts—but instead of quitting, they're fighting back. From New York to California they're taking to the streets. They're fighting for a living wage, for respect from their bosses, and in some cases, for the right to form a union.

Back in June 2012, eight immigrant workers peeling crawfish under sweatshop conditions for C.J.'s Seafood (then a Walmart supplier) went on strike in Louisiana. They stayed out for weeks, demanding an end to forced labor, wage theft, and other unfair labor practices—and they won. Following up on the C.J.'s workers' successful action, Walmart warehouse workers in California and Illinois walked out in September, calling for improved workplace safety and a fair wage. A month later, Walmart associates walked out at 28 stores in twelve cities. The strikes marked the first time in history that Walmart retail workers had ever gone on strike, and were quickly followed by more strikes and demonstrations on Black Friday, the biggest shopping day of the year.

Walmart workers took a breather after the fall strikes, as they battled an NLRB lawsuit brought by the company and strategized their next action. But low-wage workers in other cities quickly picked up the baton. On November 29, hundreds of fast-food workers staged a one-day strike in New York City. The walkout marked the launch of Fast Food Forward, a new coalition of workers, unions, and community and civil-rights groups working to increase the wages of New York City fast-food workers. By April of this year, more workers were ready to join the fight. In a wave of strikes that would last through June, fast-food and retail workers in New York, Chicago, Seattle, Milwaukee, St. Louis, and Detroit walked off the job. Pickets popped up at KFC, Jimmy John's, Chipotle, Target, McDonald's, Burger King, Popeye's, Long John Silver's, Subway, Sears, Victoria's Secret, and dozens of other establishments. On August 29, a day after the fiftieth anniversary of the March on Washington, workers took to the streets again. Thousands of workers in nearly sixty cities participated in work stoppages, demanding $15 an hour, respect from management, safe working conditions, better hours, and the right to unionize.

What has sparked this upsurge? It's hard to say. Unions have been trying to gain a foothold in the low-wage service sector for decades—a task made more difficult by the declining bargaining power of unions like the United Food and Commercial Workers union (UFCW) in the face of grocery-industry restructuring. When unions were strong, their very presence pushed up wages and working conditions across the industry, and helped inspire workers hoping to organize a union, or move into existing union jobs in restaurants and supermarkets.

But those days are long gone.

Perhaps a major catalyst to the recent strikes is the nature of the "recovery" from the Great Recession. During the downturn, 78% of jobs lost were either mid-wage or high-wage jobs and, according to the Bureau of Labor Statistics (BLS), three out of five newly created jobs are part-time, low-wage jobs. A growing number of Americans is realizing that "good jobs" aren't coming back, and that for things to get better, they're going to have to fight to turn their McJobs into something better.

Myths about Retail and Fast Food Jobs

Lousy jobs at fast-food joints and retail stores have been around for a long time. Sam Walton (of Walmart) and Ray Kroc (of McDonald's) designed their business models around underpaying their employees. But experts have always brushed off calls to improve these jobs, arguing that they were stepping-stones—summer jobs for teenagers; flexible, part-time jobs for moms; or extra-cash jobs for retirees. It didn't matter that the jobs paid low wages and offered little opportunity for advancement because they weren't designed to support a family or be a career.

But, as good jobs have steadily disappeared over the past three decades, these rationalizations are starting to sound pretty tired. A recent report by Catherine Ruetschlin at the think-tank Dēmos shows that more than 90% of retail workers are over the age of 20 and that, for the vast majority, this is their full-time, long-term occupation. Labor researchers Stephanie Luce and Naoki Fujita paint a similar picture in a study of New York City-area retail workers. According to their survey, the median age of retail workers in New York is 24 years and the average retail worker has been working in the industry for five years.

The Hamster Wheel of Low-Wage Work

Widespread coverage of the strikes suggests growing public concern over the sustainability of a McJobs economy. Dozens of newspapers, magazines, and blogs have covered the walkouts and the plight of low-wage workers, with many telling a similar story: After working for years, or even decades, at the minimum wage, workers have little to show for their efforts. They make poverty-level wages. They don't make enough money to pay their bills and provide for their families. They have to beg their bosses for more hours to put food on the table and make them eligible for healthcare, but they are often rebuffed or told that hours are contingent on working harder. Many workers try to improve their job prospects by combining work and school, but in most cases, their wages don't pay enough for tuition, so they drop out or just take one class at a time.

And many retail and fast-food workers describe horrible working conditions. They get burned by the fryers, assaulted by customers, and humiliated by their bosses. If they ask for sick days or time off to heal from injuries, or speak up about unsafe working conditions, their hours are cut, they get harassed by their supervisors, they get demerits, or they get fired. At the recent Left Forum conference, a Brooklyn KFC worker described a common scenario: While covering a late-night shift, her boss would call her from home, screaming at her to get off the clock because there were not enough customers to justify paying her. The worker would have to finish her shift without pay.

This scenario is not unique to KFC. A recent report put out by Fast Food Forward shows that, of the 500 fast-food workers surveyed, nearly 85% had experienced some form of wage theft by their employer. The report corroborates the findings of a major study conducted by the National Employment Law Project (NELP) in 2008. The NELP study demonstrated severe and widespread workplace violations in low-wage industries across the United States, ranging from minimum wage, overtime, and "off-the-clock" violations, employer retaliation and discrimination, and straight-up theft through tip-stealing, illegal payroll deductions, and pay-stub violations (see sidebar, p. 14). Sophisticated workflow software exacerbates the problem. In recent years, companies like Microsoft have put out new software that enables managers to schedule workers down to the minute, calling them in for two-to-four-hour shifts once or twice a week, and telling them to be on call all other days.

Does It Have to Be This Way?

Big companies and business organizations like the National Restaurant Association and the National Retail Association are vocal in their opposition to wage increases. Spokespeople for Walmart and Target argue that low wages are necessary to keep prices low and provide jobs in the communities where they operate. In a recent op-ed for the Washington Post, Walmart general regional manager Alex Barron argued against legislation to increase the pay of workers at big-box stores in Washington D.C., claiming higher wages would "result in fewer jobs, higher prices and fewer total retail options."

In fast food, the argument against increasing wages is slightly different. Companies like KFC (owned by Yum! Brands) and McDonald's are dominated by franchisees who rent their businesses from the parent corporation. These franchise owners claim that their margins are paper thin as a result of parent company demands, so they simply can't increase wages and stay in business. The Employment Policies Institute, a Washington, D.C., business lobbying group, reiterated this argument recently in a full-page scare ad published in USA Today. The ad warned workers that, if the $15 campaign was successful, owners would be forced to replace workers with "less-costly, automated alternatives like touch-screen ordering and payment devices."

A number of scholars have challenged these arguments, particularly Walmart's low-wages-for-low-prices ultimatum. University of Colorado-Denver management professor Wayne Cascio has shown, through a comparison of Walmart/Sam's Club and Costco, that low wages are not necessary for high profits and productivity. Costco employees average roughly $35,000 per year ($17 per hour), while Sam's Club workers average roughly $21,000 per year ($10 per hour) and Walmart workers earn an average of less than $9 an hour. Costco also provides it workers predictable, full-time work and health benefits. However, contrary to popular assumptions, Costco actually scores higher in relative financial and operating performance than Walmart. Its stores are more profitable and more productive, and its customers and employees are happier.

Costco is not exceptional. Zeynep Ton, of MIT's Sloan School of Management, has studied retail operations for a decade and argues that "the presumed trade-off between investment in employees and low prices can be broken." "High-road" employers like Trader Joe's, Wegmans, and the Container Store have all found ways to make high profits and provide decent jobs. Catherine Ruetschlin's research shows that a modest wage increase—bumping up the average annual salary of Walmart or Target workers to $25,000—would barely make a dent in big retailers' bottom line, costing them the equivalent of about 1% of total sales. Even if a company like Walmart passed on half the cost of the increase to customers, the average customer would pay roughly $17 more per year, or about 15 cents per shopping visit. And, considering most low-wage workers spend nearly their entire paycheck on necessities, the industry would see a boost in sales ($4 billion to $5 billion more per year) to its own workers. Fast-food companies are highly profitable. McDonald's alone saw profits more than double between 2007 and 2011. They could easily send some of these profits downstream to franchise owners and workers.

So why do most big retailers and fast-food chains insist on a bad-jobs or "low road" model? There are a few reasons. MIT's Ton argues that labor costs are a large, controllable expense, and retailers generally view them as a "cost-driver" rather than a "sales-driver." Store-level managers are pressured by higher-ups to control labor costs as a percentage of weekly or monthly sales. And because store managers have no control over sales (or merchandise mix, store layout, prices, etc.) they respond to pressure from above by cutting employment or forcing workers to work off-the-clock when sales dip. Another factor is financialization—the increasing dominance of finance in the economy. Firms feel a lot of pressure from Wall Street to be a Walmart and not a Costco. As Gerald Davis has argued, the rise of finance and the dominance of "shareholder value" rhetoric have resulted in an emphasis on short-term profits that register in increased share prices and big CEO bonuses.

Rampant Wage-Theft and Abuse

A 2008 study by the National Employment Law Project (NELP) sought to uncover the scope of exploitative and coercive managerial practices that violate workers' legal rights. As expected, the abuses were myriad. The most common one? Wage-theft. According to the NELP report:
- Over 25% of workers interviewed were regularly paid below the minimum wage.
- Nearly 20% did not receive proper compensation for overtime.
- Nearly 17% had not been paid for off-the-clock work in the previous week.

The managers responsible for workplace abuses exhibit a disregard for labor rights that does not stop at under-payment of wages. The NELP study found many workers still remain in harm's way:
- 12% of tipped workers had experienced tip-theft within the previous week.
- 20% of workers had withheld complaints of wage-theft, dangerous conditions, or similar violations from their employer for fear of retaliation.
- 50% of workers who had filed for workers' compensation faced illegal managerial intimidation in reaction their claim. Common tactics include: denying the claim, calling immigration, or even firing the worker. —Aaron Markiewitz

Perhaps the main reason why companies refuse to invest in creating good jobs is that they can. In this era of neoliberalism, there is little external pressure from unions, community groups, or the government forcing companies to create jobs that offer a predictable, full-time workweek paying decent wages and benefits. When ten Walmart butchers in Jacksonville, Tex., voted for a collective-bargaining agreement in 2000, the company simply negated their decision by eliminating delis from every one of its stores in the United States and switching to pre-packaged meat. Even companies with a positive image like Costco have dumped millions of dollars into fighting pro-worker legislation like the Employee Free Choice Act, preferring a paternalistic strategy over unionization.

The Alt-Labor Upsurge

The organizations behind the recent fast-food and retail actions, and even the demands of the strikers themselves, vary considerably. However, one unifying characteristic across the movement is the absence of traditional union-organizing strategies, pushing many observers to classify the movement as an alternative labor, or "alt-labor" movement. "Alt-labor" is shorthand for organizations and campaigns that eschew old-school, one-worksite, one-union strategies, in favor of less risky, and often more effective, community-based methods of organizing and outreach.

Alt-labor strategies are not actually new. Workers adopted them in the 1930s, and organizations like New Labor in New Brunswick, N.J., have been around for years, fighting against wage theft and unsafe workplaces. But as labor scholar Janice Fine notes, non-traditional labor organizations have become increasingly important during the past two decades. New organizations like Brooklyn's New York Communities for Change (out of the ashes of ACORN) have appeared on the scene and are registering real gains. NYCC worked as part of WASH New York, a hybrid labor/community group organizing washeros at Astoria Car Wash & Hi-Tek in Queens. The groundbreaking campaign resulted in the first collective-bargaining agreement for New York car-wash workers. NYCC is also behind Fast Food Forward, another hybrid group that is organizing fast-food workers in Brooklyn, using community support networks to help workers stand up for better wages, hours, and working conditions.

The wave of fast-food and retail strikes that spread from New York to St. Louis, Detroit, Seattle, and other cities in April was spearheaded by broad coalitions like Fast Food Forward. These coalitions are comprised of unions like the Service Employees International Union (SEIU), religious organizations, alt-labor groups like Jobs With Justice, community groups, and immigrant-rights groups. They also share common goals—Fast Food Forward, the St. Louis Organizing Committee, the Workers Organizing Committee of Chicago, and other coalitions in Milwaukee, Detroit, and Seattle are all calling for $15 an hour and the right to organize a union. And rather than organizing through one union, one store at a time, the coalitions are targeting the industry as a whole, staging one-day protests designed to inspire other workers and call attention to their struggle.

The Organization United for Respect at Walmart (OUR Walmart) is the grassroots organization behind the Walmart campaign. OUR Walmart gets much of its funding from UFCW and differs from the fast-food campaigns in that it is explicitly not seeking to form a union. Instead, OUR Walmart's goal is to build a worker-community support network that can pressure Walmart to improve its wages, hours, and working conditions without a collective-bargaining agreement. OUR Walmart has organized short (one-hour or one-day) simultaneous strikes that spotlight Walmart's abuses, while limiting the risk for workers involved. The strategy comes from decades of failing to crack Walmart using traditional organizing strategies.

Many labor scholars laud the actions of these coalitions, but don't see the alt-labor formations as a long-term solution. They argue that because the organizations are funded by external sources like unions, religious organizations, and grants, rather than by members, the organizations will eventually fade away after workers achieve initial successes and the public loses interest. Without a concerted, long-term strategy to unionize, workers will have no way to cement their gains, and will have to keep hitting the streets.

This may be the case, but for many workers, they've got nothing left to lose. There are so few good jobs out there that all strategies with the potential to make bad jobs better and increase wages need to be on the table. Fast-food and retail workers are showing they've got the guts to try something new, and if the past year is sign of things to come, one of these days we might finally have something to sing about on Labor Day. ❏

Sources: Catherine Ruetschlin, "Retail's Hidden Potential: How Raising Wages would Benefit Workers, the Industry and the Overall Economy," Dēmos, November 2012; Stephanie Luce and Naoki Fujita, "Discounted Jobs: How Retailers Sell Workers Short," Murphy Institute, City University of New York and Retail Action Project, 2012; Wayne F. Cascio, "Decency Means More than 'Always Low Prices': A Comparison of Costco to Walmart's Sam's Club," *Academy of Management Perspectives*, August 2006; Zeynep Ton, "Why Good Jobs are Good for Retailers," *Harvard Business Review*, January-February 2012; Gerald Davis, *Managed by the Markets: How Finance Re-Shaped America*, Oxford University Press, USA, 2009; Janice Fine, *Worker Centers: Organizing Communities at the Edge of the Dream*, ILR Press, 2006; Annette Bernhardt, et al., "Broken Laws, Unprotected Workers: Violations of Employment and Labor Laws in America's Cities," National Employment Law Project, 2008 (available at unprotectedworkers.org).

Article 6.6

DOG WALKING AND COLLEGE TEACHING
The Rise of the American Gig Economy

BY GERALD FRIEDMAN
March/April 2014

Growing numbers of Americans no longer hold a regular "job" with a long-term connection to a particular business. Instead, they work "gigs" where they are employed on a particular task or for a defined time, with little more connection to their employer than a consumer has with a particular brand of chips. Borrowed from the music industry, the word "gig" has been applied to all sorts of flexible employment (otherwise referred to as "contingent labor," "temp labor," or the "precariat"). Some have praised the rise of the gig economy for freeing workers from the grip of employers' "internal labor markets," where career advancement is tied to a particular business instead of competitive bidding between employers. Rather than being driven by worker preferences, however, the rise of the gig economy comes from employers' drive to lower costs, especially during business downturns. Gig workers experience greater insecurity than workers in traditional jobs and suffer from lack of access to established systems of social insurance.

FIGURE 1: DISTRIBUTION OF THE LABOR FORCE BY CONTRACT TYPE, 1999

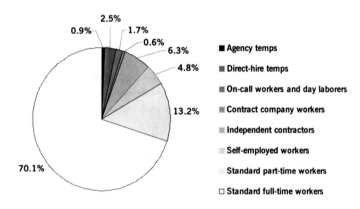

2.5%
0.9%
1.7%
0.6%
6.3%
4.8%
13.2%
70.1%

■ Agency temps
▨ Direct-hire temps
▨ On-call workers and day laborers
▨ Contract company workers
▨ Independent contractors
▨ Self-employed workers
  Standard part-time workers
☐ Standard full-time workers

Special surveys by the Bureau of Labor Statistics in 1995, 2001, and 2005, and by the General Accounting Office in 1999, yielded widely varying estimates of the scale of the gig economy. The GAO estimated that as many as 30% of workers were on some type of contingent labor contract, including some categories of workers (self-employed and part-time workers) who are not counted as contingent workers by the BLS. Using the narrower BLS definition, 12% of workers were on contingent contracts in 1999 (similar to the number estimated from more recent surveys).

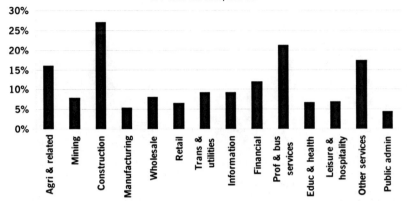

FIGURE 2: SHARE OF WORKERS ON CONTINGENT CONTRACTS, BY INDUSTRY, 2005

Contingent workers are employed throughout the economy, in all industries and in virtually all occupations. Using the BLS definition, which includes independent contractors, temporary workers, on-call workers, and workers provided by contract firms, contingent workers made up over 11% of the labor force in 2005. Some contingent workers do low-wage work in agriculture, construction, manufacturing, retail trade, and services; others are employed as highly paid financial analysts, lawyers, accountants, and physicians.

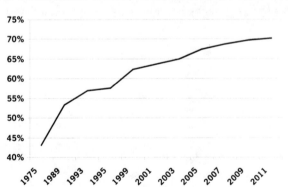

FIGURE 3: CONTINGENT LABOR, COLLEGE AND UNIVERSITY FACULTY

While many people may think of "day laborers" in construction or office "temps" when they think of contingent workers, few occupations have seen as sharp an increase in contingent labor as teaching in higher education. Adjunct and part-time professors now account for the great majority of college faculty nationwide. Tenured and tenure-track faculty now comprise less than a third of the teaching staff, and teach barely half of all classes. Colleges and universities hire adjunct faculty because they make it possible to more precisely match faculty to the demand for classes, and because adjuncts are paid substantially less.

FIGURE 4: AVERAGE EARNINGS, TRADITIONAL VS. CONTINGENT EMPLOYMENT

Employers prefer contingent labor because it is more "flexible." Workers can be laid off at any time in response to a decline in sales. Employers can also pay contingent workers less by not offering benefits. By treating many contingent workers as independent contractors, employers avoid paying for government-mandated benefits (the employer's half of Social Security, unemployment insurance, workers' compensation, etc.). They also usually exclude contingent workers from employer-provided benefits such as health insurance and pensions. Counting wages and benefits, contingent workers are paid substantially less than workers in traditional jobs and are left much more vulnerable to illness or economic downturns.

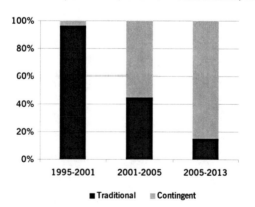

FIGURE 5: NEW JOBS, TRADITIONAL VS. CONTINGENT, 1995-2013

While a solid majority of workers is still employed under traditional arrangements, most new jobs since 2001 have been under contingent arrangements. This is in sharp contrast to the late 1990s, when unemployment rates were low and employers had to offer workers more desirable long-term contracts. With the economic recession of the early 2000s, followed by the Great Recession and the anemic recovery (2007 to the present), however, employers have shunned long-term employment contracts and workers have had to settle. ❑

Sources: General Accounting Office (GAO), Contingent Workers: Incomes and Benefits Lag Behind Those of Rest of Workforce (gao.gov); Bureau of Labor Statistics (BLS), Contingent and Alternative Employment Arrangements, February 2005 and February 2001 (bls.gov); Sharon Cohany, "Workers in Alternative Employment Arrangements." *Monthly Labor Review* (October): 31–46; U.S. Department of Education, National Center for Education Statistics, National Study of Postsecondary Faculty; John Curtis, "Trends in Faculty Employment Status, 1975-2011" (aaup.org).

Article 6.7

AFTER HORROR, APOLOGETICS
Sweatshop apologists cover for intransigent U.S. retail giants.

BY JOHN MILLER
September/October 2013

> Bangladesh just isn't rich enough to support the sort of worker safety laws that we have ourselves. ...
>
> [S]horter working hours ... , safer workplaces, unemployment protections and the rest ... are the products of wealth. ...
>
> [A]ll of us who would like to see those conditions improve ... should be cheering on the export led growth of that Bangladeshi economy.
>
> —Tim Worstall, "Sadly, Bangladesh Simply Cannot Afford Rich World Safety And Working Standards," *Forbes*, April 28, 2013.

The April 24 collapse of the Rana Plaza building, just outside of Dhaka, Bangladesh's capital city, killed over 1,100 garment workers toiling in the country's growing export sector.

The horrors of the Rana Plaza disaster, the worst ever in the garment industry, sent shockwaves across the globe. In the United States, the largest single destination for clothes made in Bangladesh, newspaper editors called on retailers whose wares are made in the country's export factories to sign the legally binding fire-and-safety accord already negotiated by mostly European major retailers. Even some of the business press chimed in. The editors of *Bloomberg Businessweek* admonished global brand-name retailers that safe factories are "not only right but also smart." But just two U.S. retailers signed on, while most opted to sign a non-legally binding ersatz accord.

The business press, however, also turned their pages over to sweatshop defenders, contrarians who refuse to let the catastrophic loss of life in Bangladesh's export factories shake their faith in neoliberal globalization. Tim Worstall, a fellow at London's free-market Adam Smith Institute, told *Forbes* readers that "Bangladesh simply cannot afford rich world safety and working standards." Economist Benjamin Powell, meanwhile, took the argument that sweatshops "improve the lives of their workers and boost growth" out for a spin on the *Forbes* op-ed pages.

The sweatshop defenders are twisting Bangladesh workers' need for more and better jobs into a case for low wages and bad working conditions. Their misleading arguments, moreover, are no excuse for major U.S. retailers to refuse to sign onto the European-initiated safety agreement, a truly positive development in the fight against sweatshops.

More Jobs, Not More Sweatshops

Bangladesh is "dirt poor," as Worstall puts it. The country is on the United Nations' list of 46 Least Developed Countries. Its gross domestic product (GDP) per capita, the most common measure of economic development, is about one-fiftieth that of the United States.

The garment industry is the leading sector of the Bangladeshi economy, responsible for some 80% of total exports by value. Bangladesh's garment exports tripled between 2005 and 2010, boosting the nation's growth rate. By 2011, Bangladesh was the third-largest exporter of clothes in the world, after China and Italy.

On top of that, the garment industry has provided much-needed jobs. Bangladesh has about 5,000 garment factories that employ 3.6 million workers, the vast majority of them women. Wages for women in the garment industry were 13.7% higher than wages for women with similar years of education and experience in other industries in Bangladesh, according to a 2012 study. And the most common alternative employments for women, such as domestic service and agriculture labor, pay far less than factory jobs.

Still, none of that is a good reason to endorse sweatshops.

While Bangladesh's garment industry boosted economic growth and added to employment, neither its horrific working conditions nor its dismally low wages improved without government intervention.

Rana Plaza was a deathtrap. But it was only the latest tragedy to have struck Bangladeshi workers sewing garments for major U.S. and European retailers. Less than five months earlier, a devastating fire at Tazreen Fashions, a garment factory not far from Rana Plaza, killed 117 workers. In addition to the 1,129 workers killed at Rana Plaza, more than 600 garment workers have died in factory fires in Bangladesh since 2005, according to *Fatal Fashion*, a 2013 report published by SOMO Centre for Research on Multinational Corporations. From 2000 to 2010, wages in the garment industry remained flat, according to a survey conducted by War on Want, a British nonprofit. Even after the minimum wage in the garment industry nearly doubled in 2010, itself part of the fight against sweatshop conditions, wages remained among the lowest in the world. A seamstress in Bangladesh earns less than $50 a month, versus $100 in Vietnam and $235 in China, according to World Bank data. The bottom line, as *Businessweek* puts it, is that "Bangladesh's $18 billion garment industry relies on super-low wages and women desperate for work."

This does not mean that trying to improve these conditions is a futile undertaking. Safer working conditions and higher wages are unlikely to stand in the way of investment in Bangladesh's garment industry and job creation.

Factory costs, including wages, make up only a small portion of the overall cost of most garments. Leading Bangladesh garment makers told *Businessweek* that their total factory costs for a $22 pair of jeans was just 90 cents. That's just 4% of the price paid by consumers. On the other hand, a 2009 study of the sales in a major New York retail store found that the company could use "social labeling" to charge up to 20% more and still expect sales revenues to rise. In other words, doubling the wages paid to Bangladeshi garment workers and at the same time improving working conditions would not have to diminish retailer revenues.

Nor does improving worker safety have to be that expensive. The Worker Rights Consortium, an independent labor-rights monitoring group, estimates that it would cost an average of $600,000 to elevate each of Bangladesh's 5,000 factories to Western safety standards, for a total of $3 billion. If the $3 billion were spread over five years, it would add an average of less than 10 cents to the price paid by retail compan each of the 7 billion garments that Bangladesh sells each year to Western brand

How to Stop Sweatshop Abuse

For sweatshop apologists like Worstall and Powell, yet more export-led growth is the key to improving working and safety conditions in Bangladesh. "Economic development, rather than legal mandates," Powell argues, "drives safety improvements." Along the same lines, Worstall claims that rapid economic growth and increasing wealth are what improved working conditions in the United States a century ago and that those same forces, if given a chance, will do the same in Bangladesh.

But their arguments distort the historical record and misrepresent the role of economic development in bringing about social improvement. Working conditions have not improved because of market-led forces alone, but due to economic growth combined with the very kind of social action that sweatshops defenders find objectionable.

U.S. economic history makes that much clear. It was the 1911 Triangle Shirtwaist fire, which cost 146 garment workers their lives, along with the hardships of the Great Depression, that inspired the unionization of garment workers and led to the imposition of government regulations to improve workplace safety. Those reforms, combined with the post-World War II economic boom, nearly eliminated U.S. sweatshops.

Since then, declining economic opportunity, severe cutbacks in inspectors, and declining union representation have paved the way for the return of sweatshops to the United States. This trend further confirms that economic development, by itself, will not eliminate inhuman working conditions.

In contrast, a combination of forces that could eliminate sweatshops is forming in Bangladesh today. Despite the government's record of repressing labor protest and detaining labor leaders, the horror of the Rana Plaza collapse has sparked massive protests and calls for unionization in Bangladesh. In reaction, the government has amended its labor laws to remove some of the obstacles to workers forming unions, although formidable obstacles remain (including the requirement that at least 30% of the workers at an entire company—not at a single workplace as in the United States—be members of a union before the government will grant recognition).

Meanwhile, 80 mostly European retail chains that sell Bangladesh-made garments have signed the legally binding Accord on Fire and Building Safety in Bangladesh. For the first time, apparel manufacturers and retailers will be held accountable for the conditions in the factories that make their clothes. This "joint liability" aspect, a long-held goal of labor-rights advocates, is precisely what makes this international accord so important.

Negotiated with worker-safety groups and labor unions, the five-year accord sets up a governing board with equal numbers of labor and retail representatives, and a chair chosen by the International Labor Organization (ILO). An independent inspector will conduct audits of factory hazards and make the results public. Corrective actions recommended by the inspector will be mandatory and retailers will be forbidden from doing business with noncompliant facilities. Each retailer will contribute to the cost of implementing the accord based on how much they produce in Bangladesh, up to a maximum of $2.5 million over five years to pay for administering the safety plan and pick up the tab for factory repairs and renovations. The accord subjects disputes between retailers and union representatives to arbitration, with decisions enforceable by a court of law in the retailer's home country.

The signatories include Swedish retailer Hennes and Mauritz, which has more of its clothes made in Bangladesh than any other company; Benetton Group S.p.A., the Italian retailer whose order forms were famously found in the rubble of the collapsed Rana Plaza factory; and Canada's Loblow Companies, whose Joe Fresh clothing was also found at Rana Plaza. Together, their clothes are made in over 1,000 of Bangladesh's 5,000 factories.

However, only two U.S. companies, Abercrombie & Fitch and PVH (parent of Tommy Hilfiger and Calvin Klein), have signed the accord. Walmart, The Gap, J.C. Penney, Sears, and the rest of the major U.S. retailers doing business in Bangladesh have refused. The industry trade group, the National Retail Federation, objected to the accord's "one-size-fits-all approach" and its "legally questionable binding arbitration provision" that could bring disputes to court in the highly litigious United States. Several of those retailers cobbled together an alternative agreement signed so far by 17 mostly U.S. retailers.

But their "company-developed and company-controlled" plan, as a coalition of labor-rights groups described it, falls well short of the European-initiated plan. It is not legally binding and lacks labor organization representatives. Moreover, while retailers contribute to the implementation of their safety plan, they will face no binding commitment to pay for improving conditions. An AFL-CIO spokesperson put it most succinctly, "This is a matter of life or death. Quite simply, non-binding is just not good enough." ❑

Sources: JSOMO Centre for Research on Multinational Corporations and Clean Clothes Campaign, *Fatal Fashion*, March 2013; International Labor Rights Forum, "Accord on Fire and Building and Safety in Bangladesh," May 13, 2012; Michael Hiscox and Nicholas Smyth, "Is There Consumer Demand for Improved Labor Standards: Evidence from Field Experiments in Social Labeling," Department of Government, Harvard University, 2012; Rachel Heath and Mushfig Mubarak, "Does Demand or Supply Constrain Investments in Education? Evidence from Garment Sector Jobs in Bangladesh," Aug. 15, 2012; Rubana Huq, "The Economics of a $6.75 Shirt," *Wall Street Journal*, May 16, 2003; "Halfhearted Labor Reform in Bangladesh," *New York Times*, July 17, 2013; "A Handbook on the Bangladesh Labour Act, 2006," International Labour Organization; Renee Dudley, "Bangladesh Fire Safety to Cost Retailers $3 Billion, Group Say," *Businessweek*, Dec. 10, 2012; Mehul Srivastava and Arun Deynath, "In Bangladesh's Paradox for Poor women Workers," *Businessweek*, May 9, 2013; Mehul Srivastava and Sarah Shannon, "Ninety Cents Buys Safety on $22 Jeans in Bangladesh," *Businessweek*, June 6, 2013; "Bloomberg View: How to Fix Bangladesh's Factories," *Businessweek*, May 02, 2013; Steven Greenhouse and Stephanie Clifford, "U.S. Retailers Offer Plan For Safety at Factories," *New York Times*, July 10, 2013; Alliance for Bangladesh Worker Safety, "Alliance of Leading Retailers in North America Join Forces in Comprehensive, Five-Year Commitment to Improve Factory Safety Conditions For Workers in Bangladesh," press release, July 10, 2013.

Article 6.8

INTERNATIONAL LABOR STANDARDS

BY ARTHUR MacEWAN
September/October 2008

> Dear Dr. Dollar:
> *U.S. activists have pushed to get foreign trade agreements to include higher labor standards. But then you hear that developing countries don't want that because cheaper labor without a lot of rules and regulations is what's helping them to bring industries in and build their economies. Is there a way to reconcile these views? Or are the activists just blind to the real needs of the countries they supposedly want to help?*
>
> —Philip Bereaud, Swampscott, Mass.

In 1971, General Emilio Medici, the then-military dictator of Brazil, commented on economic conditions in his country with the infamous line: "The economy is doing fine, but the people aren't."

Like General Medici, the government officials of many low-income countries today see the well-being of their economies in terms of overall output and the profits of firms—those profits that keep bringing in new investment, new industries that "build their economies." It is these officials who typically get to speak for their countries. When someone says that these countries "want" this or that—or "don't want" this or that—it is usually because the countries' officials have expressed this position.

Do we know what the people in these countries want? The people who work in the new, rapidly growing industries, in the mines and fields, and in the small shops and market stalls of low-income countries? Certainly they want better conditions—more to eat, better housing, security for their children, improved health and safety. The officials claim that to obtain these better conditions, they must "build their economies." But just because "the economy is doing fine" does not mean that the people are doing fine.

In fact, in many low-income countries, economic expansion comes along with severe inequality. The people who do the work are not getting a reasonable share of the rising national income (and are sometimes worse off even in absolute terms). Brazil in the early 1970s was a prime example and, in spite of major political change, remains a highly unequal country. Today, in both India and China, as in several other countries, economic growth is coming with increasingly severe inequality.

Workers in these countries struggle to improve their positions. They form—or try to form—independent unions. They demand higher wages and better working conditions. They struggle for political rights. It seems obvious that we should support those struggles, just as we support parallel struggles of workers in our own country. The first principle in supporting workers' struggles, here or anywhere else, is supporting their right to struggle—the right, in particular, to form independent unions without fear of reprisal. Indeed, in the ongoing controversy over the U.S.-

Colombia Free Trade Agreement, the assassination of trade union leaders has rightly been a major issue.

Just how we offer our support—in particular, how we incorporate that support into trade agreements—is a complicated question. Pressure from abroad can help, but applying it is a complex process. A ban on goods produced with child labor, for example, could harm the most impoverished families that depend on children's earnings, or could force some children into worse forms of work (e.g., prostitution). On the other hand, using trade agreements to pressure governments to allow unhindered union organizing efforts by workers seems perfectly legitimate. When workers are denied the right to organize, their work is just one step up from slavery. Trade agreements can also be used to support a set of basic health and safety rights for workers. (Indeed, it might be useful if a few countries refused to enter into trade agreements with the United States until we improve workers' basic organizing rights and health and safety conditions in our own country!)

There is no doubt that the pressures that come through trade sanctions (restricting or banning commerce with another country) or simply from denying free access to the U.S. market can do immediate harm to workers and the general populace of low-income countries. Any struggle for change can generate short-run costs, but the long-run gains—even the hope of those gains—can make those costs acceptable. Consider, for example, the Apartheid-era trade sanctions against South Africa. To the extent that those sanctions were effective, some South African workers were deprived of employment. Nonetheless, the sanctions were widely supported by mass organizations in South Africa. Or note that when workers in this country strike or advocate a boycott of their company in an effort to obtain better conditions, they both lose income and run the risk that their employer will close up shop.

Efforts by people in this country to use trade agreements to raise labor standards in other countries should, whenever possible, take their lead from workers in those countries. It is up to them to decide what costs are acceptable. There are times, however, when popular forces are denied even basic rights to struggle. The best thing we can do, then, is to push for those rights—particularly the right to organize independent unions—that help create the opportunity for workers in poor countries to choose what to fight for. ❑

Chapter 7

THE DISTRIBUTION
OF INCOME

INTRODUCTION

For many mainstream economists, inequality in the distribution of income is a natural outcome of the functioning of markets. If workers get paid based on productivity, wage differences simply reflect underlying differences in productivity.

People who supply other inputs—investors or lenders supplying capital, landowners supplying land—are similarly rewarded according to the marginal products of those inputs. Even poverty is largely seen as a result of low productivity, which can be interpreted more compassionately as the consequence of a lack of education and training, or, at an extreme, as a result of shirking and a whole host of moral failings. President Reagan's deliberate use of the term "welfare queen" to cast poor, black women as undeserving of society's support is perhaps the most famous example of the latter. Indeed, in this view, a high degree of equality (or measures aimed at reducing inequality) would reduce the incentives for increasing productivity, slowing overall growth. Economists also argue that because the rich tend to save more (thus swelling the pool of resources available for investment), the larger the share of the economic pie that goes to them, the better the entire economy does. Trickle on down!

Chris Tilly, in his remarkable essay "Geese, Golden Eggs, and Traps" (Article 7.1), lays out the arguments for and against income equality and then takes down the rosy view of the economic benefits of inequality. His analysis shows how economies such as the United States' can end up in an "inequality trap" where high inequality leads to low growth, which in turn can lead to even higher inequality.

Dean Baker ("Inequality: The Silly Tales Economists Like to Tell," Article 7.2) rebuts mainstream economists' claims that globalization and technological change are the causes of rising inequality (and their implicit view that, therefore, there is nothing that can be done about it). Technological change, he argues, affects both lower-income and higher-income individuals. Meanwhile, the only reason that lower-income workers have borne the brunt of globalization is that, unlike high-income professionals, they lack the political power to secure protection from global competition.

The next two articles look at patterns of inequality along lines of gender and race. In his article "The Wages of Gender" (Article 7.3), Gerald Friedman reports that the gender income gap has narrowed in recent decades, owing to increased educational and work opportunities for women. There is still, however, quite a ways to go to achieve full equality. Meanwhile, Arthur MacEwan observes, in his article "Black-White Income Differences: What's Happened?" (Article 7.4), the income gap between African Americans and whites has hardly budged since 1970. This seeming lack of change, moreover, masks an increase in income inequality among African Americans—with a small number of success stories at the top hiding a worsening of the fortunes of low-income African Americans.

In "New Welfare Policy, Same Single-Mother Poverty" (Article 7.5), Randy Albelda brings us up to date on the current collection of anti-poverty programs and evaluates their relative success or lack thereof. The "feminization of poverty" continues with the Great Recession, adding extra burdens on single mothers. Albelda suggests solutions the country can pursue if it is serious about addressing single-mother poverty as opposed to stigmatizing the poor and powerless.

The last two articles of the chapter return to the balance of power between workers and employers and its effects on the distribution of income. Arthur MacEwan points out that the income share of the richest 1% rose when the share of workers who were union members fell. To MacEwan it seems clear that restoring union size and strength would go a long way toward reducing inequality (Article 7.6).

Alejandro Reuss reflects on the attention drawn to economic inequality by the Occupy Wall Street movement and its language describing society as divided between the 1% (the richest members of society) and the 99% (everyone else). Reuss argues that we should go one step further, recognizing a sharp divide based on how people derive their incomes—from work or from property— and the resulting conflict (or "class struggle") between these two groups (Article 7.7).

Discussion Questions

1. (Article 7.1) According to Tilly, many of the mechanisms linking equality and growth are political. Should economic models incorporate political behavior as well as economic behavior? What are some ways they could do that?

2. (Article 7.1) Explain Tilly's metaphor about the "Goose that Laid the Golden Eggs." How is equality the goose?

4. (Article 7.2) Why does Baker think that increasing inequality is not simply due to unavoidable processes of globalization and technological change? How is economic inequality, in Baker's analysis, related to inequalities in political power?

5. (Article 7.3) What are the key factors explaining the decline of the wage gap between men and women? Has this always been because women's compensation has grown spectacularly?

6. (Article 7.3) According to Friedman, what have been the wider social consequences of the increase in women's educational and work opportunities, and in turn their increasing role as household "breadwinners"?

7. (Article 7.4) MacEwan notes some spectacular African American "success stories" and, more broadly, an increase in opportunities for African American professionals. Nonetheless, the black-white income gap has hardly budged. Why not? What factors does he blame for worsening the fortunes of many African Americans?

8. (Article 7.5) Can you solve the problem of poverty by simply insisting that the poor "work their way out" of poverty? Why is this approach especially hard for single mothers? Do the social stigmas against poor single mothers exact a broader social cost?

9. (Article 7.6) MacEwan shows that union strength and economic inequality are negatively associated (when one is high, the other is low). What possible explanations does MacEwan offer? Is there good reason to believe that higher unionization was the cause of greater equality in the past, and the decline of unions explains increased inequality in recent years?

10. (Article 7.7) Examine the graph that Reuss has provided. Explain what is happening in the graph over time. What does it mean to describe this as an outcome of "class struggle"?

Article 7.1

GEESE, GOLDEN EGGS, AND TRAPS
Why inequality is bad for the economy.

BY CHRIS TILLY
July/August 2004

Whenever progressives propose ways to redistribute wealth from the rich to those with low and moderate incomes, conservative politicians and economists accuse them of trying to kill the goose that lays the golden egg. The advocates of unfettered capitalism proclaim that inequality is good for the economy because it promotes economic growth. Unequal incomes, they say, provide the incentives necessary to guide productive economic decisions by businesses and individuals. Try to reduce inequality, and you'll sap growth. Furthermore, the conservatives argue, growth actually promotes equality by boosting the have-nots more than the haves. So instead of fiddling with who gets how much, the best way to help those at the bottom is to pump up growth.

But these conservative prescriptions are absolutely, dangerously wrong. Instead of the goose-killer, equality turns out to be the goose. Inequality stifles growth; equality gooses it up. Moreover, economic expansion does not necessarily promote equality—instead, it is the types of jobs and the rules of the economic game that matter most.

Inequality: Goose or Goose-Killer?

The conservative argument may be wrong, but it's straightforward. Inequality is good for the economy, conservatives say, because it provides the right incentives for innovation and economic growth. First of all, people will only have the motivation to work hard, innovate, and invest wisely if the economic system rewards them for good economic choices and penalizes bad ones. Robin Hood-style policies that collect from the wealthy and help those who are worse off violate this principle. They reduce the payoff to smart decisions and lessen the sting of dumb ones. The result: people and companies are bound to make less efficient decisions. "We must allow [individuals] to fail, as well as succeed, and we must replace the nanny state with a regime of self-reliance and self-respect," writes conservative lawyer Stephen Kinsella in *The Freeman: Ideas on Liberty* (not clear how the free woman fits in). To prove their point, conservatives point to the former state socialist countries, whose economies had become stagnant and inefficient by the time they fell at the end of the 1980s.

If you don't buy this incentive story, there's always the well-worn trickle-down theory. To grow, the economy needs productive investments: new offices, factories, computers, and machines. To finance such investments takes a pool of savings. The rich save a larger fraction of their incomes than those less well-off. So to spur growth, give more to the well-heeled (or at least take less away from them in the form of taxes), and give less to the down-and-out. The rich will save their money and then invest it, promoting growth that's good for everyone.

Unfortunately for trickle-down, the brilliant economist John Maynard Keynes debunked the theory in his *General Theory of Employment, Interest, and*

Money in 1936. Keynes, whose precepts guided liberal U.S. economic policy from the 1940s through the 1970s, agreed that investments must be financed out of savings. But he showed that most often it's changes in investment that drive savings, rather than the other way around. When businesses are optimistic about the future and invest in building and retooling, the economy booms, all of us make more money, and we put some of it in banks, 401(k)s, stocks, and so on. That is, saving grows to match investment. When companies are glum, the process runs in reverse, and savings shrink to equal investment. This leads to the "paradox of thrift": if people try to save too much, businesses will see less consumer spending, will invest less, and total savings will end up diminishing rather than growing as the economy spirals downward. A number of Keynes's followers added the next logical step: shifting money from the high-saving rich to the high-spending rest of us, and not the other way around, will spur investment and growth.

Of the two conservative arguments in favor of inequality, the incentive argument is a little weightier. Keynes himself agreed that people needed financial consequences to steer their actions, but questioned whether the differences in pay-offs needed to be so huge. Certainly state socialist countries' attempts to replace material incentives with moral exhortation have often fallen short. In 1970, the Cuban government launched the Gran Zafra (Great Harvest), an attempt to reap 10 million tons of sugar cane with (strongly encouraged) volunteer labor. Originally inspired by Che Guevara's ideal of the New Socialist Man (not clear how the New Socialist Woman fit in), the effort ended with Fidel Castro tearfully apologizing to the Cuban people in a nationally broadcast speech for letting wishful thinking guide economic policy.

But before conceding this point to the conservatives, let's look at the evidence about the connection between equality and growth. Economists William Easterly of New York University and Gary Fields of Cornell University have recently summarized this evidence:

- Countries, and regions within countries, with more equal incomes grow faster. (These growth figures do not include environmental destruction or improvement. If they knocked off points for environmental destruction and added points for environmental improvement, the correlation between equality and growth would be even stronger, since desperation drives poor people to adopt environmentally destructive practices such as rapid deforestation.)
- Countries with more equally distributed land grow faster.
- Somewhat disturbingly, more ethnically homogeneous countries and regions grow faster—presumably because there are fewer ethnically based inequalities.
- In addition, more worker rights are associated with higher rates of economic growth, according to Josh Bivens and Christian Weller, economists at two Washington think tanks, the Economic Policy Institute and the Center for American Progress.

These patterns recommend a second look at the incentive question. In fact, more equality can actually strengthen incentives and opportunities to produce.

Equality as the Goose

Equality can boost growth in several ways. Perhaps the simplest is that study after study has shown that farmland is more productive when cultivated in small plots. So organizations promoting more equal distribution of land, like Brazil's Landless Workers' Movement, are not just helping the landless poor—they're contributing to agricultural productivity!

Another reason for the link between equality and growth is what Easterly calls "match effects," which have been highlighted in research by Stanford's Paul Roemer and others in recent years. One example of a match effect is the fact that well-educated people are most productive when working with others who have lots of schooling. Likewise, people working with computers are more productive when many others have computers (so that, for example, email communication is widespread, and know-how about computer repair and software is easy to come by). In very unequal societies, highly educated, computer-using elites are surrounded by majorities with little education and no computer access, dragging down their productivity. This decreases young people's incentive to get more education and businesses' incentive to invest in computers, since the pay-off will be smaller.

Match effects can even matter at the level of a metropolitan area. Urban economist Larry Ledebur looked at income and employment growth in 85 U.S. cities and their neighboring suburbs. He found that where the income gap between those in the suburbs and those in the city was largest, income and job growth was slower for everyone.

"Pressure effects" also help explain why equality sparks growth. Policies that close off the low-road strategy of exploiting poor and working people create pressure effects, driving economic elites to search for investment opportunities that pay off by boosting productivity rather than squeezing the have-nots harder. For example, where workers have more rights, they will place greater demands on businesses. Business owners will respond by trying to increase productivity, both to remain profitable even after paying higher wages, and to find ways to produce with fewer workers. The CIO union drives in U.S. mass production industries in the 1930s and 1940s provide much of the explanation for the superb productivity growth of the 1950s and 1960s. (The absence of pressure effects may help explain why many past and present state socialist countries have seen slow growth, since they tend to offer numerous protections for workers but no right to organize independent unions.) Similarly, if a government buys out large land-holdings in order to break them up, wealthy families who simply kept their fortunes tied up in land for generations will look for new, productive investments. Industrialization in Asian "tigers" South Korea and Taiwan took off in the 1950s on the wings of funds freed up in exactly this way.

Inequality, Conflict, and Growth

Inequality hinders growth in another important way: it fuels social conflict. Stark inequality in countries such as Bolivia and Haiti has led to chronic conflict that hobbles economic growth. Moreover, inequality ties up resources in unproductive uses such as paying for large numbers of police and security guards—attempts to prevent individuals from redistributing resources through theft.

Ethnic variety is connected to slower growth because, on the average, more ethnically diverse countries are also more likely to be ethnically divided. In other words, the problem isn't ethnic variety itself, but racism and ethnic conflict that can exist among diverse populations. In nations like Guatemala, Congo, and Nigeria, ethnic strife has crippled growth—a problem alien to ethnically uniform Japan and South Korea. The reasons are similar to some of the reasons that large class divides hurt growth. Where ethnic divisions (which can take tribal, language, religious, racial, or regional forms) loom large, dominant ethnic groups seek to use government power to better themselves at the expense of other groups, rather than making broad-based investments in education and infrastructure. This can involve keeping down the underdogs—slower growth in the U.S. South for much of the country's history was linked to the Southern system of white supremacy. Or it can involve seizing the surplus of ethnic groups perceived as better off—in the extreme, Nazi Germany's expropriation and genocide of the Jews, who often held professional and commercial jobs.

Of course, the solution to such divisions is not "ethnic cleansing" so that each country has only one ethnic group—in addition to being morally abhorrent, this is simply impossible in a world with 191 countries and 5,000 ethnic groups. Rather, the solution is to diminish ethnic inequalities. Once the 1964 Civil Rights Act forced the South to drop racist laws, the New South's economic growth spurt began. Easterly reports that in countries with strong rule of law, professional bureaucracies, protection of contracts, and freedom from expropriation—all rules that make it harder for one ethnic group to economically oppress another—ethnic diversity has no negative impact on growth.

If more equality leads to faster growth so everybody benefits, why do the rich typically resist redistribution? Looking at the ways that equity seeds growth helps us understand why. The importance of pressure effects tells us that the wealthy often don't think about more productive ways to invest or reorganize their businesses until they are forced to. But also, if a country becomes very unequal, it can get stuck in an "inequality trap." Any redistribution involves a tradeoff for the rich. They lose by giving up part of their wealth, but they gain a share in increased economic growth. The bigger the disparity between the rich and the rest, the more the rich have to lose, and the less likely that the equal share of boosted growth they'll get will make up for their loss. Once the gap goes beyond a certain point, the wealthy have a strong incentive to restrict democracy, and to block spending on education which might lead the poor to challenge economic injustice—making reform that much harder.

Does Economic Growth Reduce Inequality?

If inequality isn't actually good for the economy, what about the second part of the conservatives' argument—that growth itself promotes equality? According to the conservatives, those who care about equality should simply pursue growth and wait for equality to follow.

"A rising tide lifts all boats," President John F. Kennedy famously declared. But he said nothing about which boats will rise fastest when the economic tide comes in. Growth does typically reduce poverty, according to studies reviewed by economist Gary Fields, though some "boats"—especially families with strong barriers to participating in the labor force—stay "stuck in the mud." But inequality can increase at the same time that poverty falls, if the rich gain even faster than the poor do. True, sustained periods of low unemployment, like that in the late 1990s United States, do tend to raise wages at the bottom even faster than salaries at the top. But growth after the recessions of 1991 and 2001 began with years of "jobless recoveries"—growth with inequality.

For decades the prevailing view about growth and inequality within countries was that expressed by Simon Kuznets in his 1955 presidential address to the American Economic Association. Kuznets argued that as countries grew, inequality would first increase, then decrease. The reason is that people will gradually move from the low-income agricultural sector to higher-income industrial jobs—with inequality peaking when the workforce is equally divided between low- and high-income sectors. For mature industrial economies, Kuznets's proposition counsels focusing on growth, assuming that it will bring equity. In developing countries, it calls for enduring current inequality for the sake of future equity and prosperity.

But economic growth doesn't automatically fuel equality. In 1998, economists Klaus Deininger and Lyn Squire traced inequality and growth over time in 48 countries. Five followed the Kuznets pattern, four followed the reverse pattern (decreasing inequality followed by an increase), and the rest showed no systematic pattern. In the United States, for example:

- incomes became more equal during the 1930s through 1940s New Deal period (a time that included economic decline followed by growth);
- from the 1950s through the 1970s, income gaps lessened during booms and expanded during slumps;
- from the late 1970s forward, income inequality worsened fairly consistently, whether the economy was stagnating or growing.

The reasons are not hard to guess. The New Deal introduced widespread unionization, a minimum wage, social security, unemployment insurance, and welfare. Since the late 1970s, unions have declined, the inflation-adjusted value of the minimum wage has fallen, and the social safety net has been shredded. In the United States, as elsewhere, growth only promotes equality if policies and institutions to support equity are in place.

Trapped?

Let's revisit the idea of an inequality trap. The notion is that as the gap between the rich and everybody else grows wider, the wealthy become more willing to give up overall growth in return for the larger share they're getting for themselves. The "haves" back policies to control the "have-nots," instead of devoting social resources to educating the poor so they'll be more productive.

Sound familiar? It should. After two decades of widening inequality, the last few years have brought us massive tax cuts that primarily benefit the wealthiest, at the expense of investment in infrastructure and the education, child care, and income supports that would help raise less well-off kids to be productive adults. Federal and state governments have cranked up expenditures on prisons, police, and "homeland security," and Republican campaign organizations have devoted major resources to keeping blacks and the poor away from the polls. If the economic patterns of the past are any indication, we're going to pay for these policies in slower growth and stagnation unless we can find our way out of this inequality trap. ❑

Article 7.2

INEQUALITY: THE SILLY TALES ECONOMISTS LIKE TO TELL

BY DEAN BAKER

October 2012; Al Jazeera English

There is no serious dispute that the United States has seen a massive increase in inequality over the last three decades. However there is a major dispute over the causes of this rise in inequality.

The explanation most popular in elite and policy circles is that the rise in inequality was simply the natural working of the economy. Their story is that the explosion of information technology and globalization have increased demand for highly-skilled workers while sharply reducing the demand for less-educated workers.

While the first part of this story is at best questionable, the second part should invite ridicule and derision. It doesn't pass the laugh test.

As far as the technology story, yes information technologies have displaced large amounts of less-skilled labor. So did the technologies that preceded them. There are hundreds of books and articles from the 1950s and 1960s that expressed grave concerns that automation would leave much of the workforce unemployed. Is there evidence that the displacement is taking place more rapidly today than in that era? If so, it is not showing up on our productivity data.

More germane to the issue at hand, unlike the earlier wave of technology, computerization offers the potential for displacing vast amounts of highly skilled labor. Legal research that might have previously required a highly skilled lawyer can now be done by an intelligent college grad and a good search engine. Medical diagnosis and the interpretation of test results that may have previously required a physician, and quite possibly a highly paid specialist, can now be done by technical specialists who may not even have a college education.

There is no reason to believe that current technologies are replacing comparatively more less-educated workers than highly educated workers. The fact that lawyers and doctors largely control how their professions are practiced almost certainly has much more to do with the demand for their services.

If the technology explanation for inequality is weak, the globalization part of the story is positively pernicious. The basic story is that globalization has integrated a huge labor force of billions of workers in developing countries into the world economy. These workers are able to fill many of the jobs that used to provide middle class living standards to workers in the United States and will accept a fraction of the wage. This makes many formerly middle class jobs uncompetitive in the world economy given current wages and currency values.

This part of the story is true. The part that our elite leave out is that there are tens of millions of bright and highly educated workers in the developing world who could fill most of the top paying jobs in the U.S. economy: Doctors, lawyers, accountants, etc. These workers are also willing to work for a small fraction of the wages of their U.S. counterparts since they come from poor countries with much lower standards of living.

The reason why the manufacturing workers, construction workers, and restaurant workers lose their jobs to low-paid workers from the developing world, and doctors and lawyers don't, is that doctors and lawyers use their political power to limit the extent to which they are exposed to competition from their low-paid counterparts in the developing world. Our trade policy has been explicitly designed to remove barriers that prevent General Electric and other companies from moving their manufacturing operations to Mexico, China or other developing countries. By contrast, many of the barriers that make it difficult for foreign professionals to work in the United States have actually been strengthened in the last two decades.

If economics was an honest profession, economists would focus their efforts on documenting the waste associated with protectionist barriers for professionals. They devoted endless research studies to estimating the cost to consumers of tariffs on products like shoes and tires. It speaks to the incredible corruption of the economics profession that there are not hundreds of studies showing the loss to consumers from the barriers to trade in physicians' services. If trade could bring down the wages of physicians in the United States just to European levels, it would save consumers close to $100 billion a year.

But economists are not rewarded for studying the economy. That is why almost everyone in the profession missed the $8 trillion housing bubble, the collapse of which stands to cost the country more than $7 trillion in lost output according to the Congressional Budget Office (that comes to around $60,000 per household).

Few if any economists lost their six-figure paychecks for this disastrous mistake. But most economists are not paid for knowing about the economy. They are paid for telling stories that justify giving more money to rich people. Hence we can look forward to many more people telling us that all the money going to the rich was just the natural workings of the economy. When it comes to all the government rules and regulations that shifted income upward, they just don't know what you're talking about. ❏

Article 7.3

THE WAGES OF GENDER

BY GERALD FRIEDMAN
September/October 2013 and November/December 2013

Fifty years ago, in June 1963, President John F. Kennedy signed the Equal Pay Act, forbidding what he called the "unconscionable practice of paying female employees less wages than male employees for the same job." While acknowledging that "much remains to be done to achieve full equality of economic opportunity," he pronounced the law a "significant step forward."

Women have made much progress since then because of anti-discrimination legislation and the work of millions of activists to open occupations previously closed to women. The gap between men's and women's wages has narrowed significantly, and women have gained access to a broad range of professional and managerial occupations. With these economic gains, the balance of power between the genders and within families has changed because women can support themselves and their families even without a husband.

A great deal, however, still remains to be done. Women still earn less than men for reasons tied to gender—including outright discrimination in many occupations as well as the continued expectation that women will bear the primary responsibility for childcare and other household responsibilities. The great progress made in reducing gender disparities over the past decades shows the importance of maintaining political and social movements to eliminate remaining gender inequities.

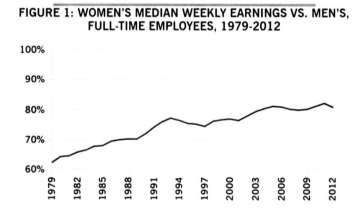

FIGURE 1: WOMEN'S MEDIAN WEEKLY EARNINGS VS. MEN'S, FULL-TIME EMPLOYEES, 1979-2012

The median weekly wage for women employed full time is 81% of the figure for men. While this is a significant shortfall, it is also a significant improvement over the 1979 figure of 62%. While there has been progress in most years, improvement may have slowed. The ratio of women's earnings to men's increased by nearly eight percentage points in the 1980s, five points in the 1990s, and only four points since 2000.

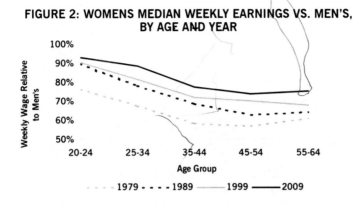

FIGURE 2: WOMENS MEDIAN WEEKLY EARNINGS VS. MEN'S, BY AGE AND YEAR

This graph shows median earnings for women compared to men, across different age groups, in 1979, 1989, 1999, and 2009. At least in part because of gender discrimination and the unequal burdens of family care work, women's wages grow more slowly with age than do those of men (reflected in the downward slope of each curve). This pattern has persisted even while women's wages have increased relative to men's for all age groups (reflected in the curve's consistent rise from one decade to the next).

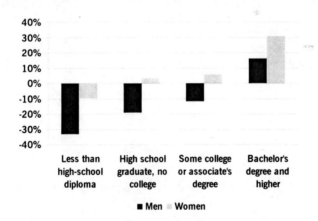

FIGURE 3: PERCENTAGE CHANGE IN INFLATION-ADJUSTED MEDIAN WEEKLY EARNINGS, BY GENDER AND EDUCATION, 1979-2011

Rising relative earnings for women reflect both the entry of women into higher-paid occupations and rising earnings for women relative to men within occupations. Women's wages have risen relative to men's for all levels of education. For less-educated workers, however, much of the narrowing of the gender wage gap has come because women's wages have fallen less than men's have. Only among college graduates has the gender gap narrowed because wages have risen for both women and men, but have risen faster for women.

FIGURE 4: WOMEN'S MEDIAN WEEKLY EARNINGS VS. MEN'S, BY POSITION IN FEMALE AND MALE INCOME RANKINGS

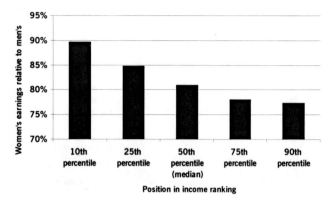

The gender pay gap is greater for higher-income workers. At low-paying jobs, women earn almost as much as men. (Women who are low in the female income ranking make almost 90% as much as men who are low in the male income ranking.) At higher income levels, however, women's pay lags further behind men's. This reflects the continuing exclusion of women from many of the highest-paid occupations and the top positions within occupations—the so-called "glass ceiling."

FIGURE 5: MARRIED WOMEN WHO EARN MORE THAN HUSBANDS, 1947-2011

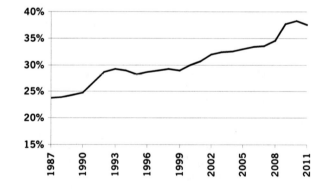

Women earn more than their husbands in a growing share of opposite-sex marriages. This increase is due not only to rising relative wages for women but also to an increase in the proportion of married women working outside the home. In addition, there has been a decline, especially since the beginning of the Great Recession, in the share of married men working outside the home—due both to higher male unemployment and more men dropping out of the labor force altogether.

FIGURE 6: BA DEGREES BY GENDER, UNITED STATES, 1964-2006

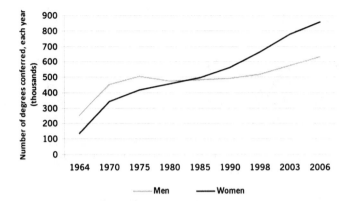

While barely a third of college degrees went to women in the early 1960s, the number of women earning BAs passed the number of men in the 1980s. Since then, college graduation numbers for women have continued to outpace the figures for men. With improvements in their educational attainment, women have gained access to more highly paid professions, like medicine and law, and their incomes have increased accordingly.

FIGURE 7: OCCUPATIONAL DISTRIBUTION, BY GENDER, UNITED STATES, 2011

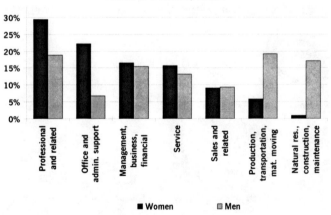

Compared to men, there are relatively few women employed in many traditional blue-collar occupations, including construction, manufacturing, mining, and transportation. To the extent that these jobs were relatively well-paid, the exclusion of women lowered their relative earnings. Over the past 40 years, however, more women have moved into higher paid professional and managerial occupations while wages for production workers have fallen relative to earnings in traditionally female service and office occupations.

FIGURE 8: HOUSEWORK TIME, BY GENDER AND MARITAL STATUS, 1976-2005

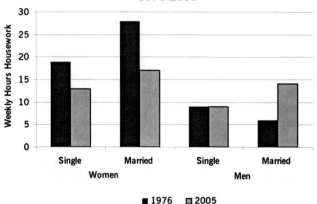

■ 1976 ▨ 2005

In the 1970s, marriage dramatically increased women's housework time while reducing men's. Since then, increasing women's economic equality has been associated with a change in the impact of marriage on housework. As of 2005, married men did more housework than unmarried men, rather than less. While married women still do more housework than men, marriage now causes a relatively small increase in the housework done by women, compared to what it did in the 1970s.

FIGURE 9: WOMEN'S LABOR FORCE PARTICIPATION RATE, BY FAMILY STATUS

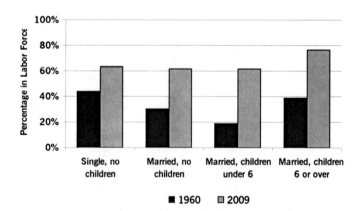

■ 1960 ▨ 2009

In 1960, fewer women were in the paid labor force, many left the labor force when they married, and most left when they had children. Family status has had much less effect on labor-force participation in more recent years. By 2009, few women left the labor force to marry and care for children. By continuing their paid employment, women are able to continue accumulating on-the-job training, remain part of work teams, and generally maintain their careers

FIGURE 10: PERCENTAGE OF TOTAL EMPLOYEES, BY GENDER

Caring Occupations   Other Occupations

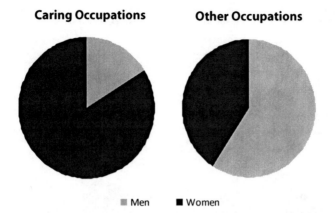

■ Men   ■ Women

Women remain in a vulnerable economic position because their employment is concentrated in a particular subset of the economy. Women are disproportionately employed in "caring" occupations, including elementary school teachers (82% female), nurses (90%), housekeepers (90%), childcare workers (94%), and personal care attendants (87%). Cutbacks in government funding and social support for these occupations could undermine many of the economic gains made by women over the past decades. ❏

Sources: Bureau of Labor Statistics (BLS), Weekly and hourly earnings data from the Current Population Survey; BLS, "Highlights of Women's Earnings in 2011," October 2012; BLS, 1988–2012 Annual Social and Economic Supplements to the Current Population Survey (CPS); BLS, Current Population Survey, Labor Force Participation, Bulletin 2307; Department of Education, National Council of Education Statistics at (nces.ed.gov); Panel Study of Income Dynamics at University of Michigan, Institute for Social Research (www.nsf.gov).

Article 7.4

BLACK-WHITE INCOME DIFFERENCES: WHAT'S HAPPENED?

BY ARTHUR MacEWAN
July/August 2013

Dear Dr. Dollar:
There is a great deal of awareness of the general increase of income inequality in the United States. But what's happened to the income inequality between African Americans and European Americans (the "Black-White" inequality)?
—Andy Druding, Richmond, Calif.

With a president who is African-American and talk of a "post-racial" society, one might think that the economic position of African Americans relative to European Americans had improved significantly over the last 40 or so years. One would be wrong.

In 2011, the median income of Black households was about $32,000; that is, half of Black households had income above this figure, and half had incomes below this figure. This was 61.7% of the 2011 median income of White households. In 1970, before the general increase of income inequality, the figure was 60.9%, just a smidgen lower. Not much change. Also, there has been virtually no change if mean incomes are used for the Black-White comparison. (The "mean" is the average—the total income all households in the group divided by the number of households.)

This lack of change over the last 40 years might come as a surprise, contrary to visible indicators of improvement in the position of Black people. We see, for example, many Black professionals in fields where 40 years ago there were few. There are also more Black executives—even a few CEOs of major corporations. And there is Barack Obama. How do these visible changes square with the lack of change in the relative income positions of Blacks and Whites?

The answer to this question is largely that the distribution of income among Black households is very unequal, even more unequal than the distribution of income among White households. So, many of the prominent Black people who appear to be doing so well are indeed doing well. At the other end are the Black households that are doing worse. Between 1970 and 2011, the upper 5% of Black households saw their average (mean) incomes rise from about $114,000 to about $215,000 (measured in 2011 dollars), while the incomes of Black households in the bottom 20% saw their average income fall from $6,465 to $6,379.

Among White households, the pattern of change was similar but not quite so extreme. The average income of the top 5% of White households rose by 83% in this period, as compared to the 88% increase for the top Black households—though that elite White group was still taking in 50% per household more than their Black counterparts. The bottom 20% of White households saw a 13% increase per household in their inflation-adjusted incomes between 1970 and 2011.

So high-income Blacks have done pretty well—even slightly improved relative to the top White households. They have to a degree benefited from the social changes of recent decades. But for a very large segment of the Black population, not only that bottom 20%, their relative position has gotten somewhat worse, and for many their absolute incomes have actually fallen. The long-term reduction of the minimum wage (in real terms) has had an especially harsh impact on low-income Blacks, and the weakening of labor unions has also harmed a broad swath of the Black community. Add the mass incarceration of young Black men and their consequent exclusion from the economic mainstream, and it is not hard to understand continuing Black-White inequality.

Two other points should be kept in mind: First, the changes between 1970 and 2011 have not been smooth. Measured by either the mean or the median, the income position of Black households relative to White households was fairly stable in the 1970s, fell off sharply in the early 1980s, and rose again to a peak in the late 1990s before falling off to its current level.

Second, income distribution is only one measure of economic inequality. The Great Recession had a devastating impact on the wealth of Black households, largely explained by the impact of the housing crisis. In 2004, the net worth of White households was about eleven times that of Black households (bad enough), about the same as it had been since the early 1980s (with a slight improvement in the mid-1990s). But by 2009, though both Black and White net worth fell from 2004, White net worth was 19 times Black net worth.

The more things change, the more they stay the same—or get worse! ❏

Sources: U.S. Census Bureau, Historical Income Tables: Income Inequality (census.org).

Article 7.5

NEW WELFARE POLICY, SAME SINGLE-MOTHER POVERTY

BY RANDY ALBELDA

January/February 2012

Four years into a period of deep recession and persistent economic crisis, only now has the p-word—poverty—finally surfaced. The Census Bureau's September 13 2011 announcement that the U.S. poverty rate had increased to 15.1% in 2010, up from 14.3% in 2009, put the issue of poverty onto page one, albeit briefly. In fact, poverty and how to address it have not been prominent items on the national agenda since the "welfare reform" debates of the 1980s and early 1990s.

"Welfare queens" may have disappeared from politicians' rhetoric, but poor people, disproportionately single mothers and their children, are still around. Single-mother families have been and continue to be particularly vulnerable to being poor. The September report showed the poverty rate for single mothers and their children rose as well: from 32.5% in 2009 to 34.2% in 2010.

It is remarkably hard to be the primary caregiver *and* garner enough income to support a family. This reality was built into the design of the first generation of federal anti-poverty programs in the United States. Developed beginning in the New Deal era, these programs were aimed at families with no able-bodied male breadwinner and hence no jobs or wages—single mothers, people with disabilities, and elders. Putting single mothers to work was thought to be undesirable. Or, white single mothers—there was much less reluctance in the case of black single mothers, who were largely excluded from the various anti-poverty programs until the 1960s.

The most important of the anti-poverty programs for single mothers was the cash assistance program, Aid to Dependent Children (later renamed Aid to Families with Dependent Children, or AFDC), established in 1935—also commonly referred to as "welfare." Other programs developed in the succeeding decades included Food Stamps, Medicaid, and housing assistance.

Then, in 1996, with the support of President Clinton, Congress abolished AFDC, replacing it with a block grant called TANF (Temporary Assistance to Needy Families), and passed a spate of other changes to related programs. The new anti-poverty regime implied a new social compact with the non-disabled, non-elder poor, supported by both conservatives and liberals: to require employment in exchange for—and ultimately be weaned off of—government support. In other words, the new mandate for poor adults, especially single mothers, was to get a job—any job.

And, in fact, in the ensuing years the number of poor families with wages from work increased. Moreover, welfare rolls dropped. And, in the first four years following welfare "reform," the official poverty rate for single-mother families fell too. (It has been increasing since 2000, although not quite back to its 1996 level.) But despite their higher wage income, many single-mother families are no better able to provide for their basic needs today than before the mid-1990s. Even the lower poverty rate may not reflect the real material well-being of many single moms and their children, given that their mix of resources has shifted to include more of the kinds of income counted by poverty measures and less of the uncounted kinds.

While TANF and the other legislative changes promote employment in theory, they did not reshape anti-poverty programs to genuinely support employment. Key programs are insufficiently funded, leaving many without access to child care and other vital work supports; income eligibility requirements and benefit levels designed for those with no earnings work poorly for low-wage earners; and the sheer amount of time it takes to apply for and keep benefits is at odds with holding down a job.

Ironically, there has been little or no talk of revisiting these policies despite the massive job losses of the Great Recession. With job creation at a standstill, in 2010 the unemployment rate for single mothers was 14.6% (more than one out of every seven). For this and other reasons it is time to "modernize" anti-poverty programs by assuring they do what policy makers and others want them to do—encourage employment while reducing poverty. And they must also serve as an important safety net when work is not available or possible. But changes to government policies are not enough. If employment is to be the route out of poverty, then wages and employer benefits must support workers at basic minimum levels.

Ending "Welfare" And Promoting Employment

Among the changes to U.S. anti-poverty programs in the 1990s, the most sweeping and highly politicized involved AFDC, the cash assistance program for poor parents. The 1996 legislative overhaul gave states tremendous leeway over eligibility rules in the new TANF program. For the first time there was a time limit: states are not allowed to allocate federal TANF money to any adult who has received TANF for 60 months—regardless of how long it took to accrue 60 months of aid. And the new law required recipients whose youngest child is over one year old to do some form of paid or unpaid work—most forms of education and job training don't count—after 24 months of receiving benefits.

To accommodate the push for employment, Congress expanded the Earned Income Tax Credit, which provides refundable tax credits for low-income wage earners; expanded the Child Care Development Block Grant, which gives states money to help provide child care to working parents with low incomes, including parents leaving TANF; and established the State Children's Health Insurance Program (S-CHIP), in part out of a recognition that single mothers entering the workforce were losing Medicaid coverage yet often working for employers who provided unaffordable health insurance coverage or none at all. Even housing assistance programs started promoting employment: the Department of Housing and Urban Development encouraged local housing authorities to redesign housing assistance so as to induce residents to increase their earnings.

The strategy of promoting employment was remarkably successful at getting single mothers into the labor force. In 1995, 63.5% of all single mothers were employed; by 2009, 67.8% were. This rate exceeds that of married mothers, at 66.3%. So with all that employment, why are poverty rates still so high for single-mother families? The answer lies in the nature of low-wage work and the mismatch between poverty reduction policies and employment.

Single Mothers and Low-Wage Jobs Don't Mix

There are two fundamental mismatches single mothers face in this new welfare regime. The first has to do with the awkward pairing of poor mothers and low-wage jobs. In 2009 over one-third of single mothers were in jobs that are low paying (defined as below two-thirds of the median hourly wage, which was $9.06). In addition to the low pay, these jobs typically lack benefits such as paid sick or vacation days and health insurance. Many low-wage jobs that mothers find in retail and hospitality have very irregular work hours, providing the employers with lots of flexibility but workers with almost none. These features of low-wage work wreak havoc for single moms. An irregular work schedule makes child care nearly impossible to arrange. A late school bus, a sick child, or a sick child-care provider can throw a wrench in the best-laid plans for getting to and staying at work. Without paid time off, a missed day of work is a missed day of pay. And too many missed days can easily cost you your job.

Medicaid, the government health insurance program for the poor, does not make up for the lack of employer-sponsored health insurance common in low-wage jobs. Medicaid income eligibility thresholds vary state by state, but are typically so low that many low-wage workers don't qualify. Only 63% of low-wage single mothers have any health insurance coverage at all, compared to 82% of all workers. The new Patient Protection and Affordable Care Act (also known as Obamacare) may help, depending on the cost of purchasing insurance, but for now many low-wage mothers go without health care coverage.

Finally, there is the ultimate reality that there are only 24 hours in a day. Low wages mean working many hours to earn enough to cover basic needs. Yet working more hours means less time with kids. This can be costly in several ways. Hiring babysitters can be expensive. Relying heavily on good-natured relatives who provide care but may not engage and motivate young children also has costs, as does leaving younger children in the care of older brothers and sisters, who in turn can miss out on important after-school learning. Long work hours coupled with a tight budget might mean little time to help do homework, meet with teachers, or participate in in- and out-of-school activities that enrich children's lives.

A New Mismatch

The first generation of anti-poverty programs were designed on the assumption that recipients would not be working outside the home. Unfortunately, their successor programs such as TANF and SNAP, despite their explicit aim of encouraging employment, still do not work well for working people.

What does it mean that these programs are not designed for those with employment? There are two important features. First, income thresholds for eligibility tend to be very low—that is, only those with extremely low earnings qualify. For example, only two states have income thresholds above the poverty line for TANF eligibility. To get any SNAP benefits, a single mother needs to have income below 130% of the poverty line. Working full-time at $10 an hour (that's about $1,600 a month in take-home pay) would make a single mother with one child ineligible for

Poverty Remeasured

According to the Census Bureau, 46.2 million Americans were poor in 2010. But what exactly does "poor" mean? The academic and policy debates over how to measure poverty fill volumes. Some questions relate to the establishment of the poverty threshold. On what basis should the poverty line be drawn? Is poverty relative or absolute—in other words, if the average standard of living in a society rises, should its poverty threshold rise as well? Other questions concern measuring income. What kinds of income should be counted? Before or after taxes and government benefits? Who is included in the poverty assessment? (For example, those in institutional settings such as prisons are excluded from the official U.S. poverty measure—not a minor point when you consider that nearly 2.3 million adults were incarcerated in the United States as of the end of 2009.)

Established in 1963 by multiplying an emergency food budget by three, and adjusted solely for inflation in the years since, the official U.S. poverty thresholds are notoriously low. A family of four bringing in over $22,314—*including* any TANF cash assistance, unemployment or workers' comp, Social Security or veterans' benefits, and child support—is not officially poor. In many parts of the United States, $22K would not be enough to keep one person, let alone four people, off the street and minimally clothed and fed.

An interagency federal effort to develop a more realistic poverty level has just released its new measure, known as the Supplemental Poverty Measure. The SPM makes many adjustments to the traditional calculation:

It counts the Earned Income Tax Credit and non-cash benefits such as food stamps and housing assistance as income.

It subtracts from income out-of-pocket medical costs, certain work-related expenses (e.g., child care), and taxes paid.

Its thresholds are adjusted for cost-of-living differences by region and are relative rather than absolute—basic expenses that are the building blocks of the threshold are pegged at the 33rd percentile of U.S. households.

The SPM poverty rate for 2009 was 15.7%, somewhat higher than the 14.5% official rate. More dramatic differences between the two poverty rates appeared in some subgroups, especially the elderly: 9.9% by the traditional measure versus 16.1% by the SPM, largely due to their high out-of-pocket medical expenses.

—Amy Gluckman

Sources: "Measure by Measure," *The Economist*, January 20, 2011; Ellen Frank, "Measures of Poverty," *Dollars & Sense*, January 2006; Center for Women's Welfare, Univ. of Wash. School of Social Work, "How Does the Self-Sufficiency Standard Compare to the New Supplemental Poverty Measure?"; U.S. Census Bureau, "How the Census Bureau Measures Poverty" and "Poverty Thresholds by Size of Family and Number of Children: 2010."

both programs in all states. Moreover, even if you are eligible, these benefits phase out sharply. With TANF (in most states), SNAP, and housing assistance, for every additional dollar you earn, you lose about 33 cents in each form of support. This means work just does not pay.

Second, applying for and maintaining benefits under these programs often takes a great deal of time. Each program has particular eligibility requirements; each requires different sets of documents to verify eligibility. While some states have tried to move to a "one-stop" system, most require separate applications for each program and, often, one or more office visits. Recertification (i.e., maintaining eligibility) can require assembling further documentation and meeting again with caseworkers. If you have ever applied for one of these programs, maybe you have experienced how time-consuming—and frustrating—the process can be.

In short, the programs were designed for applicants and recipients with plenty of time on their hands. But with employment requirements, this is not the right assumption. Missing time at work to provide more paperwork for the welfare office is just not worth it; there is considerable evidence that many eligible people do not use TANF or SNAP for that reason. Even the benefit levels assume an unlimited amount of time. Until recently, the maximum dollar amount of monthly SNAP benefits was based on a very low-cost food budget that assumed hours of home cooking.

Unlike cash assistance or food assistance, child care subsidies are obviously aimed at "working" mothers. But this program, too, often has onerous reporting requirements. Moreover, in most states the subsidy phases out very quickly especially after recipients' earnings reach the federal poverty line. This means that a worker who gets a small raise at work can suddenly face a steep increase in her child-care bill. (Of course, this is only a problem for the lucky parents who actually receive a child-care subsidy; as mentioned earlier, the lack of funding means that most eligible parents do not.)

The Earned Income Tax Credit is a notable exception. The refundable tax credit was established explicitly to help working parents with low incomes. It is relatively easy to claim (fill out a two page tax form along with the standard income tax forms), and of all the anti-poverty programs it reaches the highest up the income ladder. It even phases out differently: the credit increases as earnings rise, flattens out, and then decreases at higher levels of earnings. Most recipients get the credit in an annual lump sum and so use it very differently from other anti-poverty supports. Families often use the "windfall" to pay off a large bill or to pay for things long put off, like a visit to the dentist or a major car repair. While helpful and relatively easy to get, then, the Earned Income Tax Credit does not typically help with day-to-day expenses as the other anti-poverty programs do.

Has Employment-Promotion "Worked"?

The most striking change in the anti-poverty picture since welfare reform was enacted is that the welfare rolls have plummeted. In 1996, the last full year under the old system, there were 4.43 million families on AFDC nationwide; in 2010, amid the worst labor market in decades, the TANF caseload was only 1.86 million. In fact, when unemployment soared in 2008, only 15 states saw their TANF caseloads increase. The rest continued to experience reductions. Plus, when the TANF rolls fell sharply in the late 1990s, so did Medicaid and Food Stamps enrollments. These programs have since seen increases in usage, especially since the recession, but it's clear that when families lose cash assistance they frequently lose access to other supports as well.

Welfare reform has worked very well, then, if receiving welfare is a bad thing. Indeed, advocates of the new regime tout the rapid and steep decline in welfare use as their main indicator of its success. In and of itself, however, fewer families using anti-poverty programs does not mean less poverty, more personal responsibility, or greater self-sufficiency. During the economic expansion of the late 1990s, the official poverty rate for single mothers and their children fell from 35.8% in 1996 to 28.5% in 2000. It has risen nearly every year since, reaching 34.2% in 2010. But if a successful anti-poverty effort is measured at all by the economic well-being of the targeted families, then that slight drop in the poverty rate is swamped by the 60% decrease in the number of families using welfare over the same period. Far fewer poor families are being served. In 1996, 45.7% of all poor children received some form of income-based cash assistance; in 2009, only 18.7% did. The Great Recession pushed 800,000 additional U.S. families into poverty between 2007 and 2009, yet the TANF rolls rose by only 110,000 over this period.

Data from two federal government reports on TANF, depicted in the chart below, nicely illustrate the dilemmas of the new welfare regime. The chart shows the total average amounts of earnings and the value of major government supports ("means-tested income") for the bottom 40% of single-mother families (by total income) between 1996 and 2005. It is clear that since welfare reform, these families are relying much more on earnings. But despite the additional work effort, they find themselves essentially no better off. The bottom 20% saw their package of earnings

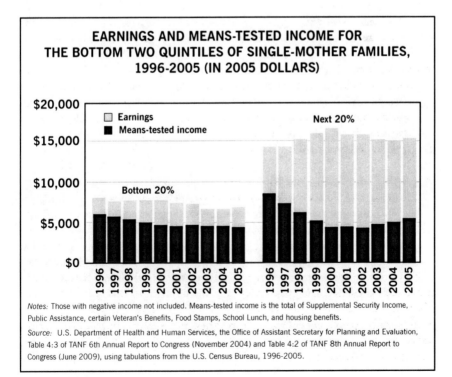

EARNINGS AND MEANS-TESTED INCOME FOR
THE BOTTOM TWO QUINTILES OF SINGLE-MOTHER FAMILIES,
1996-2005 (IN 2005 DOLLARS)

Notes: Those with negative income not included. Means-tested income is the total of Supplemental Security Income, Public Assistance, certain Veteran's Benefits, Food Stamps, School Lunch, and housing benefits.

Source: U.S. Department of Health and Human Services, the Office of Assistant Secretary for Planning and Evaluation, Table 4:3 of TANF 6th Annual Report to Congress (November 2004) and Table 4:2 of TANF 8th Annual Report to Congress (June 2009), using tabulations from the U.S. Census Bureau, 1996-2005.

and government benefits *fall*: their average earnings have not increased much while government supports have dropped off, leaving them with fewer resources on average in 2006 than in 1996. For the second quintile, earnings have increased substantially but benefits have fallen nearly as much, leaving this group only slightly better off over the period. And that is without taking into account the expenses associated with employment (e.g. child care, transportation, work clothes) and with the loss of public supports (such as increased co-payments for child care or health insurance). These women are working a lot more—in the second quintile about double—but are barely better off at all! So much for "making work pay."

More hours of work also means fewer hours with children. If the time a mother spends with her children is worth anything, then substituting earnings for benefits represents a loss of resources to her family.

What Might Be Done?

Employment, even with government supports, is unlikely to provide a substantial share of single-mother families with adequate incomes. Three factors—women's lower pay, the time and money it takes to raise children, and the primary reliance on only one adult to both earn and care for children—combine to make it nearly impossible for a sizeable number of single mothers to move to stable and sufficient levels of resources.

Addressing the time- and money-squeeze that single mothers faced in the old anti-poverty regime and still face in the new one will take thoroughgoing changes in the relations among work, family, and income.

- *Make work pay by shoring up wages and employer benefits.* To ensure that the private sector does its part, raise the minimum wage. A full-time, year-round minimum wage job pays just over the poverty income threshold for a family of two. Conservatives and the small business lobby will trot out the bogeyman of job destruction, but studies on minimum-wage increases show a zero or even positive effect on employment. In addition, mandate paid sick days for all workers and require benefit parity for part-time, temporary, and subcontracted workers. This would close a loophole that a growing number of employers use to dodge fringe benefits.

- *Reform anti-poverty programs to really support employment.* To truly support low-wage employment, anti-poverty programs should increase income eligibility limits so that a worker can receive the supports even while earning and then phase out the programs more gradually so low-wage workers keep getting them until they earn enough not to need them. Also, streamline application processes and make them more user-friendly. Many states have done this for unemployment insurance, car registration, and driver's license renewal. Why not do the same for SNAP, TANF and Medicaid?

- *Support paid and unpaid care work.* A society that expects all able-bodied adults to work—regardless of the age of their children—should also be a society that shares the costs of going to work, by offering programs to care for children and others who need care. This means universal child care and afterschool programs. It also means paid parental leave and paid time off to care for an ill relative. The federal Family and Medical Leave Act gives most workers the right to take unpaid leaves, but many can't afford to. California and New Jersey have extended their temporary disability insurance benefits to cover those facing a wide range of family needs—perhaps a helpful model.

New anti-poverty regime, but same poverty problems. Most single mothers *cannot* work their way out of poverty—definitely not without the right kinds of supplemental support. There are many possible policy steps that could be taken to help them and other low-wage workers get the most out of an inhospitable labor market. But ultimately, better designed assistance to poor and low-income families, old fashioned cash assistance, and minimal employment standards must be part of the formula. ❏

Sources: Randy Albelda and Chris Tilly, *Glass Ceilings and Bottomless Pits: Women's Work, Women's Poverty*, South End Press, 1997; U.S. Census Bureau, *Historical Tables on Poverty*; Kaiser Family Foundation, "Income Eligibility Limits for Working Adults at Application as a Percent of the Federal Poverty Level by Scope of Benefit Package," statehealthfacts.org, January 2011; U.S. Dept. of Health and Human Services, *TANF 6th and 8th Annual Report to Congress*, November 2004 and July 2009; U.S. Dept. of Health and Human Services, *Estimates of Child Care Eligibility and Receipt for Fiscal Year 2006*, April 2010; Thomas Gabe, *Trends in Welfare, Work, and the Economic Well-being of Female Headed Families with Children: 1987-2005*, Congressional Research Service Report RL30797, 2007; Randy Albelda and Heather Boushey, *Bridging the Gaps: A Picture of How Work Supports Work in Ten States*, Center for Social Policy, Univ. of Mass. Boston and Center for Economic and Policy Research, 2007; Author's calculations from the U.S. Census Bureau's Current Population Survey, various years.

Article 7.6

UNIONS AND INCOME INEQUALITY

BY ARTHUR MacEWAN
November/December 2011

Dear Dr. Dollar:
I know unions have shrunk in the United States, but by how much? And how best to respond to my right-wing friends who claim that unions are bad for the economy?
—Rich Sanford, Hardwick, Mass.

Take a look at the graph below. The two lines on the graph show for the period 1917 through 2007 (1) labor union membership as a percentage of the total U.S. work force and (2) the percentage of all income obtained by the highest 1% of income recipients. So the lines show, roughly, the strength of unions and the distribution of income for the past century. (John Miller and I developed this graph for our book *Economic Collapse, Economic Change.*)

The picture is pretty clear. In periods when unions have been strong, income distribution has been less unequal. In periods when unions have been weak, income distribution has been more unequal. In the post-World War II era, union members were about 25% of the labor force; today the figure is about 10%. In those postwar years, the highest-income 1% got 10% to 12% of all income; today they get about 25%.

The causation between union strength and income distribution is not simple. Nonetheless, there are some fairly direct connections. For example, when unions are

UNION MEMBERSHIP AND INCOME INEQUALITY, 1917-2007

Union Membership as a Share of Civilian Labor Force

Share of All Income Going to the Highest-Income 1%

Source: Arthur MacEwan and John A. Miller, *Economic Collapse, Economic Change: Getting to the Root of the Crisis* (M.E. Sharpe, 2011).

strong, they can push for higher wages and thus we see a more equal distribution of income. Also, strong unions can have an impact on the political process, bringing about policies that are more favorable to workers.

But causation can work in the other direction as well. Great income inequality puts more power in the hands of the rich, and they can use that power to get policies put in place that weaken unions—for example, getting people who are hostile to unions appointed to the National Labor Relations Board.

And then there are other factors that affect both union strength and income distribution—for example, the changing structure of the global economy, which places U.S. workers in competition with poorly paid workers elsewhere. Yet the structure of the global economy is itself affected by the distribution of political power. For example, the "free trade" agreements that the United States has established with other countries generally ignore workers' rights (to say nothing of the environment) and go to great lengths to protect the rights of corporations. So, again, causation works in complex ways, and there are certainly other factors that need to be taken account of to explain the relationship shown in the graph.

However one explains the relationship, it is hard to imagine that we can return to a more equal distribution of income while unions remain weak. This means, at the very least, that the interests of unions and of people at the bottom of the income distribution are bound up with one another. Building stronger unions is an important part of fighting poverty—and the hunger and homelessness that are the clear manifestations of poverty.

One important thing to notice in the graph: In the post-World War II years, economic growth was the best we have seen. Certainly no one can claim that it is impossible for strong unions and a more equal distribution of income to co-exist with fairly rapid economic growth. Indeed, we might even argue that strong unions and a more equal distribution of income create favorable conditions for economic growth!

Stronger unions, it turns out, could be good preventive medicine for much of what ails our economy. ❏

Article 7.7

THE 99%, THE 1%, AND CLASS STRUGGLE

BY ALEJANDRO REUSS
November/December 2011

Between 1979 and 2007, the income share of the top 1% of U.S. households (by income rank) more than doubled, to over 17% of total U.S. income. Meanwhile, the income share of the bottom 80% dropped from 57% to 48% of total income. "We are the 99%," the rallying cry of the Occupy Wall Street movement, does a good job at calling attention to the dramatic increase of incomes for those at the very top—and the stagnation of incomes for the majority.

This way of looking at income distribution, however, does not explicitly focus on the different *sources* of people's incomes. Most people get nearly all of their incomes—wages and salaries, as well as employment benefits—by working for someone else. A few people, on the other hand, get much of their income not from work but from ownership of property—profits from a business, dividends from stock, interest income from bonds, rents on land or structures, and so on. People with large property incomes may also draw large salaries or bonuses, especially from managerial jobs. Executive pay, though treated in official government statistics as labor income, derives from control over business firms and really should be counted as property income.

Over the last forty years, the distribution of income in the United States has tilted in favor of capitalists (including business owners, stock- and bond-holders, and corporate executives) and against workers. Between the 1940s and 1960s, U.S. workers' hourly output ("average labor productivity") and workers' real hourly compensation both grew at about 3% per year, so the distribution of income between workers and capitalists changed relatively little. (If the size of a pie doubles and the size

GROWING GAP BETWEEN PRODUCTIVITY AND PAY, 1947-2010

Source: Bureau of Labor Statistics, Real Hourly Compensation, Private Business Sector, Series ID number: PRS84006153; Bureau of Labor Statistics, Output Per Hour, Private Business Sector, Series ID number: PRS84006093.

of your slice also doubles, your share of the pie does not change.) Since the 1970s, productivity has kept growing at over 2% per year. Average hourly compensation, however, has stagnated—growing only about 1% per year (see figure). As the gap between what workers produce and what they get paid has increased, workers' share of total income has fallen, and capitalists' share has increased. Since income from property is overwhelmingly concentrated at the top of the income scale, this has helped fuel the rising income share of "the 1%."

The spectacular rise in some types of income—like bank profits or executive compensation—has provoked widespread outrage. Lower financial profits or CEO pay, however, will not reverse the trend toward greater inequality if the result is only to swell, say, profits for nonfinancial corporations or dividends for wealthy shareholders. Focusing too much on one or another kind of property income distracts from the fact that the overall property-income share has been growing at workers' expense.

Workers and employers—whether they like it or not, recognize it or not, prepare for it or not—are locked in a class struggle. Employers in the United States and other countries, over the last few decades, have recognized that they were in a war and prepared for it. They have been fighting and winning. Workers will only regain what they have lost if they can rebuild their collective fighting strength. In the era of globalized capitalism, this means not only building up labor movements in individual countries, but also creating practical solidarity between workers around the world.

A labor resurgence could end workers' decades-long losing streak at the hands of employers and help reverse the tide of rising inequality. Ultimately, though, this struggle should be about more than just getting a better deal. It should be—and can be—about the possibility of building a new kind of society. The monstrous inequalities of capitalism are plain to see. The need for an appealing alternative—a vision of a cooperative, democratic, and egalitarian way of life—is equally stark. ❑

Sources: Bureau of Labor Statistics, Real Hourly Compensation, Private Business Sector, Series ID number: PRS84006153; Bureau of Labor Statistics, Output Per Hour, Private Business Sector, Series ID number: PRS84006093; Congressional Budget Office, Trends in the Distribution of Household Income Between 1979 and 2007 (October 2011) (www.cbo.gov); James Heintz, "Unpacking the U.S. Labor Share," *Capitalism on Trial: A Conference in Honor of Thomas A. Weisskopf*, Political Economy Research Institute, University of Massachusetts-Amherst (September 2011).

Chapter 8

MARKET FAILURE AND GOVERNMENT POLICY

INTRODUCTION

Markets sometimes fail. Mainstream economists typically focus on cases in which existing markets fail to facilitate exchanges that would make both parties better off. When a factory pollutes the air, people downwind suffer a cost. They might be willing to pay the polluter to curb emissions, but there is no market for clean air. In cases like this, one solution is for the government to step in with regulations that ban industries from imposing pollution costs on others. The same goes when private markets do not provide sufficient amounts of public goods, such as vaccines, from which everyone benefits whether they contribute to paying for them or not. Again, government must step in. But what percentage of pollution should industries be required to eliminate? How much should be spent on public health? To decide how much government should step in, economists propose cost-benefit analysis, suggesting that the government weigh costs against benefits, in much the same way a firm decides how many cars to produce.

Orthodox economists typically see market failures as fairly limited in scope. In fact, they deny that many negative consequences of markets are market failures at all. When workers are paid wages too low to meet their basic needs, economists do not usually call their poverty and overwork market failures, but "incentives" to get a higher-paying job. As we saw in the last chapter, mainstream economists are less concerned about how equally the pie is distributed than the overall size of the pie, although most would agree that governments should help those most in need. Still, when economists do recognize market failures, most argue that they are best solved by markets themselves. So pollution, for example, should be reduced by allowing firms to trade for the right to pollute. Finally, orthodox economists worry about government failure—the possibility that government responses to market failures may cause more problems than they solve. They conclude that the "invisible hand" of the market works pretty well, and that the alternatives, especially the "visible hand" of the state, will only make matters worse.

In "Pricing the Priceless: Inside the Strange World of Cost-Benefit Analysis" (Article 8.1), Lisa Heinzerling and Frank Ackerman point out key flaws in the use of cost-benefit analysis to guide government action. While weighing the costs of a course of action (like pollution limits) against the benefits has a superficial plausibility, cost-benefit analysis fails to make the nature of public choices clearer. It fails, for example, to account for all relevant costs or benefits, it downgrades the importance of the future, and it does not deal with the problem of how costs and benefits are distributed.

The most common complaint from industry and their legions of lobbyists is that there is a rigid trade-off between environmental protection and employment. In "The Phantom Menace: Environmental Regulations are Not 'Job Killers'"(Article 8.2), Garrett-Peltier shows this is a false dichotomy. Enforcing environmental rules and "going green" not only might not cost net jobs, but in fact might create significant new employment, especially in weaning ourselves off hydrocarbon fuels.

In his article "Frackonomics: The Science and Economics of the Gas Boom" (Article 8.3), economist Rob Larson looks at the environmental impacts of this controversial new form of natural-gas extraction. He finds harms including everything from toxic pollution to increased seismic instabiliy. Moreover, he argues, these problems are not well dealt with by neoclassical economics' usual prescription of strengthened private-property rights.

Next, Patricia Rodrgiuez covers large-scale trash dumping, and the grassroots movements against it. In "Lake Country, Not Trash Country!" (Article 8.4), she describes the expansion of trash hauling from major eastern cities to rural areas like the Finger Lakes region of upstate New York, and the environmental problems surrounding it. Local residents, fighting the trash importing, are confronting the waste disposal companies and political elites at all levels.

Finally, in "Universal Healthcare: Can We Afford Anything Less?" (Article 8.6), Gerald Friedman graphically illustrates that a single-payer health care system is entirely affordable and cost-effective. Since the benefits of such a plan outweigh the costs, why do we not have such a system?

Discussion Questions

1. (Article 8.1) Lisa Heinzerling and Frank Ackerman point out a number of flaws in cost-benefit analysis. These weaknesses suggest that the cost-benefit approach will work better in some situations, worse in others. Describe when you would expect it to work better or worse, and explain.

2. (Article 8.1) Make a list of types of goods that are harder to put a price on (valuate) than others. Why is it so hard to price these types of goods?

3. (Article 8.2) Do environmental regulations "kill jobs"? Is this a false dichotomy? If so, why? Why is the concept "net jobs" important here?

4. (Article 8.3) What are the main harms, in Larson's view, from gas extraction by hydraulic fracturing ("fracking")? What are some possible solutions? Why does Larson doubt the viability of solutions based purely on private property and private legal action?

5. (Article 8.4) Rodriguez describes the struggles of Finger Lakes region residents against large-scale trash hauling. Does her account fit with the idea that government acts to protect the general public interest, and therefore will intervene to prevent negative environmental spillovers?

6. (Article 8.5) Should health care be treated as a private commodity or as a public good? What does Friedman think? What is your view?

Article 8.1

PRICING THE PRICELESS
Inside the Strange World of Cost-Benefit Analysis

BY LISA HEINZERLING AND FRANK ACKERMAN
March/April 2003

How strictly should we regulate arsenic in drinking water? Or carbon dioxide in the atmosphere? Or pesticides in our food? Or oil drilling in scenic places? The list of environmental harms and potential regulatory remedies often appears to be endless. In evaluating a proposed new initiative, how do we know if it is worth doing or not? Is there an objective way to decide how to proceed? Cost-benefit analysis promises to provide the solution—to add up the benefits of a public policy and compare them to the costs.

The costs of protecting health and the environment through pollution control devices and other approaches are, by their very nature, measured in dollars. The other side of the balance—calculating the benefits of life, health, and nature in dollars and cents—is far more problematic. Since there are no natural prices for a healthy environment, cost-benefit analysis creates artificial ones. Researchers, for example, may ask a cross-section of the affected population how much they would pay to preserve or protect something that can't be bought in a store. The average American household is supposedly willing to pay $257 to prevent the extinction of bald eagles, $208 to protect humpback whales, and $80 to protect gray wolves.

Costs and benefits of a policy, however, frequently fall at different times. When the analysis spans a number of years, future costs and benefits are *discounted,* or treated as equivalent to smaller amounts of money in today's dollars. The case for discounting begins with the observation that money received today is worth a little more than money received in the future. (For example, if the interest rate is 3%, you only need to deposit about $97 today to get $100 next year. Economists would say that, at a *3% discount rate,* $100 next year has a *present value* of $97.) For longer periods of time, or higher discount rates, the effect is magnified. The important issue for environmental policy is whether this logic also applies to outcomes far in the future, and to opportunities—like long life and good health—that are not naturally stated in dollar terms.

Why Cost-Benefit Analysis Doesn't Work

The case for cost-benefit analysis of environmental protection is, at best, wildly optimistic and, at worst, demonstrably wrong. The method simply does not offer the policy-making panacea its adherents promise. In practice, cost-benefit analysis frequently produces false and misleading results. Moreover, there is no quick fix, because these failures are intrinsic to the methodology, appearing whenever it is applied to any complex environmental problem.

It puts dollar figures on values that are not commodities, and have no price.
Artificial prices have been estimated for many benefits of environmental regulation. Preventing retardation due to childhood lead poisoning comes in at about $9,000 per lost IQ point. Saving a life is ostensibly worth $6.3 million. But what can it mean to say that one life is worth $6.3 million? You cannot buy the right to kill someone for $6.3 million, nor for any other price. If analysts calculated the value of life itself by asking people what it is worth to them (the most common method of valuation of other environmental benefits), the answer would be infinite. The standard response is that a value like $6.3 million is not actually a price on an individual's life or death. Rather, it is a way of expressing the value of small risks of death. If people are willing to pay $6.30 to avoid a one in a million increase in the risk of death, then the "value of a statistical life" is $6.3 million.

It ignores the collective choice presented to society by most public health and environmental problems.
Under the cost-benefit approach, valuation of environmental benefits is based on individuals' private decisions as consumers or workers, not on their public values as citizens. However, policies that protect the environment are often public goods, and are not available for purchase in individual portions. In a classic example of this distinction, the philosopher Mark Sagoff found that his students, in their role as citizens, opposed commercial ski development in a nearby wilderness area, but, in their role as consumers, would plan to go skiing there if the development was built. There is no contradiction between these two views: as individual consumers, the students would have no way to express their collective preference for wilderness preservation. Their individual willingness to pay for skiing would send a misleading signal about their views as citizens.

It is often impossible to arrive at a meaningful social valuation by adding up the willingness to pay expressed by individuals. What could it mean to ask how much you personally are willing to pay to clean up a major oil spill? If no one else contributes, the clean-up won't happen regardless of your decision. As the Nobel Prize-winning economist Amartya Sen has pointed out, if your willingness to pay for a large-scale public initiative is independent of what others are paying, then you probably have not understood the nature of the problem.

It systematically downgrades the importance of the future.
One of the great triumphs of environmental law is that it seeks to avert harms to people and to natural resources in the future, and not only within this generation, but in future generations as well. Indeed, one of the primary objectives of the National Environmental Policy Act, which has been called our basic charter of environmental protection, is to nudge the nation into "fulfill[ing] the responsibilities of each generation as trustee of the environment for succeeding generations."

The time periods involved in protecting the environment are often enormous—even many centuries, in such cases as climate change, radioactive waste, etc. With time spans this long, any discounting will make even global catastrophes seem trivial. At a discount rate of 5%, for example, the deaths of a billion people 500 years from now become less serious than the death of one person today. Seen in this way, discounting looks like a fancy justification for foisting our problems off onto the people who come after us.

It ignores considerations of distribution and fairness.
Cost-benefit analysis adds up all the costs of a policy, adds up all the benefits, and compares the totals. Implicit in this innocuous-sounding procedure is the assumption that it doesn't matter who gets the benefits and who pays the costs. Yet isn't there is an important difference between spending state tax revenues, say, to improve the parks in rich communities, and spending the same revenues to clean up pollution in poor communities?

The problem of equity runs even deeper. Benefits are typically measured by willingness to pay for environmental improvement, and the rich are able and willing to pay for more than the poor. Imagine a cost-benefit analysis of locating an undesirable facility, such as a landfill or incinerator. Wealthy communities are willing to pay more for the benefit of not having the facility in their backyards; thus, under the logic of cost-benefit analysis, the net benefits to society will be maximized by putting the facility in a low-income area. In reality, pollution is typically dumped on the poor without waiting for formal analysis. Still, cost-benefit analysis rationalizes and reinforces the problem, allowing environmental burdens to flow downhill along the income slopes of an unequal society.

Conclusion

There is nothing objective about the basic premises of cost-benefit analysis. Treating individuals solely as consumers, rather than as citizens with a sense of moral responsibility, represents a distinct and highly questionable worldview. Likewise, discounting reflects judgments about the nature of environmental risks and citizens' responsibilities toward future generations.

These assumptions beg fundamental questions about ethics and equity, and one cannot decide whether to embrace them without thinking through the whole range of moral issues they raise. Yet once one has thought through these issues, there is no need then to collapse the complex moral inquiry into a series of numbers. Pricing the priceless just translates our inquiry into a different language, one with a painfully impoverished vocabulary. ❏

This article is a condensed version of the report Pricing the Priceless, *published by the Georgetown Environmental Law and Policy Institute at Georgetown University Law Center. The full report is available on-line at www. ase.tufts.edu/gdae. See also Ackerman and Heinzerling's book on these and related issues,* Priceless: Human Health, the Environment, and the Limits of the Market, *The New Press, January 2004.*

Article 8.2

THE PHANTOM MENACE

Environmental regulations are not "job-killers."

BY HEIDI GARRETT-PELTIER

July/August 2011

Polluting industries, along with the legislators who are in their pockets, consistently claim that environmental regulation will be a "job killer." They counter efforts to control pollution and to protect the environment by claiming that any such measures would increase costs and destroy jobs. But these are empty threats. In fact, the bulk of the evidence shows that environmental regulations do not hinder economic growth or employment and may actually stimulate both.

One recent example of this, the Northeast Regional Greenhouse Gas Initiative (RGGI), is an emissions-allowance program that caps and reduces emissions in ten northeast and mid-Atlantic states. Under RGGI, allowances are auctioned to power companies and the majority of the revenues are used to offset increases in consumer energy bills and to invest in energy efficiency and renewable energy. A report released in February 2011 shows that RGGI has created an economic return of $3 to $4 for every $1 invested, and has created jobs throughout the region. Yet this successful program has come under attack by right-wing ideologues, including the Koch brothers-funded "Americans for Prosperity"; as a result, the state of New Hampshire recently pulled out of the program.

The allegation that environmental regulation is a job-killer is based on a mischaracterization of costs, both by firms and by economists. Firms often frame spending on environmental controls or energy-efficient machinery as a pure cost—wasted spending that reduces profitability. But such expenses should instead be seen as investments that enhance productivity and in turn promote economic development. Not only can these investments lead to lower costs for energy use and waste disposal, they may also direct innovations in the production process itself that could increase the firm's long-run profits. This is the Porter Hypothesis, named after Harvard Business School professor Michael Porter. According to studies conducted by Porter, properly and flexibly designed environmental regulation can trigger innovation that partly or completely offsets the costs of complying with the regulation.

The positive aspects of environmental regulation are overlooked not only by firms, but also by economists who model the costs of compliance without including its widespread benefits. These include reduced mortality, fewer sick days for workers and school children, reduced health-care costs, increased biodiversity, and mitigation of climate change. But most mainstream models leave these benefits out of their calculations. The Environmental Protection Agency, which recently released a study of the impacts of the Clean Air Act from 1990 to 2020, compared the effects of a "cost-only" model with those of a more complete model. In the version which only incorporated the costs of compliance, both GDP and overall economic welfare were expected to decline by 2020 due to Clean Air Act regulations. However, once the costs of compliance were coupled with the benefits, the model showed that both GDP and economic welfare would increase over time, and that by 2020 the economic benefits would outweigh the costs. Likewise, the Office of Management and Budget found that to date the benefits of the law have far exceeded the cost, with an economic return of between $4 and $8 for every $1 invested in compliance.

Environmental regulations do affect jobs. But contrary to claims by polluting industries and congressional Republicans, efforts to protect our environment can actually create jobs. In order to reduce harmful pollution from power plants, for example, an electric company would have to equip plants with scrubbers and other technologies. These technologies would need to be manufactured and installed, creating jobs for people in the manufacturing and construction industries.

The official unemployment rate in the United States is still quite high, hovering around 9%. In this economic climate, politicians are more sensitive than ever to claims that environmental regulation could be a job-killer. By framing investments as wasted costs and relying on incomplete economic models, polluting industries have consistently tried to fight environmental standards. It's time to change the terms of the debate. We need to move beyond fear-mongering about the costs and start capturing the benefits. ❏

Article 8.3

FRACKONOMICS
The Science and Economics of the Gas Boom

BY ROBERT LARSON
July/August 2013

Between 1868 and 1969, Cleveland's Cuyahoga River caught fire at least ten times, including one blaze that reached the Standard Oil refinery where storage tanks detonated. Ultimately, the seemingly impossible and unnatural phenomenon of burning water came to represent the dangers of unregulated industrial development and generated popular support for the environmental laws of the 1970s, including the Clean Water Act and the Safe Drinking Water Act.

Today the unsettling sight of burning water has returned, from a new industry that is exempt from both these laws. In homes near installations using the drilling technique known as hydraulic fracturing, or "fracking," the tap water has been known to ignite with the touch of a lighter. The industry is relatively new, so the scientific literature yields only tentative results and provisional research conclusions. But the early research suggests fracking has serious negative consequences for public health and local ecology, from flaming tap water to toxic chemicals to ground tremors. Industry spokesmen insist that the negative side-effects of fracking are insignificant. But there's one positive side-effect everyone should be able to agree upon: fracking is an ideal vehicle for explaining key economic concepts of market failure and market power, including *externalities, asymmetrical information*, and *regulatory capture*, along with brand-new ones, like *science capture*. Let's start with the firewater.

Liar Liar, Taps on Fire

In the fracking process, natural gas (methane) is released from shale rock strata up to a mile underground, by injecting millions of gallons of water, along with sand and a variety of synthetic chemicals. The huge pressure of the water makes new cracks in the rock, allowing the gas to dissolve and be extracted. Natural gas is now responsible for 30% of U.S. electricity production and for heating half of all U.S. homes. The national and business media have breathlessly reported huge growth in gas production, and the oil-and-gas industry projects that North America will return to exporting energy by 2025. Besides the sheer growth in production, the *Wall Street Journal* reported earlier this year, the fracking boom has brought other economic benefits, "improving employment in some regions and a rebound in U.S.-based manufacturing," and "greater defense against overseas turmoil that can disrupt energy supplies."

As made notorious by the documentary *Gasland*, water supplies are a major focus of concern about fracking, especially since the emergence of dramatic footage of a number of Pennsylvania homes, near fracking pads above the Marcellus Shale formation, producing fireballs from the kitchen tap. Duke University earth scientists conducted a more rigorous exploration of this phenomenon, published in the *Proceedings of the National Academy of the Sciences*. They surveyed rural Pennsylvanian water wells for residential use, measuring concentrations of methane, the main chemical component of natural gas. Concentrations rose far above natural levels closer to drill pads, spiking within one kilometer of active gas development sites to a level that "represents a potential explosion hazard." It was also found that the specific gas chemistry in the wells matched those produced through drilling, rather than through naturally occurring compounds. As the gas boom goes "boom," the cautious scientists conclude: "Greater stewardship, knowledge, and—possibly—regulation are needed to ensure the sustainable future of shale-gas extraction."

In parts of the country where water is scarcer, the issue is more ominous. The Environmental Protection Agency (EPA) and U.S. Geological Survey have found toxic alcohols, glycols, and carcinogenic benzene in underground aquifers in Wyoming, evidence that fracking has tainted precious underground water supplies. In press accounts, local residents who requested the study "expressed gratitude to the EPA, and perhaps a bit of veiled doubt about the zeal of local and state regulators." In parched Texas, the volume of water adequate for irrigating $200,000 worth of crops can be used to frack $2.5 billion-worth of gas or oil. The *Wall Street Journal* reports that "companies have been on a buying spree, snapping up rights to scarce river water—easily outbidding traditional users such as farmers and cities." A Texan rancher relates: "They're just so much bigger and more powerful than we are…We're just kind of the little ant that gets squashed."

Top-Secret Ingredients

The heavy use of often-secret synthetic chemicals has also cast a shadow over the fracking debate. Bloomberg News reported in 2012 that energy companies and well operators were refusing to disclose the chemical formulas of thousands of substances used in the fracking process, enough to "keep [the] U.S. clueless on wells." Many states have instituted a self-reporting law, modeled on one first developed in Texas, allowing drillers to withhold the ingredients used in their chemical mixes. Bloomberg reports that drillers "claimed similar exemptions about 19,000 times" in the first eight months of 2012 alone. The congressional exemption of the industry from federal water requirements (discussed below) makes this non-disclosure possible, so that "neighbors of fracked wells … can't use the disclosures to watch for frack fluids migrating into creeks, rivers and aquifers, because they don't know what to look for."

This development is a perfect example of what economists call *asymmetric information*, where one participant in a transaction knows relevant information that is unknown to the other party. The lack of information on one side can put the other party at an advantage, like the seller of a used car who knows more about the car's problems than the prospective buyer. For example, a team of Colorado endocrinologists set out to catalogue these synthetic compounds used in wells across the country, based on regulatory filings. The survey was limited due to the "void of environmental authority" to compel chemical disclosure, and thus the data sheets and reports are "fraught with gaps in information about the formulation of the products." Many of these reports only specify the general chemical class or use the label "proprietary," providing no additional information. Ultimately, the scientists found that over 75% of the chemicals were harmful for the sensory organs, nearly half could affect the nervous and immune systems, and 25% could cause "cancer and mutations."

Another report by Colorado scientists observed that fracking development is increasingly located "near where people live, work, and play." The study used air sampling to find strongly elevated health risks within a radius of about half a mile from fracking sites. The effects ranged from "headaches and eye irritation" up to "tremors, temporary limb paralysis, and unconsciousness at higher exposures." A larger review by Pennsylvania scientists reached similar conclusions, based on local resident reporting and finding a match of over two-thirds "between known health effects of chemicals detected and symptoms reported."

The scientists caution that their findings "do not constitute definitive proof of cause and effect," but they do "indicate the strong likelihood that the health of people living in proximity to gas facilities is being affected by exposure to pollutants from those facilities." They frequently advocate the *precautionary principle*—that careful study showing that a product or process is *not* harmful should precede its use—as when they recommend "health impact assessments before permitting begins," and note that "scientific knowledge about the health and environmental impacts of shale gas development … are proceeding at a far slower pace than the development itself." These conclusions contradict the industry's claim that fracking is both safe for public health and not in need of any further study. Especially considering the earthquakes.

Tectonic Economics

Perhaps more alarming than the burning water and secret chemicals is the association of fracking with earthquakes. An early report of this development came from the Oklahoma Geological Survey, which surveyed the timing of tremors and their proximity to fracking sites and found a "strong correlation in time and space" and thus "a possibility these earthquakes were induced by hydraulic fracturing." Earthquake epicenters were mostly within two miles of wells, and any earthquake disruption or damage caused by fracking-related activities represents an *externality*, a side effect of an economic transaction that affects parties outside the transaction.

These findings are backed up by a review in the prestigious research journal *Science*, in which cautious scientists note that fracking *itself* is not responsible for "the earthquakes that have been shaking previously calm regions." Yet they find that the induced earthquakes do arise from "all manner of other energy-related fluid injection—including deep disposal of fracking's wastewater, extraction of methane from coal beds, and creation of geothermal energy reservoirs." A surveyed area in Arkansas typically had about two quakes a year, before the beginning of fracking-water disposal. The year water disposal began, the number rose to ten. The next year, to 54. After water injection was halted, the quakes tapered off. The *Science* authors observe the "strongly suggestive" correlation between water disposal and seismic activity: "The quakes began only after injection began, surged when the rate of injection surged, were limited to the vicinity of the wells, and trailed off after injection was stopped." The scientists' main conclusion is the adoption of the precautionary principle: "look before you leap ... Stopping injection has stopped significant earthquakes within days to a year. ... The new regulations in Ohio and Arkansas at least move in the direction of such a learn-as-you-go approach."

Fracknapping

You might wonder why the EPA has not limited or regulated fracking operations, in light of the combustible water, cancer-causing chemicals, and earthquake clusters. The EPA might well have adopted significant national policies on fracking by now, had the practice not been made exempt from the main national environmental laws in the Energy Policy Act of 2005, an offspring of Dick Cheney's secretive energy committee. The exemptions from the Clean Water Act, the Safe Drinking Water Act, the Clean Air Act, and the Superfund law drastically limit the agency's authority to act on fracking.

The drive to limit even EPA *research* into fracking is decades old. An extensive *New York Times* report, based on interviews with scientists and reviews of confidential files, found that "more than a quarter-century of efforts by some lawmakers and regulators to force the federal government to police the industry better have been thwarted, as EPA studies have been repeatedly narrowed in scope and important findings have been removed." When Congress first directed the EPA to investigate fracking in the 1980s, the *Times* reported, EPA scientists found that some fracking waste was "hazardous and should be tightly controlled." But the final report sent to Congress eliminated these conclusions. An agency scientist relates, "It was like science didn't matter. ... The industry was going to get what it wanted, and we were not supposed to stand in the way."

Similarly, when an EPA public-advisory letter to the state of New York called for a moratorium on drilling, the advice was stripped from the released version. A staff scientist said the redaction was due to "politics," but could as well have said "business power." More importantly, the first major EPA review of fracking found "little or no threat to drinking water." This was an eyebrow-raising claim, given that five of seven members of the peer review panel had current or former energy industry affiliations, a detail noted by agency whistle-blower Weston Wilson. Other studies have been narrowed in scope or colored by similar conflicts of interest. More recently, the agency announced that its study finding contamination of Wyoming groundwater will not be subjected to outside peer review, and that further work instead will be funded directly by industry. As the EPA is presently drafting a brand-new report on the subject, these past embarrassments should be kept in mind.

This brings up the problem of *regulatory capture*, where an industry to be monitored gains major influence over regulators' policies. As mentioned above, fracking is very loosely regulated by the states, which is always a favorite outcome for corporate America since the regulatory resources of state governments are far smaller and the regulators are even more easily dominated than those of the federal government. The industry-sponsored FracFocus website is the state-sanctioned chemical-information clearing house, and a masterpiece of smooth PR design, suggesting clear water and full transparency. But Bloomberg News reports that "more than 40 percent of wells fracked in eight major drilling states last year had been omitted from the voluntary site."

Other state reactions have varied. In 2010, the New York State legislature voted to ban fracking, but then-Governor Paterson vetoed the bill and instead issued a temporary moratorium on the practice, though fracking remains illegal in the New York City watershed. Finally, while the EPA's main study is still pending, the agency has taken some steps, as in 2012 when it required well operators to reduce methane gas emissions from wells and storage pits to limit air pollution. But even here the regulation wears kid gloves: The new moves do not cut into industry profits. In fact, capturing the "fugitive" methane, the agency estimates, will *save* the industry $11 to $19 million annually. Also, the regulation won't take effect until 2015.

Neoclassical Gas

Mainstream, or "neoclassical," economic theory considers itself to have solutions to these problems—solutions centered as always on "free markets." The idea is that if firms create chronic health problems or combustible tap water, market forces should drive up their costs, as landowners learn of these firms' practices and demand higher payment for drilling. But as seen above, even households that have already leased their land for gas development remain unaware of the identities and effects of the obscure synthetic chemicals to which they are exposed. This *informational asymmetry*—the firms know things the landowners don't—significantly attenuates the ability of landowners to make informed choices.

On the other hand, households that are located near a drill pad but uninvolved in licensing the drilling will experience the ill effects as externalities. Neoclassicals suggest these can be fixed through a better property-rights system, where surrounding individuals can sue drillers for injuring their health. But this solution runs up against another problem: proving cause-and-effect from a drilling pad to a particular individual's health problems is extremely difficult. The tobacco industry notoriously made this point in court for many years, arguing that it was impossible to prove if a man's lung cancer was caused by a four-pack-a-day cigarette habit, as opposed to, say, local auto exhaust. If cause-and-effect is hard to prove in court for cigarettes, doing so for air-delivered volatile organic compounds will be almost impossible.

This problem is aggravated by the use of corporate resources to influence research. The showcase example is a study produced by the University of Texas, "Fact-Based Regulation for Environmental Protection in Shale Gas Development." The study gave fracking a guardedly positive bill of health, finding no evidence of negative health impacts. The commercial media gave the study a good deal of favorable attention, until the revelation that the lead researcher, Dr. Charles G. Groat, formerly of USGS, sits on the board of the Plains Exploration & Production Company, a Houston-based energy firm heavily invested in gas development. His compensation from the board was several times his academic salary, and he also held 40,000 shares of its stock. An in-house review by the university was outspoken, saying "the term 'fact-based' would not apply" to the paper, which was "inappropriately selective ... such that they seemed to suggest that public concerns were without scientific basis and largely resulted from media bias." Groat retired from the university the day the review was released, but this practice has become increasingly common from industries under fire for environmental or public-health impacts. Bloomberg News flatly stated that "producers are taking a page from the tobacco industry playbook: funding research at established universities that arrives at conclusions that counter concerns raised by critics." This raises the ugly possibility of *science capture*.

No Frackin' Way

Not that Americans are taking it lying down. A diverse popular coalition successfully fought to block a Gulf Coast gas terminal that stood to inflict major damage on local wildlife. The *Oil & Gas Journal* reports on the "firestorm" of activism: "In an unlikely but massive undertaking, environmental activists, sports fishermen, local politicians, media groups, and other citizens formed a coalition known as the 'Gumbo Alliance' that united opposition to the technology." The Louisiana governor vetoed the project "under considerable public pressure." Elsewhere, local residents have taken action to keep fracking and its negative externalities out of their communities. New York State "fractivists" have won an impressive 55 municipal bans and 105 local moratoriums against fracking, to date. The state's Court of Appeals—New York's highest court—recently upheld the bans against an industry lawsuit. These activist successes are an early challenge to what the *Wall Street Journal* called the new "shale barons."

American job markets remain highly depressed and state budgets are strained. What we need, instead of dogged extraction of every particle of fossil fuels from the ground, is a public employment program geared toward the construction of a new sustainable energy system. This would be a far superior alternative to fracking—on grounds of health, ecology, and employment. It could also serve as a springboard for a broader questioning of the suitability of capitalism for the challenges of the 21st century. That kind of radical approach would see the glass of water as half full, not half on fire. ❏

Sources: Russel Gold, "Gas Boom Projected to Grow for Decades," *Wall Street Journal*, February 28, 2013; Tom Fowler, "US Oil Sector Notches Historic Annual Gusher," *Wall Street Journal*, January 19, 2013; Stephen Osborn, Avner Vengosh, Nathaniel Warner, and Robert Jackson, "Methane contamination of drinking water accompanying gas-well drilling and hydraulic fracturing," *Proceedings of the National Academy of the Sciences*, Vol. 108, No. 20, May 17, 2011; Kirk Johnson, "EPA Links Tainted Water in Wyoming to Hydraulic Fracturing for Natural Gas," *New York Times*, December 8, 2011; Tennille Tracy, "New EPA Findings Test Fracking Site," *Wall Street Journal*, October 11, 2012; Felicity Barringer, "Spread of Hydrofracking Could Strain Water Resources in West, Study Finds," *New York Times*, May 2, 2013; Russel Gold and Ana Campoy, "Oil's Growing Thirst for Water," *Wall Street Journal*, December 6, 2011; Ben Elgin, Benjamin Haas and Phil Kuntz, "Fracking Secrets by Thousands Keep US Clueless on Wells," Bloomberg News, November 30, 2012; Theo Colborn, Carol Kwiatkowski, Kim Schultz and Mary Bachran, "Natural Gas Operations form a Public Health Perspective," *Human and Ecological Risk Assessment: An International Journal*, Vol. 17, No. 5, September 20, 2011; Lisa McKenzie,

Roxana Witter, Lee Newman, John Adgate, "Human health risk assessment of air emissions from development of unconventional natural gas resources," *Science of the Total Environment*, Vol. 424, May 1 2012; Nadia Steinzor, Wilma Subra, and Lisa Sumi, "Investigating Links between Shale Gas Development and Health Impacts Through a Community Survey Project in Pennsylvania," *New Solutions*, Vol. 23, No. 1, 2013; Austin Holland, Oklahoma Geological Survey, "Examination of Possibly Induced Seismicity from Hydraulic Fracturing in the Eolga Field, Garvin County, Oklahoma, August 2011; Richard Kerr, "Learning How NOT to Make Your Own Earthquakes," *Science*, Vol. 335, No. 6075, March 23 2012; Zoe Corbyn, "Method predicts size of fracking earthquakes," *Nature* News, December 9, 2011; Ian Urbina, "Pressure Limits Efforts to Police Drilling for Gas," *New York Times*, March 3, 2011; Devlin Barrett and Ryan Dezember, "Regulators Back 'Fracking' in New York," *Wall Street Journal*, July 1, 2011; John Broder, "US Caps Emissions in Drilling for Fuel," *New York Times*, February 4, 2012; Norman Augustine, Rita Colwell, and James Duderstadt, "A Review of the Processes of Preparation and Distribution of the report 'Fact-Based Regulation for Environmental Protection in Shale Gas Development,'" University of Texas at Austin, November 30, 2012; Jim Efsthathiou, "Frackers Fund University Research That Proves Their Case," Bloomberg News, July 23, 2012; Daron Threet, "US offshore LNG terminals face technical, legal maze," *Oil & Gas Journal*, December 24, 2007; Ellen Cantarow, "New York's Zoning Ban Movement Fracks Big Gas," Truthout, May 9, 2013 (Truthout.org); Alyssa Abkowitz, "The New Texas Land Rush," *Wall Street Journal*, April 25, 2013; Daron Threet, "US offshore LNG terminals face technical, legal maze," *Oil & Gas Journal*, December 24, 2007.

Article 8.4

LAKE COUNTRY, NOT TRASH COUNTRY!
The Struggle for Environmental Protection in New York's Finger Lakes Region

BY PATRICIA RODRIGUEZ
March/April 2014

I t seemed like a typical meeting of Concerned Citizens of Seneca County (CCSC), but on the evening of September 11, 2013, there was a lot to share among the twenty or so in attendance. Glen Silver and Karen Rothfuss, two local residents who have been organizing resistance against landfill expansions in the Finger Lakes region of upstate New York told fellow CCSC members about the previous night's meeting of the Seneca County Board of Supervisors (BOS).

A month before, the board had passed two resolutions. The first requested a reconsideration of the sales and use tax exemptions provided by the Seneca County Industrial Development Agency to the local landfill company Seneca Meadows. The second, by a vote of 11-0, rejected a railroad spur project that would bring garbage-by-rail to the Waterloo, N.Y., landfill. Both Silver and Rothfuss had spoken out at the August meeting to challenge representatives of the landfill company who were pleading against the two resolutions. Seneca Meadows is owned by the Canadian company Progressive Waste Solutions, which operates landfills both in Canada and in many southern and northeastern U.S. states.

Located five hours away from big cities like New York and Toronto, a few hours from medium-sized cities like Rochester (to the northwest), and just an hour away from Ithaca, the Finger Lakes region contains beautiful glacial lakes, national forests, and numerous wineries. Despite the region's relatively stable income from tourism, many of the rural townships in the Finger Lakes are desperately in need of economic investment and revenue. According to Department of Environmental Conservation data, the region including the Finger Lakes (region 8) takes in the largest percentage (45%) of the total waste disposed throughout the state. Besides the Seneca Meadows landfill in Seneca County, the town of Flint in neighboring Ontario County hosts a landfill operated by Casella Waste Services.

The Railroad Spur and Other Concerns

CCSC folks certainly celebrated the two BOS resolutions at their September 11 meeting, but at the same time they understood that the unanimous vote on the railroad spur line was simply one victory. They will need to keep fighting other attempts to push through the rail extension, which would involve the additional construction of two industrial rail yards (four and eight parallel tracks respectively) located at one of the busiest traffic cross-roads in the area.

Seneca Meadows already brings in 6,000 tons of garbage a day from New Jersey, Pennsylvania, several New England states, and Canada. (In 2001, the landfill was permitted to increase its capacity from 4,700 tons, according to CCSC members.) Every year, more than 75,000 18-wheeler trucks transport the trash into the landfill, and will continue to do so at least until 2023, when the company's dumping permit expires. Over the past decade, 14 landfills in New York State have reached capacity, according to the 2013 documentary *Trashed: No Place for Waste*. Considering this trend, future requests from landfill companies for permit renovations and landfill expansions are highly probable.

Seneca Meadows argues that the rail plan will take hundreds of trash trucks off local roads and transport waste and materials in more energy-efficient and environmentally friendly ways, while not increasing the amount of trash the landfill is allowed to receive under its permit. Company executives also argue that the plan will bring jobs to the community, and help continue low-cost electricity and heat generation for local schools and homes (from garbage-generated methane gas). Seneca Meadows currently offers 150 local jobs, provides tax revenue that keeps local residents' taxes from increasing, and makes contributions to area schools, a local hospice, a food distribution campaign for children in need, and environmental educational workshops for the community. It also has created the Seneca Meadows Wetlands Preserve, with trails open to the public throughout the year. These are not minor issues for cash-strapped, low-income communities. Such considerations give the company a lot of leverage to keep its operations going, and push for expansion.

Concerned Citizens of Seneca County has raised the question of why Seneca Meadows would want to begin garbage by rail, if not to increase dumping capacity. One of the group's fears is that the rail will enable the other trash company operating in the area, Casella Waste, to bring increased trash to the region as well. "With the rail," they argue, "all options are open."

CCSC argues that there are better economic development options than to turn the region into "ground zero for trash"—and for water and air pollution. For one, they argue that much of what goes into the landfill can be sorted out for reuse, and between 50-60% could be composted, thus providing more and better-paying jobs to the local population, also reducing methane emissions—a major contributor to global climate change. Changing consumer habits, like reducing wasteful packaging or one-time-use items, is also part of the new zero-waste philosophy they want to help instill. Furthermore, they argue, local government should not be in the business of subsidizing corporations; instead, officials at every level of government could push for product stewardship, where the cost of disposing of used products is paid by the manufacturer, not the communities.

Town, County, State, and Nation

The Seneca County Board of Supervisors is just one of the many local and state institutions where decisions are made about this type of project. The layers of overlapping jurisdictions are complex. Town, county, and state institutions are numerous, and the company seems determined to push their interests in one venue and then another, inevitably requiring local activists to try to figure out how to navigate myriad different institutions. One of these venues is the Seneca Falls Town Planning Board, which had approved a smaller portion of the railroad plans in 2007 (before CCSC was formed). Seneca County planning units, particularly the Industrial Development Agency, are also key.

In 2009, Seneca County applied for two grants for stimulus funds to build permanent rail infrastructure to the Seneca Meadows landfill—one through the New York State Department of Transportation (for $2.4 million dollars), the other, for a portion of a federal Transportation Investment Generating Economic Recovery (TIGER) grant (for over $17 million dollars). Nothing came of the rail expansion then, perhaps because the Finger Lakes Zero Waste Coalition (FLZWC) and CCSC sent several letters opposing the rail plan to the governor and other state and local officials.

Local residents are certainly worried about local government support for the renewed rail plan. When landfill officials began pushing the railroad expansion in town council meetings, residents got active and raised concerns. Yet, the plans do not seem to fade away, creating a war of attrition between the landfill company, the local government, and local businesses and residents. The latest iteration of this conflict involves a complaint filed December 2013 in Seneca County Court by a local business seeking to annul the decision of the Seneca Falls Town Board to approve the zoning change from a commercial and agricultural zone to a manufacturing zone. The August 6, 2013, approval of the change was made upon request by Seneca Meadows, in order to let the company begin soil excavations (to provide top-layer covering of the garbage). The challenger, William Lutz, president of the bottle company Waterloo Containers, alleges that the Town Board failed to follow legal procedures and environmental guidelines that require citizen input. He argues that "an abbreviated, closely held review allowed the zoning change to proceed unchallenged. We are seeking to have the town conduct the proper review with full citizen participation."

So far, local activism has been able to keep construction of the railroad spur at bay. Part of the story behind the recent Board of Supervisors vote, for example, is the pressure activists have brought to bear on the different boards. "A lot of the work behind the 11-0 vote was done behind the scenes, contacting officials," explains Glen Silver. "In the past, the Seneca County Board of Supervisors had pushed for the TIGER grant application [to bring trash by train], and now three years later they have largely gone in our direction [against the railroad spur project]."

The Harm Done

Landfills and the transportation of garbage to these landfills do not just create minor nuisances. Though New York state has 18 landfills that are operated by local governments and that handle only refuse generated locally, the eight larger landfills in the state are operated privately, and take in solid waste, as well as contaminated soil, incinerator ash, sewage sludge, industrial and medical waste, pieces of shredded cars, storm debris, and other materials. The landfill companies in the area allege that the collection of landfill materials adheres to state regulations, that they use state-of-the-art systems such as bottom plastic liners to contain seepage, and that many companies have environmentally sound ways to generate electricity from methane gas collected in pipes that lie beneath the waste. But both the companies and the federal Environmental Protection Agency (EPA) also acknowledge that some gas escapes the pipe system and some seepage escapes liners. This means emissions of hazardous gases known to cause cancer and other diseases and of toxic liquid "leachates" that seep into the recreational waterways and lakes, contaminating the local drinking water systems. A big concern for the CCSC is that many residential areas and schools are close to and downwind from the landfill, which means that children and seniors (some of the most vulnerable populations) are exposed to the dangerous gases during the entire year, 24 hours a day.

Other problems have also been raised by residents in Seneca County, like the company's application for a permit to operate a clay mine to dig up soil for the landfill on the north side of Waterloo. The mine would be about 45 feet deep and located on portions of a 120-acre parcel of farmland directly across the road from Waterloo village residential neighborhoods, a middle/high school, and three youth-league ball fields. CCSC has had several state regulatory hearings on this issue, which is still on the table for town officials to decide, despite a stamp of approval from the New York State Department of Environmental Conservation (DEC). One of the nearly 60 letters submitted against the mine project during the public comment period reads: "Seneca Meadows continues to try and convince us what a good neighbor they are to the community ... But in the greater community we recognize that these donations are only a thinly veiled enticement to purchase compliance and support for their next project." At the same time, other residents (including employees of Seneca Meadows), wrote letters of support, one of which reads: "Seneca Meadows has always operated within the best interests of its neighbors, and always listens and responds to reasonable concerns of the community."

If past experiences with the consequences of garbage by rail are any indication, there are serious negative effects on communities all along the rail lines (not just near the landfill site). In 2010, residents in Middle Village (Queens, N.Y.), began a steady campaign of complaints about noise and odor when a landfill on Staten Island was closed and local garbage began to be transported through their community by rail en route to Virginia.

More recently, local citizen groups have noted problems with the lack of disclosure of what comes into the landfill, and from where. A recent news article in a Rochester newspaper discusses a lawsuit being brought by Canadian local authorities against WeCare Organics. The local authorities and residents of a town near Toronto had paid $6 million over the span of a few years for their organic waste to be turned into compost at a WeCare Organics facility in Massachusetts. Instead, the lawsuit alleges, the company dumped the waste into the Seneca Meadows landfill. Incidentally, the WeCare sister company in Massachusetts is also being sued in federal court by City of Marlborough authorities for "violating environmental laws and unleashing a foul odor on neighbors."

The Battle in Ontario County

Less than 15 miles from the Seneca County landfill, in neighboring Ontario County, the Finger Lakes Zero Waste Coalition (FLZWC) is waging a similar fight against a landfill, this one operated by Casella Waste Services. Casella Waste is a Vermont-based company that operates several landfills in the northeast United States. The Ontario County landfill has become the target of complaints about odor and air pollution.

FLZWC, an all-volunteer organization dedicated to promoting sustainable waste management, filed a petition in December 2012 for the EPA to intervene to stop excessive toxic emissions from the Casella Waste landfill. According to the petition, the excessive toxic pollution results from underreporting in county and company emission reports of toxic releases from materials such as contaminated soil, industrial sludge, construction and demolition debris, and incinerator ash used as cover at the landfill. The same underreporting is alleged for the landfill's gas-to-energy program. The petition was based on information gathered by members of FLZWC coalition from documents obtained under the Freedom of Information Act (FOIA). The petitioners requested that the EPA enforce the controls necessary to adequately destroy toxic emissions stemming from all of the landfill operations. The petition is still in process, as is a similar petition by the CCSC; to date, neither group has heard back from EPA officials. The two groups are working together to challenge the lack of regulations on landfill corporations in the Finger Lakes.

Ontario County receives $2 million per year under its long-term operating agreement with Casella Waste Services (possibly more, since the county gets paid extra if county officials approve an excess over the limit of 100,000 tons a year allowed under the agreement). Casella Waste, like Seneca Meadows, has contributed to many local government projects, including a local jail expansion and a 911 telephone system, with an additional $18 million promised if an expansion permit is approved. There are, however, tremendous costs for residents living near the landfill, in terms of traffic, noise, contamination, smell, and reduced property values. County officials have adopted some input from concerned citizens, submitted in venues like public commentaries on a ten-year Ontario County Solid Waste Management Plan. Local officials, however, appear to be taking cues from state officials, especially the Department of Environmental Conservation (DEC) environmental and health requirements.

For instance, at a January 2014 meeting of the Ontario County Environmental Quality Committee (EQC, a committee of the county's Board of Supervisors), its representatives favorably assessed a state initiative to reduce waste exported from New York to other states like New Jersey, Pennsylvania, and Ohio. This is a budget-cutting measure, since the export of waste requires shipping-related spending by the state. But the implementation of these initiatives is still at a very early stage: Ontario County committee members noted that not enough data has yet been collected about what and how much goes into the waste stream from local municipalities. The EQC meeting ended with the approval of a plan to ask each municipality in the county to attempt its own measurements. The committee also urged municipalities to figure out how they could take part in a state revenue-sharing plan to reduce waste going into the solid-waste system, a plan that the administrators emphasized had been approved by the DEC.

According to FLZWC activist Katherine Bennet Roll, however, it is unclear that state funding would be forthcoming, as there seems to be a constant push from the state to create more room for trash. In the meantime, the Board of Supervisors continues to consider an expansion of the Ontario County landfill (to around 43 acres), even though the last expansion was granted only in 2007-2008. Back then, county officials approved a 49.9% increase in the amount of trash the landfill could accept each year (50% would have necessitated greater citizen approval processes).

If the expansion is approved, Ontario County's landfill could add a total of another 11.8 million cubic yards of trash (to the existing 11.5 million cubic yards), a sum which would be equivalent to seven times the volume of the Egypt's Great Pyramid of Giza, according to FLZWC. To compound the problem, even if the companies leave at the end of the contract in 2023, there is a potential threat for hundreds of years, as the technique of layering clay beneath the usual liner as a barrier to toxic seepage has repeatedly proven flawed. Combined, the two Finger Lakes area landfills produce over 47 million gallons of toxic liquid run-off a year that pass through waste-water treatment plants and end up in the nearby lakes. Meanwhile, the landfills produce methane, some of which is used for electricity or heat. The EPA estimates, however, that the collection process only captures about 75% of the gas—the rest goes into the air as pollution. As FLZWC member Katie Bennet Roll explained in an op-ed in the *Finger Lakes Times* (March 24, 2013), "Any expansion [of the landfills] will only increase the amount of pollutants in the air we breathe every day."

Citizens in Action

It should come as no surprise that concerned local residents express very little trust in most state and local officials. At a meeting during a "Landfill Summit" held at Hobart and William Smith College (Geneva, N.Y.) in April 2013, members of FLZWC and CCSC had a long list of concerns related to official accountability. For instance, Ontario County administrators had failed to implement a mandatory recycling law that took effect in 1992 (Local Law #6). State officials did not create any disincentives for counties to export their waste to the Finger Lakes landfills (like calling attention to negative impacts on local communities). The DEC refused to impose sanctions on the landfill companies for violating laws prohibiting odor outside the landfill's geographic footprint. In essence, activists demanded accountability from officials at all levels.

What is more of a (welcome) surprise is the work being done by these local activist organizations, and how it may further the search for solutions to the problems created by landfills and, largely, by consumerism. As Glen Silver, president of CCSC and vice president of FLZWC, explains, "Neither the DEC nor anyone is there to protect us; instead, the local community can and must make changes itself, but only if awakened." Despite the recent victories, the groups recognize the need for ongoing vigilance. Seneca Meadows is currently sending mass mailings of glossy literature to all of the local residents, trying to convince them of what a "valued partner, trusted neighbor" they are. CCSC and FLZWC, in response, have alerted local residents to write letters to the editor and join in local fundraisers to raise money to pay for upcoming court filings and other legal challenges.

Activism is difficult and costly. Town meetings are often called or rescheduled at the last minute, making it hard for citizens to attend important decision-making meetings. Citizens have to make time to litigate in the courts (and to learn how). They may pay out of their own pockets for litigation or for independent environmental studies that allow them to challenge company claims. Despite these obstacles, they fight for the community, and results—such as the 2009 creation of the first-ever "green citizen committees" for Seneca County and neighboring Wayne County—are often promising. The legacy they want to leave is the preservation of their neighborhoods for future inhabitants, and not for companies who profit from dumping urban wastes on rural lands.

The Big Picture

At the national level, the EPA reports that the average American discards almost 4.5 pounds of garbage every day. Accounting also for construction and demolition waste, and non-hazardous industrial waste, those figures expand tremendously: the solid-waste industry manages nearly 545 million tons of solid waste each year, equal to the weight of 2.3 million Boeing 747s.

According to the documentary film *Trashed*, which portrays the global problem of landfills, the world's population and environment currently co-exist with 200 billion plastic bottles, 58 billion disposable cups, and many billions of plastic bags. Municipal-level figures from the EPA note that more than 30% of municipal solid waste is packaging, and 40% of that waste is plastic.

Zero-waste can be a local development alternative to landfill and incinerator-based waste systems. As the DEC has itself noted: "for every job required to operate a landfill or municipal waste combustor, ten jobs can be created to process recyclable materials and prepare them for market." Many local initiatives around zero waste have been incredibly successful, such as San Francisco's source separation and community compost program (which produces organic material used in local agriculture). Besides, the emphasis of zero-waste initiatives in general on reduction, reuse, recycling, and renewable energy is extremely timely, considering the alarming national-level waste figures.

Research on landfill location suggests that low potential for citizen litigation and long-term multi-leveled institutional openness to landfill companies are key factors in future sitings. Company officials operating in the Finger Lakes, though, may have failed to do their homework fully. Recently, local citizens celebrated the prevention of a new landfill in Arcadia, Wayne County, N.Y. Meanwhile, the coalitions and groups of activists in the Finger Lakes will continue to press for greater regulation, environmentally minded and just policies, greater public accountability, and an end to the expansion of landfills in the region. As Glen Silver notes, "there is an exciting thing about community action … there are amazing things that people can do—many times beyond what they ever thought possible—when they become committed to these issues." ❏

Sources: Rulings of the Administrative Law Judge on Issues and Party Status, Seneca Meadows, Inc. application for a Mined Land Reclamation Permit, Application No. 8-4538-00094-00001, March 26, 2012 (dec.ny.gov); David Shaw, 'Waterloo Container Sues Seneca Falls Over Zoning Change for Rail-Spur Project', Finger Lakes Times, December 15, 2013; Steve Orr, 'Watchdog: Rochester Region King of the Hill in Trash', *Democrat and Chronicle*, November 11, 2013; Steve Orr, 'Lawsuits Raise Stink over Firm's Cross-border Composting Deal,' *Democrat and Chronicle*, January 3, 2014; Concerned Citizens of Seneca county (ccseneca.org); Finger Lakes Zero Waste Coalition (flzw.org); *Trashed: No Place for Waste* website (trashedfilm.com).

Article 8.6

UNIVERSAL HEALTH CARE: CAN WE AFFORD ANYTHING LESS?

Why only a single-payer system can solve America's health-care mess.

BY GERALD FRIEDMAN
July/August 2011

America's broken health-care system suffers from what appear to be two separate problems. From the right, a chorus warns of the dangers of rising costs; we on the left focus on the growing number of people going without health care because they lack adequate insurance. This division of labor allows the right to dismiss attempts to extend coverage while crying crocodile tears for the 40 million uninsured. But the division between problem of cost and the problem of coverage is misguided. It is founded on the assumption, common among neoclassical economists, that the current market system is efficient. Instead, however, the current system is inherently inefficient; it is the very source of the rising cost pressures. In fact, the only way we can control health-care costs and avoid fiscal and economic catastrophe is to establish a single-payer system with universal coverage.

The rising cost of health care threatens the U.S. economy. For decades, the cost of health insurance has been rising at over twice the general rate of inflation; the share of American income going to pay for health care has more than doubled since 1970 from 7% to 17%. By driving up costs for employees, retirees, the needy, the young, and the old, rising health-care costs have become a major problem for governments at every level. Health costs are squeezing public spending needed for education and infrastructure. Rising costs threaten all Americans by squeezing the income available for other activities. Indeed, if current trends continued, the entire economy would be absorbed by health care by the 2050s.

Conservatives argue that providing universal coverage would bring this fiscal Armageddon on even sooner by increasing the number of people receiving care. Following this logic, their policy has been to restrict access to health care by raising insurance deductibles, copayments, and cost sharing and by reducing access to insurance. Even before the Great Recession, growing numbers of American adults were uninsured or underinsured. Between 2003 and 2007, the share of non-elderly adults without adequate health insurance rose from 35% to 42%, reaching 75 million. This number has grown substantially since then, with the recession reducing employment and with the continued decline in employer-provided health insurance. Content to believe that our current health-care system is efficient, conservatives assume that costs would have risen more had these millions not lost access, and likewise believe that extending health-insurance coverage to tens of millions using a plan like the Affordable Care Act would drive up costs even further. Attacks on employee health insurance and on Medicare and Medicaid come from this same logic—the idea that the only way to control health-care costs is to reduce the number of people with access to health care. If we do not find a way to control costs by increasing access, there will be more proposals like that of Rep. Paul Ryan (R-Wisc.) and the Republicans in the House of Representatives to slash Medicaid and abolish Medicare.

The Problem of Cost in a Private, For-Profit Health Insurance System

If health insurance were like other commodities, like shoes or bow ties, then reducing access might lower costs by reducing demands on suppliers for time and materials. But health care is different because so much of the cost of providing it is in the administration of the payment system rather than in the actual work of doctors, nurses, and other providers, and because coordination and cooperation among different providers is essential for effective and efficient health care. It is not cost pressures on providers that are driving up health-care costs; instead, costs are rising because of what economists call transaction costs, the rising cost of administering and coordinating a system that is designed to reduce access.

The health-insurance and health-care markets are different from most other markets because private companies selling insurance do not want to sell to everyone, but only to those unlikely to need care (and, therefore, most likely to drop coverage if prices rise). As much as 70% of the "losses" suffered by health-insurance providers—that is, the money they pay out in claims—goes to as few as 10% of their subscribers. This creates a powerful incentive for companies to screen subscribers, to identify those likely to submit claims, and to harass them so that they will drop their coverage and go elsewhere. The collection of insurance-related information has become a major source of waste in the American economy because it is not organized to improve patient care but to harass and to drive away needy subscribers and their health-care providers. Because driving away the sick is so profitable for health insurers, they are doing it more and more, creating the enormous bureaucratic waste that characterizes the process of billing and insurance handling. Rising by over 10% a year for the past 25 years, health insurers' administrative costs are among the fastest-growing in the U.S. health-care sector. Doctors in private practice now spend as much as 25% of their revenue on administration, nearly $70,000 per physician for billing and insurance costs.

For-profit health insurance also creates waste by discouraging people from receiving preventive care and by driving the sick into more expensive care settings. Almost a third of Americans with "adequate" health insurance go without care every year due to costs, and the proportion going without care rises to over half of those with "inadequate" insurance and over two-thirds for those without insurance. Nearly half of the uninsured have no regular source of care, and a third did not fill a prescription in the 2010 because of cost. All of this unutilized care might appear to save the system money. But it doesn't. Reducing access does not reduce health-care expenditures when it makes people sicker and pushes them into hospitals and emergency rooms, which are the most expensive settings for health care and are often the least efficient because care provided in these settings rarely has continuity or follow-up.

The great waste in our current private insurance system is an opportunity for policy because it makes it possible to economize on spending by replacing our current system with one providing universal access. I have estimated that in Massachusetts, a state with a relatively efficient health-insurance system, it would be possible to lower the cost of providing health care by nearly 16% even after providing coverage to everyone in the state currently without insurance (see Table 1). This could be done largely by reducing the cost of administering the private insurance system, with most of the savings coming within providers' offices by reducing the costs of billing and processing insurance claims. This is a conservative estimate made for a state with a relatively efficient health-insurance system. In a report prepared for the state of Vermont, William Hsiao of the Harvard School of Public Health and MIT economist Jonathan Gruber estimate that shifting to a single-payer system could lead to savings of around 25% through reduced administrative cost and improved delivery of care. (They have also noted that administrative savings would be even larger if the entire country shifted to a single-payer system because this would save the cost of billing people with private, out-of-state insurance plans.) In Massachusetts, my conservative estimates suggests that as much as $10 billion a year could be saved by shifting to a single-payer system.

Single-Payer Systems Control Costs by Providing Better Care

Adoption of a single-payer health-insurance program with universal coverage could also save money and improve care by allowing better coordination of care among different providers and by providing a continuity of care that is not possible with competing insurance plans. A comparison of health care in the United States with health care in other countries shows how large these cost savings might be. When Canada first adopted its current health-care financing system in 1968, the health-care share of the national gross domestic product in the United States (7.1%) was nearly the same as in Canada (6.9%), and only a little higher than in other advanced

---

TABLE 1: SOURCES OF SAVINGS AND ADDED COSTS FOR A HYP-THETICAL MASSACHUSETTS SINGLE-PAYER HEALTH SYSTEM

Change in health-care expenditures	Size of change as share of total health-care expenditures
Savings from single-payer system	
Administration costs within health-insurance system	-2.0%
Administrative costs within providers' offices	-10.1%
Reduction in provider prices through reducing market leverage for privileged providers	-5.0%
Savings:	-17.1%
Increased costs from single-payer	
Expansion in coverage to the uninsured	+1.35%
Increased utilization because of elimination of copayments, balanced by improvements in preventive care	+/- 0.0%
Total increased costs:	+1.35%
Net change in health-care expenditures:	-15.75%

Source: Calculations by the author from data in OECD Health Data 2010 (oecd.org).

economies. Since then, however, health care has become dramatically more expensive in the United States. In the United States, per capita health-care spending since 1971 has risen by over $6,900 compared with an increase of less than $3,600 in Canada and barely $3,200 elsewhere (see Table 2). Physician Steffie Woolhandler and others have shown how much of this discrepancy between the experience of the United States and Canada can be associated with the lower administrative costs of Canada's single-payer system; she has found that administrative costs are nearly twice as high in the United States as in Canada—31% of costs versus 17%.

The United States is unique among advanced economies both for its reliance on private health insurance and for rapid inflation in health-care costs. Health-care costs have risen faster in the United States than in any other advanced economy: twice as fast as in Canada, France, Germany, Sweden, or the United Kingdom. We might accept higher and rapidly rising costs had Americans experienced better health outcomes. But using life expectancy at birth as a measure of general health, we have gone from a relatively healthy country to a relatively unhealthy one. Our gain in life expectancy since 1971 (5.4 years for women) is impressive except when put beside other advanced economies (where the average increase is 7.3 years).

The relatively slow increase in life expectancy in the United States highlights the gross inefficiency of our private health-care system. Had the United States increased life expectancy at the same dollar cost as in other countries, we would have saved nearly $4,500 per person. Or, put another way, had we increased life expectancy at the same rate as other countries, our spending increase since 1971 would have bought an extra 15 years of life expectancy, 10 years more than we have. The failure of American

TABLE 2: GREATER INCREASE IN COST FOR U.S. HEALTH-CARE SYSTEM, 1971-2007

	U.S. vs. Canada		U.S. vs. 5-country average	
	Dollars	Share of GDP	Dollars	Share of GDP
Extra increase 1971-2007	$3,356	5.40%	$3,690	4.72%
Extra adjusted for smaller life expectancy gain	$4,006	5.98%	$4,480	5.73%
	As share of national health expenditures			
Extra increase 1971-2007	45%		49%	
Extra adjusted for smaller life expectancy gain	53%		59%	

Note: The first line shows how much faster health-care spending rose per person and as a share of gross domestic product in the United States compared with Canada and with the average of five countries (Canada, France, Germany, Sweden, and the United Kingdom). The second row adjusts this increase for the slower rate of growth in life expectancy in the United States than in these other countries. The third and fourth rows estimate the degree of waste in our health-care system as the proportion of total expenditures accounted for by the extra increases in health-care expenditures in the United States. Source: Calculations by the author from data in OECD Health Data 2010 (oecd.org).

life expectancy to rise as fast as life expectancy elsewhere can be directly tied to the inequitable provision of health care through our private, for-profit health-insurance system. Increases in life expectancy since 1990 have been largely restricted to relatively affluent Americans with better health insurance. Since 1990, men in the top 50% of the income distribution have had a six-year increase in life expectancy at age 65 compared with an increase of only one year for men earning below the median.

R ising health-care costs reflect in part the greater costs of caring for an aging population with more chronic conditions. As such, the United States looks especially bad because our population is aging less quickly than that of other countries because of high rates of immigration, relatively higher fertility, and the slower increase in life expectancy in the United States. Countries also buy higher life expectancy by spending

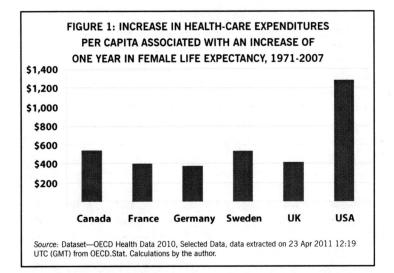

FIGURE 1: INCREASE IN HEALTH-CARE EXPENDITURES PER CAPITA ASSOCIATED WITH AN INCREASE OF ONE YEAR IN FEMALE LIFE EXPECTANCY, 1971-2007

Source: Dataset—OECD Health Data 2010, Selected Data, data extracted on 23 Apr 2011 12:19 UTC (GMT) from OECD.Stat. Calculations by the author.

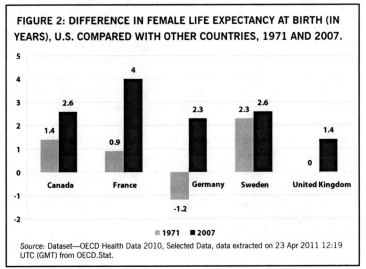

FIGURE 2: DIFFERENCE IN FEMALE LIFE EXPECTANCY AT BIRTH (IN YEARS), U.S. COMPARED WITH OTHER COUNTRIES, 1971 AND 2007.

Source: Dataset—OECD Health Data 2010, Selected Data, data extracted on 23 Apr 2011 12:19 UTC (GMT) from OECD.Stat.

on health care; rising health expenditures have funded improvements in treatment that have contributed to rising life expectancy throughout the world. Female life expectancy at birth has increased by nearly nine years in Germany since 1971, by over eight years in France, by seven years in Canada and the United Kingdom, and by six years in Sweden. By contrast, the United States, where female life expectancy increased by a little over five years, has done relatively poorly despite increasing health-care expenditures that dwarf those of other countries. In other countries, increasing expenditures by about $500 per person is associated with an extra year of life expectancy. With our privatized health-insurance system, we need spending increases over twice as large to gain an extra year of life (see Figure 1, previous page).

The international comparison also provides another perspective on any supposed trade-off between containing costs and expanding coverage. In countries other than the United States, almost all of the increase in health-care spending as a share of national income is due to better quality health care as measured by improvements in life expectancy (see Figure 2, previous page). The problem of rising health-care costs is almost unique to the United States, the only advanced industrialized country without universal coverage and without any effective national health plan.

In short, the question is not whether we can afford a single-payer health-insurance system that would provide adequate health care for all Americans. The real question is: can we afford anything else? ❏

Sources: Cathy Shoen, "How Many Are Underinsured? Trends Among U.S. Adults, 2003 and 2007," *Health Affairs*, June 10, 2008; "Insured but Poorly Protected: How Many Are Underinsured? U. S. Adults Trends, 2003 to 2007," Commonwealth Fund, June 10, 2008 (commonwealthfund. org); David Cutler and Dan Ly, "The (Paper) Work of Medicine: Understanding International Medical Costs," *Journal of Economic Perspectives*, Spring 2011; Stephen M. Davidson, Still Broken: Understanding the U.S. Health Care System, Stanford Business Books, 2010; P Franks and C M Clancy, "Health insurance and mortality. Evidence from a national cohort," *The Journal of the American Medical Association*, August 11, 1993; Allan Garber and Jonathan Skinner, "Is American Health Care Uniquely Inefficient?" *Journal of Economic Perspectives*, Fall 2008; Jonathan Gruber, "The Role of Consumer Co-payments for Health Care: Lessons from the RAND Health Insurance Experiment and Beyond," Kaiser Family Foundation, October 2006 (kff.org); David Himmelstein and Steffie Woolhandler, "Administrative Waste in the U.S. Health Care System in 2003," *International Journal of Health Services*, 2004; "The Uninsured: A Primer: Supplemental Data Tables," Kaiser Family Foundation, December 2010; Karen Davis and Cathy Shoen, "Slowing the Growth of U.S. Health Care Expenditures: What are the Options?" Commonwealth Fund, January 2007 (commonwealthfund.org); "Accounting for the Cost of Health Care in the United States," McKinsey Global Institute, January 2007 (mckinsey.com); "Investigation of Health Care Cost Trends and Cost Drivers," Office of Massachusetts Attorney General Martha Coakley, January 29, 2010 (mass.gov); Hilary Waldron, "Trends in Mortality Differentials and Life Expectancy for Male Social Security-Covered Workers, by Average Relative Earnings," Social Security Administration, October 2007; Richard G. Wilkinson, *The Spirit Level*, Bloomsbury Press, 2010; William Hsiao and Steven Kappel, "Act 128: Health System Reform Design. Achieving Affordable Universal Health Care in Vermont," January 21, 2011 (leg.state.vt.us); Steffie Woolhandler and Terry Campbell, "Cost of Health Care Administration in the United States and Canada," *New England Journal of Medicine*, 2003.

Chapter 9

TAXATION

INTRODUCTION

"Only the little people pay taxes." —*Leona Helmsley*

"Taxes are the price we pay for civilization." —*Oliver Wendell Holmes, Jr.*

Taxation is a fascinating subject. It is perhaps the clearest manifestation of class struggle one can find. How a modern government funds itself in order to provide services is an elaborate study in power. The contentious tango of taxes and their inverse, subsidies, plays out daily at all three levels of government—federal, state and local. Who pays taxes and at what rates? What is taxed? Who bears the burden of taxation? And how are tax revenues collected? These are questions that this chapter will address.

In the Reagan era, "supply-side" economist Arthur Laffer famously claimed that high marginal tax rates discourage work and saving, and that cutting tax rates on the rich would spur investment and economic growth. We start the chapter with two articles on the subject: In "Can Tax Cuts Really Increase Government Revenue?" (Article 9.1), economist Ellen Frank reviews the basic arguments made by Laffer and the other supply-siders, and why there is reason to be skeptical. Gerald Friedman puts these arguments to the test, and finds that cutting taxes on the very rich, as the U.S. government has been doing for decades, has not led to the promised investment or economic growth (Article 9.2).

As John Miller points out in "No Fooling—Corporations Evade Taxes" (Article 9.3), *Forbes* magazine finally acknowledged a case of a large corporation gaming the tax code, reporting that General Electric generated $10.3 billion in pretax income but ended up owing nothing to Uncle Sam. What is worse, the company received a tax benefit of $1.1 billion from American taxpayers as gratitude for its clever accounting.

Next, economist Arthur MacEwan answers the question "What's Wrong With a Flat Tax?" (Article 9.4). As MacEwan points out, an income tax that takes the same percentage from everyone may sound even-handed. However, it would eliminate the main "progressive" federal tax (which takes a larger percentage from those with higher incomes), while leaving in place "regressive" taxes that take a larger share of income from those with lower incomes (like payroll taxes). That, MacEwan argues, would just shift the tax burden from rich to poor.

In "Transaction Tax: Sand in the Wheels, Not in the Face" (Article 9.5), economist John Miller makes the case for a tax on stock and other securities trades. This kind of tax, he argues, will not only raise revenue, but also reduce speculation in financial markets and help restore a focus on longer-term planning and job creation in the economy.

Next, in "State Income Taxes and the Footloose Taxpayer" (Article 9.6), Miller debunks claims that high state income taxes drive "tax flight" or stifle economic growth. In fact, he argues, high-tax states have actually prospered more than low-tax states.

Finally, Gerald Friedman asks "Who Are the 47%?" (Article 9.7). Friedman refutes the view, first, that nearly half the U.S. population pays no taxes. The "47%" actually pay various state and local taxes, as well as federal taxes (especially payroll taxes) besides the income tax. Moreover, the main reasons that people do not pay federal income taxes are that they are elderly, disabled, or simply have very low incomes.

Discussion Questions

1. (Articles 9.1 and 9.2) What is the basis of supply-siders' claim that lowering the highest marginal tax rate will generate more tax revenue? What are the main arguments against this view?

2. (Article 9.2) In what way have tax policies contributed to growing inequality in the United States? Do you think there is a case for remaking tax policy to be more progressive?

3. (Article 9.3) What are the three key corporate "loopholes" from which corporations have traditionally avoided paying their full marginal tax rate?

4. (Articles 9.3) Why do corporations complain about a corporate marginal tax rate of 35% when in fact no company actually pays that rate?

5. (Article 9.4) In MacEwan's view, why is a "flat" income tax not desirable? What are some arguments in favor of progressive taxation?

6. (Article 9.5) What is a "Tobin Tax"? Why is this a "two birds with one stone" form of taxation?

7. (Article 9.6) If, as Miller argues, high state income taxes neither provoke tax flight nor reduce economic growth, why not?

8. (Article 9.7) Is it bad that nearly half of the population does not pay federal income taxes? Does it affect your opinion to know that almost all of these individuals pay other kinds of (local, state, and federal) taxes?

9. (Article 9.7) Are the reasons that people do not pay federal income tax justified? That is, would it be desirable to change the tax code to make sure more people did pay federal income taxes? To this end, would it be desirable to reduce other taxes?

Article 9.1

CAN TAX CUTS REALLY INCREASE GOVERNMENT REVENUE?

BY ELLEN FRANK
November/December 2003

> Dear Dr. Dollar:
> *A Republican friend tells me that the huge new tax cuts will actually produce more revenue than the government would have collected before the cut, because once rich beneficiaries invest the money, they will pay taxes on every transaction. He suggested that the increase could be as much as 50% more than the originally scheduled revenues. Is this possible?*
> —Judith Walker, New York, N.Y.

Back in the 1970s, conservative economist Arthur Laffer proposed that high marginal tax rates discouraged people from earning additional income. By cutting taxes, especially on those with the highest incomes, Laffer argued, governments would spur individuals to work harder and invest more, stoking economic growth. Though the government would get a smaller bite from every dollar the economy generated, there would be so many more dollars to tax that government revenues would actually rise. Ronald Reagan invoked the "Laffer curve" in the 1980s, insisting he could cut taxes, hike defense spending, and still balance the budget.

Bush's 2001 and 2003 tax packages are eerily reminiscent of the Reagan cuts. They reduce rates levied on ordinary income, with the largest rate cut going to the wealthiest taxpayers. They extend business tax write-offs and increase the child tax credit (though only for two years and only for families who earn enough to pay federal income taxes). They cut the tax on capital gains from 28% to 15%; dividend income, previously taxed at the same rate as ordinary income, now faces a top rate of 15%.

Citizens for Tax Justice estimates that two-thirds of the 2003 tax cut will accrue to the richest 10% of taxpayers. By 2006, the increased child credit will be phased out and nine out of ten taxpayers will find their taxes cut by less than $100. The top 1%, in contrast, will save an average $24,000 annually over the next four years, thanks to the 2003 cut alone.

Though inspired by the same "supply-side" vision that guided Reagan, Bush officials have not explicitly cited Laffer's arguments in defense of their tax packages. Probably, they wish to avoid ridicule. After the Reagan tax cut, the U.S. economy sank into recession and federal tax collections dropped nearly 10%. The deficit soared and economic growth was tepid through much of Reagan's presidency, despite sharp hikes in military spending. Some of the Republican faithful continue to argue that tax cuts will unleash enough growth to pay for themselves, but most are embarrassed to raise the now discredited Laffer curve.

The problem with your friend's assertion is fairly simple. If the government cuts projected taxes by $1.5 trillion over the next decade, those dollars will recirculate through the economy. The $1.5 trillion tax cut becomes $1.5 trillion in taxable income and is itself taxed, as your friend suggests. But this would be just as true if, instead of cutting taxes, the government spent $1.5 trillion on highways or national defense or schools or, for that matter, if it trimmed $1.5 trillion from the tax liability of low- and middle-income households. All tax cuts become income, are re-spent, and taxed. That reality is already factored into everyone's economic projections. But the new income, taxed at a lower rate, will generate lower overall tax collections.

To conclude that revenues will rise rather than fall following a tax cut, one must maintain that the tax cut causes the economy to grow faster than it would have otherwise—that cutting taxes on the upper crust stimulates enough additional growth to offset the lower tax rates, more growth than would be propelled by, say, building roads or reducing payroll taxes. Free-marketeers insist that this is indeed the case. Spend $1.5 trillion on highways and you get $1.5 trillion worth of highways. Give it to Wall Street and investors will develop new technologies, improve productivity, and spur the economy to new heights.

Critics of the Bush cuts contend, however, that faster growth arises from robust demand for goods and from solid, well-maintained public infrastructure. Give $1.5 to Wall Street and you get inflated stock prices and real estate bubbles. Give it to working families or state governments and you get crowded malls, ringing cash registers, and businesses busily investing to keep up with their customers.

Who is right? Die-hard supply-siders insist that the Reagan tax cuts worked as planned—the payoff just didn't arrive until the mid-1990s! But the Bush administration's own budget office is predicting sizable deficits for the next several years. Maybe, like your friend, they believe the tax cuts will pay for themselves—but they're not banking on it. ❑

Article 9.2

THE GREAT TAX-CUT EXPERIMENT
Has cutting tax rates for the rich helped the economy?

BY GERALD FRIEDMAN
January/February 2013

Since the late 1970s, during the Carter Administration, conservative economists have been warning that high taxes retard economic growth by discouraging productive work and investment. These arguments have resonated with politicians, who have steadily cut income taxes, especially those borne by the richest Americans. The highest marginal tax rate, which stood at 70% by the end of the 1970s, was cut to less than 30% in less than a decade. (The marginal rate for a person is the one applied to his or her last dollar of income. A marginal rate that applies to, say, the bracket above $250,000, then, is paid only on that portion of income. The portion of a person's income below that threshold is taxed at the lower rates applying to lower tax brackets.) Despite increases in the early 1990s, the top marginal rate remained below 40%, when it was cut further during the administration of George W. Bush. These dramatic cuts in tax rates, however, have not led to an acceleration in economic growth, investment, or productivity.

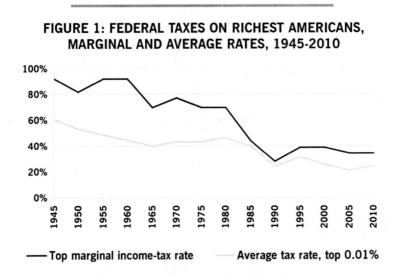

FIGURE 1: FEDERAL TAXES ON RICHEST AMERICANS, MARGINAL AND AVERAGE RATES, 1945-2010

—— Top marginal income-tax rate   —— Average tax rate, top 0.01%

The federal government has been cutting taxes on the richest Americans since the end of World War II. The average tax paid by the richest taxpayers, as a percentage of income, is typically less than the top marginal rate. Some of their income (the portion below the threshold for the top marginal rate, any capital-gains income, etc.) is taxed at lower rates. Some is not subject to federal income tax because of deductions for state and local taxes, health-care costs, and other expenses. The decline in the average tax rate for the richest, however, does follow the cuts in the top marginal income-tax rate.

FIGURE 2: TAX REVENUE AS A PERCENTAGE OF GDP, 2008

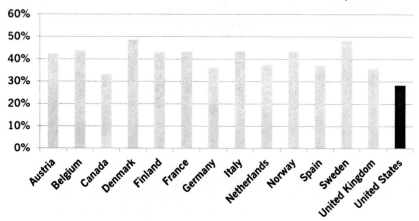

Americans pay a smaller proportion of total income in taxes than do people in any other advanced capitalist economy. As recently as the late 1960s, taxes accounted for as high a share of national income in the United States as in Western European countries. After decades of tax cuts, however, the United States now stands out for its low taxes and small government sector.

FIGURE 3: AVERAGE TAX RATES ON RICHEST AND REAL GDP GROWTH, BY PRESIDENT, 1947-2010

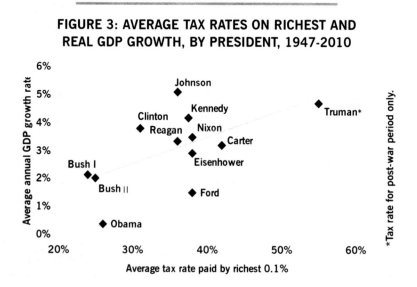

On average, the economy has grown faster during presidential administrations with higher tax rates on the richest Americans. Growth was unusually slow during George W. Bush's two terms (Bush II) and during Obama's first term, when the Bush tax cuts remained in effect. On average, every 10 percentage-point rise in the average tax rate on the richest has been associated with an increase in annual GDP growth of almost one percentage point.

FIGURE 4: TOP MARGINAL TAX RATE AND INVESTMENT,1963-2011

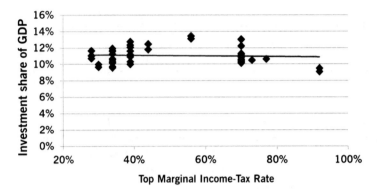

Cutting taxes on the richest Americans has not led them to invest more in plant and equipment. Over the past 50 years, as tax rates have declined, there has been no increase in investment spending as a percentage of GDP. (The flat trend line shows that changes in the highest marginal income-tax rate have not affected investment much, one way or the other.) Instead, the investment share of the economy has been determined by other factors, such as aggregate demand, rather than tax policy.

FIGURE 5: TAX SHARE OF GDP AND PRODUCTIVITY GROWTH

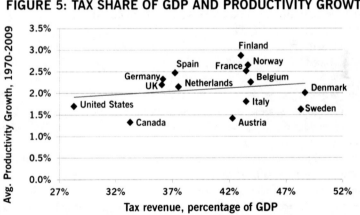

Despite lower and declining tax rates, especially on the rich, the United States has had slower productivity growth over the last several decades than other advanced economies. Overall, lower taxes are associated with slower growth in GDP per hour worked. A 10 percentage point increase in taxes as a share of GDP is associated with an increase in the productivity growth rate of 0.2 percentage points. ❑

Sources: Tom Petska and Mike Strudler, "Income, Taxes, and Tax Progressivity: An Examination of Recent Trends in the Distribution of Individual Income and Taxes" (Statistics of Income Division, Internal Revenue Service, 1997); Thomas Hungerford, "Taxes and the Economy: An Economic Analysis of the Top Tax Rates Since 1945" (Congressional Research Service, 2012); Economic Report of the President, 2012; Bureau of Economic Analysis (bea.gov); Organization of Economic Cooperation and Development, OECD STAT.

Article 9.3

NO FOOLING—CORPORATIONS EVADE TAXES

Forbes *finally notices what has been obvious for years.*

BY JOHN MILLER
May/June 2011

> WHAT THE TOP U.S. COMPANIES PAY IN TAXES
>
> Some of the world's biggest, most profitable corporations enjoy a far lower tax rate than you do—that is, if they pay taxes at all.
>
> The most egregious example is General Electric. Last year the conglomerate generated $10.3 billion in pretax income, but ended up owing nothing to Uncle Sam. In fact, it recorded a tax benefit of $1.1 billion.
>
> Over the last two years, GE Capital [one of the two divisions of General Electric] has displayed an uncanny ability to lose lots of money in the U.S. (posting a $6.5 billion loss in 2009), and make lots of money overseas (a $4.3 billion gain).
>
> It only makes sense that multinationals "put costs in high-tax countries and profits in low-tax countries," says Scott Hodge, president of the Tax Foundation. Those low-tax countries are almost anywhere but the U.S. "When you add in state taxes, the U.S. has the highest tax burden among industrialized countries," says Hodge. In contrast, China's rate is just 25%; Ireland's is 12.5%.
>
> —Christopher Helman, "What the Top U.S. Companies Pay in Taxes," *Forbes*, April 1, 2011

When *Forbes* magazine, the keeper of the list of the 400 richest Americans, warns that corporations not paying taxes on their profits will raise your hackles, you might wonder about the article's April 1 dateline. If it turns out *not* to be an April Fool's joke, things must be *really* bad.

And indeed they are. As *Forbes* reports, General Electric, the third largest U.S. corporation, turned a profit of $10.3 billion in 2010, paid no corporate income taxes, and got a "tax benefit" of $1.1 billion on taxes owed on past profits. And from 2005 to 2009, according to its own filings, GE paid a consolidated tax rate of just 11.6% on its corporate rates, including state, local, and foreign taxes. That's a far cry from the 35% rate nominally levied on corporate profits above $10 million.

Nor was GE alone among the top ten U.S. corporations with no tax obligations. Bank of America (BofA), the seventh largest U.S. corporation, racked up $4.4 billion in profits in 2010 and also paid no corporate income taxes (or in 2009 for that matter). Like GE, BofA has hauled in a whopping "tax benefit"—$1.9 billion.

For BofA, much like for GE, losses incurred during the financial crisis erased it tax liabilities. BofA, of course, contributed mightily to the crisis. It was one of four banks that controlled 95% of commercial bank derivatives activity, mortgage-based securities that inflated the housing bubble and brought on the crisis.

And when the crisis hit, U.S. taxpayers bailed them out, not once but several times. All told BofA received $45 billion of government money from the Troubled

Asset Relief Program (TARP) as well as other government guarantees. And while BofA paid no taxes on their over $4 billion of profits, they nonetheless managed to pay out $3.3 billion in bonuses to corporate executives. All of that has made BofA a prime target for US Uncut protests (see p. 6) against corporate tax dodging that has cost the federal government revenues well beyond the $39 billion saved by the punishing spending cuts in the recent 2011 budget deal.

These two corporate behemoths and other many other major corporations paid no corporate income taxes last year, even though 2010 U.S. corporate profits had returned their level in 2005 in the midst the profits-heavy Bush expansion before the crisis hit.

An Old Story

But why is *Forbes* suddenly noticing corporate tax evasion? After all, corporations not paying taxes on their profits is an old story. Let's take a look at the track record of major corporations paying corporate income before the crisis hit and the losses that supposedly explain their not paying taxes.

The Government Accounting Office conducted a detailed study of the burden of the corporate income tax from 1998 to 2005. The results were stunning. Over half (55%) of large U.S. corporations reported no tax liability for at least one of those eight years. And in 2005 alone 25% of those corporations paid no corporate income taxes, even though corporate profits had more than doubled from 2001 to 2005.

In another careful study, the Treasury Department found that from 2000 to 2005, the share of corporate operating surplus that that U.S. corporations pay in taxes—a proxy for the average tax rate—was 16.7% thanks to various corporate loopholes, especially three key mechanisms:

- Accelerated Depreciation: allows corporations to write off machinery and equipment or other assets more quickly than they actually deteriorate.
- Stock Options: by giving their executives the option to buy the company's stock at a favorable price, corporations can take a tax deduction for the difference between what the employees pay for the stock and what it's worth.
- Debt Financing: offers a lower effective tax rate for corporate investment than equity (or stock) financing because the interest payments on debt (usually incurred by issuing bonds) get added to corporate costs and reduce reported profits.

Corporate income taxes are levied against reported corporate profits, and each of these mechanisms allows corporations to inflate their reported costs and thereby reduce their taxable profits.

And then there are overseas profits. U.S.-based corporations don't pay U.S. corporate taxes on their foreign income until it is "repatriated," or sent back to the parent corporation from abroad. That allows multinational corporations to defer payment of U.S. corporate income taxes on their overseas profits indefinitely or repatriate their profits from foreign subsidiaries when their losses from domestic operations can offset those profits and wipe out any tax liability, as GE did in 2010.

Hardly Overtaxed

Nonetheless, Scott Hodge, the president of the right-wing Tax Foundation, stead-fastly maintains that U.S. corporations are overtaxed, and that that is what driving U.S. corporations to park their profits abroad (and lower their U.S. taxes). Looking at nominal corporate tax rates, Hodge would seem to have a case. Among the 19 OECD countries, only the statutory corporate tax rates in Japan surpass the (aver-age combined federal and state) 39.3% rate on U.S. corporate profits. And the U.S. rate is well above the OECD average of 27.6%.

But these sorts of comparisons misrepresent where U.S. corporate taxes stand with respect to tax rates actually paid by corporations in other advanced countries. Why? The tax analyst's answer is that the U.S. corporate income tax has a "narrow base," or in plain English, is riddled with loopholes. As a result U.S. effective cor-porate tax rates—the proportion of corporate profits actually paid out in taxes—are not only far lower than the nominal rate but below the effective rates in several other countries. The Congressional Budget Office, for instance, found that U.S. effective corporate tax rates were near the OECD average for equity-financed investments, and below the OECD average for debt-financed investments. And for the years from 2000 to 2005, the Treasury Department found the average corporate tax rate among OECD countries was 21.6%, well above the U.S. 16.7% rate.

Current U.S. corporate tax rates are also extremely low by historical standards. In 1953, government revenue from the U.S. corporate income taxes were the equal of 5.6% of GDP; the figure was 4.0% of GDP in 1969, 2.2% of GDP from 2000 to 2005, and is currently running at about 2.0% of GDP.

By all these measures U.S. corporations are hardly over-taxed. And some major corporations are barely taxed, if taxed at all.

Closing corporate loopholes so that corporate income tax revenues in the United States match the 3.4% of GDP collected on average by OECD corporate income taxes would add close to $200 billion to federal government revenues—more than five times the $39 billion of devastating spending cuts just made in the federal bud-get in 2011. Returning the corporate income tax revenues to the 4.0% of GDP level of four decades ago would add close to $300 billion a year to government revenues.

The cost of not shutting down those corporate loopholes would be to let major cor-porations go untaxed, to rob the federal government of revenues that could, with enough political will, reverse devastating budget cuts, and to leave the rest of us to pay more and more of the taxes necessary to support a government that does less and less for us. ❏

Sources: "Corporate Tax Reform: Issues for Congress," by Jane G. Gravelle and Thomas L. Hungerford, CRS Report for Congress, October 31, 2007; "Treasury Conference On Business Taxation and Global Competitiveness," U.S. Department of the Treasury, Background Paper, July 23, 2007; "Six Tests for Corporate Tax Reform," by Chuck Marr and Brian Highsmith, Center on Budget and Policy Priorities, February 28, 2011; "Tax Holiday For Overseas Corporate Profits Would Increase Deficits, Fail To Boost The Economy, And Ultimately Shift More Investment And Jobs Overseas," by Chuck Marr and Brian Highsmith, Center on Budget and Policy Priorities, April 8, 2011; and, "Comparison of the Reported Tax Liabilities of Foreign and U.S.-Controlled Corporations, 1998-2005," Government Accounting Office, July 2008.

Article 9.4

WHAT'S WRONG WITH A FLAT TAX?

BY ARTHUR MacEWAN
September/October 2012

Dear Dr. Dollar:

Today a minister asked me why a flat tax, where "everybody pays their fair share," is not the best idea. I did not have a short, convincing explanation. Can you help? —Arthur Milholland, Silver Springs, MD

Although flat tax proposals differ, they have one basic thing in common: they would all reduce the tax rates for people with high incomes. Thus they would either shift the tax burden to people with lower incomes or lead to a reduction in government services or both.

Currently, the federal personal income tax is quite progressive on paper and somewhat progressive in fact. A "progressive" income tax system is one where people with higher incomes pay a larger percentage of their income as taxes than do people with lower incomes. (A "regressive" system is one where people with lower incomes pay a higher share of their income as taxes; a "proportional" system is one where everyone pays the same proportion of their income as taxes. A flat tax and a proportional tax are the same.)

The justification for a progressive tax system is fairness: people with higher incomes have a greater ability to pay taxes and therefore should be subject to a higher tax rate. For example (to take an extreme case), a family with an income of $2 million can pay $200,000 in taxes more easily (i.e., with less impact on their circumstances) than a family with an income of $20,000 can pay $2,000 in taxes. Also, the principle of fairness suggests that high-income families should pay higher rates to support a system that provides so well for them. These concepts of fairness have been long established in the U.S. personal income-tax system.

Even today, with rates for high-income people lowered from earlier years, the system still has a significant element of progressivity. For example, a family with taxable income of $20,000 would supposedly pay $2,150 (10.75%), while a family with taxable income of $1 million would supposedly pay $320,000 (32%). Of course many people, especially those with high-incomes, find various "loopholes," and do not end up paying as much in taxes as they otherwise would. Many loopholes are in the deductions that allow people to keep their taxable income—and therefore their taxes—down. At the same time, many people with low incomes have their taxes greatly reduced—sometimes resulting in payments *from* the government rather than tax payments *to* the government.

The Tax Policy Center has estimated that in 2010 people in the lowest 40% of the income distribution on average got money back from the government (because of the Earned Income Tax Credit and the Child Tax Credit), while people in the highest-income 20% on average paid taxes at a rate of 13.6%. People at the very top, the highest-income 1%, paid on average 18.6%.

Conservative ideologues like to jump on the fact that many low-income people pay no federal income tax at all. Yet federal income taxes are only part of the tax story. Low-income people still pay Social Security and Medicare taxes, sales taxes at the state level, and various other taxes. Overall, the U.S. tax system is hardly progressive at all, and may even be regressive.

Advocates of a flat tax claim it would be better to get rid of all the complications in the federal income tax—the adjustments, the credits, the deductions, etc.—and just charge everyone the same rate. Also, they argue that a flat tax would boost the economy because the current high rates on people with high incomes harm the incentive to invest and to work. Yet there is no way around the simple arithmetic: to lower the top rate and to obtain the same amount of revenue from a flat tax as from the current system, people below the top would have to have their tax rates increased. (While advocates of a flat tax generally reject the principles of fairness on which the progressivity of the U.S. tax code has long been based, it would be possible to introduce an element of progressivity into a flat tax by exempting all income below a certain level. Still, except for those people near the bottom, tax rates would have to be raised for most people—though not for those at the top.)

Furthermore, the claim that with a flat tax all the adjustments, credits, deductions, etc. would be eliminated is not credible. Indeed, since a flat tax would increase the after-tax income of those at the top, it would increase the amount of money they would have to buy influence to get their favorite "complications" reinstated (as if they didn't have enough influence already!). As to the argument that reducing the tax rate on people with high incomes would boost the economy, well, we have seen how well that has worked since the Bush tax cuts for the wealthy were put in place in 2001.

So a flat tax would be one more break for the rich, increasing their income on the backs of the great majority of the populace. Not fair at all. That's what's wrong with a flat tax. ❑

Article 9.5

TRANSACTION TAX: SAND IN THE WHEELS, NOT IN THE FACE

*Why a transaction tax is a really **good** idea.*

BY JOHN MILLER
March/April 2010

WHY TAXING STOCK TRADES IS A REALLY BAD IDEA

[S]urely it is "socially useful" to let free people transact freely, without regulators and legislators micromanaging them. ... It's Economics 101 that the free actions of market participants cause supply and demand to reach equilibrium. And isn't that what investors—indeed even speculators—do? Can they do it as well when facing the dead-weight costs of a transaction tax?

If not, then trading volume in our stock markets will fall. Beyond the tax, everyone—investors and speculator, great and small—who buys or sells stocks will pay more to transact in markets that are less liquid. In such a world, markets would necessarily be more risky, and the cost of capital for business would necessarily rise. The consequence of that is that innovation, growth, and jobs would necessarily fall. That would be the full and true cost of the trading tax.

—Donald L. Luskin and Chris Hynes, "Why Taxing Stock Trades Is a Really Bad Idea," *Wall Street Journal*, January 5, 2010

"Some financial activities which proliferated over the last 10 years were socially useless," Britain's Finance Service Authority Chairman Adiar Turner told a black-tie gathering of financial executives in London in September 2009. That is why he had proposed a transaction tax for the United Kingdom and why British Prime Minister Gordon Brown would propose an international transaction tax at the November G-20 summit.

The gathered bankers "saw red," as one report described their reaction. Investment bankers Donald L. Luskin and Chris Hynes are still irate.

In some ways their reaction is surprising. A financial transaction tax is nothing other than a sales tax on trading stocks and other securities. Transaction taxes are already in place in about 30 countries, and a transaction tax applied to the sale of stock in the United States from 1914 to 1964.

In addition, the transaction tax rates on a single trade are typically quite low. For instance, the "Let Wall Street Pay for the Restoration of Main Street Act of 2009," proposed by U.S. Representative Peter DeFazio (D-Ore.), would assess a one quarter of one percent (.25%) tax on the value of stock transactions, and two one hundredths of one percent (.02%) tax on the sale on a variety of derivative assets—including credit default swaps, which played such a large role in the mortgage crisis. To target speculators, the bill exempts retirement accounts, mutual funds, education and health savings accounts, and the first $100,000 of transactions annually.

In other ways, Luskin's and Hynes's reaction is not surprising at all. At its heart, a transaction tax is a radical measure. Its premise is that faster-acting financial markets driven by speculation don't bring relief to the economy—instead, they loot the economy. Its purpose, as Nobel Prize-winning economist James Tobin put it when he proposed his original transaction tax on international money markets during the 1970s, is to "throw sand in the wheels" of our financial markets.

Also, while its tax rate is low, the burden of a transaction tax adds up as securities are repeatedly traded, as is the practice on Wall Street today. For instance, even after accounting for its exemptions and allowing for a sizable decline in trading, the DeFazio bill would still raise $63.5 billion annually, according to the estimates of Dean Baker, co-director of the Center for Economic Policy Research.

Luskin and Hynes have two main objections to the transaction tax. The first is that a transaction tax would affect every single person who owns and invests in stocks, not just speculators. Customers would not have to pay a tax to buy or sell mutual funds, but, as Luskin and Hynes emphasize, the mutual funds themselves would have to pay a tax every time they trade stocks. So everyone holding mutual funds would still end up paying the tax.

What Luskin and Hynes don't say is this: Mutual funds that actively trade stocks would pay three times the transaction taxes of an average fund, as the Investment Company Institute, the fund industry trade group, reports. And stock index funds, which hold a sample of all stocks but seldom trade them, are taxed the least. Those funds have historically outperformed other mutual funds. So a transaction tax would work to push mutual fund customers to invest their savings more wisely, providing some with higher rates of return with a transaction tax than their previous funds provided without it. And that would mean fewer broker fees and lower profits for the fund industry.

But what really sticks in Luskin's and Hynes's craw is the assertion that financial trading is not socially useful. That claim flies in face of the long-held contention, buttressed by much of finance theory, that the equilibrium outcomes of financial markets are efficient. And if financial markets are efficient, there is no need for a tax that will reduce trading.

But much of what Luskin and Hynes have to say is not right. First, as anyone who *paid attention* in Economics 101 would know, reaching an equilibrium is not in and of itself desirable. To endorse the outcomes of today's speculative financial markets as desirable because they reach an equilibrium is the equivalent of describing a gambler in a poker game raking in a big pot as desirable because it clears the table. And the gamblers in our financial markets did rake in some awfully big pots betting that subprime borrowers would default on their loans. The last few years show us just how undesirable that equilibrium turned out to be.

Second, speculation dwarfs financing investment in U.S. stock markets. During the 1970s, for every dollar of new investment in plants and equipment, $1.30 in stocks were traded on the U.S. exchanges, reports Robert Pollin, co-director of the Political Economy Research Institute. But from 1998 to 2007, $27 in stocks were traded on the U.S. exchanges for every dollar of corporate investment in plant equipment. Such a rapid stock turnover has diverted the attention of managers of enterprises from long-term planning. Whatever damage that churning caused on Main Street, it paid off handsomely on Wall Street. From 1973 to 2007, the size of the financial (and insurance) sector relative to the economy doubled, financial sector profits went from one-quarter to two-fifths of domestic profits, and compensation in the finance industry went from just about average to 180% of the private industry average.

By counteracting these trends, a transactions tax can actually enhance, not diminish, the efficiency of financial markets. If it forces the financial sector to fulfill its function of transferring savings to investment with less short-term churning, then the tax will have freed up resources for more productive uses.

A transaction tax would surely be a step in the right direction toward reducing the bloat of the finance industry, righting the balance of speculation over enterprise, and restoring the focus on long-term planning and job-creation in the economy.

None of that will happen unless every last grain of the decades' worth of sand the bullies on Wall Street have kicked in our faces gets thrown into the wheels of finance. That is a tall order. But as DeFazio's and Turner's example shows, some of today's policymakers are up to the task. ❑

Sources: Dean Baker, "The Benefits of a Financial Transaction Tax," Center For Economic and Policy Research, December 2008; Robert Pollin and Dean Baker, "Public Investment, Industrial Policy, and U.S. Economic Renewal," Political Economy Research Institute, December 2009; Caroline Binham, "Turner Plan on 'Socially Useless' Trades Make Bankers See Red," Bloomberg. com; Yaiman Onaran, "Taxing Wall Street Today Wins Support for Keynes Idea (Update 1)," Bloomberg.com; Dean Baker, Robert Pollin, Travis McArthur, and Matt Sherman, "The Potential Revenue from Financial Transactions Taxes, Political Economy Research Institute, Working paper no. 212, December 2009; Donald L. Luskin and Chris Hynes, "Why Taxing Stock Trades Is a Really Bad Idea," *Wall Street Journal*, January 5, 2010; John McKinnon, "Lawmakers Weigh A Wall Street Tax," *Wall Street Journal*, December 19, 2009; Tobin Tax, freerisk.org/wiki/index. php/Tobin_tax; text of HR 4191—"Let Wall Street Pay for the Restoration of Main Street Act of 2009," www.govtrack.us.

Article 9.6

THE STATE INCOME TAX AND THE FOOTLOOSE TAXPAYER

BY JOHN MILLER
March/April 2013

> Nine states ... have no income tax, and the race is on to see which will be the tenth, and perhaps the 11th and 12th. ...
>
> Nebraska Governor Dave Heineman ... wants to eliminate the state income tax and replace it with a broader sales tax. ... Louisiana Governor Bobby Jindal wants to zero out his state's [income and corporate taxes] and replace them by raising the state's current 4% sales tax. ...
>
> As an economic matter, this swap makes sense. Income taxes generally do more economic harm because they are a direct penalty on saving, investment and labor that create new wealth.
> —"The State Tax Reformers," *Wall Street Journal*, Jan. 29, 2013.

> America's top-grossing golfer Phil Mickelson said that federal and California state tax hikes had made him contemplate making "drastic changes" in his life—including, it was widely assumed, moving to a no-income-tax state such as Texas or Florida.
> —"Mickelson and the Sports Star Tax Migration," *Wall Street Journal*, Jan. 27, 2013

Perhaps we are not so different from the rich and famous after all. Income tax rates go up in California, and PGA star Phil Mickelson contemplates hightailing it for Florida. And if your state jacks up its income-tax rate, you ought to be out of there as well, off to amass your fortune in a no-income-tax state. Or better still, your state might become the next to abolish its income tax, and you can hit the jackpot in the comfort of your own home.

I have some bad news for you. The mega-wealthy who own houses in multiple states—any one of which they could designate as their tax home—really are different from us. We're not so footloose when it comes to escaping state income taxes. And despite the insistence otherwise of the *Wall Street Journal* editors, the state income tax is not what stands between you and prosperity.

But there is good news as well. State governments are not actually held hostage by hordes of taxpayers ready to depart if their income gets taxed. A few just act that way—no wonder given the anti-income-tax snow job of the *WSJ* editors. But the truth is that junking the income tax and ratcheting up sales-tax rates, thrusting more of the tax burden onto middle- and low-income taxpayers, is no prerequisite for prosperity. Rather, the states with the most progressive state income taxes are more prosperous than those without a state income tax, and do a better job of adequately funding the state services on which we all depend.

The Rich Don't Move That Much

Let's start with the rich. Every report of millionaires stampeding for the exit because a state threatens higher income taxes turns out to be an urban legend.

In 2004, New Jersey raised the tax rate on income over $500,000 by 2.6 percentage points. A few years later, citing a Chamber of Commerce study, Gov. Chris Christie warned that "if you tax them, they will leave." But it turns out that no more than 70 taxpayers in that bracket left New Jersey between 2004 and 2007, and the tax increase added nearly $4 billion in state revenues over those years.

In 2005, California passed a 1% tax on income over $1 million to finance mental-health services. A study conducted last year by sociologists Charles Varner and Cristóbal Young found "no observable tax flight" in response to the millionaire tax. As they noted, net migration accounted for a change of just 50-120 people in California's millionaire population, or about 1% of the total 10,000-person change.

In Maryland, a 2008 tax increase on income over $1 million brought reports that "Millionaires Go Missing," in the *Wall Street Journal*. That may have helped convince the state legislature to let the increase expire in 2011. But a follow-up study by the Institute on Taxation and Economic Policy (ITEP), the research wing of Citizens for Tax Justice, found that nearly the entire decline in the number of millionaires was due to a drop in their incomes (from the stock-market crash and Great Recession), not to out-migration. Those former millionaires remained on the tax rolls, but in a lower tax bracket.

Part of the reason that these state income taxes provoked little migration among the wealthy is that state-to-state migration is uncommon. Most people, even the rich, have strong ties to their states and are reluctant to leave. In the years from 2001 to 2010, just 1.7% of U.S. residents moved from one state to another for any reason.

Income Taxes and the Rest of Us

But wouldn't moving to a non-income-tax state, or better yet getting your state to gut its income tax, do you a world of good?

That's the message that Arthur Laffer, the supply-side economist who for decades has oversold federal pro-rich tax cuts as an elixir of economic growth, is peddling to state governments. And it's one that the *Journal* editors are only too happy to endorse.

According to the editors, the latest edition of Laffer's *Rich States, Poor States* report demonstrates that taxing the rich, through progressive taxation, is counterproductive. The report, a publication of the conservative American Legislative Exchange Council (ALEC), claims to show that the economies of the nine states with no income tax (Alaska, Florida, Nevada, New Hampshire, South Dakota, Tennessee, Texas, Washington, and Wyoming) outperform the economies of the nine states with high income-tax rates (California, Hawaii, Maine, Maryland, New Jersey, New York, Ohio, Oregon, and Vermont). But that conclusion is sustained only by "cherry picking" the data, as a recent ITEP critique of Laffer's report puts it.

To begin with, the nine states with high income taxes are more prosperous than the nine states without an income tax. In 2011, per-capita personal income in the no-income-tax states averaged just over $42,000, less than the $44,000 average in the high-tax states.

What about Laffer's claim that the no-income-tax states are more dynamic than the high-income-tax states? That comparison doesn't favor the no-income-tax states either, once you correct the flaws in Laffer's analysis. A disproportionate amount of the economic growth and job creation of the nation in the last decade was, indeed, concentrated in the no-income-tax states. But Laffer's conclusions depend on his ignoring population growth. On economic growth, Laffer reports that, over the ten years from 2001 to 2010, output increased by almost 60% in the nine no-income-tax states, compared to just over 40% in the high-income-tax states. But, as even Laffer admits, those results are driven largely by higher population growth in the no-income-tax states. When the ITEP report corrected Laffer's figures for population growth, it found that real per-capita income growth rates in the no-income-tax states (5.2%) were far lower than those in high-income-tax states (8.2%) from 2002 to 2011.

Laffer's job-creation numbers are just as misleading. First off, more than two-thirds of the net job creation in the no-income-tax states from 2002 to 2011 occurred in just one state, Texas. Five of the nine states contributed less than 1% of national net job creation over that period. On top of that, the average unemployment in the no-income-tax states from 2002 to 2011 was 6.0%—hardly different from the 6.1% average in the high-income-tax states. Things are no better in Texas; its average unemployment rate was 6.2% from 2002 to 2011, and its per capita income was below the national average at the end of that period.

Finally, it is true that revenues from progressive state income taxes are more volatile than those from highly regressive state sales taxes. But abandoning the income tax for a sales tax, as the *WSJ* editors counsel, would not improve the finances of state governments. That's because the personal income tax is the only major state tax that generates revenues that keep pace with the growth of the economy. A 2005 study conducted by Legislative Analyst's Office of cash-strapped California found that, "any rebalancing which reduces the state's dependence on California's progressive PIT [personal income tax] would likely result in less growth in revenues over the long term." Beyond worsening state finances, any policy that lowers income-tax rates and increases the share of state revenues collected from sales taxes would shift more of the burden of state taxes onto middle- and low-income taxpayers.

The Choice Before Us

The actual choice between no-income-tax and high-income-tax states is far different than the one the *Journal* editors suggest. No-income-tax states levy regressive taxes unlikely to be able to fund state services, while high-income-tax states levy more progressive taxes that are more volatile but will do a better job of funding state government over time. The economies of no-income-tax states offer a lower standard of living and slower economic growth per capita than the economies in the high-income-tax states. The no-income-tax states have higher but uneven job creation and unemployment rates no lower than the high-income-tax states.

That hardly constitutes a persuasive case for giving up on progressive taxation. And despite the "if you tax them, they will leave" scare tactics, it is clear that states can impose graduated income taxes without their people heading for the door.

If your state has an income tax, it should stick with it and might even raise its top rate to fund much-needed programs, if you don't mind a couple of PGA superstars moving out of the neighborhood. ❏

Sources: James B. Stewart, "The Myth of the Rich Who Flee From Taxes," *The New York Times*, Feb. 15, 2013; Elizabeth G. Hall, "Revenue Volatility in California," California Legislative Analyst's Office, January 2005; "States with 'High Rate' Income Taxes Are Still Outperforming No-Tax States," Institute on Taxation and Economic Policy (ITEP), Feb. 28, 2013; "Laffer's Latest Job Growth Factoid is All Rhetoric," ITEP, Feb. 27, 2013; Robert Tannenwald, Jon Shure, and Nicholas Johnson, "Tax Flight Is A Myth," Center for Budget and Policy Priorities (CBPP), Aug. 4, 2011; Cristóbal Young and Charles Varner, "Millionaire Migration and State Taxation on Top Incomes," *National Tax Journal*, June 2011; Charles Varner and Cristóbal Young, "Millionaire Migration in California," 2012; Arthur Laffer, Stephen Moore, Jonathan Williams, *Rich States, Poor States*, 5th ed., American Legislative Exchange Council (ALEC), 2012.

Article 9.7

WHO ARE "THE 47%"?

And why don't they pay (income) taxes?

BY GERALD FRIEDMAN
November/December 2012

"There are 47% of the people ... who are dependent upon government, who believe that they are victims, who believe the government has a responsibility to care for them, who believe that they are entitled to health care, to food, to housing, to you-name-it .... These are people who pay no income tax."

While Mitt Romney did not intend for the general public to hear his candid remarks to his wealthy donors, his dismissal of nearly half of the American public as irresponsible dependents mooching off hard-working taxpayers is common among American conservatives. It is also wrong.

Virtually all of those who pay no federal income tax pay other taxes, including federal payroll taxes and state and local sales and property taxes, and many pay a higher share of their income in taxes than do Mitt Romney and his wealthy friends. (The latter avoid payroll taxes and much of their income tax by taking their salary as capital gains.) Furthermore, most of "the 47%" owe no federal income tax for good and sensible reasons: they are disabled, elderly, or have a very low income.

FIGURE 1: SHARE OF HOUSEHOLDS BY TAX STATUS

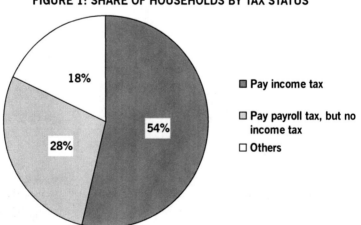

- ■ Pay income tax
- ☐ Pay payroll tax, but no income tax
- ☐ Others

18%

54%

28%

While just over 46% of Americans paid no income tax last year, over half of them (over 28% of the total) paid payroll taxes (e.g., Social Security and Medicare taxes), most paid federal excise taxes (on phones and other services), and almost all paid sales and other state and local taxes.

FIGURE 2: REASONS FOR NOT PAYING INCOME TAX

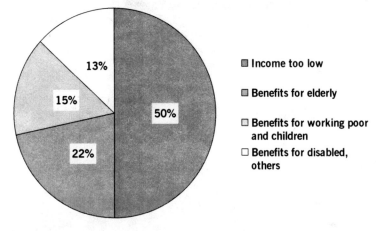

- ▨ Income too low
- ▨ Benefits for elderly
- ☐ Benefits for working poor and children
- ☐ Benefits for disabled, others

Those who are not paying income tax include the elderly, the disabled, many children, and the poorest Americans. Almost a third have household incomes under $10,000, and almost two thirds have incomes under $20,000. Only 5% have household incomes of as much as $50,000.

FIGURE 3: PERCENTAGE NOT PAYING INCOME TAX, BY INCOME CLASS

The proportion of returns without income tax liability falls quickly from almost 100% for the lowest incomes down to a negligible percentage for high income returns.

Many Americans do not pay income tax because of provisions inserted into the tax code, including some under Republican icons like Richard Nixon and Ronald Reagan, to encourage low-income Americans to seek paid work— such as the Earned

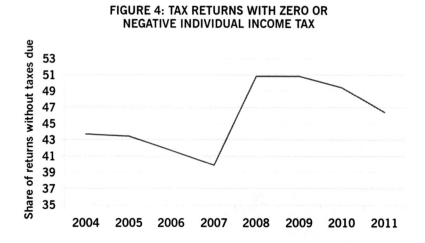

FIGURE 4: TAX RETURNS WITH ZERO OR
NEGATIVE INDIVIDUAL INCOME TAX

Income Tax Credit and the high minimum income threshold before income taxes are due. Because of provisions like these, when incomes fall, the income of a larger share of Americans falls below the level at which they pay income taxes. This is why the share not paying income tax increased sharply during the Great Recession, and has been decreasing (slowly) with the (slow) recovery since.

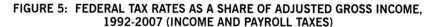

FIGURE 5: FEDERAL TAX RATES AS A SHARE OF ADJUSTED GROSS INCOME,
1992-2007 (INCOME AND PAYROLL TAXES)

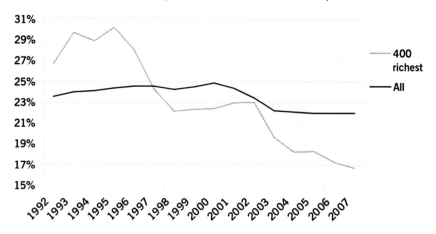

The real tax evaders are not the disabled, elderly, or the poor who earn too little to pay federal income tax. They are the super-rich who shift income into tax shelters, offshore accounts, and get paid in capital gains taxed at a preferential rate. Such evasions have allowed the wealthiest Americans to lower their total federal tax bill to well below the rate paid by other Americans. ❑

Source: Tax Policy Center.

Chapter 10

TRADE AND DEVELOPMENT

INTRODUCTION

Given the economic turmoil of the last four years in the developed world, it is ironic that the developing world is still being urged to adopt free markets and increased privatization as the keys to catching up with the West. These neoliberal policy prescriptions have been applied across the developing world, over the last few decades, as a one-size-fits-all solution to problems such as poverty, malnutrition, and political conflict. While spiking unemployment in the United States led to a (temporary) surge in government spending, developing countries with double-digit unemployment were routinely told that macroeconomic crises could only be dealt with by "tightening their belts." And while the West, having experienced a financial crisis, now embraced some new financial regulations, similar calls for more regulation from developing countries were dismissed as misguided.

The contributors to this section take on different aspects of the neoliberal (or "free market") policy mix, raising questions that recur through this entire volume. Where do the limits of the market lie? At what point do we decide that markets are no longer serving the general public, whose well-being economists claim to champion? And to what extent should communities, via politically representative bodies of all kinds, be able to regulate and control markets?

The first tenet of the neoliberal faith is the belief that openness to international trade is the key to growth and development. Ramaa Vasudevan, in the primer "Comparative Advantage" (Article 10.1), starts off this chapter with a critique of the Ricardian theory of comparative advantage that is central to the neoclassical argument for free trade.

Thomas Palley offers a concise and useful metaphor for the effect of globalization and outsourcing on productive industry in the United States. "The Globalization Clock" (Article 10.2) describes how globalization and outsourcing pick off domestic industries one by one, based on the relative exportability of the goods or services and the skill level of the workers. This metaphor also illustrates why, at any given period of time, there has not been a majority consensus against outsourcing: The majority of people (consumers) benefit through lower prices from the outsourced industry; only those acutely affected through the loss of their jobs are against it. But as the clock ticks forward, more and more industries at higher and higher levels of skill become outsourced.

Ellen Frank's "Should Developing Countries Embrace Protectionism?" (Article 10.3), points out that, contrary to the claims of globalization advocates and the theory of comparative advantage, the historical record suggests that protectionism may be a better strategy for economic development. In fact, it is hard to provide an example of successful economic growth and development from countries that "got prices right" as opposed to those that "got prices wrong"—but to their trading advantage.

Tim Wise's "How Beer Explains 20 Years of NAFTA's Devastating Effects on Mexico" (Article 10.4) explores the flip side of the question: What can happen to a developing country that embraces the neoliberal "free trade" agenda? Wise's answer is that its own productive capacity can be devastated, while it increasingly specializes in low domestic-input assembly industry.

Next, Elissa Dennis describes an intriguing policy proposal from the government of Ecuador, which would give the country needed funds for economic development in exchange for *not* extracting its oil (Article 10.5). Recognizing the environmental damage done by petroleum extraction (especially right around drilling sites) and consumption (globally), Ecuador has offered to "keep it in the ground." It would forego some of the revenues it could gain from extraction, while asking international contributors to pay the rest.

The relationship between two economic giants, the United States and China, powerfully shapes the global economy. Exports are the engine of China's recent rapid growth, and the United States is its biggest customer. Arthur MacEwan examines accusations against the Chinese government of "currency manipulation"—a policy of actively pushing down the value of its currency, the yuan, relative to the dollar, and therefore keeping its exports cheaper. By examining why the United States, which has lost manufacturing jobs, does not protest more strenuously against this policy, MacEwan exposes the mutual dependence of the Chinese and U.S. economic strategies (Article 10.6).

A major change in China's economy, and therefore in the entire global economy, may be coming from Chinese workers. John Miller explains, in this chapter's final article, how the combination of tighter labor markets and labor militancy has been pushing up wages in China since 2009. Miller reports on the labor unrest in China's export factories and argues that improving conditions for workers in China is good news for factory workers around the globe (Article 10.7).

Discussion Questions

1. (Article 10.1) Under what conditions might the mainstream argument about the advantages of specialization based on comparative advantage break down?

2. (Article 10.2) Thomas Palley argues that the relative benefits and costs of globalization are not evenly distributed. Some folks gain from globalization and others lose. What is "Palley's Clock"? Explain in detail the metaphor and mechanism.

3. (Article 10.2) Does Palley's assessment of globalization differ at all from your textbook's? What time is it in the United States according to "Palley's Clock"?

4. (Article 10.3) What is the basic argument in favor of free trade? Ellen Frank argues that free trade can prevent poorer countries from developing, rather than helping them do so. (The same argument applies to poorer regions within richer countries like the United States.) What is her reasoning? How do you think a pro-free-trade economist would respond?

5. (Article 10.4) In Wise's view, how has NAFTA "devastated" the Mexican economy? How is beer an example of economic tends characterizing the Mexican economy more broadly, since the passage of NAFTA?

6. (Article 10.5) How does the development strategy proposed by the government of Ecuador differ from the neoliberal development path common in poor countries that possess valuable natural resources? How does it differ even from the paths of other countries in which the government plays a large role in resource development?

7. (Article 10.6) How does China's government keep down the prices of its exports? Why does the U.S. government not protest more strenuously against this policy?

8. (Article 10.7) What explains rising wages in Chinese export factories? How do Miller's and the *Wall Street Journal*'s definition of the virtuous cycle of development differ?

Article 10.1

COMPARATIVE ADVANTAGE

BY RAMAA VASUDEVAN
July/August 2007

Dear Dr. Dollar:
When economists argue that the outsourcing of jobs might be a plus for the U.S. economy, they often mention the idea of comparative advantage. So free trade would allow the United States to specialize in higher-end service-sector businesses, creating higher-paying jobs than the ones that would be outsourced. But is it really true that free trade leads to universal benefits?
—David Goodman, Boston, Mass.

You're right: The purveyors of the free trade gospel do invoke the doctrine of comparative advantage to dismiss widespread concerns about the export of jobs. Attributed to 19th-century British political-economist David Ricardo, the doctrine says that a nation always stands to gain if it exports the goods it produces *relatively* more cheaply in exchange for goods that it can get *comparatively* more cheaply from abroad. Free trade would lead to each country specializing in the products it can produce at *relatively* lower costs. Such specialization allows both trading partners to gain from trade, the theory goes, even if in one of the countries production of *both* goods costs more in absolute terms.

For instance, suppose that in the United States the cost to produce one car equals the cost to produce 10 bags of cotton, while in the Philippines the cost to produce one car equals the cost to produce 100 bags of cotton. The Philippines would then have a comparative advantage in the production of cotton, producing one bag at a cost equal to the production cost of 1/100 of a car, versus 1/10 of a car in the United States; likewise, the United States would hold a comparative advantage in the production of cars. Whatever the prices of cars and cotton in the global market, the theory goes, the Philippines would be better off producing only cotton and importing all its cars from the United States, and the United States would be better off producing only cars and importing all of its cotton from the Philippines. If the international terms of trade—the relative price—is one car for 50 bags, then the United States will take in 50 bags of cotton for each car it exports, 40 more than the 10 bags it forgoes by putting its productive resources into making the car rather than growing cotton. The Philippines is also better off: it can import a car in exchange for the export of 50 bags of cotton, whereas it would have had to forgo the production of 100 bags of cotton in order to produce that car domestically. If the price of cars goes up in the global marketplace, the Philippines will lose out in relative terms—but will still be better off than if it tried to produce its own cars.

The real world, unfortunately, does not always conform to the assumptions underlying comparative-advantage theory. One assumption is that trade is balanced. But many countries are running persistent deficits, notably the United States, whose trade deficit is now at nearly 7% of its GDP. A second premise, that there is full employment within the trading nations, is also patently unrealistic. As global trade intensifies, jobs created in the export sector do not necessarily compensate for the jobs lost in the sectors wiped out by foreign competition.

The comparative advantage story faces more direct empirical challenges as well. Nearly 70% of U.S. trade is trade in similar goods, known as *intra-industry trade*: for example, exporting Fords and importing BMWs. And about one third of U.S. trade as of the late 1990s was trade between branches of a single corporation located in different countries (*intra-firm trade*). Comparative advantage cannot explain these patterns.

Comparative advantage is a static concept that identifies immediate gains from trade but is a poor guide to economic development, a process of structural change over time which is by definition dynamic. Thus the comparative advantage tale is particularly pernicious when preached to developing countries, consigning many to "specialize" in agricultural goods or be forced into a race to the bottom where cheap sweatshop labor is their sole source of competitiveness.

The irony, of course, is that none of the rich countries got that way by following the maxim that they now preach. These countries historically relied on tariff walls and other forms of protectionism to build their industrial base. And even now, they continue to protect sectors like agriculture with subsidies. The countries now touted as new models of the benefits of free trade—South Korea and the other "Asian tigers," for instance—actually flouted this economic wisdom, nurturing their technological capabilities in specific manufacturing sectors and taking advantage of their lower wage costs to *gradually* become effective competitors of the United States and Europe in manufacturing.

The fundamental point is this: contrary to the comparative-advantage claim that trade is universally beneficial, nations as a whole do not prosper from free trade. Free trade creates winners and losers, both within and between countries. In today's context it is the global corporate giants that are propelling and profiting from "free trade": not only outsourcing white-collar jobs, but creating global commodity chains linking sweatshop labor in the developing countries of Latin America and Asia (Africa being largely left out of the game aside from the export of natural resources such as oil) with ever-more insecure consumers in the developed world. Promoting "free trade" as a political cause enables this process to continue.

It is a process with real human costs in terms of both wages and work. People in developing countries across the globe continue to face these costs as trade liberalization measures are enforced; and the working class in the United States is also being forced to bear the brunt of the relentless logic of competition. ❏

Sources: Arthur MacEwan, "The Gospel of Free Trade: The New Evangelists," *Dollars & Sense*, July/August 2002; Ha-Joon Chang, *Kicking away the Ladder: The Real History of Fair Trade*, Foreign Policy in Focus, 2003; Anwar Shaikh, "Globalization and the Myths of Free Trade," in *Globalization and the Myths of Free Trade: History, Theory, and Empirical Evidence*, ed. Anwar Shaikh, Routledge 2007.

Article 10.2

THE GLOBALIZATION CLOCK
Why corporations are winning and workers are losing.

BY THOMAS PALLEY
May/June 2006

Political economy has historically been constructed around the divide between capital and labor, with firms and workers at odds over the division of the economic pie. Within this construct, labor is usually represented as a monolithic interest, yet the reality is that labor has always suffered from internal divisions—by race, by occupational status, and along many other fault lines. Neoliberal globalization has in many ways sharpened these divisions, which helps to explain why corporations have been winning and workers losing.

One of these fault lines divides workers from themselves: since workers are also consumers, they face a divide between the desire for higher wages and the desire for lower prices. Historically, this identity split has been exploited to divide union from nonunion workers, with anti-labor advocates accusing union workers of causing higher prices. Today, globalization is amplifying the divide between people's interests as workers and their interests as consumers through its promise of ever-lower prices.

Consider the debate over Wal-Mart's low-road labor policies. While Wal-Mart's low wages and skimpy benefits have recently faced scrutiny, even some liberal commentators argue that Wal-Mart is actually good for low-wage workers because they gain more as consumers from its "low, low prices" than they lose as workers from its low wages. But this static, snapshot analysis fails to capture the full impact of globalization, past and future.

Globalization affects the economy unevenly, hitting some sectors first and others later. The process can be understood in terms of the hands of a clock. At one o'clock is the apparel sector; at two o'clock the textile sector; at three the steel sector; at six the auto sector. Workers in the apparel sector are the first to have their jobs shifted to lower-wage venues; at the same time, though, all other workers get price reductions. Next, the process picks off textile sector workers at two o'clock. Meanwhile, workers from three o'clock onward get price cuts, as do the apparel workers at one o'clock. Each time the hands of the clock move, the workers taking the hit are isolated. In this fashion globalization moves around the clock, with labor perennially divided.

Manufacturing was first to experience this process, but technological innovations associated with the Internet are putting service and knowledge workers in the firing line as well. Online business models are making even retail workers vulnerable—consider Amazon.com, for example, which has opened a customer support center and two technology development centers in India. Public sector wages are also in play, at least indirectly, since falling wages mean falling tax revenues. The problem is that each time the hands on the globalization clock move forward, workers are divided: the majority is made slightly better off while the few are made much worse off.

Globalization also alters the historical divisions within capital, creating a new split between bigger internationalized firms and smaller firms that remain nationally centered. This division has been brought into sharp focus with the debate over the trade deficit and the overvalued dollar. In previous decades, manufacturing as a whole opposed running trade deficits and maintaining an overvalued dollar because of the adverse impact of increased imports. The one major business sector with a different view was retailing, which benefited from cheap imports.

However, the spread of multinational production and outsourcing has divided manufacturing in wealthy countries into two camps. In one camp are larger multinational corporations that have gone global and benefit from cheap imports; in the other are smaller businesses that remain nationally centered in terms of sales, production and input sourcing. Multinational corporations tend to support an overvalued dollar since this makes imports produced in their foreign factories cheaper. Conversely, domestic manufacturers are hurt by an overvalued dollar, which advantages import competition.

This division opens the possibility of a new alliance between labor and those manufacturers and businesses that remain nationally based—potentially a potent one, since there are approximately seven million enterprises with sales of less than $10 million in the United States, versus only 200,000 with sales greater than $10 million. However, such an alliance will always be unstable as the inherent labor-capital conflict over income distribution can always reassert itself. Indeed, this pattern is already evident in the internal politics of the National Association of Manufacturers, whose members have been significantly divided regarding the overvalued dollar. As one way to address this division, the group is promoting a domestic "competitiveness" agenda aimed at weakening regulation, reducing corporate legal liability, and lowering employee benefit costs—an agenda designed to appeal to both camps, but at the expense of workers.

Solidarity has always been key to political and economic advance by working families, and it is key to mastering the politics of globalization. Developing a coherent story about the economics of neoliberal globalization around which working families can coalesce is a key ingredient for solidarity. So too is understanding how globalization divides labor. These narratives and analyses can help counter deep cultural proclivities to individualism, as well as other historic divides such as racism. However, as if this were not difficult enough, globalization creates additional challenges. National political solutions that worked in the past are not adequate to the task of controlling international competition. That means the solidarity bar is further raised, calling for international solidarity that supports new forms of international economic regulation. ❑

Article 10.3

SHOULD DEVELOPING COUNTRIES EMBRACE PROTECTIONISM?

BY ELLEN FRANK
July 2004

> Dear Dr. Dollar:
> *Supposedly, countries should produce what they are best at. If the United States makes computers and China produces rice, then the theory of free trade says China should trade its rice for computers. But if China puts tariffs on U.S.-made computers and builds up its own computer industry, then it will become best at making them and can buy rice from Vietnam. Isn't it advantageous for poor countries to practice protectionism and become industrial powers themselves, rather than simply producing mono-crop commodities? I'm asking because local alternative currencies like Ithaca Hours benefit local businesses, though they restrict consumers to local goods that may be more expensive than goods from further away.*
> —Matt Cary, Hollywood, Fla.

The modern theory of free trade argues that countries are "endowed" with certain quantities of labor, capital, and natural resources. A country with lots of labor but little capital should specialize in the production of labor-intensive goods, like hand-woven rugs, hand-sewn garments, or hand-picked fruit. By ramping up produc-tion of these goods, a developing country can trade on world markets, earning the foreign exchange to purchase capital-intensive products like computers and cars. Free trade thus permits poor countries (or, to be more precise, their most well-off citizens) to *consume* high-tech goods that they lack the ability to *produce* and so obtain higher living standards. "Capital-rich" countries like the United States benefit from relatively cheap fruit and garments, freeing up their workforce to focus on high-tech goods. Free trade, according to this story, is a win-win game for everyone.

The flaw in this tale, which you have hit upon exactly, is that being "capital-rich" or "capital-poor" is not a natural phenomenon like having lots of oil. Capital is created—typically with plenty of government assistance and protection.

Developing countries can create industrial capacity and train their citizens to manufacture high-tech goods. But doing so takes time. Building up the capacity to manufacture computers, for example, at prices that are competitive with firms in developed countries may take several years. To buy this time, a government needs to keep foreign-made computers from flooding its market and undercutting less-established local producers. It also needs to limit inflows of foreign capital. Studies show that when foreign firms set up production facilities in developing countries, they are unlikely to share their latest techniques, so such foreign investment does not typically build local expertise or benefit local entrepreneurs.

The United States and other rich countries employed these protectionist strategies. In the 1800s, American entrepreneurs traveled to England and France to learn the latest manufacturing techniques and freely appropriated designs for cutting-edge industrial equipment. The U.S. government protected its nascent industries with high tariff walls until they could compete with European manufacturers.

After World War II, Japan effectively froze out foreign goods while building up world-class auto, computer, and electronics industries. Korea later followed Japan's strategy; in recent years, so has China. There, "infant industries" are heavily protected by tariffs, quotas, and other trade barriers. Foreign producers are welcome only if they establish high-tech facilities in which Chinese engineers and production workers can garner the most modern skills.

Development economists like Alice Amsden and Dani Rodrik are increasingly reaching the conclusion that carefully designed industrial policies, combined with protections for infant industries, are most effective in promoting internal development in poor countries. "Free-trade" policies, on the other hand, seem to lock poor countries into producing low-tech goods like garments and agricultural commodities, whose prices tend to decline on world markets due to intense competition with other poor countries.

In the contemporary global economy, however, there are three difficulties with implementing a local development strategy. First, some countries have bargained away their right to protect local firms by entering into free-trade agreements. Second, protectionism means that local consumers are denied the benefits of cheap manufactured goods from abroad, at least in the short run.

Finally, in many parts of the world the floodgates of foreign-made goods have already been opened and, with the middle and upper classes enjoying their computers and cell phones, it may be impossible to build the political consensus to close them. This last concern bears on the prospects for local alternative currencies. Since it is impos-sible to "close off" the local economy, the success of local currencies in bolstering hometown businesses depends on the willingness of local residents to deny themselves the benefits of cheaper nonlocal goods. Like national protectionist polices, local currencies restrict consumer choice.

Ultimately, the success or failure of such ventures rests on the degree of public support for local business. With local currencies, participation is voluntary and attitudes toward local producers often favorable. National protectionist polices, however, entail coerced public participation and generally fail when governments are corrupt and unable to command public support. ❑

Article 10.4

HOW BEER EXPLAINS 20 YEARS OF NAFTA'S DEVASTATING EFFECTS ON MEXICO

BY TIMOTHY A. WISE
January 2014; Global Post

Mexico's largest agribusiness association invited me to Aguascalientes to participate in its annual forum in October. The theme for this year's gathering was "New Perspectives on the Challenge of Feeding the World."

But it was unclear why Mexico, which now imports 42% of its food, would be worried about feeding the world. It wasn't doing so well feeding its own people.

In part, you can thank the North American Free Trade Agreement (NAFTA) for that. Twenty years ago, on January 1, 1994, NAFTA took effect, and Mexico was the poster child for the wonders of free trade. The promises seemed endless.

Mexico would enter the "First World" of developed countries on the crest of rising trade and foreign investment. Its dynamic manufacturing sector would create so many jobs it would not only end the U.S. immigration problem but absorb millions of peasant farmers freed from their unproductive toil in the fields. Mexico could import cheap corn and export electronics.

So much for promises.

NAFTA produced a devastating one-two punch. For the first 10 years, the flood of U.S. exports of corn, wheat, meat and other staples drove Mexican producer prices well below the costs of production.

Mexico's three million small-scale corn farmers saw prices for their crops fall 66%, largely because the United States increased corn exports by 400%, exporting at prices 19% below even U.S. farmers' costs of production. Call it the Age of Agricultural Dumping.

Soybeans, wheat, cotton and rice saw similar export surges under NAFTA, with similar drops in producer prices. Mexico's agricultural exports to the United States increased as well, but it takes a lot of tomatoes and strawberries to make up for the surge in staple-food imports.

By the mid-2000s, Mexico was importing 42% of its food, mostly from the United States. Corn import dependence had grown from 8% before NAFTA to 32%. Mexico was importing nearly 60% of its wheat where before it had imported less than 20%. Import dependence was more than 70% for soybeans, rice and cotton.

Then came the sucker punch. In 2007, international prices for many staple crops doubled or tripled, and so did the cost of importing them. Countries like Mexico that had gotten hooked on cheap imports paid a heavy price. Call it the Age of Dependency.

U.S. policies had as much to do with these high and volatile prices as they had with the Age of Dumping. Now, instead of price-depressing surpluses caused by

U.S. agricultural policies, U.S. subsidies and incentives were diverting 40% of U.S. corn—15% of the global supply—into ethanol production.

This drove up the price of corn, but also prices for related crops, like soybeans and wheat, and the livestock products that had relied for so long on cheap feed.

Compounding the price volatility, U.S. deregulation of financial markets in the early 2000s had brought agricultural commodity markets into the global casino. Financial speculators, fleeing the collapsing U.S. housing and stock markets in 2007, went "all in" on commodities, driving prices to disruptive highs, then lows, then highs again.

This was devastating for countries dependent on imported food. The world's Least Developed Countries, which had exported more than they imported in the early 1980s, saw their food import bills skyrocket to more than $25 billion, driving their collective agricultural trade deficit to more than $19 billion.

Mexico's agricultural imports topped $20 billion following the price spikes, with its agricultural trade deficit jumping to more than $4 billion. Corn imports accounted for more than half the bill.

And most telling: twenty years into NAFTA, 55 million Mexicans—about half the population—are estimated to be in poverty, many without secure access to food.

The night before my talk in Aguascalientes, in which I would gently call attention to the high cost of Mexico's failed cheap-food experiment under NAFTA, I ended up at a lush cocktail reception talking to the U.S. Embassy's agricultural attaché. I must have said something about Mexico's agricultural trade deficit, and he immediately took offense.

"This year," he proclaimed, "Mexico may actually run a surplus."

I knew better; I'd seen this statistical sleight-of-hand many times.

"Do you mean the 'agri-food' trade balance?" I asked.

He nodded.

"The one that has beer as one of Mexico's biggest agricultural exports?"

He nodded again, and not sheepishly. Beer has undoubtedly been a NAFTA success story for Mexico.

"Beer is a product of agriculture," he said, with conviction.

I took a sip of my margarita.

"Don't you think including beer distorts how Mexican agriculture is really doing under NAFTA?" I asked.

Not at all, he replied, the beer sector is a perfect example of the kind of integration NAFTA can achieve.

"Look, Mexico's even importing the barley malt from us to make its beer!" I said.

I took another sip.

"So Mexico's agricultural contribution to its beer exports is … what?" I asked.

Nervous laughter.

Here is a case where NAFTA has gotten the United States to open its market to something of value that Mexico can export, and Mexico can't even capture the value from it. The industry's growth benefits U.S. barley growers and U.S. malt makers. Mexico can't even import the barley and make the malt themselves.

So the country is basically a maquiladora for beer bottling. I guess Mexico contributes the water. Which it doesn't have enough of.

This has been Mexico under NAFTA in a nutshell. Giving away everything of value, then deluding yourself that your farm sector is doing fine because your Corona beer, bottled from U.S. ingredients, is a big hit in the States.

Meanwhile, hungry corn farmers wait for their government to invest in producing more of its own food. ❑

Article 10.5

KEEP IT IN THE GROUND

An alternative vision for petroleum emerges in Ecuador. But will Big Oil win the day?

BY ELISSA DENNIS
July/August 2010

In the far eastern reaches of Ecuador, in the Amazon basin rain forest, lies a land of incredible beauty and biological diversity. More than 2,200 varieties of trees reach for the sky, providing a habitat for more species of birds, bats, insects, frogs, and fish than can be found almost anywhere else in the world. Indigenous Waorani people have made the land their home for millennia, including the last two tribes living in voluntary isolation in the country. The land was established as Yasuní National Park in 1979, and recognized as a UNESCO World Biosphere Reserve in 1989.

Underneath this landscape lies a different type of natural resource: petroleum. Since 1972, oil has been Ecuador's primary export, representing 57% of the country's exports in 2008; oil revenues comprised on average 26% of the government's revenue between 2000 and 2007. More than 1.1 billion barrels of heavy crude oil have been extracted from Yasuní, about one quarter of the nation's production to date.

At this economic, environmental, and political intersection lie two distinct visions for Yasuní's, and Ecuador's, next 25 years. Petroecuador, the state-owned oil company, has concluded that 846 million barrels of oil could be extracted from proven reserves at the Ishpingo, Tambococha, and Tiputini (ITT) wells in an approximately 200,000 hectare area covering about 20% of the parkland. Extracting this petroleum, either alone or in partnership with interested oil companies in Brazil, Venezuela, or China, would generate approximately $7 billion, primarily in the first 13 years of extraction and continuing with declining productivity for another 12 years.

The alternative vision is the simple but profound choice to leave the oil in the ground.

Environmentalists and indigenous communities have been organizing for years to restrict drilling in Yasuní. But the vision became much more real when President Rafael Correa presented a challenge to the world community at a September 24, 2007 meeting of the United Nations General Assembly: if governments, companies, international organizations, and individuals pledge a total of $350 million per year for 10 years, equal to half of the forgone revenues from ITT, then Ecuador will chip in the other half and keep the oil underground indefinitely, as this nation's contribution to halting global climate change.

The Yasuní-ITT Initiative would preserve the fragile environment, leave the voluntarily isolated tribes in peace, and prevent the emission of an estimated 407 million metric tons of carbon dioxide into the atmosphere. This "big idea from a small country" has even broader implications, as Alberto Acosta, former Energy Minister and one of the architects of the proposal, notes in his new book, *La Maldición de la Abundancia* (*The Curse of Abundance*). The Initiative is a "*punto de ruptura*," he writes, a turning point in environmental history which "questions the logic of extractive (exporter of raw material) development," while introducing the possibility of global "*sumak kawsay*," the indigenous Kichwa concept of "good living" in harmony with nature.

Ecuador, like much of Latin America, has long been an exporter of raw materials: cacao in the 19th century, bananas in the 20th century, and now petroleum. The nation dove into the oil boom of the 1970s, investing in infrastructure and building up external debt. When oil prices plummeted in the 1980s while interest rates on that debt ballooned, Ecuador was trapped in the debt crisis that affected much of the region. Thus began what Correa calls "the long night of neoliberalism:" IMF-mandated privatizations of utilities and mining sectors, with a concomitant decline of revenues from the nation's natural resources to the Ecuadorian people. By 1986, all of the nation's petroleum revenues were going to pay external debt.

Close to 40 years of oil production has failed to improve the living standards of the majority of Ecuadorians. "Petroleum has not helped this country," notes Ana Cecilia Salazar, director of the Department of Social Sciences in the College of Economics of the University of Cuenca. "It has been corrupt. It has not diminished poverty. It has not industrialized this country. It has just made a few people rich."

Currently 38% of the population lives in poverty, with 13% in extreme poverty. The nation's per capita income growth between 1982 and 2007 was only .7% per year. And although the unemployment rate of 10% may seem moderate, an estimated 53% of the population is considered "underemployed."

Petroleum extraction has brought significant environmental damage. Each year 198,000 hectares of land in the Amazon are deforested for oil production. A verdict is expected this year in an Ecuadorian court in the 17-year-old class action suit brought by 30,000 victims of Texaco/Chevron's drilling operations in the area northwest of Yasuní between 1964 and 1990. The unprecedented $27 billion lawsuit alleges that thousands of cancers and other health problems were caused by Texaco's use of outdated and dangerous practices, including the dumping of 18 billion gallons of toxic wastewater into local water supplies.

Regardless of its economic or environmental impacts, the oil is running out. With 4.16 billion barrels in proven reserves nationwide, and another half billion "probable" barrels, best-case projections, including the discovery of new reserves, indicate the nation will stop exporting oil within 28 years, and stop producing oil within 35 years.

"At this moment we have an opportunity to rethink the extractive economy that for many years has constrained the economy and politics in the country," says Esperanza Martinez, a biologist, environmental activist, and author of the book *Yasuní: El tortuoso camino de Kioto a Quito.* "This proposal intends to change the terms of the North-South relationship in climate change negotiations."

As such, the Initiative fits into the emerging idea of "climate debt." The North's voracious energy consumption in the past has destroyed natural resources in the South; the South is currently bearing the brunt of global warming effects like floods and drought; and the South needs to adapt expensive new energy technology for the future instead of industrializing with the cheap fossil fuels that built the North. Bolivian president Evo Morales proposed at the Copenhagen climate talks last December that developed nations pay 1% of GDP, totaling $700 billion/year, into a compensation fund that poor nations could use to adapt their energy systems.

"Clearly in the future, it will not be possible to extract all the petroleum in the world because that would create a very serious world problem, so we need to create measures of compensation to pay the ecological debt to the countries," says Malki Sáenz, formerly Coordinator of the Yasuní-ITT Initiative within the Ministry of Foreign Relations. The Initiative "is a way to show the international community that real compensation mechanisms exist for not extracting petroleum."

Indigenous and environmental movements in Latin America and Africa are raising possibilities of leaving oil in the ground elsewhere. But the Yasuní-ITT proposal is the furthest along in detail, government sponsorship, and ongoing negotiations. The Initiative proposes that governments, international institutions, civil associations, companies, and individuals contribute to a fund administered through an international organization such as the United Nations Development Program (UNDP). Contributions could include swaps of Ecuador's external debt, as well as resources generated from emissions auctions in the European Union and carbon emission taxes such as those implemented in Sweden and Slovakia.

Contributors of at least $10,000 would receive a Yasuní Guarantee Certificate (CGY), redeemable only in the event that a future government decides to extract the oil. The total dollar value of the CGYs issued would equal the calculated value of the 407 million metric tons of non-emitted carbon dioxide.

The money would be invested in fixed income shares of renewable energy projects with a guaranteed yield, such as hydroelectric, geothermal, wind, and solar power, thus helping to reduce the country's dependence on fossil fuels. The interest payments generated by these investments would be designated for: 1) conservation projects, preventing deforestation of almost 10 million hectares in 40 protected areas covering 38% of Ecuador's territory; 2) reforestation and natural regeneration projects on another one million hectares of forest land; 3) national energy efficiency improvements; and 4) education, health, employment, and training programs in sustainable activities like ecotourism and agro forestry in the affected areas. The first three activities could prevent an additional 820 million metric tons of carbon dioxide emissions, tripling the Initiative's effectiveness.

These nationwide conservation efforts, as well as the proposal's mention of "monitoring" throughout Yasuní and possibly shutting down existing oil production, are particularly disconcerting to Ecuadorian and international oil and wood interests. Many speculate that political pressure from these economic powerhouses was behind a major blow to the Initiative this past January, when Correa, in one of his regular Saturday radio broadcasts, suddenly blasted the negotiations as "shameful," and a threat to the nation's "sovereignty" and "dignity." He threatened that if the full package of international commitments was not in place by this June, he would begin extracting oil from ITT.

Correa's comments spurred the resignations of four critical members of the negotiating commission, including Chancellor Fander Falconí, a longtime ally in Correa's PAIS party, and Roque Sevilla, an ecologist, businessman, and ex-Mayor of Quito whom Correa had picked to lead the commission. Ecuador's Ambassador to the UN Francisco Carrion also resigned from the commission, as did World Wildlife Fund president Yolanda Kakabadse.

Correa has been clear from the outset that the government has a Plan B, to extract the oil, and that the non-extraction "first option" is contingent on the mandated monetary commitments. But oddly his outburst came as the negotiating team's efforts were bearing fruit. Sevilla told the press in January of commitments in various stages of approval from Germany, Spain, Belgium, France, and Switzerland, totaling at least $1.5 billion. The team was poised to sign an agreement with UNDP last December in Copenhagen to administer the fund. Correa called off the signing at the last minute, questioning the breadth of the Initiative's conservation efforts and UNDP's proposed six-person administrative body, three appointed by Ecuador, two by contributing nations, and one by UNDP. This joint control structure apparently sparked Correa's tirade about shame and dignity.

Within a couple of weeks of the blowup, the government had backpedaled, withdrawing the June deadline, appointing a new negotiating team, and reasserting the position that the government's "first option" is to leave the oil in the ground. At the same time, Petroecuador began work on a new pipeline near Yasuní, part of the infrastructure needed for ITT production, pursuant to a 2007 Memorandum of Understanding with several foreign oil companies.

Amid the doubts and mixed messages, proponents are fighting to save the Initiative as a cornerstone in the creation of a post-petroleum Ecuador and ultimately a post-petroleum world. In media interviews after his resignation, Sevilla stressed that he would keep working to ensure that the Initiative would not fail. The Constitution provides for a public referendum prior to extracting oil from protected areas like Yasuní, he noted. "If the president doesn't want to assume his responsibility as leader…let's pass the responsibility to the public." In fact, 75% of respondents in a January poll in Quito and Guayaquil, the country's two largest cities, indicated that they would vote to not extract the ITT oil.

Martinez and Sáenz concur that just as the Initiative emerged from widespread organizing efforts, its success will come from the people. "This is the moment to define ourselves and develop an economic model not based on petroleum," Salazar says. "We have other knowledge, we have minerals, water. We need to change our consciousness and end the economic dependence on one resource." ❑

Resources: Live Yasuní, Finding Species, Inc., liveYasuní.org; "S.O.S. Yasuní" sosYasuní.org; "Yasuní-ITT: An Initiative to Change History," Government of Ecuador, Yasuní-itt.gov.ec.

Update, November 2013

Declaring "the world has failed us," Ecuador's President Rafael Correa signaled the termination of the Yasuní ITT Initiative in August 2013. Citing a meager $116 million in pledges, he announced the decision to move forward with the Plan B that was always in the background: extraction of oil from the Ishpingo, Tambococha, and Tiputini fields in the eastern section of Yasuní National Park. The drilling will only impact 0.1% of the parklands, Correa contends, noting that the estimated value of oil in the targeted area has increased from $7 billion to $18 billion. Despite street demonstrations in Quito and Cuenca and calls for a national referendum, the National Assembly ratified Correa's action in October 2013.

Correa, a U.S. trained economist, has consistently ridiculed "infantile" environmentalists, and is clearly most comfortable with a pragmatic economic development model of extractivism with equitable distribution of resources. Like his Bolivian counterpart Evo Morales, Correa has run afoul of indigenous communities and the environmental left through efforts to transform the nation from exploited exporter of raw materials into savvy user of natural resources to fuel economic growth and social programs.

"We can't be beggars sitting on a sack of gold," is Correa's constant refrain. The 2012 signing of a five-year $1.4 billion contract with the Chinese-owned mining company Ecuacorriente for development of the El Mirador copper mine in the southern Amazon is emblematic of this approach. While industry analysts cringed at the 52% of revenues slated for taxes and royalties to the state, advocates for the environment and indigenous Amazon community representatives took to the streets in protest at this launch of what the Correa government boasts will be a new era of mining in Ecuador.

Correa's critics say his government never wholeheartedly supported the Yasuní effort, and point to a growing Chinese political and economic influence. Since Correa's 2008 move to default on the nation's IMF debt, China has provided billions of dollars to Ecuador, with oil production pledged as repayment of some of that debt. China is also a key investor in Ecuador's oil industry, including links to ITT.

Ecuador's debt situation with China today is more "colonizing" than it was with the United States, says University of Cuenca professor Ana Cecilia Salazar, noting a $19 billion debt level in 2011 compared with $14.55 billion in 2004. She sees that as one reflection of a government long on populist rhetoric but short on progressive economic transformation. "We are living an illusion that has generated social backing for the government, but basically a policy of redistribution of wealth doesn't exist, rather a populist administration based on grants and subsidies that is not true social justice," she says.

Salazar acknowledges there has been some lessening of poverty during Correa's tenure, and some marginalized groups have benefited from government programs made possible by the high price of oil. But she notes "there is no change in the dynamics of concentration," with economic inequality growing, as 40% of the nation's wealth sits in the hands of 15% of the population. While 27,000 acres of land have been distributed to *campesinos*, millions of acres have been ceded to mining companies, she says.

Correa's strategy of moving from neoliberalism to "neo-Keynesianism," just creates a mirage of "green capitalism," Salazar says. With Yasuní, even if the drilling is contained in a small area, it is impossible to not impact the vulnerable megadiverse environment and the communities that have been living there in voluntary isolation. Opening up the area to oil necessitates new highways which expose the region to indiscriminate logging, a problem the government has not been able to control elsewhere in the Amazon region. With the end of the Yasuní initiative, the vision of a post-petroleum Ecuador is fading, Salazar says. "The government model that initially made us dream about overcoming the extractivist economy has disappeared." ❏

Article 10.6

IS CHINA'S CURRENCY MANIPULATION HURTING THE U.S.?

BY ARTHUR MacEWAN

November/December 2010

Dear Dr. Dollar:
Is it true that China has been harming the U.S. economy by keeping its currency "undervalued"? Shouldn't the U.S. government do something about this situation?
—Jenny Boyd, Edmond, W.Va.

The Chinese government, operating through the Chinese central bank, does keep its currency unit—the yuan—cheap relative to the dollar. This means that goods imported *from* China cost less (in terms of dollars) than they would otherwise, while U.S. exports *to* China cost more (in terms of yuan). So we in the United States buy a lot of Chinese-made goods and the Chinese don't buy much from us. In the 2007 to 2009 period, the United States purchased $253 billion more in goods annually from China than it sold to China.

This looks bad for U.S workers. For example, when money gets spent in the United States, much of it is spent on Chinese-made goods, and fewer jobs are then created in the United States. So the Chinese government's currency policy is at least partly to blame for our employment woes. Reacting to this situation, many people are calling for the U.S. government to do something to get the Chinese government to change its policy.

But things are not so simple.

First of all, there is an additional reason for the low cost of Chinese goods— low Chinese wages. The Chinese government's policy of repressing labor probably accounts for the low cost of Chinese goods at least as much as does its currency policy. Moreover, there is a lot more going on in the global economy. Both currency problems and job losses involve much more than Chinese government actions— though China provides a convenient target for ire.

And the currency story itself is complex. In order to keep the value of its currency low relative to the dollar, the Chinese government increases the supply of yuan, uses these yuan to buy dollars, then uses the dollars to buy U.S. securities, largely government bonds but also private securities. In early 2009, China held $764 billion in U.S. Treasury securities, making it the largest foreign holder of U.S. government debt. By buying U.S. government bonds, the Chinese have been financing the federal deficit. More generally, by supplying funds to the United States, the Chinese government has been keeping interest rates low in this country.

If the Chinese were to act differently, allowing the value of their currency to rise relative to the dollar, both the cost of capital and the prices of the many goods imported from China would rise. The rising cost of capital would probably not be a serious problem, as the Federal Reserve could take counteraction to keep interest rates low. So, an increase in the value of the yuan would net the United States some jobs, but also raise some prices for U.S. consumers.

It is pretty clear that right now what the United States needs is jobs. Moreover, low-cost Chinese goods have contributed to the declining role of manufacturing in the United States, a phenomenon that both weakens important segments of organized labor and threatens to inhibit technological progress, which has often been centered in manufacturing or based on applications in manufacturing (e.g., robotics).

So why doesn't the U.S. government place more pressure on China to raise the value of the yuan? Part of the reason may lie in concern about losing Chinese financing of the U.S. federal deficit. For several years the two governments have been co-dependent: The U.S. government gets financing for its deficits, and the Chinese government gains by maintaining an undervalued currency. Not an easy relationship to change.

Probably more important, however, many large and politically powerful U.S.-based firms depend directly on the low-cost goods imported from China. Wal-mart and Target, as any shopper knows, are filled with Chinese-made goods. Then there are the less visible products from China, including a power device that goes into the Microsoft Xbox, computer keyboards for Dell, and many other goods for many other U.S. corporations. If the yuan's value rose and these firms had to pay more dollars to buy these items, they could probably not pass all the increase on to consumers and their profits would suffer.

Still, in spite of the interests of these firms, the U.S. government may take some action, either by pressing harder for China to let the value of the yuan rise relative to the dollar or by placing some restrictions on imports from China. But don't expect too big a change. ❏

Article 10.7

CHINESE WORKERS STAND UP
What is the real cause of increasing wages in China?

BY JOHN MILLER
September/October 2010

> "THE RISE OF CHINESE LABOR:
> WAGE HIKES ARE PART OF A VIRTUOUS CYCLE OF DEVELOPMENT"

> The recent strikes at Honda factories in southern China represent another data point in an emerging trend: Cheap labor won't be the source of the Chinese economy's competitive advantage much longer.
>   The auto maker has caved and given workers a 24% pay increase to restart one assembly line. Foxconn, the electronics producer that has experienced a string of worker suicides, has also announced big raises. This is all part of the virtuous cycle of development: Productivity increases, which drive wages higher, forcing businesses to adjust, leading to more productivity growth.
> —*Wall Street Journal* op-ed, June 9, 2010

Wages in China are in fact rising. But that hardly constitutes a "virtuous cycle of development" that is the inevitable result of market-led economic growth, as the *Wall Street Journal* editors contend.

Rather, higher wages in China are the hard-fought gains of militant workers who have used tightening labor markets as a lever to pry wage gains out of employers whose coffers have long been brimming with cash.

Labor unrest taking advantage of tightening labor markets is the story in China today—not abstract economic forces lifting wages, the tale the *Journal's* editors want to pass off as a paean to free-market economics.

A Changing Labor Outlook

In recent years rapid economic growth has indeed tightened the Chinese labor market, drying up the seemingly bottomless pool of jobseekers from the countryside. As of May 2010, job vacancies in China outnumbered the number of job applicants, according to the Chinese Labor Market Information Center.

And wages are rising for many. Pay for China's 150 million or so internal-migrant workers increased 16% in 2009 despite the global financial crisis, according to Cai Fang, head of the Institute of Population and Labor Economics at the Chinese Academy of Social Sciences.

Higher wages aren't about to break the corporate piggybank. In recent years the biggest increase in China's extraordinarily high national savings (which includes household and business savings) has come from retained earnings—the undistributed profits of Chinese corporations. Retained earnings did so much to boost the country's savings because low wages kept corporate profits high. For more than a decade, labor's share of national income has been on the decline in China as the corporate share has increased dramatically. On top of that, the strong productivity growth that the *Journal* editors laud has offset wage increases, keeping labor costs per unit of output in check. At the beginning of 2010 Chinese unit labor costs were no higher than in 2004.

Wage increases notwithstanding, working conditions in China remain oppressive, as even the *Journal* editors seem to recognize. In May 2010 a thirteenth worker attempted to commit suicide at a Foxconn factory in southern China. The world's largest maker of computer components, Foxconn supplies Apple, Dell, and Hewlett-Packard, among others. While working conditions at this Taiwanese-owned company are far from the worst in China, the hours are long, the assembly line moves too fast, and managers enforce military-style discipline.

Foxconn's string of suicides is just the tip of the iceberg. Early in 2008, the *New York Times* reported that worker abuse is still commonplace in many of the Chinese factories that supply Western companies. The *Times* quoted labor activists who reported unfair labor practices—child labor, enforced 16-hour days, and sub-minimum wages, among others—in factories supplying several U.S. firms including Wal-Mart, Disney, and Dell. The activists also reported that factories routinely withhold health benefits, employ dangerous machinery, and expose workers to lead, mercury, and other hazardous chemicals. According to government statistics, an average of 187 Chinese workers die each day in industrial accidents; the equivalent U.S. figure is three.

The Real Virtuous Cycle

Rapid economic growth and rising productivity undoubtedly laid the groundwork for higher wages. But it is labor militancy that has exploited workers' improved bargaining position. The number of labor disputes in China doubled from 2006 to 2009. Workers have won wage increases in excess of 20% at several large export factories, including Foshan Fengfu Autoparts, the company that supplies exhaust pipes to Japanese automaker Honda, and Hon Hai Precision Industry Co., the Taiwan-based electronics manufacturer that supplies iPads and iPhones for Apple and a range of gadgets for Hewlett-Packard and Nintendo.

Predictably, the editors misrepresent how social improvement comes about with economic development. Not just in China but in the developed economies as well, improvements in working conditions have come about not due to market-led forces alone, but when economic growth was combined with social action and worker militancy.

The history of sweatshops in the United States makes that clear. The shirtwaist strike of 1909, the tragedy of the Triangle Shirtwaist fire two years later, and the hardships of the Great Depression inspired garment workers to unionize and led to the imposition of government regulations on the garment industry and other industries, beginning with the New York Factory Acts and extending to the Fair Labor Standards Act of 1938. The power of those reforms along with the postwar boom nearly eradicated sweatshops in the United States.

Since then, sweatshops have returned with a vengeance to the U.S. garment industry. Why? Declining economic opportunity is part of the answer. But severe cutbacks in the number of inspectors and a drop-off in union density paved the way as well. The U.S. experience confirms the take-away message from rising Chinese wages: Economic development by itself will not eliminate inhuman working conditions. Improve-ments in working conditions are neither inevitable nor irreversible.

Not only is labor organizing crucial for improving working conditions, but those organizing efforts need to be international if workers are to succeed in reaping durable gains from economic development.

China's case makes that clear. Rising wages in China have prompted footwear and apparel firms to shift their manufacturing elsewhere—to Indonesia, Bangladesh, and Vietnam, for example. Jim Sciabarrasi, head of sourcing and procurement at U.S.-based sneaker company New Balance, was clear about the reason for the firm's move. "Indonesia has a ready supply of workers and their wages are not going up as fast as in China," he told the *Boston Globe*.

Chinese workers attempting to organize and improve their situation always face the threat that their employer will simply pack up and depart for even lower-cost countries. This kind of threat, which helps employers resist demands for better wages and working conditions not just in China but elsewhere in global South and in the developed economies as well, has been increasingly effective as globalization has weakened limits on the mobility of corporations. It throws into sharp relief the common interests of workers in all countries in improving conditions at the bottom, in robust full-employment programs that raise their incomes and enhance their bargaining power.

In that way, the rise of China's workers and the bold labor unrest there should benefit manufacturing workers across the globe, a virtuous cycle the *Wall Street Journal* editors would not only be loathe to recognize but have gone out of their way to obscure. ❏

Sources: David Barboza, "In Chinese Factories, Lost Fingers and Low Pay," *New York Times*, Jan. 5, 2008; William Foreman, "13th worker attempts suicide at Foxconn tech factory in southern China, report says," *Los Angeles Times*, May 27, 2010; Jenn Abelson, "Local sneaker firms are making it in Indonesia," *Boston Globe*, May 29, 2010; Norihiko Shirouzo, "Chinese Workers Challenge Beijing's Authority," *WSJ*, June 13, 2010; Elizabeth Holmes, "U.S. Apparel Retailers Turn Their Gaze beyond China," *WSJ*, June 15, 2010; "NW: Wage disputes in China put world on notice," NIKKEI, June 14, 2010; Aileen Wang and Simon Rabinovitch, "Why labor unrest is good for China and the world," Reuters, June 2, 2010; World Bank, China Quarterly Update, June 2010; James Areddy, "Accidents Plague China's Workplaces," *WSJ*, July 28, 2010.

Chapter 11

POLICY SPOTLIGHT: A COMING GENERATIONAL WAR?

INTRODUCTION

If you follow economic news and commentary, you will have heard arguments that there is a "generational war" afoot. What does this mean? Mainly, it is an argument that what we are doing economically today, especially what benefits the current working generation or the generation that has already retired, will harm the economic prospects of today's young people and those who are yet to be born. As some of the articles in this chapter argue, this view is very misleading when it comes to government debt (and has been used as a way to attack popular programs, like Social Security and Medicare, that ensure people will not be left destitute late in life).

The term "generational war" is certainly melodramatic. We would be better off referring to issues of "intergenerational distribution" or "intergenerational equity." While the notion that the current generation is doing future generations wrong may be incorrect when it comes to government finance, issues of intergenerational equity (whether the actions of the current generation are fair to future generations) are worth taking seriously. We do have to think about the world we will leave to our children, grandchildren, and so on.

The chapter begins with Dean Baker's refutation of the "generational war" idea, as it is commonly stated in relation to government spending. In "Are Our Parents Stealing From Our Kids? No, They Are Not" (Article 11.1), Baker points out that higher public spending on programs that benefit seniors actually goes hand in hand with higher spending on programs that benefit the young (both in U.S. history and across different countries). So much for a "zero-sum" game pitting one generation against the other.

The next three articles focus on education. To be sure, young people are getting short shrift in some ways, both in terms of the kind of education they are receiving and the ways it is paid for. (But seniors are not to blame.)

As Arthur MacEwan explains in "Education: Not Just 'Human Capital'" (Article 11.2), corporate-inspired education reforms are focused on making schools more effective "human capital" factories. The students should be tested, the "free market" reformers say, as a measure of quality. The teachers who do not perform should be fired, and "failing" schools should be shut down. This agenda,

MacEwan argues, reduces education to the production of an adequately skilled and obedient workforce, underestimates the successes of public schools (when they have adequate resources), and ignores the bigger social problems that impede greater educational achievement.

Student debt burdens, Molly Cusano and Zachary Santamaria show (Article 11.3), have been surging even as the average incomes of college graduates have stagnated. As a result, millions of graduates remain under a cloud of debt well into their thirties and beyond.

Instead of advocating for an education-financing system that would reduce this burden, explains John Miller (Article 11.4), the business press has been fighting for a further reduction in federal higher-education grants (Pell Grants) for low- and middle-income students. Far from being cut, Miller argues, Pell Grants should be made a "near universal" support for students.

Meanwhile, seniors also find themselves under the gun, especially due to attacks on retirement security—from shifts to pensions that shift risk from employers onto workers to attacks on Social Security and other federal "entitlement" programs. The next two articles tackle these issues.

In "What Happened to Defined-Benefit Pensions?" (Article 11.5), Arthur MacEwan takes on the dramatic shift from "defined-benefit" pensions, which guarantee workers' retirement income for life, to "defined-contribution" pensions, which make workers actual retirement incomes dependent on stock market returns. The shift in risk from employers to workers, MacEwan argues, reflects a larger shift in bargaining power in employers' favor.

Next, in "Myths of the Deficit" (Article 11.6), Marty Wolfson refutes the idea that federal budget deficits are creating a "burden" on future generations. Debts run up today will be paid back later. Those doing the paying, through future taxes, will be our grandchildren. But most of the people receiving the payments will also be our grandchildren, since most of the debt is owed to the U.S. public. (Current bond owners will leave these assets to their heirs.) The real issues, in other words, are not really between, but within, generations.

Finally, Frank Ackerman puts intergenerational equity issues in a different light: focusing on the issue of long-term environmental sustainability and climate change. In his article, "Climate Economics in Four Easy Pieces" (Article 11.7), he argues that a key reason for aggressive action to avert climate change now is that "our grandchildren's lives are important."

Discussion Questions

1. (Article 11.1) Baker argues that, far from being in opposition to one another, spending on programs for the young and for the old tend to go hand in hand. Why would this be the case? How does this fact relate to other articles in this chapter (which emphasize attacks on both affordable education and secure retirement)?

2. (Article 11.2) Why does MacEwan argue that education is (and should be) about more than "human capital" formation? Why does he think that even

employers are not interested only in the technical skills that future workers learn in school?

3.   (Article 11.2) Why does MacEwan think that the narrative about public schools failure is wrong? In what ways are public schools successful and in what ways not? How can we tell, if they are not completely successful, *why* this is the case?

4.   (Articles 11.3 and 11.4) Why have student debt burdens increased so much in recent years? What policy responses would you propose?

5.   (Article 11.5) Explain the contrast between "defined-benefit" and "defined-contribution" pensions. What does MacEwan mean when he argues that this is the result of a more general "power shift" in favor of employers and against workers?

6.   (Article 11.6) If Wolfson is right, and the main distributional effects of government debt are within (rather than between) generations, why is the "generational war" interpretation so widespread? Is this a simple mistake? Or does it reflect some political agenda?

7.   (Article 11.7) Ackerman argues that a key issue in making climate policy today is how we weigh the interests of future generations against those of the current generation. Why is this so important? What kind of formula would you use in weighing these different interests?

Articke 11.1

ARE OUR PARENTS STEALING FROM OUR KIDS? NO, THEY'RE NOT

BY DEAN BAKER
October 2013; The Business Desk (PBS NewsHour)

A common refrain in debates over Social Security and Medicare is that these programs are putting seniors ahead of children. The implication is that there is a fixed pool of tax revenue. If more of this revenue goes to seniors to pay for their benefits, there is less to cover the cost of child nutrition and health care, daycare, education and other programs that benefit the young. To put in crudely, in this view, a dollar spent on the elderly is a dollar taken away from spending on children.

There is an alternative perspective. The amount of money that the government collects in tax revenue may not be fixed. Understood this way, people's willingness to pay taxes may depend on their perception of the usefulness of the services provided. This could mean, for example, that if the public believes that the government services being provided to both seniors and children are valuable and should be expanded, they would be willing to pay higher taxes to support those services.

If we look at the situation historically in the United States, we have vastly increased the share of GDP going to government programs for both seniors and the young over the last 60 years. In 1950, Social Security payments were less than 1 percent of GDP and Medicare and Medicaid did not even exist. By comparison, we are now spending almost 5 percent of GDP on Social Security, and more than 5 percent of GDP on Medicare and Medicaid.

PER PERSON SPENDING ON KIDS AND SENIORS, PERCENTAGE OF PER CAPITA INCOME

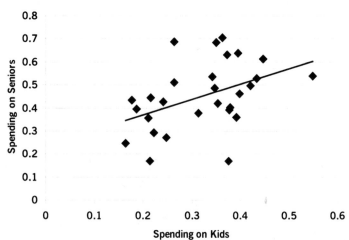

This growth in federal spending for programs that primarily benefit seniors has been accompanied by a huge expansion in programs intended to primarily benefit the young, such as Head Start; the Women, Infants and Children Nutrition Program; and the State Children's Health Insurance Program. In addition, state and local funding for education and other programs that benefit the young has also hugely increased relative to the size of the economy over the last six decades. People have been willing to pay more in taxes to finance programs that benefit both the elderly and the young.

There is a similar story if we look across countries. If the tradeoff view were correct, we should find that countries that are more generous in their support of seniors are stingier when it comes to public support for their children and vice versa. However, the opposite appears to be the case. If we control for the relative income of different countries, it turns out that a dollar of additional spending per kid is associated with 67 cents of additional spending for each senior. (This relationship is statistically significant at the 5% confidence level.)

In short, the data suggest that more spending on seniors is associated with more spending on kids. Presumably this indicates that countries where people rely on the government to ensure that their seniors have a decent standard of living are also inclined to provide the government with resources necessary to ensure that their children's needs are also met.

This evidence suggests that cuts to programs for seniors may be unlikely to end up benefitting our kids. Rather such cuts may be associated with reduced spending on kids as well. If the public does not trust the government to provide good care for seniors, it may also not trust the government to provide good care for children.

In that case, there would be no tradeoff between spending on seniors and spending on kids. If we care about both our seniors and our kids, and trust the government programs designed to provide support at both ends of life, then both sets of programs are likely to be adequately funded. In the opposite case, neither set of programs is likely to be adequately funded. The world where just one set of programs, either those supporting seniors or those supporting kids, receives adequate funding seems largely the invention of politicians. ❏

Article 11.2

EDUCATION: NOT JUST "HUMAN CAPITAL"

BY ARTHUR MacEWAN
January/February 2013

Dear Dr. Dollar:
What's going on with the economics of education? It all seems to be about impos-
ing "standards" to motivate and punish educators. And then there is privatization,
which is supposed to force schools to shape up or die. Help me out here!
    —Nancy Hernandez, Colorado Springs, Colo.

A great deal of the economics of education reduces schooling to the creation of
"human capital." Economists tend to view education as a way of making the
individual more productive—like a better-functioning machine that can generate more output. As with any piece of equipment coming off the production line,
human capital is subjected to quality control—through standardized testing.

Of course, people are not machines, which presents employers with a problem.
A good machine does what it is supposed to do and has no ideas about fair wages
and decent working conditions. So in creating human capital, schools have the task
of turning out well-behaved workers, people who follow orders and accept their
employers' authority. In other words, in economists' human-capital view of education, schools need to prepare pupils for the discipline of the capitalist workplace.
Thus, testing is not simply quality-control for technical skills (reading and math)
but also for test-taking ability, which teaches discipline, endurance, and not asking
too many questions.

Education has—or should have—goals that are much more complex than
those involved in building a machine. Education is about the passing on of culture.
It is about preparing people both to get the most out of and make the greatest contribution to society. Enabling people to be more economically productive, while
important, is only a part of this process. Reducing schooling to its narrowest economic function obscures and undermines the larger roles of education.

But from the perspective of business executives, the narrowest economic function is the important thing, at least in the short run. Complaining that our public
schools are failing, elite business groups have pushed an education agenda that would
standardize the "products" of the schools, especially through high-stakes standardized testing. These groups (often private foundations, most prominently the Gates
Foundation) and many economists argue that testing can create appropriate incentives for the students and their teachers. Students who fail the tests can't graduate
and teachers whose students do poorly on the tests don't get raises or get fired.

Likewise, the argument continues, schools with low test scores should be closed
down and replaced by other schools—just as private firms that don't produce good
products are replaced by other firms. This is the root of the argument for school
privatization—sometimes in the form of (formally public) charter schools and sometimes through private schools. Privatized schools eliminate the supposed causes of

public schools' failures—public bureaucracy and teachers' unions.

Beyond this ideological drive for privatization, there is also money to be made. For-profit firms such as EdisonLearning, Inc., and Educational Services of America, which run schools and provide services for school systems, are cashing in on the education market. As one consultant recently told a group of potential investors in education: "You start to see entire ecosystems of investment opportunity lining up. It could get really, really big."

There are many problems with the kind of school reform being pushed by many economists and elite business groups. For example:

Our public schools are not failing. We have some marvelous public schools. We also have some terrible schools. No surprise: the good schools tend to be in wealthy areas, the terrible schools in poverty-stricken areas.

To a large extent, the poor academic performance of many kids—in both traditional public schools and charter schools—is rooted in the larger problems of economic inequality and poverty. Poverty undermines children's ability to come to school ready to learn. Poor health, overworked parents, dangerous communities—all this undermines teachers' efforts.

In states where teachers unions exist, both good schools and terrible schools are unionized. Likewise, both good and terrible public schools operate under similar—sometimes the same—bureaucratic structures.

Incentives directed toward the wrong goal (the narrowest economic function) lead people in negative directions. Teaching to the test does not create students who are effective contributors to society.

Charter schools have been operating for decades. Yet there is no evidence that they produce better outcomes than traditional public schools.

Public schools are one of the great social support programs of our society. By themselves, they cannot eliminate poverty and other social ills, but they can move things in a positive direction. However, for the public schools to be an effective social support program, they need effective social support. ❏

Article 11.3

STUDENT-LOAN DEBT BY THE NUMBERS

Rising costs and declining job prospects spell trouble.

BY MOLLY CUSANO AND ZACHARY SANTAMARIA
May/June 2012

The total amount of student-loan debt in the United States passed the $1 trillion mark in April 2012, according to the Federal Reserve Bank of New York. Since early 2011, student-loan debt has exceeded total consumer credit-card debt and auto-loan debt combined.

Obtaining a college degree has long been viewed as a secure a path to financial stability, but with the rising cost of tuition, students must ask themselves whether a college degree is still worth the financial commitment. Students are paying more for college than ever before, even as job prospects and incomes for recent graduates diminish, leaving the average college graduate laden with debt. Not only are students borrowing more money to finance their educations, but they're also choosing more private loans instead of federal loans because federal loan subsidies have not kept up with tuition increases. Also, new legislation has lowered the maximum income threshold (from $30,000 to $23,000) for students to be eligible for Pell Grants, which do not have to be paid back. This means fewer incoming 2012-2013 students will qualify for these grants.

The first figure below compares the rising cost of attending a four-year private university to the stagnating median income of new graduates with bachelor's degrees. The second figure gives a breakdown of past-due student-loan balance by age group, showing that those under 40 account for most defaults, but that people continue to default on student loans into their 40s, 50s, and even 60s.

FIGURE 1: MEDIAN INCOME, NEW GRADUATES WITH BACHELOR'S DEGREE, AND COST OF PRIVATE FOUR-YEAR COLLEGE, 1990-2008

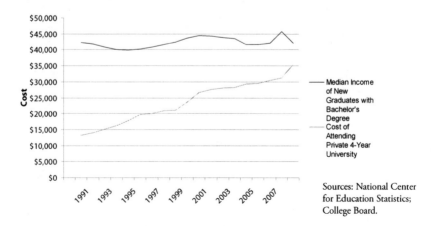

Sources: National Center for Education Statistics; College Board.

Since the early 1990s, the price of attending college has increased dramatically even as the median starting salary for grads has stagnated. The graph shows a pending convergence of the two numbers, which could earn a year at a private school would cost the same as the first-year salary of a newly hired college graduate. Private college costs have gone from just over $13,000 a year to more than $35,000, while median starting income for college grads has actually gone down slightly from $42,300 to $42,100.

FIGURE 2: PAST-DUE STUDENT DEBT, BY AGE OF DEBTOR, 2011

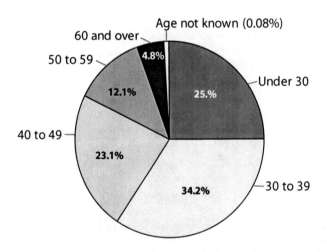

Sources: Federal Reserve Bank of New York Consumer Credit Panel; Equifax.

The total past-due balance of student loans in the United States is now $85 billion, with over 34% of the debt held by people ages 30-39. This shows that excessive student-loan debt, which borrowers are having trouble paying off, is not only owed by recent twenty-something college grads, but also by people further on in their careers. Some 23% of past-due balances are owed by people ages 40-49, and almost 5% of the $85 billion is owed by those age 60 and over. It is becoming clear that some student debt will never be paid off. ❏

Article 11.4

PUTTING THE SCREWS TO GENERATION SCREWED

Wall Street Journal *editors oppose expanded Pell grants.*

BY JOHN MILLER
September/October 2012

- Pell Grants are now so broad that more than half of all undergrads benefit.
- Better-off students often receive the large Pell Grants and apply them to more expensive schools.
- Pell Grants and other student aid are contributing to the ever-higher tuition spiral. Write 100 times on the chalkboard: Student aid raises tuition.
- Overall graduation rates were lower for students who received Pell Grants than for those who didn't.
- The best thing Mr. Obama could do for students, and taxpayers, is to get Pell Grants away from being a broad entitlement and back to their core mission of helping the poorest students.

> —Claims from "Pell Grants Flunk Out: The subsidy program has strayed far from its origins," *Wall Street Journal*, June 18, 2012.

More than $1 trillion of U.S. student debt. Better than nine of ten college graduates with student debt. Over one quarter of the repayments on those loans past due.

"A Generation Hobbled by the Soaring Cost of College" is how the *New York Times* put it in their recent exposé on college debt. And if you mix in the worst economy since the Great Depression, one that has hit those without a college degree especially hard and has left the employment prospects of even college graduates much diminished, this generation is not just hobbled but screwed. Apparently, however, not screwed enough for the editors of the *Wall Street Journal*. The editors rail against the ongoing expansion of Pell Grants, the chief form of federal aid to low- and middle-income students that can reduce the debt burden students incur.

The prospect of Pell Grants becoming an ever-more-universal entitlement must really have the *Wall Street Journal* editors spooked.

Below is a closer look at the predicament of students and former students burdened by debt and exactly why expanding Pell Grants should be supported, not opposed.

Generation Screwed

The cost of college tuition and fees has skyrocketed and student debt along with it. Since 1978, the cost of college tuition and fees has increased eleven-fold, rising faster than even the cost of medical care, and many times faster than family incomes.

Since 1999, student loan debt has increased fivefold. It has eclipsed credit-card debt and is now second only to mortgage debt.

With bankruptcy not an option, borrowers can be stuck repaying their student loans long after leaving college. The federal government is now garnishing the Social Security benefits of an increasing number of retirees with student debt. The Treasury Department reports that in the first seven months of this year, the federal government withheld money from roughly 115,000 retirees' Social Security checks because they had fallen behind on federal student loans. That's nearly double the 60,000 cases in all of 2007. There were just six cases in 2000.

A college degree is now the minimum credential needed for entrance into much of today's economy. "In the mid 1970s, less than 30% of jobs in America required any education beyond high school," reports Jamie P. Merisotis, president and chief executive officer of Lumina Foundation, a private foundation dedicated to expanding higher-education opportunity. "Today, the majority of U.S. jobs require a postsecondary degree or credential." A recent study conducted by the Georgetown Center on Education and the Workforce projects that 63% of job openings in 2018 will require at least some college education.

On top of that, the penalty for not obtaining a college degree has increased dramatically over the last three decades. Beginning with the loss of manufacturing jobs beginning in the late 1970s, the gap between the earnings of college graduates and those with just high school education has steadily widened. The Georgetown study calculated that in 1980 college graduates' lifetime earnings were 44% higher than those of high-school graduates. In 2010 college graduates' lifetime earnings were nearly twice (97% more than) those of high school graduates.

At the same time, the employment prospects of even college graduates are far from bright. First off, having graduated from college is no guarantee of full-time employment. The Economic Policy Institute Briefing Paper on "The Class of 2012" found that the unemployment rate for young college graduates (ages 21 to 24) averaged 9.4% from April 2011 to March 2012. Another 19.1% of of this group was underemployed--unable to find full-time work--during that time period. Second, pay for college grads is down. On average, wages for full-time workers with four-year college degrees fell by 5.4% (adjusted for inflation) between 2000 and 2011. Finally, many graduates do not find the kinds of jobs they wanted. More than a third (37.8%) of college graduates under 25, reports a recent study by economist Andrew Sum of Northeastern University's Center for Labor Market Studies, were working at jobs that did not require a college degree.

For workers without a college degree the numbers are even worse. In May 2012 about one quarter (24%) of new high school graduates from 17 to 20 years old were unemployed, and about half (54% for April 2011 to March 212) were underemployed, unable to get a full time job. Finally, average hourly wages for young high-school graduates plummeted from 2000 to 2011, falling 11.1% after adjusting for inflation.

Pell-Mell

The *WSJ* editors stand four square against providing relief for those hobbled by student debt, especially by expanding Pell Grants to an ever-wider swath of college students. But there is plenty wrong with the editors' long list of complaints about Pell Grants.

To start with, contrary to the editors' complaints, Pell Grants are well targeted. The evidence from a report by the conservative John William Pope Center, which is the source of many of the editors' claims, shows as much. In academic year 2009-2010, a year when the median household income was $51,190, some 94.2% of Pell grant recipients had a family income less than $50,000, and the majority (58.9%) had a family income of less than $20,000.

Nor is it surprising that the graduation rates for Pell Grant recipients are lower than other students. Proportionally, nearly twice as many Pell recipients have parents with only a high school diploma and nearly twice as many come from non-English-speaking homes as other undergraduates. Even the Pope Center recognizes that these are risk factors for dropping out.

The size of Pell Grants is another reason why it is hardly surprising that the graduation rates of Pell recipients are lower than those of other undergraduates. Award amounts for Pell recipients have remained relatively flat in real terms, but covered less and less of college costs. The $5,550 maximum Pell Grant in 2011 covered just one-third of the average cost of attending a public four-year college, just one half the level it covered in 1980-81, according to the Institute for College Access and Success. [Add something like: If Pell Grants covered more of college costs, students from lower-income families would be less likely to drop out due to economic hardship--like being unable to make tuition due to tight family budgets.

In addition, better-off students do not often receive large Pell Grants, as the editors contend. The College Board reports that in academic year 2010-2011 just 1.6% of recipients from families with an income above $60,000 received the maximum Pell Grant of $5,550, well below the 33.8% of the recipients from families with incomes between $15,000 and $20,000 who got the maximum grant. While a bit more than one-fifth of those high-income recipients did apply their Pell Grants to schools that cost $30,000 or more, that amounts to less than one half of one percent of all Pell Grants going to help these high-income recipients attend "more expensive" colleges.

Finally, writing 100 times on the chalkboard "student aid raises tuition," as the editors have suggested, might convince some readers that Pell Grants are driving up tuition. But the evidence is far from conclusive. The Pope Center report states that, "most studies show at least some effect of aid on tuition," which implies that other studies show that student aid has had zero effect on tuition. Indeed they do. For instance, David L. Warren, president of the National Association of Independent Colleges and Universities, reports, "Studies conducted during three successive administrations—Bill Clinton, George W. Bush, and Barack Obama—have found no link between student aid and tuition increases."

One must also ask how Pell Grants with a maximum grant that now covers just one third of the cost of attending a public four-year college, could have fueled the rise in college tuition. What's more, the College Board reports that the average inflation-adjusted net tuition and fees (published tuition and fees minus grants from all sources and federal tax benefits) at private, nonprofit colleges and universities actually dropped from 2006-07 to 2011-12, even as total Pell Grant expenditures more than doubled after correcting for inflation.

A Universal Entitlement

The Obama administration has undertaken some positive steps to expand access to Pell Grants and toward providing debt relief for students. In 2010, the President signed legislation that converted all federally guaranteed student loans (loans issued by private banks to students, with the federal government promising to pay back the loan if the debtor failed to do so) to direct loans administered by the government. This change eliminated fees paid to the private banks that had acted as intermediaries, saving nearly $68 billion over the next 11 years, $36 billion of which is to be used to expand Pell Grants. This year, the Obama Consumer Financial Protection Bureau issued a report recommending that Congress enact legislation letting borrowers discharge their private student loans (those not backed by the federal government) through bankruptcy.

But much more needs to be done. Private student loans account for just 10% of student loans. A good first step toward genuine debt relief would be for Congress to pass the Student Loan Forgiveness Act of 2012, introduced by Representative Hansen Clarke, a Michigan Democrat, which would allow "existing borrowers" to be forgiven up to $45,000 in student debt after the borrower has made ten years of income-based payments (no more than 10% of income).

Pell Grants need to be not only a entitlement, but expanded to a near universal entitlement A recent report from the Pell Institute's newsletter, Postsecondary Education Opportunity, throws into to sharp relief the need to do yet more. Only 10.7% of students from families in the bottom fourth by family income, below $33,050, had attained a bachelor's degree by 24 years of age; among students from families in the second fourth by family income, with incomes between $33,050 and $61,600, only 15%. At the same time, 79.1% of students from the top fourth by family income, above $98,875, had a bachelor's degree by age 24.

As more and more families rely on Pell Grants to reduce the cost of a college education for their children, the more likely it is that Pell Grants will continue to withstand the budget cuts likely to come in the upcoming years. And more fulsome and the more universal Pell Grants will help make merit, not economic means, the determinant of who gets a college degree. ❑

Sources: Anthony Carnevale, Tamara Jayasundera, and Ban Cheah, "The College Advantage: Weathering the Economic Storm," Center on Education and the Workforce, Georgetown University, August 15, 2012; Jenna Ashley Robinson and Duke Cheston, "Pell Grants: Where Does All the Money Go?" John W. Pope Center for Higher Education Policy, June 2012; Rep. Hansen Clarke, The Student Loan Forgiveness Act of 2012; "Public Policy Analysis of Opportunity for Postsecondary Education," Postsecondary Education Opportunity newsletter, January 2012; Heidi Shierholz, Natalie Sabadish, and Hilary Wething, "The Class Of 2012: Labor market for young graduates remains grim," Economic Policy Institute Briefing Paper, May 3, 2012; Meta Brown, Andrew Haughwout, Donghoon Lee, Maricar Mabutas, and Wilbert van der Klaauw, "Federal Student Financial Aid: Grading Student Loans," Federal Reserve Bank of New York, March 05, 2012; Charley Stone, Carl Van Horn, Cliff Zukin, and John J. Heldrich, "Chasing the American Dream: Recent College Graduates and the Great Recession," Center for Workforce Development, May 2012.

Article 11.5

WHAT HAPPENED TO DEFINED-BENEFIT PENSIONS?

BY ARTHUR MacEWAN
September/October 2013

> Dear Dr. Dollar:
> *What has happened to the defined benefit pensions? Why are they being replaced by defined contribution programs? What are the implications for us (workers!) as we grow older and live longer?* —Susan A. Titus, Detroit, Mich.

In large part, the shift from defined benefit pensions to defined contribution pensions is explained by employers shifting risk from themselves to their employees. Increasingly, in recent decades, for the same reasons that employers have been able to hold down wages, employers have shifted pension plans because they have had the power to do so. (See box for definitions of the two types of plans.)

The shift has been dramatic. In 1975, 71% of active workers participating in pension plans had defined benefit plans, and 29% had defined contribution plans. By 2010, the figures had more than reversed: 19% were in defined benefit plans; 81%, in defined contribution plans. Even though the labor force grew by 64% over this 45-year period, the number of workers in defined benefit plans fell by 37%. (See graph.)

In a defined benefit pension system, the employer is obligated to pay the fixed pension regardless of what happens to the economy. The risk for the employer is that bad economic times can make it difficult to make the payments—because the

PERCENTAGE OF NON-RETIRED PENSION-PLAN PARTICIPANTS, DEFINED BENEFIT (DB) VS. DEFINED CONTRIBUTION (DC) PLANS, 1975-2010*

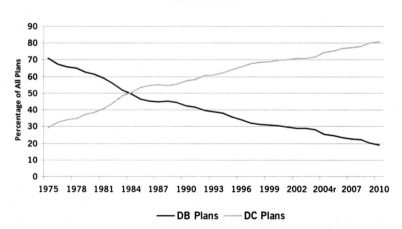

— DB Plans — DC Plans

*Many people participate in more than one plan. In 2004 (shown twice) definitions changed.
Sources: U.S. Dept. of Labor, Private Pension Plan Bulletin Historical Tables and Graphs, Nov. 2012.

> **DEFINED BENEFIT:** Employer and employees make contributions to a general pension fund managed by the employer. Based on a formula including years of employment and level of salary, each employee receives a fixed annual amount of money after retirement; that fixed amount does not depend on how well the investment of the fund does. The quality of the plan from the perspective of the employee depends on the amount of employee and employer contributions and on the particulars of the formula for determining benefits.
>
> **DEFINED CONTRIBUTION:** Employer and employee make contributions to a fund that is identified with the individual and is managed by an investment firm. The money that the employee receives after retirement depends on the amount of money in the individual's fund. The quality of the plan from the perspective of the employee depends on the amount of employee and employer contributions and on how well the investment does, both up to and after the time of retirement.

investments made with the pension fund have done poorly, because the firm's revenues are less than anticipated, or both. Even if a private firm goes broke, defined benefit pensions are insured by the federal government, so the private-sector employee bears little or no risk. However, for public sector employees, who now account for most defined benefit plans, there is risk in extreme cases such as—you know it well!—Detroit in 2013. When a public employer goes bankrupt, the pensioners and active workers in the pension system are put in line behind the employer's creditors—mainly banks. (The Detroit situation is being disputed in the courts at this writing, but it does not appear likely that things will come out well for people in the public pension system.)

In defined contribution plans, the risk falls on the employee. The contributions (from both the employee and the employer) go into an investment fund for the individual worker, generally with taxes deferred until the money is taken out of the fund (as in a 401k). But if the economy goes sour— for example, if the stock market crashes—the employee has far less for retirement. This is exactly what happened with the crash of 2008.

There could hardly be a clearer case of conflict of interests between employees and employers. As employers have been able to hold down wages over the last several decades, they have shifted the burden of risk onto employees. There are several aspects of this power shift that have favored employers: the large decline in union membership, the way globalization has been structured to favor large firms, the general shift in political power (of which the decline in the minimum wage is a clear marker), and the way technological changes have been used to displace labor. The result has been a worsening of what workers get—stagnant wages and higher risk.

Social Security alone certainly does not provide a good standard of living. In 2012, the average annual Social Security payment from the Old-Age and Survivors Insurance trust fund was a little more than $14,000 per recipient. A person retiring in 2013 at age 65 who had been earning an annual salary of $70,000 (a bit more than the median family income), would receive about $21,000 annually. Even if all the efforts in Washington to cut Social Security benefits fail, it is easy to see why people need some additional form of retirement income to provide them with a reasonable standard of living during retirement.

Beyond Social Security, in 2010, active workers held 90.6 million pension plans, 17.2 million defined benefit plans and 73.4 million defined contribution plans. These figures involve some double counting, as many people have more than one pension plan, but, with a 2010 labor force of 153.9 million, this means that at least 41% of workers had no pension plan at all (other than Social Security). In fact, according to progressive pension expert Teresa Ghilarducci, a majority of workers do not have pension plans at work and over 75% of Americans nearing retirement age in 2010 had less than $30,000 in their retirement accounts.

While the pressure from business groups in Washington is to reduce Social Security, the current dismal state of retirement prospects for the majority of people in fact provides a strong case for a more extensive public pension system. ❑

Sources: Teresa Ghilarducci, "Don't Cut Pensions, Expand Them," *New York Times*, March 15, 2012; Teresa Ghilarducci, "Our Ridiculous Approach to Retirement, *New York Times*, July 21, 2012; Employee Benefit Research Institute, "The Basics of Social Security, Updated With the 2013 Board of Trustees Report," July 2013.

Article 11.6

MYTHS OF THE DEFICIT

BY MARTY WOLFSON
May/June 2010

Nearly 15 million people are officially counted as unemployed in the United States, and more than 6 million of these have been unemployed for more than 26 weeks. Another 11 million are the "hidden" unemployed: jobless workers who have given up looking for work and part-time workers who want full-time jobs. Unemployment has especially affected minority communities; the official black teenage unemployment rate, for example, stands at 42%.

The *moral* case for urgently addressing the unemployment issue is clear. The costs of unemployment, especially prolonged unemployment, are devastating. Self-worth is questioned, homes are lost, families stressed, communities disrupted. Across the land, the number one issue is jobs, jobs, jobs.

The *economic* case for how to address the jobs issue is also clear. As Keynes argued during the Great Depression, federal government spending can directly create jobs. And the $787 billion stimulus package approved by Congress in February 2009 did help pull the economy back from disaster, when it was shedding 20,000 jobs *a day* in late 2008 and early 2009.

But we still have a long way to go. To get back just to where we were when the recession began in December 2007, the economy would need to create 11.1 million jobs: 8.4 million to replace the jobs lost and 2.7 million to absorb new workers who have entered the labor market since then.

Despite a pickup of economic activity recently, long-term projections are that the unemployment rate will fall only gradually over the next several years. The Congressional Budget Office forecast for the unemployment rate for 2012 is a stubbornly high 8%. So why are we not moving more aggressively to reduce unemployment?

The *ideological* opposition to government spending remains a major obstacle. There are those who see an increase in the role of government as something to be avoided at all costs—even if the cost is the jobs of the unemployed.

Even among those who are not subject to such ideological blinders, there is still a *political* argument that resonates strongly. The argument is that government spending to create jobs will create large budget deficits, which will have terrible consequences for the American people. Politicians, pundits, and other commentators—in a frenzied drumbeat of speeches, op-eds, and articles—have asserted that the most urgent priority *now* is to reduce the budget deficit.

It is important to note that this argument is focused on current policy, not just the long-term budgetary situation. There is room for debate about long-term budget deficits, but these are affected more by the explosive growth of health-care costs than by government discretionary spending to create jobs.

Why, then, are people taken in by an argument that says it is more important to reduce the budget deficit now than for the government to spend money to create jobs? Two myths constantly repeated in the public debate have contributed to this situation:

1) Families can't spend more than they have; neither should the government.

It seems to be common sense that a family can't spend more than it has. But of course that is exactly what the family does when it takes out a car loan or a student loan, or does any other kind of borrowing. The government, just like families, should be able to borrow. The real issue is whether or not the debt is affordable. For families, and for the government, that depends on the size of the debt relative to the income available to service the debt; it also depends on the nature of the borrowing.

For the federal government, the relevant debt-income measure is the ratio of outstanding debt of the federal government to gross domestic product. (*Outstanding debt* is the total amount owed at a particular time, roughly the result of debt accumulated over time by annual budget deficits; GDP, the value of goods and services produced, is equal to total income.) In 2009, this ratio was 53%. Although higher than the recent low point of 33% at the end of the 1990s expansion, the ratio in 2009 was still far lower than the record peak of 109% in 1946—after which the U.S. economy in the post-World War II period experienced the strongest economic growth in its history.

The U.S. ratio of 53% actually compares favorably to those of other advanced industrial countries. For example, IMF data indicate the following debt-to-GDP ratios for 2009: France (67%), Germany (70%), Japan (105%), and Italy (113%).

The nature of the borrowing also affects affordability. If a family runs up credit-card debt to finance a lavish lifestyle, after the fancy dinners are eaten the family still needs to figure out how to pay its debt. But if a family member borrows to buy a car to get to work, presumably the job will help provide the income to service the debt.

Likewise for the federal government: If the government borrows to finance tax cuts for the rich, and the rich use their tax cuts to purchase imported luxury goods, then the government still needs to figure out how to pay its debt. On the other hand, if the government borrows to put people to work creating long-term investments that increase the productivity of the U.S. economy, like infrastructure and education, then it is in a much better situation. The income generated by the more productive economy, as well as by the newly employed workers, can help to provide the tax revenue to service the debt.

So it is a myth to say that families can't spend more than they have. They can, and so can the government. And both are justified in borrowing if the size of the debt is manageable and if so doing helps to provide the income necessary to service the debt.

2) Large budget deficits create a burden for our grandchildren.

This is the issue that probably resonates most forcefully with public opinion. If we in the current generation run up a big debt, it may be left to our grandchildren to repay. The only difficulty with this reasoning is that the grandchildren who may be asked to repay the debt are paying it to other grandchildren. When the government incurs a debt, it issues a bond, an obligation to repay the debt to the holder of the bond. If the holders of the bond are U.S. residents, then paying off the debt means paying money to U.S. residents. In other words, debt that is an obligation of future U.S. taxpayers is also a source of income to the U.S. holders of that debt. Thus there is not a generational burden that we today are imposing on "our grandchildren" as a collective entity.

Of course, the obvious exception to this reasoning is the debt held by non-U.S. residents. In that case, it is indeed true that future generations of Americans will need to pay interest to foreign holders of U.S. debt. But the basic reason for this situation is the trade deficit, not the budget deficit. When we pay more for imports than we receive from exports, and when U.S. multinational companies ship production abroad to take advantage of low-cost labor, foreigners are provided with dollars that they can use to invest in U.S. assets. And the real burden that this causes is the same whether foreigners invest in U.S. government debt or whether they invest in U.S. companies, real estate, the U.S. stock market, etc.

Borrowing by the federal government can in some situations create a real burden, but it has less to do with generational transfers and more to do with distributional issues and the nature of economic growth (discussed above). If the grandchildren who are taxed in the future to pay off government debt are poorer than the grandchildren who are paid, the distribution of income becomes more unequal.

Also, cutting taxes for the rich and spending money on wars in Iraq and Afghanistan do not lead to the kind of productive economic growth that generates strong tax revenue. So financing these by debt *does* create a real distributional burden: The rich and military contractors benefit, but the losers are those who might be taxed, or those whose government programs might be squeezed out of the budget, because of the need to pay interest on the debt.

Borrowing money to put people back to work does make sense. It helps people most in need, the unemployed. It provides them with income that they can use to pay taxes and to buy goods and services that create more jobs, more income, and more tax revenue. Indeed, our inability thus far to seriously tackle the unemployment problem is what has worsened the budget problem, as tax receipts have fallen and spending for unemployment benefits and food stamps have risen. An analysis by the Economic Policy Institute reveals that the largest source of the 2009 budget deficit (42%) was actually the recession itself.

We *will* leave a burden for our grandchildren if we don't address the urgent problem of unemployment, if we let parents and grandparents suffer the indignities and financial hardships of lost jobs. We *will* leave a burden for our grandchildren if we don't rebuild our aging infrastructure, break our reliance on fossil fuels, and provide all our children with an excellent education. It makes perfect sense to borrow money now to address these problems, and we shouldn't let myths about budget deficits get in the way of meeting these real needs. ❑

Sources: Congressional Budget Office, "The Budget and Economic Outlook: Fiscal Years 2010 to 2020," January 2010; John Irons, Kathryn Edwards, and Anna Turner, "The 2009 Budget Deficit: How Did We Get Here?" Economic Policy Institute, August 20, 2009; Dean Baker, "The Budget Deficit Scare Story and the Great Recession," Center for Economic and Policy Research, February 2010; Office of Management and Budget, "The President's Budget For Fiscal Year 2011, Historical Tables: Table 7.1, Federal Debt at the End of Year: 1940-2015," February 2010.

CLIMATE ECONOMICS IN FOUR EASY PIECES

Conventional cost-benefit models cannot inform our decisions about how to address the threat of climate change.

FRANK ACKERMAN
November/December 2008

Once upon a time, debates about climate policy were primarily about the science. An inordinate amount of attention was focused on the handful of "climate skeptics" who challenged the scientific understanding of climate change. The influence of the skeptics, however, is rapidly fading; few people were swayed by their arguments, and doubt about the major results of climate science is no longer important in shaping public policy.

As the climate *science* debate is reaching closure, the climate *economics* debate is heating up. The controversial issue now is the fear that overly ambitious climate initiatives could hurt the economy. Mainstream economists emphasizing that fear have, in effect, replaced the climate skeptics as the intellectual enablers of inaction.

For example, William Nordhaus, the U.S. economist best known for his work on climate change, pays lip service to scientists' calls for decisive action. He finds, however, that the "optimal" policy is a very small carbon tax that would reduce greenhouse gas emissions only 25% below "business-as-usual" levels by 2050—that would, in other words, allow emissions to rise well above current levels by mid-century. Richard Tol, a European economist who has written widely on climate change, favors an even smaller carbon tax of just $2 per ton of carbon dioxide. That would amount to all of $0.02 per gallon of gasoline, a microscopic "incentive" for change that consumers would never notice.

There are other voices in the climate economics debate; in particular, the British government's Stern Review offers a different perspective. Economist Nicholas Stern's analysis is much less wrong than the traditional Nordhaus-Tol approach, but even Stern has not challenged the conventional view enough.

What will it take to build a better economics of climate change, one that is consistent with the urgency expressed by the latest climate science? The issues that matter are big, non-technical principles, capable of being expressed in bumper-sticker format. Here are the four bumper stickers for a better climate economics:

1. Our grandchildren's lives are important.

2. We need to buy insurance for the planet.

3. Climate damages are too valuable to have prices.

4. Some costs are better than others.

1. Our grandchildren's lives are important.

The most widely debated challenge of climate economics is the valuation of the very long run. For ordinary loans and investments, both the costs today and the resulting future benefits typically occur within a single lifetime. In such cases, it makes sense to think in terms of the same person experiencing and comparing the costs and the benefits.

In the case of climate change, the time spans involved are well beyond those encountered in most areas of economics. The most important consequences of today's choices will be felt by generations to come, long after all of us making those choices have passed away. As a result, the costs of reducing emissions today and the benefits in the far future will not be experienced by the same people. The economics of climate change is centrally concerned with our relationship to our descendants whom we will never meet. As a bridge to that unknowable future, consider our grandchildren—the last generation most of us will ever know.

Suppose that you want your grandchildren to receive $100 (in today's dollars, corrected for inflation), 60 years from now. How much would you have to put in a bank account today, to ensure that the $100 will be there 60 years from now? The answer is $55 at 1% interest, or just over $5 at 5%.

In parallel fashion, economists routinely deal with future costs and benefits by "discounting" them, or converting them to "present values"—a process that is simply compound interest in reverse. In the standard jargon, the *present value* of $100, to be received 60 years from now, is $55 at a 1% *discount rate*, or about $5 at a 5% discount rate. As this example shows, a higher discount rate implies a smaller present value.

The central problem of climate economics, in a cost-benefit framework, is deciding how much to spend today on preventing future harms. What should we spend to prevent $100 of climate damages 60 years from now? The standard answer is, no more than the present value of that future loss: $55 at a discount rate of 1%, or $5 at 5%. The higher the discount rate, the less it is "worth" spending today on protecting our grandchildren.

The effect of a change in the discount rate becomes much more pronounced as the time period lengthens. Damages of $1 million occurring 200 years from now have a present value of only about $60 at a 5% discount rate, versus more than $130,000 at a 1% discount rate. The choice of the discount rate is all-important to our stance toward the far future: should we spend as much as $130,000, or as little as $60, to avoid one million dollars of climate damages in the early twenty-third century?

For financial transactions within a single lifetime, it makes sense to use market interest rates as the discount rate. Climate change, however, involves public policy decisions with impacts spanning centuries; there is no market in which public resources are traded from one century to the next. The choice of an intergenerational discount rate is a matter of ethics and policy, not a market-determined result.

Economists commonly identify two separate aspects of long-term discounting, each contributing to the discount rate.

One component of the discount rate is based on the assumption of an upward trend in income and wealth. If future generations will be richer than we are, they will need less help from us, and they will get less benefit from an additional dollar of income than we do. So we can discount benefits that will flow to our wealthier descendants, at a rate based on the expected growth of per capita incomes. Among economists, the income-related motive for discounting may be the least controversial part of the picture.

Setting aside changes in per capita income from one generation to the next, there may still be a reason to discount a sum many years in the future. This component of the discount rate, known as "pure time preference," is the subject of longstanding ethical, philosophical, and economic debate. On the one hand, there are reasons to think that pure time preference is greater than zero: both psychological experiments and common sense suggest that people are impatient, and prefer money now to money later. On the other hand, a pure time preference of zero expresses the equal worth of people of all generations, and the equal importance of reducing climate impacts and other burdens on them (assuming that all generations have equal incomes).

The Stern Review provides an excellent discussion of the debate, explaining Stern's assumption of pure time preference close to zero and an overall discount rate of 1.4%. This discount rate alone is sufficient to explain Stern's support for a substantial program of climate protection: at the higher discount rates used in more traditional analyses, the Stern program would look "inefficient," since the costs would outweigh the present value of the benefits.

2. We need to buy insurance for the planet.

Does climate science predict that things are certain to get worse? Or does it tell us that we are uncertain about what will happen next? Unfortunately, the answer seems to be yes to both questions. For example, the most likely level of sea level rise in this century, according to the latest Intergovernmental Panel on Climate Change reports, is no more than one meter or so—a real threat to low-lying coastal areas and islands that will face increasing storm damages, but survivable, with some adaptation efforts, for most of the world. On the other hand, there is a worst-case risk of an abrupt loss of the Greenland ice sheet, or perhaps of a large portion of the West Antarctic ice sheet. Either one could cause an eventual seven-meter rise in sea level—a catastrophic impact on coastal communities, economic activity, and infrastructure everywhere, and well beyond the range of plausible adaptation efforts in most places.

The evaluation of climate damages thus depends on whether we focus on the most likely outcomes or the credible worst-case risks; the latter, of course, are much larger.

Cost-benefit analysis conventionally rests on average or expected outcomes. But this is not the only way that people make decisions. When faced with uncertain, potentially large risks, people do not normally act on the basis of average outcomes; instead, they typically focus on protection against worst-case scenarios. When you go to the airport, do you leave just enough time for the average traffic delay (so that you would catch your plane, on average, half of the time)? Or do you allow time for some estimate of worst-case traffic jams? Once you get there, of course, you will experience additional delays due to security, which is all about worst cases: your *average* fellow passenger is not a threat to anyone's safety.

The very existence of the insurance industry is evidence of the desire to avoid or control worst-case scenarios. It is impossible for an insurance company to pay out in claims as much as its customers pay in premiums; if it did, there would be no money left to pay the costs of running the company, or the profits received by its owners. People who buy insurance are therefore guaranteed to get back less than they, on average, have paid; they (we) are paying for the security that insurance provides in case the worst should happen. This way of thinking does not apply to every decision: in casino games, people make bets based on averages and probabilities, and no one has any insurance against losing the next round. But life is not a casino, and public policy should not be a gamble.

Should climate policy be based on the most likely outcomes, or on the worst-case risks? Should we be investing in climate protection as if we expect sea level rise of one meter, or as if we are buying insurance to be sure of preventing a seven-meters rise?

In fact, the worst-case climate risks are even more unknown than the individual risks of fire and death that motivate insurance purchases. You do not know whether or not you will have a fire next year or die before the year is over, but you have very good information about the likelihood of these tragic events. So does the insurance industry, which is why they are willing to insure you. In contrast, there is no body of statistical information about the probability of Greenland-sized ice sheets collapsing at various temperatures; it's not an experiment that anyone can perform over and over again.

A recent analysis by Martin Weitzman argues that the probabilities of the worst outcomes are inescapably unknowable—and this deep uncertainty is more important than anything we do know in motivating concern about climate change. There is a technical sense in which the expected value of future climate damages can be infinite because we know so little about the probability of the worst, most damaging possibilities. The practical implication of infinite expected damages is that the most likely outcome is irrelevant; what matters is buying insurance for the planet, i.e., doing our best to understand and prevent the worst-case risks.

3. Climate damages are too valuable to have prices.

To decide whether climate protection is worthwhile, in cost-benefit terms, we would need to know the monetary value of everything important that is being protected. Even if we could price everything affected by climate change, the prices would conceal a critical form of international inequity. The emissions that cause climate change have come predominantly from rich countries, while the damages will be felt first and worst in some of the world's poorest, tropical countries (although no one will be immune from harm for long). There are, however, no meaningful prices for many of the benefits of health and environmental protection. What is the dollar value of a human life saved? How much is it worth to save an endangered species from extinction, or to preserve a unique location or ecosystem? Economists have made up price tags for such priceless values, but the results do not always pass the laugh test.

Is a human life worth $6.1 million, as estimated by the Clinton administration, based on small differences in the wages paid for more and less risky jobs? Or is it worth $3.7 million, as the (second) Bush administration concluded on the basis of questionnaires about people's willingness to pay for reducing small, hypothetical risks? Are lives of people in rich countries worth much more than those in poor countries, as some economists infamously argued in the IPCC's 1995 report? Can the value of an endangered species be determined by survey research on how much people would pay to protect it? If, as one study found, the U.S. population as a whole would pay $18 billion to protect the existence of humpback whales, would it be acceptable for someone to pay $36 billion for the right to hunt and kill the entire species?

The only sensible response to such nonsensical questions is that there are many crucially important values that do not have meaningful prices. This is not a new idea: as the eighteenth-century philosopher Immanuel Kant put it, some things have a price, or relative worth, while other things have a dignity, or inner worth. No price tag does justice to the dignity of human life or the natural world.

Since some of the most important benefits of climate protection are priceless, any monetary value for total benefits will necessarily be incomplete. The corollary is that preventive action may be justified even in the absence of a complete monetary measure of the benefits of doing so.

4. Some costs are better than others.

The language of cost-benefit analysis embodies a clear normative slant: benefits are good, costs are bad. The goal is always to have larger benefits and smaller costs. In some respects, measurement and monetary valuation are easier for costs than for benefits: implementing pollution control measures typically involves changes in such areas as manufacturing, construction, and fuel use, all of which have well-defined prices. Yet conventional economic theory distorts the interpretation of costs in ways that exaggerate the burdens of environmental protection and hide the positive features of some of the "costs."

Average Risks or Worst-Case Scenarios?

You don't have to look far to find situations in which the sensible policy is to address worst-case outcomes rather than average outcomes. The annual number of residential fires in the United States is about 0.4% of the number of housing units. This means that a fire occurs, on average, about once every 250 years in each home—not even close to once per lifetime. By far the most likely number of fires a homeowner will experience next year, or even in a lifetime, is zero. Why don't these statistics inspire you to cancel your fire insurance? Unless you are extremely wealthy, the loss of your home in a fire would be a devastating financial blow; despite the low probability, you cannot afford to take any chances on it.

What are the chances of the ultimate loss? The probability that you will die next year is under 0.1% if you are in your twenties, under 0.2% in your thirties, under 0.4% in your forties. It is not until age 61 that you have as much as a 1% chance of death within the coming year. Yet most U.S. families with dependent children buy life insurance. Without it, the risk to children of losing their parents' income would be too great—even though the parents are, on average, extraordinarily likely to survive.

For instance, empirical studies of energy use and carbon emissions repeatedly find significant opportunities for emissions reduction at zero or negative net cost—the so-called "no regrets" options.

According to a longstanding tradition in economic theory, however, cost-free energy savings are impossible. The textbook theory of competitive markets assumes that every resource is productively employed in its most valuable use—in other words, that every no-regrets option must already have been taken. As the saying goes, there are no free lunches; there cannot be any $20 bills on the sidewalk because someone would have picked them up already. Any new emissions reduction measures, then, must have positive costs. This leads to greater estimates of climate policy costs than the bottom-up studies that reveal extensive opportunities for costless savings.

In the medium term, we will need to move beyond the no-regrets options; how much will it cost to finish the job of climate protection? Again, there are rival interpretations of the costs based on rival assumptions about the economy. The same economic theory that proclaimed the absence of $20 bills on the sidewalk is responsible for the idea that all costs are bad. Since the free market lets everyone spend their money in whatever way they choose, any new cost must represent a loss: it leaves people with less to spend on whatever purchases they had previously selected to maximize their satisfaction in life. Climate damages are one source of loss, and spending on climate protection is another; both reduce the resources available for the desirable things in life.

But are the two kinds of costs really comparable? Is it really a matter of indifference whether we spend $1 billion on bigger and better levees or lose $1 billion to storm damages? In the real-world economy, money spent on building levees creates jobs and incomes. The construction workers buy groceries, clothing, and so on, indirectly creating other jobs. With more people working, tax revenues increase while unemployment compensation payments decrease.

None of this happens if the levees are not built and the storm damages are allowed to occur. The costs of prevention are good costs, with numerous indirect benefits; the costs of climate damages are bad costs, representing pure physical destruction. One worthwhile goal is to keep total costs as low as possible; another is to have as much as possible of good costs rather than bad costs. Think of it as the cholesterol theory of climate costs.

In the long run, the deep reductions in carbon emissions needed for climate stabilization will require new technologies that have not yet been invented, or at best exist only in small, expensive prototypes. How much will it cost to invent, develop, and implement the low-carbon technologies of the future?

Lacking a rigorous theory of innovation, economists modeling climate change have often assumed that new technologies simply appear, making the economy inexorably more efficient over time. A more realistic view observes that the costs of producing a new product typically decline as industry gains more experience with it, in a pattern called "learning by doing" or the "learning curve" effect. Public investment is often necessary to support the innovation process in its early, expensive stages. Wind power is now relatively cheap and competitive, in suitable locations; this is a direct result of decades of public investment in the United States and Europe, starting when wind turbines were still quite expensive. The costs of climate policy, in the long run, will include doing the same for other promising new technologies, investing public resources in jump-starting a set of slightly different industries than we might have chosen in the absence of climate change. If this is a cost, many communities would be better off with more of it.

Saving the Planet

A widely publicized, conventional economic analysis recommends inaction on climate change, claiming that the costs currently outweigh the benefits for anything more than the smallest steps toward reducing carbon emissions. Put our "four easy pieces" together, and we have the outline of an economics that complements the science of climate change and endorses active, large-scale climate protection.

How realistic is it to expect that the world will shake off its inertia and act boldly and rapidly enough to make a difference? This may be the last generation that will have a real chance at protecting the earth's climate. Projections from the latest IPCC reports, the Stern Review, and other sources suggest that it is still possible to save the planet—if we start at once. ❑

Sources: Frank Ackerman, *Can We Afford the Future? Economics for a Warming World*, Zed Books, 2008; Frank Ackerman, *Poisoned for Pennies: The Economics of Toxics and Precaution*, Island Press, 2008; Frank Ackerman and Lisa Heinzerling, *Priceless: On Knowing the Price of Everything and the Value of Nothing*, The New Press, 2004; J. Creyts, A. Derkach, S. Nyquist, K. Ostrowski and J. Stephenson, *Reducing U.S. Greenhouse Gas Emissions: How Much at What Cost?*, McKinsey & Co., 2007; P.-A. Enkvist, T. Naucler and J. Rosander, "A Cost Curve for Greenhouse Gas Reduction," *The McKinsey Quarterly*, 2007; Immanuel Kant, *Groundwork for the Metaphysics of Morals*, translated by Thomas K. Abbot, with revisions by Lara Denis, Broadview Press, 2005 [1785]; B. Lomborg, *Cool It: The Skeptical Environmentalist's Guide to Global Warming*, Alfred A. Knopf, 2007; W.D. Nordhaus, *A Question of Balance: Economic Modeling of Global Warming*, Yale University Press, 2008; F.P. Ramsey, "A mathematical theory of saving," *The Economic Journal* 138(152): 543-59, 1928; Nicholas Stern *et al.*, *The Stern Review: The Economics of Climate Change*, HM Treasury, 2006; U.S. Census Bureau, "Statistical Abstract of the United States." 127th edition. 2008; M.L. Weitzman, "On Modeling and Interpreting the Economics of Catastrophic Climate Change," December 5, 2007 version, www.economics.harvard.edu/faculty/weitzman/files/modeling.pdf.

CONTRIBUTORS

Frank Ackerman is an economist with Synapse Energy Economics and a founder of *Dollars & Sense*.

Randy Albelda, a *Dollars & Sense* Associate, teaches economics at the University of Massachusetts-Boston.

Gar Alperovitz is a professor of political economy at the University of Maryland and co-author, with Lew Daly, of *Unjust Deserts: How the Rich Are Taking Our Common Inheritance and Why We Should Take It Back* (New Press, 2009).

Dean Baker is co-director of the Center for Economic and Policy Research.

Peter Barnes, co-founder of Working Assets, is a senior fellow at the Tomales Bay Institute.

Joe Berry has been active in the campus labor movement nationally and is a retired labor educator.

Sarah Blaskey is a student at the University of Wisconsin-Madison and a member of the Student Labor Action Coalition.

Marc Breslow is co-chair of the Massachusetts Climate Action Network and a former *Dollars & Sense* collective member.

Jim Campen is professor emeritus of economics at the University of Massachusetts-Boston, and former executive director of Americans for Fairness in Lending.

Esther Cervantes is a former *Dollars & Sense* business and circulation manager.

Molly Cusano is a former *Dollars & Sense* intern.

Lew Daly is a senior fellow at Demos and co-author, with Gar Alperovitz, of *Unjust Deserts: How the Rich Are Taking Our Common Inheritance and Why We Should Take It Back* (New Press, 2009).

Elissa Dennis is a consultant to nonprofit affordable housing developers with Community Economics, Inc. in Oakland, Calif.

Alan Durning founded Sightline Institute (formerly Northwest Environment Watch) and is a former senior researcher at the Worldwatch Institute.

Anne Fischel teaches media and community studies at Evergreen State College in Olympia, Wash.

Ellen Frank teaches economics at the University of Massachusetts-Boston and is a *Dollars & Sense* collective member.

Gerald Friedman is a professor of economics at the University of Massachusetts-Amherst.

Heidi Garrett-Peltier is a research fellow at the Political Economy Research Institute at the University of Massachusetts-Amherst.

Phil Gasper teaches at Madison College and writes the "Critical Thinking" column for *International Socialist Review*.

Lisa Heinzerling is a professor of law at Georgetown University Law School, specializing in environmental law.

Edward Herman is an economist and co-author of *The Global Media: The New Missionaries of Corporate Capitalism* (Continuum, 1997).

Mara Kardas-Nelson is a freelance writer currently based in Capetown, South Africa. She has written on health, the environment, and human rights for the *Globe & Mail* and the *Mail & Guardian*.

Marie Kennedy is professor emerita of Community Planning at the University of Massachusetts-Boston and visiting professor in Urban Planning at UCLA. She is a member of the board of directors of Grassroots International.

Rob Larson teaches economics at Tacoma Community College in Tacoma, Wash., and is the author of *Bleakonomics* (Pluto Press).

Jonathan Latham, PhD, is co-founder and executive director of the Bioscience Resource Project, publisher of Independent Science News (independentsciencenews.org).

Arthur MacEwan, a *Dollars & Sense* Associate, is professor emeritus of economics at the University of Massachusetts-Boston.

Aaron Markiewicz is a *Dollars & Sense* intern.

John Miller, a *Dollars & Sense* collective member, teaches economics at Wheaton College.

William G. Moseley is a professor of geography at Macalester College.

Lin Nelson teaches environmental and community studies at the Evergreen State College in Olympia, Wash.

Thomas Palley is an economist who has held positions at the AFL-CIO, Open Society Institute, and the U.S./China Economic and Security Review Commission.

Alejandro Reuss (co-editor of this volume) is co-editor of *Dollars & Sense* and an instructor at the Labor Relations and Research Center at UMass-Amherst.

Zachary Santamaria is a former *Dollars & Sense* intern.

Helen Scharber is an assistant professor of economics at Hampshire College in Amherst, Mass.

Dan Schneider is a freelance journalist and a member of the *Dollars & Sense* collective.

Bryan Snyder (co-editor of this volume) is a senior lecturer in economics at Bentley University.

Chris Sturr (co-editor of this volume) is co-editor of *Dollars & Sense*.

Chris Tilly is a *Dollars & Sense* Associate and director of UCLA's Institute for Research on Labor and Employment and professor in the Urban Planning Department.

Ramaa Vasudevan teaches economics at Colorado State University and is a *Dollars & Sense* Associate.

Brian Walsh is a public-school teacher, union activist, and graduate student at the Labor Relations and Research Center at UMass-Amherst.

Jeannette Wicks-Lim is an economist and research fellow at the Political Economy Research Institute at the University of Massachusetts-Amherst.

Thad Williamson, a *Dollars & Sense* Associate, is assistant professor of leadership studies at the University of Richmond. He is the author of four books, including *Sprawl, Justice, and Citizenship: The Civic Costs of the American Way of Life* (Oxford, 2010).

Richard Wolff is professor of economics at the University of Massachusetts, Amherst. He is co-author of *Knowledge and Class: A Critique of Political Economy*, *Economics: Marxian vs. Neoclassical*, and *Bringing It All Back Home: Class, Gender, and Power in the Modern Household*.

Marty Wolfson is a professor of economics at the University of Notre Dame.

Helena Worthen has been active in the campus labor movement nationally and is a retired labor educator.

CPSIA information can be obtained at www.ICGtesting.com
Printed in the USA
BVOW04s1232050115

381928BV00004B/7/P